CW00505130

A Modern Approach to the Incidental Question

A Modern Approach to the Incidental Question

by

Dr. Rhona Schuz

LONDON – THE HAGUE – BOSTON

Published by
Kluwer Law International Ltd
Sterling House
66 Wilton Road
London SW1V 1DE
United Kingdom

Sold and distributed in the USA
and Canada by
Kluwer Law International
675 Massachusetts Avenue
Cambridge MA 02139
USA

Kluwer Law International Ltd incorporates
the publishing programmes of
Graham & Trotman Ltd,
Kluwer Law & Taxation Publishers
and Martinus Nijhoff Publishers

In all other countries, sold and
distributed by
Kluwer Law International
P.O. Box 322
3300 AH Dordrecht
The Netherlands

ISBN 90-411-0668-5

First published 1997

British Library Cataloguing Publication Data

A catalogue record for this book is available from the British Library.

Library of Congress Cataloguing in Publication Data is available.

Typeset in Times 11/12 pt by Doyle & Co, Colchester.
Printed and bound in Great Britain by Hartnolls Ltd, Bodmin, Cornwall

Contents

Index of Cases – England and Wales

Index of Cases – Other Jurisdictions

Index of Statutes – England and Wales

Index of Statutes – Other Jurisdictions

Preface

Much academic ink has been spilt by conflicts lawyers over the past 60 years in seeking a solution to the incidental question. However, no consensus has emerged either in the literature or in case law as to how cases in which the incidental question arises should be solved.

This book aims to develop a new approach to the incidental question based on a shift in the method of analysis of the problem and on result selecting techniques. Using a clearly defined methodology, preference rules are deduced which will determine the outcome of the incidental question in each particular type of situation.

Throughout the book, it is assumed that the forum which has to solve the incidental question is England. As the preference rules are based on forum policy, it might therefore be thought that the book is only relevant to those who have an interest in English law. Such a view would be misconceived for two reasons. Firstly, the methodology can be adapted to any legal system. All that is necessary is to substitute an analysis of the local forum's policy for that presented in the book. Secondly, other countries may agree with the English policy in relation to at least some of the topics. The harmonisation of some of the Private International Rules in family law matters by means of Hague Conventions is an indication of a decrease in the differences between the policies of the various countries in these areas. Indeed, I would suggest that, the ideal solution would be for the preference rules recommended in this book to be incorporated into Hague Conventions dealing with the topics in question.

This book is based on the thesis written to obtain my doctorate at the London School of Economics. As many others have discovered before me, converting a thesis into a book is a far more demanding task than anticipated. As well as adapting and updating the original text, I have added three additional chapters and the conclusion in order to provide a more comprehensive coverage of the problem.

This book is dedicated to my family.

Rhona Schuz

Acknowledgements

Perhaps logically, the first word of thanks should go to Dr. Celia Fasberg of the Faculty of Law at the Hebrew University of Jerusalem. It was as a result of a conversation with her in 1990 that I started writing an article, which became the basis of this research project. Taking the "chain of causation" further back, I would like to mention the late Dr J H C Morris, who taught me conflict of laws for the LLM (then called the LLB) at the University of Cambridge in 1979-80. His fascination with the conflict of laws was infectious and I am grateful to him for the particular interest he took in my early attempts to come to grips with the subject.

I would like to thank Professor Trevor Hartley for his time and patience in reading successive drafts and for his helpful and constructive comments and encouragement.

Gratitude should be expressed to the London School of Economics, the Hebrew University of Jerusalem and Bar Ilan University for the assistance and facilities afforded to me during the course of my research.

The help of the staff of the following libraries is gratefully acknowledged: Bar Ilan University Law Library, the British Library of Political and Economic Science Hebrew University of Jerusalem Law Library and the Institute of Advanced Legal Studies Library. I am also grateful to my mother, Mrs. Sheila Levitt for making arrangements for me to obtain copies of material not available in Israel, and to my research assistant Naama Heller Tal for her help in preparing the final manuscript.

I would like to take this opportunity to thank all those, too numerous to mention, who have helped me at various stages during my career.

My thanks are due to Kluwer Law International and particularly Selma Hoedt for undertaking the publication of this work, to Ruth Garrett for her editorial management and to those responsible for the typesetting and cover design.

Finally, I would like to express my appreciation to my family: to my parents and parents-in-law for their support and encouragement; to Annabel Simms (nee Lanzer), whose devoted attention as nanny to my children for many years enabled me to pursue my research; to my children (Yitzi, Asher, Gila, Miriam and Simcha) for their patience and understanding, while I was finishing the manuscript; to the latest addition to the family, Ranan, for waiting to be born until after I had dispatched the manuscript to the publishers and, above all, to my husband, Tony (David), for his initial stimulation to embark on this project and for his continued and invaluable support and encouragement.

"Blessed are you, Lord our God, King of the Universe who has kept us in life, and has preserved us, and enabled us to reach this season."

Rhona Schuz

PART I

PRELIMINARY MATTERS

Chapter 1

Presentation of the Problem

I. THE SCOPE OF THE INCIDENTAL QUESTION

Three aspects of scope need to be considered. Firstly, what conditions are required for the incidental question to arise? Secondly, in what sort of areas of law will the problem arise? Thirdly, to what extent is universal treatment possible?

A. Pre-requisities

An incidental question will arise in any case where it is necessary to determine a subsidiary question in order to apply the relevant legal rule to the main question.[1] However, the term "*the* incidental question"[2] is reserved for the occurrence of the phenomenon in private international law. Thus, *the* incidental question[3] can only arise where the main question involves foreign elements and under the forum's choice of law rules is governed by a foreign law (the *lex causae*). The question to be decided is whether the incidental question should be determined by the conflict rules of the law governing the main question[4] or by the conflict rules of the forum.[5] It will only be necessary to confront this problem if the answer to the incidental question obtained by application of the conflict rules of the *lex causae* is different from that obtained by application of the forum's conflicts rules.

Leading English textbooks state[6] that in order for a "true incidental question" to be "squarely presented" three conditions are necessary: (i) the main question must by the English conflicts rule be governed by the law of some foreign

1 See Schmidt, "The Incidental Question in Private International Law" (1992) vol 233 Receuil Des Cours p 309.

2 The problem of the incidental question was discovered by the German author Melchior in 1932 in his book on the fundamental problems of German private international law.

3 This term is in more common use than the alternative term "the preliminary question", which has been criticised as misleading. See Schmidt (n 1, *supra*) at pp 322-323.

4 This is sometimes called "dependent application" (Ehrenzweig and Jayne, Private International Law vol 1 (1967) (hereinafter "Ehrenzweig") at p 170) or the "wide reference" approach (Hartley (1967) 16 ICLQ 680 at p 682) and those supporting it are sometimes called "*lex causards*" (Gottlieb (1977) 26 ICLQ 734 at p 752).

5 The corresponding terminology to that in n 4, *supra*, is "independent determination"; the "narrow reference" approach and "*lex foristes*".

6 J D McClean, *Morris: The Conflict of Laws* (1993) 4th edn (hereinafter referred to as "Morris") at p 424; L Collins *et al*, *Dicey and Morris, The Conflict of Laws* (1993) 12th edn (hereinafter referred to as "Dicey and Morris") at pp 48-49; North and Fawcett, *Cheshire and North's Private International Law* (1987) 12th edn (hereinafter referred to as "Cheshire and North") at pp 53-54. Schmidt (n 1, *supra*) at p 316 formulates his three conditions slightly differently.

country; (ii) a subsidiary question involving foreign elements must arise which is capable of arising in its own right or in other contexts and for which there is a separate conflict rule; and (iii) the English conflict rule for the determination of the subsidiary question must lead to a different result from the corresponding conflict rule of the country whose law governs the main question.

The simplest illustration is the well-known situation where the validity of a remarriage (the main question) is dependent on whether a divorce decree dissolving one party's previous marriage is recognised (the incidental question).[7] The question is whether the recognition of the divorce should be governed by the recognition rules of the forum or the recognition rules of the *lex causae* of the main question. Thus, the conflict is perceived as a conflict between the conflict rules of the *lex causae* and the conflict rules of the forum.

B. Subject-matter

In principle, the problem of the incidental question can arise in almost any area of law. However, in practice, whilst there is some variety in the subject matter of the main question,[8] the incidental question itself invariably concerns a matter of either marital status or the status of a child as legitimate, legitimated or adopted.[9]

Whilst it may be argued that the incidental question is of little practical relevance,[10] in reality the problem is of far more practical interest[11] than is suggested by the paucity of case law.[12] This will be demonstrated in Parts II and III of this book, where at the beginning of each chapter, consideration is given to the factual scope of the problem in relation to each issue.

In many cases, the problem may not be recognised.[13] Even where it is recognised, the uncertainty of the present law may be a deterrent to litigation and an incentive to out of court settlement.[14] Thus, this book treats the incidental question as a real problem requiring pragmatic solutions. Therefore, whilst

7 See example M1, *infra*, and the classic case of *Schwebel v Ungar* (1963) 42 DLR (2d) 622. Although Levontin, *Choice of Law and Conflict of Laws* (1976) maintains that there is no incidental question in the "remarriage" cases. See explanation at n 34, *infra*.

8 Eg, liability in tort and ownership of property as well as validity of marriage and succession.

9 See Schmidt n 1, *supra* at p 321.

10 Thus Nygh claims that the incidental question is "a problem which has agitated law professors for years though judges have remained blissfully unaware of its existence" (Nygh, *Conflict of Laws in Australia*, Butterworths (5th edn, 1991) at p 233 (hereinafter "Nygh") and Juenger suggests the the problem is a rare flower which "blooms almost exclusively in academic greenhouses" (Receuil de Cours vol 193 (1985-IV) at p 196).

11 The Malmstrom Report on the Hague Convention on the Celebration and Recognition of marriages states that the problem "is of great importance for the practical effects of rules set up to regulate the recognition of the validity of marriages" (Actes et documents de la troizieme session Tome III at p 306) and art 12 of the Convention specicially relates to the problem (see below, ch 9, at text accompanying n 39).

12 Gottlieb (1977) 26 ICLQ 734 analyses the Commonwealth authority. Ehrenzweig (n 4, *supra*) at p 171 claims that there are very few pertinent American cases. See also Robertson (1939) 55 LQR 565 at p 577. Schmidt (n 1, *supra*) discusses some of the Continental cases at pp 396 *et seq*.

13 Eg, *Perrini v Perrini* [1979] Fam 84.

14 Similar arguments have been advanced to explain the paucity of English case law involving choice of law in tort.

there is some reference to hypothetical examples not involving questions of personal status, most of the book focuses on the more likely family law scenarios.

C. Universality

The incidental question is of a universal nature and can arise in any country. Thus, academic analysis has been of general application and not limited to a particular jurisdiction or type of legal system, although writers naturally tend to bring examples from their own or similar systems.

It might be thought that because this book advocates a result-selecting approach based on the policy of the forum, it is in fact only relevant to those who have an interest in English law. Such a view would be misconceived for two reasons. Firstly, the methodology can be adapted to any legal system. All that is necessary is to substitute an analysis of the local forum's policy for that presented in the book. Secondly, other countries may well agree with the English policy in relation to at least some of the topics. The harmonisation of some of the private international rules in family law matters by means of Hague Conventions[15] is some indication of a decrease in the differences between the policies of the various countries in these areas. Indeed, in the author's opinion the ideal solution would be for the preference rules recommended in this book to be incorporated into Hague Conventions dealing with the topics in question.

II. THE TRADITIONAL ANALYSIS OF THE INCIDENTAL QUESTION

There is a wealth of academic literature on this famous[16] issue in many languages, which is reviewed thoroughly by Gottlieb,[17] Wengler[18] and Schmidt.[19] It is not necessary to repeat their work here and it will be sufficient to mention briefly the views of each of the three main groups of writers: the *lex foristes*,[20] the *lex causards*,[21] and those who believe that there is no general rule.

Earlier writers were more prepared to commit themselves to the *lex fori* or *lex causae* approaches. For example, Robertson[22] concluded that—

> "the preliminary question should be determined by the conflicts rules of that system of law which is selected as appropriate to determine the principal question. The reason for this is . . . that this is the only way of respecting the determination already made that the selected proper law is to govern the question in dispute."

15 Of course, if all private international rules were harmonised the problem of the incidental question would disappear.
16 See Special Commission Report on draft Hague Convention on Celebration and Recognition of Validity of Marriages n 11, *supra*, at p 136.
17 (1977) 26 ICLQ 734 at pp 751 *et seq.*
18 International Encyclopedia of Comparative Law, vol III, ch 7.
19 See n 1, *supra*..
20 See n 5, *supra*.
21 See n 4, *supra*.
22 (1939) 55 LQR 565 at pp 583-584.

Later writers, especially from the common law world, have been more reluctant to support either approach.[23] For example, Ehrenzweig, like others, points out that the *lex foristes* give priority to "conformity of decision" in the forum[24] whilst the *lex causards* give priority to "uniformity of decision" among different fora.[25] He claims that there can be no general rule favouring one of the above stances, but:

> "Rather, the answer must hinge on the interpretation of the rule of decision, be it that of the forum or a foreign country, as to whether it gives priority to conformity within its own legal system . . . or to any international uniformity in the decision of the particular issue."[26]

Gottlieb[27] himself points out that where total *renvoi*[28] is adopted, then the incidental question must be decided by the *lex causae*. This does not help at all in cases where *renvoi* would not be applied. Gottlieb declines to give any overall solution to the Incidental Question on the basis that—

> "there is really no problem of the incidental question, but as many problems as there are cases in which the incidental question may arise."[29]

In his first article on the subject he concluded that:

> "In each case the acceptance or rejection of the *renvoi*, the general purpose behind each choice-of-law rule, the factors of consistency of decision and the public policy of the forum may all be important to consider . . . I have attempted not so much to provide solutions to all the problems discussed as to suggest methods by which reasonably satisfactory results may be achieved."[30]

Gottlieb's second article, whilst providing an excellent analysis of the case law and literature on the subject, and demonstrating a methodology, does not purport to formulate any solution to the incidental question.

It is submitted that despite the quantity of writing on the subject, the present state of the jurisprudence in relation to the incidental question is unsatisfactory. The lack of clear case law or academic support for any single approach results in almost complete uncertainty as to how a court, faced with an incidental

23 See, eg, the change in approach between the earlier editions of Dicey and Morris (eg 6th edn, 1949, the first in which the problem was discussed, at p 76) and the later editions (eg 12th edn, 1993 at p 55). Cf the Danish Professor Schmidt (n 1, *supra*) who advocated the *lex causae* approach as recently as 1992.

24 This is often referred to as "internal harmony" or "internal consistency". See, eg, Khan-Freund, *Problems in Private International Law* (1977) at p 291.

25 Often referred to as "international harmony" (*ibid*).

26 Ehrenzweig (n 4, *supra*) at p 170, para 92. See also Khan-Freund, *The Growth of Internationalism in Private International Law* (1960) at pp 9 *et seq*, who sees this dichotomy as a pervasive one in the conflict of laws.

27 (1955) 33 Can Bar R 523 at p 547.

28 See Section VII, *infra*.

29 Gottlieb (1955) 33 Can Bar Rev 523 at p 555.

30 *Ibid*.

question, would decide the case. It is submitted that this flaw is particularly serious in relation to questions of status because parties and administrative officials may need to be able to ascertain the status of individuals[31] without resort to court. Thus, there is a need for a novel approach to these problems which is both theoretically sound and suitable for practical application. The purpose of this book is to seek such an approach.

III. THE "CONFLICT OF RULES"[32] ANALYSIS

A. The Analysis Outlined

Under this analysis, there is seen to be a conflict as to which of two different conflicts rules of the forum should determine the so-called incidental question. However, it is recognised that this question is not really "incidental" or "subsidiary" at all,[33] but is the question which is at the heart of the problem and the answer to which will determine the outcome of the dispute. Thus, the focus is on this question which may be referred to as the "critical question". In order to ensure the correct approach, it is essential that the latter is formulated precisely. Thus, in the classic remarriage situation, the critical question is whether the party remarrying is single[34] for the purposes of entering the second marriage?[35] This question can be answered by the forum either by applying the relevant *choice of law rules* or by using its *recognition rules* which determine the validity of the divorce or nullity decree. Hence where the two relevant rules would produce different results there is a "conflict of rules". In order to determine which of the two competing rules prevails, there needs to be a "preference rule". The purpose of this book is to construct appropriate preference rules to solve the most common types of incidental question.

Analysing the conflict as a conflict between two conflicts rules of the forum may appear to be pure semantics, since application of the forum's choice rules will result in the application of the recognition or choice rules of the *lex causae*. However, it is suggested that the difference in analysis is significant for a number of reasons. Firstly, if the conflict is seen as being between two different conflicts rules of the forum, the use of forum policy[36] to solve the conflict is easily justified. Secondly, formulation of the "critical question" facilitates

31 See Law Com WP No 89, para 2.35.

32 "Conflict of conflict rules" would be a more precise description but was rejected as being too clumsy. It is necessary to distinguish Khan-Freund's use of the term "conflict of rules" (n 24, *supra*, at p 285) to refer to the *renvoi* situation where the *lex fori*'s choice rule is different from the *lex causae*'s.

33 Schmidt (n 1, *supra*) at p 361-362 states that the Belgian author Rigaux also recognised that "logically the incidental question is the first as it governs the main question in the same way as a cause precedes its effects". However, this led him to advocate the application of the *lex fori*.

34 See Levontin (n 7, *supra*) at p 106. His view is that no incidental question arises in this situation because the only question is whether the particular party is single and free to remarry. Previous events including obtaining a divorce or nullity decree in respect of a prior marriage are "ingredients that feed the answer to this question" rather than being a question in their own right.

35 In relation to succession, the question would be whether the first spouse is still married for the purposes of succession as spouse. An appropriate question can be formulated for each situation.

36 See Ehrenzweig (n 4, *supra*) at p 170.

adoption of a "separate issue" approach[37] and identification of the relevant policy considerations. Thirdly, the traditional *lex causae* approach assumes that the *lex causae* will apply its conflict rules to determine the incidental question; whereas in fact it might apply its internal law. Under the "conflict of rules" analysis the concern is only with the ultimate result of the application of the *lex causae*. Fourthly, and ironically, although the advocated approach appears to be more parochial because it analyses the conflict purely in terms of the forum's rules, in fact it should prevent an arbitrary bias in favour of application of the *lex fori*.[38]

Whilst other writers[39] have presented the incidental question as a conflict between different conflict rules of the forum, none has considered the opportunities offered by such a presentation of providing a framework for analysis which can produce rational solutions. Thus, for example, whilst the Law Commissions[40] identify the problem of validity of a remarriage after a foreign divorce or nullity decree as a conflict between the choice of law rule and the recognition rule, they simply assert, without any real explanation, that the recognition rule should be favoured.

B. The Distinction Between Incidental Questions Involving Recognition Issues and Those Involving Choice of Law Issues

1. The Distinction

The "conflict of rules" analysis was originally developed by the author[41] in order to solve incidental question cases involving recognition of foreign judgments or decrees concerning status. In this type of case, as in the remarriage example given above, the conflict was perceived as a conflict between the forum's choice of law rules and its recognition rules. This subject was chosen because in modern times the incidental question is most likely to arise in relation to a foreign decree determining status whose validity is disputed.[42] Also, where the subsidiary question involves recognition of a foreign judgment or decree (hereinafter referred to as the "recognition situation"), the "conflict of rules" analysis is conceptually clearer because the conflict is between two different types of conflict rules (ie choice of law rules and recognition rules) and the search is for a preference rule which will determine whether the choice rule or the recognition rule will take precedence.

37 Reese (1977) 26 ICLQ 954 advocates a "separate issue" approach to the choice of law rule for validity of marriage.

38 This is referred to by Kahn-Freund (n 24, *supra*) at p 321 as the "homeward trend".

39 See, eg, Dicey and Morris (n 6, *supra*) at p 758; Cheshire and North (n 6, *supra*) at p 603; North, *The Private International Law of Matrimonial Causes in the British Isles and the Republic of Ireland* (1977) pp 224-225 and Law Com 137, para 1.12; Gordon, *Foreign Divorces: English Law and Practice* (1988) at p 150 and Gottlieb (1955) 33 Can Bar R 523 at p 525.

40 Law Com No 137, para 6.60.

41 In a Doctoral thesis presented to the University of London entitled "Conflicts between Choice of Law Rules and Recognition of Judgments Rules in Private International Law with Particular Reference to Cases Involving Determination of Status" (1994).

42 See L Pallsson, *Marriage in Comparative Conflict of Laws: Substantive Conditions* (1971) at p 95.

However, in this book, the analysis is taken a stage further and extended to cover all incidental question situations. Where no recognition issue is involved, the conflict is seen as one between two choice of law rules of the forum. For example, assume that succession under a will (the main question) depends on whether the claimant is legitimate (the incidental question) and that the *lex causae* governing the succession considers him legitimate and the *lex fori* does not. Under the "conflict of rules" analysis, the critical question is whether the claimant is treated as legitimate[43] for the purposes of this succession and the conflict is seen as one between the choice of law rule governing succession and the choice of law rule governing legitimacy. If the former applies, the claimant is treated as legitimate and can take; whereas if the latter applies, the opposite result is reached. Thus, it can be seen that in cases which do not involve a recognition issue, the preference rule must determine which of the two choice of law rules will take precedence.

The structure of the book reflects the fundamental difference between these two categories of cases. Thus, the result-orientated methodology which is developed in Chapter 3 as a mechanism for solving the "conflict of rules" is applied in Part II to five different situations involving a conflict between a choice of law rule and a recognition rule. Once the effectiveness of the approach is demonstrated in relation to these cases, it will be easier to show in Part III how the approach can also be used to develop preference rules where there is a conflict between two different choice of law rules.

2. Non-Judicial Changes of Status

In most situations, it is obvious whether or not recognition of a judgment or decree is involved and therefore with which of the two categories we are concerned. However, there is some difficulty in determining to what extent the rules determining whether non-judicial changes of status should be recognised should be treated as recognition rules.[44] At first sight, it might seem that since there is no judgment involved, these cases fall within the second category. However, this approach ignores the fact that in some areas of law, the very same rules govern the recognition of judicial and non-judicial changes of status. For example, overseas formal extra-judicial divorces are recognised on the same basis as judicial decrees and the rules in respect of informal divorces, although different, are contained in the same statutory section as those for recognition of formal decrees.[45] On the other hand, in other areas, such as legitimation, the rules for recognition are not treated like recognition of judgments rules and on the contrary are perceived as choice of law rules.[46]

43 If legitimacy depends on the validity of the parents' marriage a sub-incidental question will arise.

44 This difficulty does not arise under the traditional analysis (Section II, *supra*) because the concern is whether the incidental question should be governed by the *conflicts* rules of the forum or of the *lex causae*. It does not matter whether these conflicts rules are recognition of judgments rules or choice of law rules.

45 See Section IV A 2, *infra*.

46 In the same way as the rules governing recognition of the validity of marriages.

No doubt this apparently anomalous situation can be explained in practical terms. Where it is common for a particular status to be created or determined by judicial decree and the same or similar rules apply to non-judicial terminations, as with adoptions and divorces, the rules are treated as recognition of judgments rules, even though there is no judgment or decree. In any event, this is the distinction that will be adopted in this book for the purposes of classification between the two categories of cases.

Thus, the rules for determining the validity of extra-judicial dissolutions, annulments and adoptions will be treated as recognition rules and therefore within the first category. Other non-judicial changes of status[47] will be included within the second category.[48]

C. Distinguishing Between the "Conflict of Rules" Situation and the "Pure Recognition" Situation

In relation to the cases involving recognition rules, it is crucial to distinguish between:

1. the "conflict of rules" situation described above, which has traditionally been analysed in terms of the incidental question; and
2. the "pure recognition" case, where the foreign judgment for which recognition and/or enforcement is sought is inconsistent with the decision which would have been reached by an English court on the same facts applying English choice of law rules.

In the former, the actual issue before the court has not itself been determined by a foreign court, although its outcome depends on whether a foreign judgment is recognised. The issue can be decided either by reference to the recognition rules of the forum or by reference to the law chosen by the forum's choice of law rules. In contrast, in the second category of case, the situation is not perceived or treated as one involving conflict between the two types of rule. The reason for this is that, in deciding whether to recognise the foreign judgment, the court refers only to recognition rules. Since it is forbidden to examine the merits of the case,[49] the choice of law rules are not even called into play.

Once this distinction is grasped, it will be appreciated that without further analysis there should be no assumption that recognition rules should prevail in the "conflict of rules" situation, with which this book is concerned.

47 Although frequently the issue of recognition of a "marriage" can be converted into a recognition of judgments question by obtaining a nullity decree in the jurisdiction which considers the marriage void.

48 The question of recognition of parental orders obtained by commissioning parents in relation to a child born to surrogate mother will, for convenience, be discussed in ch 11, which mainly deals with choice of law rules governing the paternity and maternity of children born as a result of artificial reproduction techniques.

49 *Goddard v Grey* (1870) LR 6 QB 139. In some jurisdictions, only those judgments which closely approximate to the results which would have been achieved by application of the forum's choice of law rules will be recognised (see *Von Mehren v Trautman* (1968) 81 Harv LR 1601, 1605).

D. Notation and Terminology

The following notation and terminology will be adopted throughout the book:

1. Where there is a dispute between the *lex causae* and *lex fori* concerning the validity of a decree or resulting status, this will be indicated by the use of quotation marks, eg "divorce", "spouse", "adopter".
2. While the spouse in relation to whom a "divorce" or "annulment" was obtained may not be the first spouse, s(he) will be referred to as the first spouse[50] to distinguish him/her from the subsequent spouse (who will be called the second spouse) where there has been a remarriage following the "divorce" or "annulment". Similarly, where there is a marriage which is of doubtful validity *ab initio*, this will be referred to as the "first" marriage even though there may have been previous marriage or this may be the only marriage.
3. For most purposes it will not matter whether the disputed decree is a divorce decree or a nullity decree. Thus, for convenience, unless stated to the contrary references to divorce will include annulments.
4. A rule which determines which conflict rule should prevail in a particular "conflict of rules" situation will be referred to as a preference rule.[51]

IV. THE PROBLEM ILLUSTRATED

A. Recognition Rules

In order to illustrate the "conflict of rules" scenario, we need to understand the various recognition and choice rules which will produce the conflict. It will be convenient at this point to summarise briefly the rules for recognition of foreign judgments *in personam* and foreign matrimonial decrees.[52] The relevant choice of law rules will be stated as and when required.

1. In actions in personam[53]

There are now four main sets of recognition rules, three of which are statutory. The common law rules apply to any judgments which are not within the scope of any of the statutes. At common law, a judgment can only be recognised if the court granting it has jurisdictional competence either on the basis of the defendant's residence[54] or submission to the foreign court.

Other connections with the foreign court, such as nationality or that the law of that country is the *lex causae* of the issue in dispute, are not sufficient. A

50 And the marriage will be referred to as the first marriage.
51 The expression "choice of rule" rule is a more specific description but was felt to be too clumsy.
52 The rules for recognition of foreign adoptions will be discussed in ch 8.
53 For detailed exposition see Cheshire and North (ch 1, n 6, *supra*), chs 15 and 16.
54 Recently, the Court of Appeal has stated that mere presence is sufficient, *Adams v Cape Industries* [1990] Ch 433.

judgment which is *prima facie* entitled to recognition will not be recognised where the defendant successfully pleads one of a number of defences.[55]

The Administration of Justice Act 1920, and the Foreign Judgments (Reciprocal Enforcement) Act 1933 make provision for recognition and enforcement of judgments given in courts to whom the Acts are extended,[56] where the foreign court acted with jurisdiction,[57] unless one of a limited number of defences[58] is established. The 1920 Act only applied to Commonwealth countries, but the 1933 Act can be extended to any country.[59]

The Civil Jurisdiction and Judgments Acts 1982 and 1991 brought into force in England and Wales the Brussels and Lugano Conventions respectively. The aim of these Conventions is to provide for "free movement of judgments" throughout Europe.[60] Thus, all judgments of contracting states, which come within the scope of the Conventions[61] must be recognised without review of the merits and without review of whether the judgment granting court had jurisdiction, subject to certain specific exceptions.[62] A limited number of defences are provided.[63] The 1982 Act also provides for recognition and enforcement of judgments given in other parts of the United Kingdom.[64]

2. *Matrimonial Decrees*

Recognition of divorces, annulments and legal separations (hereinafter referred to as divorces) is now governed by the Family Law Act 1986, Part II, which (subject to saving provisions) supersedes the common law rules for recognition and the Recognition of Divorces and Legal Separations Act 1971. It is possible for marriages to be terminated by law without there being any divorce or annulment,[65] in which case the common law rules would still apply.[66] Under the Act, divorces are divided into three categories: (i) divorces granted in the British Isles; (ii) overseas divorces obtained by means of judicial or other proceedings (which will be referred to as formal divorces); and (iii) overseas divorces obtained otherwise than by mean of judicial or other proceedings

55 For list of the defences, see Cheshire and North (ch 1, n 6, *supra*) pp 377 *et seq* and ch 2, *infra*, Section IV.
56 Extension is by Order in Council in respect of countries with whom Her Majesty's Government is satisfied that reciprocal arrangements exist for enforcement of UK judgments.
57 There is no definition of this in the 1920 Act and therefore the common law rules must apply. Section 4(2) of the 1933 Act sets out jurisdiction rules (see ch 2, n 70, *infra*).
58 See s 9(2) of the 1920 Act and s 4(2) of the 1933 Act.
59 Commonwealth countries can also join and since 1933, the 1920 Act has not been extended to any more countries.
60 Both within the EC and EFTA areas.
61 See art 1.
62 See art 28.
63 Arts 27 and 28.
64 See ss. 18 and 19 and Schs 6 and 7.
65 Eg, a court order of presumption of death and dissolution of marriage (as in *Szemik v Gryla* (1965) 109 SJ 175).
66 *Viswallingham v Viswallingham* [1980] 1 FLR 15, where according to the religious law, the marriage was terminated automatically by the conversion of one party to a different religion. The termination was not recognised on grounds of public policy.

(which will be referred to as informal divorces). It will be convenient to treat transnational divorces as an additional category. In relation to each category, a limited number of grounds for refusal of recognition are provided,[67] which are set out and analysed in Chapter 2, *infra*. The recognition provisions are as follows.

(A) DIVORCES GRANTED IN THE BRITISH ISLES

Decrees obtained in a court of civil jurisdiction in the British Isles are automatically recognised.[68] Section 44(2) states that "no divorce or annulment obtained in any part of the British Islands shall be regarded as effective in any part of the United Kingdom unless granted by a court of civil jurisdiction."

The predecessor to this provision[69] reversed the position at common law.[70]

(B) OVERSEAS DIVORCES OBTAINED BY MEANS OF JUDICIAL OR OTHER PROCEEDINGS[71]

Such divorces will be recognised if the following conditions are fulfilled:

(i) they are effective in the country in which they are obtained *and*
(ii) one of the parties is either habitually resident in, domiciled[72] in or a national of the country in which the divorce is obtained.

The crucial distinction between divorces which come within this category and those which fall within the third category is whether the divorce was obtained by means of judicial or other proceedings. There is no statutory definition of proceedings. There would not seem to be any problem in ascertaining whether there have been judicial proceedings. The difficulty arises in determining whether the steps involved in obtaining an extra-judicial divorce are sufficient to constitute proceedings.

The most helpful guidance to emerge from the case law can be found in the speech of Oliver LJ in *Chaudhary v Chaudhary*.[73]

> In the context . . . of a solemn change of status, [proceedings] must import a degree of formality and at least the involvement of some agency, whether lay or religious, of or recognised by the state having a function that is more than simply probative, although *Quazi* . . . clearly shows that it need have no power of veto."

Applying this definition,[74] it is clear that a Pakistani Muslim Family Ordinance *talaq*,[75] a Jewish *get*[76] and a Ghanian Customary Arbitration Tribunal divorce[77]

67 See s 51 of the Family Law Act 1986.
68 Family Law Act 1986, s 44(1).
69 Domicile and Matrimonial Proceedings Act 1973, s 16(1).
70 See eg *Qureshi v Qureshi* [1972] Fam 173.
71 See Family Law Act 1986, s 46(1).
72 Either in the sense used in the foreign country or in the English sense (Family Law Act 1986, s 46(5)).
73 [1985] 3 All ER 1017 at 1031.

are obtained by means of proceedings; whereas classical Muslim law "bare" *talaqs,*[78] other non-judicial Muslim divorces and Thai consensual divorces are not obtained by means of proceedings. Which category Hindu and African and Asian customary divorces come into must be decided in each case, depending on whether there is involvement by a state recognised third party, such as a recognised *panchayat* or tribal elders.

(C) OVERSEAS DIVORCES OBTAINED OTHERWISE THAN BY MEANS OF PROCEEDINGS[79]

Informal divorces will be recognised if the following conditions are fulfilled:

(i) they are effective in the country in which they are obtained *and*
(ii) they are obtained in the country of domicile of the spouses[80] *and*
(iii) *neither* party was habitually resident in the United Kingdom for one year before the divorce was obtained.

Thus, it can be seen that recognition of informal divorces is more restrictive than that of formal divorces in two main ways.[81] Firstly, there are less jurisdictional bases available.[82] Secondly, in relation to formal divorces there is no restriction on the connection of the parties with the United Kingdom.

(D) TRANSNATIONAL DIVORCES

Transnational divorces are those obtained by means of steps taken in more than one country. In *R v Secretary of State for the Home Department, ex p Ghulam Fatima*[83] the question arose whether a talaq obtained in accordance with the provisions of the Pakistani Muslim Family Law Ordinance could be recognised under the Recognition of Divorces and Legal Separations Act 1971, where the *talaq* itself was pronounced in England and all the subsequent steps took place in Pakistan. The House of Lords held that the divorce was not an overseas divorce because the wording of the statute[84] indicated that a divorce would only be treated as an overseas divorce where all proceedings took place in the same foreign jurisdiction.

74 Gordon (n 39, *supra*) at p 115 provides a helpful table with suggested classification of divorces.
75 *Quazi v Quazi* [1980] AC 744.
76 See Berkovits (1980) 104 LQR 60.
77 *D v D (Recognition of Foreign Divorce)* [1994] 1 FLR 38.
78 *Chaudhary v Chaudhary* [1984] 3 All ER 1017.
79 See Family Law Act 1986, s 46(2).
80 Where the spouses are domiciled in separate countries, it is sufficient that the divorce is obtained in a country where one is domiciled, provided that it is recognised by the domicile of the other.
81 In addition, informal divorces are more likely to be refused recognition on the basis of public policy. See derogatory comments of Cumming-Bruce LJ about bare *talaqs* in *Chaudhary v Chaudhary* [1984] 3 WLR 1017 at 1032.
82 For formal divorces there are up to eight different countries (in the unlikely event that each party has habitual residence, domicile in the English sense, domicile in the foreign sense and nationality in different countries) where the divorce may be obtained and recognised. For informal divorces there are only four possibilities (domicile in both senses for each party).
83 [1986] AC 527.
84 Recognition of Divorces and Legal Separations Act 1971, s 2.

Until recently, the majority of commentators held that the provisions of Family Law Act 1986 could not be construed in this way[85] and that, therefore, whilst there does not appear to have been any intention to overrule the *Fatima* decision,[86] this was the result of the change in the drafting.

However, in *Berkovits v A-G, ex p Grinburg*,[87] Wall J held that s 46 of the new Act was to be construed in the same way as in the 1971 Act and that an overseas divorce could only be recognised if the proceedings all took place in the same overseas country. In this case, therefore, the transnational *get,* which had been initiated by the preparation of the *get* (the document of divorce) in England but obtained in Israel when the *get* (the document of divorce) was officially handed to the wife at a Rabbinical Court in Israel, could not be recognised.

With respect, the reasoning of his Lordship is not convincing and it would be open to another court to find that the wording of the 1986 Act is ambiguous. Therefore, the Act should be construed in such a way as to remedy the mischief which it was designed to cure, which was to avoid the creation of limping marriages.

A noteworthy difference between the *Fatima* and *Grinburg* cases is that in the latter, Wall J accepted the policy arguments in favour of recognition of the *get* in this case. Whereas in *Fatima*, there were *dicta* which suggest that even if the transnational *talaq* had fitted within the scheme of the 1971 Act, it would have been refused recognition on public policy grounds because it was effectively a "mail order" extra-judicial divorce obtained in England, which was contrary to the policy[88] of what is now s 44(2) of the Family Law Act 1986.[89]

Thus, it is submitted that the position in relation to recognition of transnational divorces remains unclear.

B. Examples of the "Conflict of Rules" Scenario

The examples given below, most of which are based on variations of the facts of decided cases, illustrate a wide range of situations where the "conflict of rules" scenario arises. In the first two examples, there is reference to a number of different problems which may arise. Thereafter, each example concentrates on one particular issue. Extensive reference to these problems will be made throughout this book. Whilst this means that the reader will need to refer back to this section, it was decided that the scope of the problem could be better illustrated at this stage by setting out all the examples together.

85 See Berkovits (1988) 104 LQR 60 at 79-80; Pilkington (1988) 37 ICLQ 131 at 133-136 and Gordon (ch n 39, *supra*) p 103, p 668 at n 18.

86 The Law Commission in Rep No 137 at para 6.11 treat *Fatima* as having settled the law on transnational divorces. As Parliament took a harsher line than the Law Commission in respect of extra-judicial divorces, it seems unlikely that they intended to take a more benevolent view of transnational divorces.

87 [1995] 2 All ER 683.

88 Cf Berkovits (1988) 104 LQR 60 at 75-78.

Example M1[90]
Alexander and Natasha are Jews who were born and brought up in Russia, where they married. In 1991, they leave Russia to emigrate to Israel. Whilst in a transit camp in Vienna, they get divorced by means of a Jewish *get* issued under the auspices of the Rabbinical Court in Vienna. The get is not recognised in Austria or Russia and so would not be recognised in England. In 1992 Alexander and Natasha arrive and acquire a domicile in Israel, where the *get* is recognised. Alexander marries Bella, an Israeli domiciliary, in Israel where they set up their home.

The following questions may arise:
(a) Is Alexander's marriage to Bella recognised in England?
(b) On Alexander's death intestate can Natasha succeed to movable and immovable property of Alexander's situated in England?
(c) What are Natasha's rights under the marriage settlement entered into between her and Alexander when they married?

In each situation if the *recognition rule* prevails Natasha is treated as still validly married to Alexander. If the *choice rule* prevails, the position will depend on which law governs the particular issue. Thus, in relation to issues governed by English law, such as succession to immovables in England, the first marriage is still valid. Whereas, in relation to issues governed by Israeli law, such as Alexander's capacity to remarry and intestate succession to movables, the first marriage will not be regarded as still subsisting.

Example M2[91]
Pedro is a national of, domiciled and habitually resident in Brazil. He is married to Evita, who is a national of and domiciled in Argentina. When the marriage breaks down Evita becomes habitually resident in Mexico, where she later obtains a divorce from Pedro. This divorce is not recognised in Brazil or Argentina, but is effective under Mexican law and *prima facie* entitled to recognition under English law. Evita then marries Juan, an Argentinian domiciliary, in Mexico. They then return to live in Argentina.
(a) Is Evita's marriage to Juan recognised in England?
(b) On Evita's death intestate can Pedro succeed to property of Evita's situated in England?
(c) What are Evita's rights under the marriage settlement entered into between her and Pedro when they married?

If the recognition rules prevail, then for all purposes Evita is considered as no longer married to Pedro, but instead validly married to Juan. If the choice rule prevails, then the marriage to Pedro still subsists in relation to all issues governed by Argentinian law and that to Juan is not recognised at all; whereas it does not subsist in relation to issues governed by Mexican or English law.

89 Previously the Domicile and Matrimonial Proceedings Act 1973, s 16(1).
90 Based on *Schwebel v Ungar* (1963) 42 DLR (2d) 622 (discussed at ch 4 II A, *infra*).
91 Based on *Lawrence v Lawrence* [1985] Fam 106 (discussed in ch 4 II B, *infra)*.

Example M3 (reverse of M1)
Assume that the *get* is obtained after Alexander and Natasha have become domiciled and habitually resident in Israel. After a short period of time, Alexander returns to Russia. He resumes his Russian domicile and marries Bella, a Russian domiciliary. Assume that the Israeli *get* is not recognised under Russian law, but is recognised under English law.

If the recognition rules apply, the first marriage no longer subsists and the second marriage will be valid for all purposes; whereas if the choice rules apply, the first marriage will be regarded as valid in relation to all matters governed by Russian law.

Example M4 (reverse of M2)
Assume that Evita does not become habitually resident in Mexico, but obtains the Mexican divorce by proxy[92] and so the divorce is not entitled to recognition in England. However, assume that it is entitled to recognition in Argentina by virtue of a bilateral treaty with Mexico.

If the recognition rules apply, the first marriage will subsist for all purposes; whereas if the choice rules apply, the second marriage will be valid in relation to all issues governed by Argentinian law but the first marriage will subsist in relation to issues governed by English law.

Example M5[93]
Maria, who is domiciled in and a national of Belgium marries Herbert, who is domiciled in Ontario. The marriage, which takes place in Ontario, is a marriage of convenience with the sole aim of enabling Maria, an illegal immigrant, to remain in Ontario. The parties have no intention of and do not in fact cohabit. The marriage is valid in Ontario. Later Maria obtains a nullity decree in Belgium on the basis that the marriage is a sham. Assume that this decree is entitled to recognition in England, but is refused recognition in Ontario on public policy grounds. Maria marries Andrew, a domiciliary of Ontario. Although the ceremony takes place in Belgium, the parties return to live in Ontario.

If the recognition rules are applied, the first marriage will have been annulled and the second will be valid for all purposes. If the choice of law rules are applied, then the first marriage still subsists in relation to all issues governed by Ontario law. Since the validity of the second marriage is governed by Ontario law[94] it will accordingly be void.

This example also involves the "pure recognition" situation referred to above.[95] The result of the Belgium decision is inconsistent with that which would have been achieved in an English Court, in which Ontario law, as the *lex loci celebrationis*, would have been applied to determine whether the sham marriage was valid. Strictly speaking, this point should not be relevant when

92 See *Padolecchia v Padolecchia* [1969] P 314.
93 Based on *Vervaeke v Smith* [1981] Fam 77 (discussed at ch II, Section VI, *infra).*
94 Either as the law of Andrew's domicile (which would prevent him from marrying a married woman) or as the law of the intended matrimonial home.
95 Section I B, *supra.*

recognition of the decree is sought because it relates to the merits. However, the courts may well be influenced by the point and might either refuse recognition on the ground of public policy[96] or else achieve the result of non-recognition by preferring the choice rules.[97]

Example M6[98]
Don and Isabella are first cousins. They are both habitually resident and domiciled in New York, where they marry. Don is a United States national, but Isabella is a Portugese national. The marriage is valid by the law of New York, but not by the law of Portugal which forbids marriages between first cousin. A few years after the marriage, Don travels to Portugal where he acquires a nullity decree on the basis that under Portugese law capacity to marry is governed by the law of the nationality and that the marriage was *void ab initio*. The nullity decree is not recognised in New York. Don dies intestate domiciled in New York leaving movable property in England.

If the choice rule is applied to the question of whether Isabella is entitled to succeed as spouse, New York law will apply and she will be entitled. If the recognition rule is applied, the Portugese decree is entitled to recognition under the Family Law Act 1986 by virtue of the wife's Portugese nationality. Thus, she would not be entitled.

Example M7
Ahmed divorces his wife Bina by bare *talaq* in India. At the time, Ahmed is domiciled in Saudi Arabia and Bina is domiciled in Dubai. The *talaq* is recognised by both countries of domicile. Subsequently, Ahmed marries Hussana in England and Bina marries Mohammed in India. Since neither of the parties is domiciled in India, where the divorce is obtained, the *talaq* will not be recognised in England. However, the remarriages are valid by the law of the parties' domiciles.

If the recognition rule is applied, the second marriages will not be valid;[99] whereas if the choice rule is applied, they will be valid.

Example M8
Shimon and Talia are domiciliaries and nationals of Israel. After they separated, Shimon comes to live in England. He institutes proceedings to divorce his wife by Jewish *get* in the Court of the Chief Rabbi in London. The *get* is handed to Talia in Haifa

96 As in *Gray v Formosa* [1963] P 259 and *per obiter dicta* in *Vervaeke v Smith* [1983] AC 145 (both analysed in detail at ch 2 VI, *infra*). However, in this example, there is little connection with England and thus English public policy may not be infringed.
97 It is arguable that this is what happened in *R v Brentwood Superintendant Registrar of Marriages, ex p Arias* [1968] 2 QB 596 (discussed at ch 4 II A, *infra*). The English court did not approve of the grant of a divorce decree in Switzerland which had the effective consequence that the wife could remarry and the husband could not (because the decree was not recognised by the law of his nationality). The English court's decision not to allow the remarriage of the husband by applying choice of law rules resulted in effective non-recognition of the Swiss divorce. The difficulty with this analysis is that the English decision continues the unfairness of the original Swiss decree.
98 Based on facts of *Sottomeyer v De Barros* (1879) 5 PD 94.
99 Whilst Ahmed has capacity to take a second wife by the law of his domicile, a polygamous marriage contracted in England is void.
100 See II B 4, *supra*.

by an agent. The *get* is recognised in Israel. Shimon then marries Rina in Israel. Assume that the transnational *get* will not be recognised in England.[100]

If the recognition rule prevails, Shimon is still treated as married to Talia and the second marriage is invalid; whereas if the choice rule prevails the second marriage is valid.

Example M9[101]
Anthony, who is a domiciliary and national of Malta, married Susan, an English domiciliary and national in an English register office. A few years later, Anthony obtains a nullity decree in Malta on the basis that the marriage was not celebrated in church. Anthony subsequently marries Rosa, a Maltese domiciliary and national, in a church ceremony in Malta. Assume that the Maltese nullity decree is not recognised in England on public policy grounds.[102] Anthony dies intestate leaving property in England.

If the recognition rule prevails then the first marriage is still valid and Susan may claim as Anthony's widow. If the choice rule prevails then the second marriage is valid and Rosa may claim as Anthony's widow.

Example M10
John and Theresa are domiciled in Puerto Rica and are nationals of the United States. John owns substantial assets in England. They travel to the Dominican Republic for the weekend, where they obtain a divorce. Assume that the divorce is recognised in Puerto Rico,[103] but not in England. The parties' matrimonial property is subject to a community regime.

If the choice rule prevails, the parties shares in the assets in England are calculated and may be claimed from the date of the divorce. If the recognition rule prevails, the parties are still regarded as married and the community still continues.[104]

Example M11
Patrick and Queenie get married in a consular marriage in Ruritania in conformity with the provisions of the Foreign Marriages Act.[105] Later, Patrick, who is now domiciled in Utopia wishes to remarry in Utopia without dissolving the marriage with Queenie. Under Utopian law, the first marriage is invalid because the formalities of Ruritanian law are not satisfied.

If the conflict rules governing formality of foreign marriages are applied, Patrick is validly married and may not remarry. Whereas, if the choice of law

101 Based on *Grey v Formosa [1963] P 259, Lepre v Lepre [1965] P 52 and Papadopoulos v Papadopoulos* [1930] P 55.
102 The cases of *Grey v Formosa, ibid* and *Lepre v Lepre, ibid* (discussed at ch 2 VI, *infra*) were decided under the common law rules. However, although they have been criticised, it seems likely that the same result would be achieved using the statutory public policy defence in Family Law Act 1986, s 51(3).
103 See ch 4 I B 2, *infra*.
104 See ch 6 I 2 (b), *infra*.
105 See ch 9 II B, *infra*.

rule governing capacity to marry is applied, Patrick is considered as a bachelor who is free to marry.

Example T1
Jane and Kevin are domiciled in Florida. Jane is a US citizen, but Kevin is a national of Haiti, although he has never had any real connection with that country. When their marriage breaks down, Kevin returns to Haiti and obtains an *ex parte* divorce there. Assume that this divorce is recognised in England, but not in the USA. Kevin later comes to live in England, but on a trip to Florida, negligently causes injury Jane. Under the law of Florida, there is inter-spousal immunity in tort. Assume that this immunity continues after separation of the spouses until divorce.

The question to be answered is whether Jane is single or still married for the purposes of suing Kevin in tort. If the recognition rule is applied she is no longer married to Kevin and thus the immunity does not apply. If the choice rule governing tort applies, which in this case is the place where the injury takes place,[106] Jane is still treated as married therefore Kevin can claim the immunity.

Example T2[107]
Lily and Michael, who are domiciled in New York, obtained a "weekend" *inter partes* divorce in Haiti. Michael is subsequently killed in New Jersey by the negligence of Norman, who is resident in England. Assume that the divorce is recognised in New Jersey[108] but not in England and that according to the law of New Jersey a wife, but not a former wife, can claim wrongful death compensation.

If the recognition rule is applied, Lilly is eligible for wrongful death compensation because she is still married to Michael. However if the choice rule applies, she is no longer the wife under the New Jersey *lex loci delicti* and cannot claim.

Example A1[109]
Alistair and his wife, who are at all material times domiciled in Zimbabwe, adopt two children in South Africa. Alistair's mother, Dorothy, who is at all material times domiciled in Zimbabwe, makes a bequest of movables in favour of the issue of Alistair. Assume that the adoption is not recognised by the law of Zimbabwe, but is recognised as an "overseas" adoption by English law.[110]

If the choice rule prevails, the children will not be able to take under Dorothy's will, which is governed by Zimbabwe law. However, if the recognition rule prevails they can take as the children of Alistair.

106 See Private International Law (Miscellaneous Provisions) Act 1995, s 11.
107 Based on the US case of *Meisenholder v Chicago and NW Ry* 213 NW 32 (1927) and see *Harper* (1959) 59 Col LR 440 at 456.
108 See ch 4 I B 2, *infra*.
109 Based on *Re Valentine's Settlement* [1965] Ch 831.
110 See ch 8 I B 4, *infra*.

Example A2 (reverse of A1)
In example A1 above, assume that Dorothy is at all material times domiciled in South Africa and that the adoptions are valid by the law of South Africa but are not recognised in Zimbabwe or in England.

If the choice rule prevails, the children can take, as the adoption is recognised in South Africa; whereas, if the recognition rule is applied, they will not succeed.

Example L1
Cuthbert is born to Albert and Brenda before they get married. At the time of the marriage, Albert is domiciled in Utopia and a national of Plutonia. Albert later dies domiciled in Ruritania, leaving movables in England. By the law of Ruritania, only a legitimate(d) child may share in the intestacy of his father.

In Utopia, but not Plutonia, a child is legitimated by the subsequent marriage of his parents. Under Ruritanian law legitimation by subsequent marriage is governed by the nationality of the father at the date of the marriage, whereas by English law, the law of the domicile at that date applies.

Thus, if the choice rule governing legitimation is applied, Cuthbert is legitimated and may share in the succession; whereas if the choice of law rule governing succession is applied (which is Ruritanian law), Cuthbert's legitimation is not recognised and he will not be able to take.

Example L2
Assume the same facts as in L1, but the laws of Plutonia and Utopia are reversed, ie in Plutonia subsequent marriage legitimates, but not in Utopia.

Thus, if the choice rule governing legitimation is applied, Cuthbert does not take; whereas if the choice rule governing succession is applied, he will take.

Example AID1
Alan is born as a result of artificial insemination by donor in Quickland, where his mother, Beth is domiciled. According to the law of Quickland, Beth's husband, Cyril is treated as Alan's father. However, at the date of birth, Cyril is domiciled in Zebraland, according to which only the biological father is treated as the father. Later Cyril dies intestate domiciled in Illinois. According to the law of Illinois the question of paternity of a child born by artificial insemination is determined by the law which has the most significant relationship to the child and the parent,[110a] which in the present case would be the law of Quickland. Assume that under English conflicts rules paternity is be governed by the law of the domicile of the man whose paternity is in issue at the date of the birth.

If the choice of law rule governing the succession is preferred, Alan is treated as Cyril's son and can succeed as a beneficiary of his estate; whereas if the forum's choice of law rule governing parenthood is preferred, Alan cannot succeed.

110a See *Re Marriage of Adams* 133 Ill 2d 437, 141 Ill Dec 448, 551 NE 2d 635 discussed at ch 11 I C 2, *infra*.

Example AID2
Assume that, in example AID1 above, Beth and Cyril are unmarried cohabitees and that the semen was obtained from Dennis, a friend, who is domiciled in Zebraland. Assume that by the law of Quickland either Cyril is treated as the father or no person is treated as the father. Dennis later dies intestate domiciled in Illinois.

If the choice of law rule governing the succession is preferred, Alan is not treated as Dennis's son and so cannot succeed; whereas if the forum's choice rule governing parenthood is preferred, Alan can succeed as beneficiary of Dennis's estate.

Example P1[111]
A painting is stolen from Winkworth's house in England. It is taken to Italy where it is sold in market overt to Yves, who is resident in Ruritania. Yves acquires good title under Italian law. This title is recognised under English choice of law rules. Suppose that in an action between Winkworth and Yves in Ruritania, the Ruritanian Court decides that the valuable painting is owned by Winkworth. This judgment is entitled to recognition in England.[112] However, Yves ignores the judgment and brings the painting from Italy to England, where Winkworth seeks return of the painting.

If the English Court applies its recognition rule, Winkworth will succeed; whereas if it applies its choice of law rule, Yves will succeed.

Example P2
Assume the same facts as in example P1 except that Yves hands the painting over to Winkworth in Ruritania. Winkworth then takes the painting back to Italy where he sells it to Zeldon. Zeldon brings it to England and Yves claims the painting from him. Applying English choice of law rules, whether Zeldon acquires good title is governed by the law of the situs, which is Italian law. Assume that under Italian law, a transferee cannot obtain better title than the transferor (unless he buys in market overt) and that the Ruritanian judgment is not recognised in Italy.

Thus, again if the English court applies its recognition rule, Zeldon (Winkworth's assignee) will succeed; whereas if it applies its choice rule Yves will succeed.

Example P3 (variation of example P2)
Assume that in P2 above, the Ruritanian judgment is not entitled to recognition in England, but that Winkworth transfers the painting to Zeldon in Ruritania.

If we apply the recognition rule, then since the Ruritanian judgment is not recognised, Winkworth never acquires title. Thus, Yves who acquired good title in Italy, still owns the painting. Whereas, if we apply the choice of law rule Winkworth obtains title by virtue of the judgment of the Ruritanian court[113]

111 Based on *Winkworth v Christie, Manson and Woods Ltd* [1980] Ch 496.
112 For a discussion of the issues which may arise in this sort of situation where the judgment is not recognised in England, see ch 2 IV B, *infra*.
113 It is assumed that the Ruritanian judgment is not merely declaratory but actually has the effect in Ruritanian law of vesting title in Winkworth.

while the painting is in Ruritania. He can therefore pass on good title when he sells the painting to Zeldon in Ruritania.

Example P4 (variation of P3)
Suppose that Yves does not hand over the painting to Winkworth in accordance with the judgment, but sells it to Zeldon in Ruritania and Zeldon brings it to England.

If we apply the *lex situs* choice rule, then it appears that Zeldon cannot acquire good title from Yves because the effect of the Ruritanian judgment is to vest title in Winkworth. If we apply the recognition rule, Zeldon acquires good title from Yves because the judgment is of no effect.

Example P5[114]
Oliver acquires property from Nancy in Plutonia and takes it to Utopia where he sells it. However, she now claims that the transaction was invalid and sues Oliver in England for conversion of her property in Utopia. In defence, Oliver claims that the transaction was valid and that therefore he was the true owner of the property at the time of the alleged conversion. Assume that the Plutonian transaction is not considered effective to transfer property rights by Plutonian law, but that under Utopian law Oliver is treated as the true owner because he obtained a valid import licence.

The critical question is whether Nancy is the owner at the date of the "conversion". If we apply the choice of law rule governing ownership, the *lex situs* at the time of transaction which is alleged to have transferred ownership, then Plutonian law governs and the answer is in the affirmative; whereas if we apply the choice of law rule governing the tort, the *lex loci delicti*, then Utopian law governs and the answer is negative.

V. CONFLICTS BETWEEN CHOICE OF LAW RULES AND FORUM DECREES/ DOMESTIC RULES

A problem similar to the incidental question may arise where a decree of the forum is not recognised by the *lex causae* or where the incidental question does not involve any foreign elements, although the main question is governed by foreign law. In such situations, there may be a conflict between the forum's choice of law rule and one of its domestic rules.[115] It is submitted that this conflict has similar

114 Based on the example referred to by Schmidt (n 1, *supra*) at pp 376-377.
115 An apparently similar conflict may arise where the main question is governed by the *lex fori*, but the incidental question has foreign elements. Thus, the question arises whether the forum's conflicts rules or its domestic law rules should determine the incidental question. On the Continent, this problem seems to be part of the "Substitution Problem" (see Schmidt, n 1, *supra* at pp 335-341). In England, the problem seems to be treated as one of construction: ie does the substantive rule of the *lex fori* intend that the particular legal concept referred to therein (eg marriage or legitimacy) be understood in the domestic law sense of the word or in accordance with the forum's private international law rules. Mann (1963) LQR 525 refers to "the primary question of construction" and claims that it is "one of the darkest corners of the conflict of laws" (at p 531). It is suggested that the construction approach highlights the fact that this situation is essentially purely a question of interpretation of domestic law and therefore fundamentally different from the "conflict of rules" or "quasi conflict of rules" situations referred to in the text.

features[116] to the true "conflict of rules" situation and can conveniently be referred to as the "quasi conflict of rules". In order to assess whether the approach advocated in this book is also appropriate for the "quasi conflict of rules" scenario, it is first necessary to consider when this conflict will arise both in respect of forum decrees and forum domestic rules.

A. Forum Decrees

In relation to issues governed by the domicile,[117] there can only be a conflict between a forum matrimonial decree and the *lex causae* where:

(a) there has been a change of domicile between decree and the relevant event,[118] or
(b) (i) jurisdiction is taken on grounds other than the domicile of both parties and
 (ii) the choice of law rule for granting the decree is other than the *lex domicilii*[119] of both parties.[120]

Requirement (a) is purely factual. However, the two requirements necessary to satisfy (b) are legal and merit further examination.

(i) Until 1937, English courts only had jurisdiction in matrimonial cases where the parties were domiciled in England. However, jurisdiction was gradually widened by statute[121] and today English courts can entertain applications for matrimonial decrees where *either* party is domiciled or has been habitually resident

116 Although according to the Austinian conception of status (as explained by Engdahl (1969) 55 Iowa L Rev 56, 57 *et seq*) the fact that the decree has validity by virtue of domestic law rather than "conflicts" recognition rules is a fundamental distinction.

117 Eg, capacity to remarry (but see ch 4 I C, *infra*), succession to movables.

118 Eg, remarriage or death.

119 In some European countries, the law of the nationality is still used to govern divorce In its unmodified form, this principle requires that a decree not be granted unless both parties are entitled to a decree under the law of their nationality. Alternatively, whilst a decree is granted on the basis of the national law of one, it is only considered effective in relation to that party and the other spouse is still considered as married. This used to be the case in France (see Hartley (1967) 16 ICLQ 680 at p 688). Under these theories, there can be no conflict between the choice rule and the forum decree. In practice, however, many countries have modified the exclusive application of the law of the nationality (see Palsson, International Encyclopedia of Comparative Law, vol III, ch 16, paras 129 *et seq).*

120 Where the divorce is governed by the personal law of one spouse only, there may be a conflict where the decree is not recognised by the personal law of the other. See examples in relation to German law given by Palsson, *Marriage in Comparative Conflict of Laws: Substantive Conditions* (1971) pp 229-232 and 244-250. The German choice of law rule in divorce has now been reformed (see Dickson (1985) 34 ICLQ 231) and it is now more likely that the divorce will be governed by a law which is not the national law of one or both parties (where there has not been a common nationality retained by one spouse, the divorce will be governed by the last common habitual residence, provided that this is retained by one and otherwise by the law with which the spouses are together most closely connected).

121 It will be remembered that until 1973 a married woman's domicile was dependent on her husband's. Thus, a wife could only petition for divorce if her husband was domiciled in England. The hardship caused by this state of affairs was mitigated by two provisions. The Matrimonial Causes Act 1937, s 13 provided for jurisdiction in a divorce case at the petition of the wife if she had been deserted by her husband or he had been deported and immediately prior to that he had been domiciled in England. The Law Reform (Miscellaneous Provisions) Act 1949 provided for jurisdiction where the wife had been ordinarily resident for three years in England and her husband was not domiciled in the United Kingdom, Channel Islands or Isle of Man.

in the jurisdiction for one year.[122] Thus, there are many decrees granted in England to parties of whom at least one is not domiciled in the forum.

(ii) In England and Wales, the choice of law rule for divorce is the *lex fori*.[123] The position in nullity is more complicated.[124] Whilst the orthodox approach is that the dual domicile test applies to most issues, the position in relation to non-consummation[125] has never been clear. Also, there are now some indications that, at least in some circumstances, capacity is governed by the intended matrimonial home or real and substantial connection test.[126] Even where domicile is the relevant connecting factor, it is domicile at the date of the first marriage which is relevant in determining whether a nullity decree should be granted. Whereas the question of capacity to enter into the second marriage is governed by the law of the domicile at the date of the latter.

In relation to issues not governed by the lex *domicili*, the problem can arise whenever the forum decree is not recognised by the *lex causae*.[127] It might be surprising, therefore, that there is no reported case[128] in which an English[129] court has had to face this conflict between its own matrimonial decree and its choice rules. Whilst s 50 of the Family Law Act 1986 now provides for a re-marriage of either party to a forum decree to be recognised, the problem may still arise in relation to other issues such as succession.

It might be argued that as a matter of policy the forum decree always prevails.[130] However, it seems implicit from the judgments in *Breen v Breen*[131] that this is not the case as the court would apparently have been prepared to refuse to recognise the second marriage if the English divorce decree had not been recognised in Ireland, even though the only connection that Ireland had with the case was that it was the *lex loci celebrationis*. If, therefore, there is no global preference for the forum decree, there is room for application of the specific result-orientated approach, explained and illustrated in Part II. In particular, it should be noted that this method bases the preference rule on forum policy.

B. Forum Domestic Rules

Firstly, it is necessary to distinguish between the situation where a domestic rule of law is applied *qua* domestic rule and where it is applied because the choice of law rule selects the domestic law to provide the rule of determination.

122 Domicile and Matrimonial Proceedings Act 1973, s 5.
123 *Zanelli v Zanelli* (1948) 64 TLR 556.
124 See Law Commission WP No 89, Part V.
125 See Bishop (1978) 41 MLR 512.
126 See ch 4 I C, *infra*.
127 Eg, the *lex situs* in relation to intestate succession to immovables.
128 The conflict would have arisen in *Breen v Breen* [1964] P 144 if the English decree had not been recognised in Ireland and one of the parties was now domiciled in Ireland.
129 There are a number of cases on the Continent of Europe in which the problem has had to be decided directly (see Palsson (n 43, *supra*) pp 229 *et seq* and Shmidt (n 1, *supra*) pp 397-402) but they do not provide any consistent guidance.
130 This seems to be the view of Lagarde as reported in Schmidt (n 1, *supra*) at p 359.
131 [1964] P 144.

The latter situation can easily be illustrated. Assume[132] that the incidental question involves the validity of a marriage celebrated in England between two cousins who are nationals of Portugal but domiciled in England. The relevant forum choice of law rule is the *lex domicili*, which happens to be English law. Assume that the main question concerns succession to immovables and is governed by Portugese law as the *lex situs*. Assume further that under Portugese law the validity of the marriage is governed by the law of the nationality, according to which it is invalid. In this case, under the traditional analysis the question is whether the forum's choice rules or the *lex causae*'s choice of law rules should determine which law governs the essential validity of marriage and thus a true incidental question is presented. Under the "conflict of rules analysis", there is a conflict between the forum's choice of law governing succession and its choice of law rule governing validity of marriage and thus the conflict comes squarely within the "conflict of rules" situation. The fact that the English choice of law rule governing validity of marriage points to an English rule of determination does not detract from this and is not in itself relevant to the conflict between the two choice of law rules.[133]

The former situation is harder to illustrate because the incidental question will only be governed by an English internal rule where there are no foreign elements at all. In which case, it seems most unlikely that the *lex causae* will apply any law other than English law to determine the incidental question because no other law has any connections with the facts. One exception would be where the *lex causae* applies its own law *qua lex fori* to the incidental question or its choice of law rule does not depend on factual connections. The common law choice of law rule for legitimacy[134] comes into one of these two categories and so provides a suitable basis for an example.

Assume[135] that a testator, X, who is domiciled in Ruritania leaves property to the legitimate children of A, his niece. A's only child is C, who was born to A and B, who had been though a ceremony of marriage. Unbeknown to A, B was still married to D and therefore their marriage was void for bigamy. Assume that A, B and C are all domiciled, national and resident in England. Thus, there are no foreign elements involved in the incidental question of whether C is

132 This example is a variation of the facts of *Sottomayor v De Barros* (1877) 3 PD 1.

133 The only relevance is that the English rule of determination selected by the choice of law rule governing capacity to marry gives a different answer than the Portugese rule of determination which is selected by the choice of law rule governing succession to immovables. But this would equally be the case if the couple were domiciled in another country according to whose law they had capacity to marry each other.

134 Ie that a child is legitimate if and only if his/her parents marriage is valid. Whilst this was presented as a choice of law rule, some commentators argued that it was simply the application of the domestic law rule *qua lex fori*. To the extent that it was a choice of law rule it did not rely on any factual connections existing at the time of or in relation to the birth of the child. The *lex domicili* of the parents at the time of the marriage would determine whether the marriage was essentially valid and the *lex loci celebrationis* whether it was formally valid. Since the case of *Re Bischoffsheim* [1948] Ch 79, it seems that a child will be legitimate even if his/her parents marriage is not valid provided that (s)he is legitimate according to the domicile of both of his/her parents. This rider adds in factual connections relevant at the time of the birth.

135 This example is based on the facts of *Shaw v Gould* (1868) LR 3 HL 55. The case would have appeared like this *mutatis mutandis* if it had come before a Scottish court.

legitimate. Under English domestic law, C will be treated as legitimate under the putative marriage doctrine.[136] Assume that under Ruritanian law, the question of whether a child is legitimate depends on whether the parents marriage is valid. Thus, a "quasi conflict of rules" is presented between the Ruritanian choice of law rule for legitimacy and the English domestic law rule.

Again, it might be decided that as a matter of policy the English domestic rule should take precedence. However, it is suggested that there is no more justification for such a position where English law applies to the incidental question purely by virtue of an internal rule than where it applies by virtue of application of a choice of law rule. We have already seen that the latter falls squarely within the "conflict of rules" analysis. Thus, again it is submitted that the result-orientated approach advocated in relation to the true "conflict of rules" is appropriate to solve "quasi conflict of rules" in the choice of law, as well as the recognition, situation.

VI. THE APPLICATION OF THE CHOICE RULE AND *RENVOI*

We have seen that under the "conflict of rules" analysis, a preference for the choice rule governing the main question results in application of the choice or recognition rules of the *lex causae* to determine the "critical question". This might be seen as an application of the doctrine of *renvoi*, because application of the *lex causae* to the problem means application of the whole *lex causae*, including its conflicts rules,[137] which may be choice rules or recognition rules.

Writers have commented on the interrelationship between *renvoi* and the incidental question. Ehrenzweig[138] states that the incidental question is "closely related to that of *renvoi*".[139]

Gottlieb[140] suggests that *renvoi* relates to the "qualitative meaning of the word 'law'", whilst the incidental question relates to the "quantitative interpretation of the word 'law'". However, he claims that whilst the two concepts bear similarities, they must be distinguished by their "relationship in time".[141] Thus, *renvoi* concerns the determination of the law which is to govern the issue. Where *renvoi* applies, there is a remission or transmission from the initial *lex causae* either back to the forum or to a third country, which becomes the real *lex causae*. Thus, *renvoi* deals with the selection of the law governing

136 Legitimacy Act, 1976 s 1. It should be noted that while the Family Law Reform Act 1987, s 1(1) provides that references in statutes "to any relationship between two persons shall, unless the contrary intention appears, be construed without regard to whetheror not the father and mother of either of them, or the father and mother of any person through whom the relationship is deduced, have or had been married to each other at any time", the Act does not abolish the status of illegitimacy.

137 It is suggested that the essence of the problem of *renvoi* is whether application of the *lex causae* requires application of only internal law or also its conflicts rules (ie the whole of the *lex causae*). This is what Robertson (1939) 55 LQR 565 at p 571 calls "*renvoi* in the wider sense". Thus, the issue of remission/transmission is not the central issue, although application of the whole of the *lex causae may result* in a transmission or remission to the law of another country. This seems to be what Robertson refers to as "*renvoi* in the narrower sense".

138 *Op cit* n 4, *supra*, at p 170.

139 See also Robertson (1939) 55 LQR 565 at p 568.

140 (1955) 33 Can BR 523 at p 543.

141 Gottlieb (1977) 26 ICLQ 734 at p 750.

the main question.[142] Whereas, the incidental question applies *after* the selection of the law governing the main question.[143]

It is suggested that this distinction is inappropriate under the "conflict of rules" analysis. Since the focus is on the "critical question", then reference by the *lex causae* to its own conflict rules (including its recognition rules) in order to answer this question can be seen as an application of the doctrine of *renvoi.* For example, assume that in the *Schwebel* situation (example M1[144]), the forum refers to Israeli law to determine whether Natasha is single. This question must be answered by Israeli recognition rules, which will have to determine whether the *get* obtained in Austria can be recognised.

The doctrine of *renvoi* has been subject to considerable academic controversy.[145] Thus, it is appropriate to examine the criticisms which have been levelled at the doctrine generally and to analyse whether they are equally pertinent to the use of the doctrine in the "conflict of rules" scenario with which we are concerned.[146]

In relation to some of the arguments, it will be necessary to distinguish between cases which involve recognition issues and those which do not. It will be found that, because of the distinction between the two types of rules in the former category, the problems associated with *renvoi* are less relevant.

1. Renvoi Causes Unnecessary Complication

Renvoi has generally been used where there is a conflict between the choice rule of the forum and the choice rule of the *lex causae.* The forum has two options before it:

(i) to apply the internal law of the *lex causae* ignoring completely that this is not the law which would be applied by the *lex causae* to such a case because of the foreign element involved;
(ii) to apply the choice rule of the *lex causae* and thus decide the case according to the internal law of the country directed by that choice rule.

If the court fails to perceive the problem of the conflict between the two choice rules, it will simply choose the first option and thus the doctrine of renvoi is not applied, by default.[147] The advantage of this is simplicity.

In the "conflict of rules" situation, the problem cannot so easily be ignored. In the recognition situation, in order to determine the outcome of the case it is necessary to decide whether the relevant foreign judgment should be recognised. Thus, a court cannot really ignore the problem, unless it simply applies the

142 *Ibid* at p 750.
143 *Ibid* and Robertson (1939) 55 LQR 565 at p 567; Khan-Freund (n 24, *supra*) at p 291 and Schmidt (n 1, *supra*) at pp 34-35.
144 Section III, *supra*.
145 See, eg, Cheshire and North (n 6, *supra*) pp 62-67; McClean, *Morris: The Conflict of Laws* (4th edn, 1993) (hereinafter "Morris") at pp 478-480; and Collier, *Conflict of Laws* (2nd edn, 1994) pp 24-28.
146 Although it should be borne in mind that most authors seem to have been primarily concerned with *renvoi* in the narrow sense.
147 Cheshire and North (n 6, *supra*) at p 60 cite a few decisions where the first option was chosen, but claim that it has been "unconsciously adopted in a multitude of decisions".
148 This is what happened in *Perrini v Perrini* [1979] Fam 84.

recognition rule without making any reference to the choice of law issue.[148] Similarly, where there is no recognition issue, it is clear that there are two potentially applicable choice rules, the application of which will lead to inconsistent results. The very fact that there exists a "conflict of rules" situation means that there is complexity. Using *renvoi* does not substantially add to this complexity.

2. The Doctrine does not Produce Uniformity of Result unless it is Applied in one of the Countries Concerned and not the Other[149]

Where there is a "conflict of rules" situation, it is inevitable that there will be some lack of uniformity between the position in different countries.[150] Thus, application of *renvoi* here is not primarily designed to achieve uniformity of result.

3. The Doctrine[151] *Involves Surrendering the Forum's Conflicts Rules to Foreign Ones*

We saw above that this argument was used in relation to the incidental question to justify referring the incidental question to the *lex fori* rather than the *lex causae*. The need to avoid treating English conflicts rules as subservient to foreign rules may appear to be a valid reason for preferring the recognition rule where there is a recognition issue and the choice rule governing the subsidiary question (which does not involve considering the *lex causae*'s conflicts rules) where there is no recognition issue.

It is suggested, however, that this reasoning can be easily countered. English choice rules direct that the law of another jurisdiction should apply because[152] of the quality and degree of connection between the issues in the case and that jurisdiction. Once the forum law has chosen the *lex causae*, it has fulfilled its function. Thus, applying the recognition or the choice rules of the *lex causae* in the "conflict of rules" situation is not an abrogation of the forum's choice rules. On the contrary, it is taking the application of those rules to their logical conclusion.[153]

4. The Doctrine is Difficult to Apply

There are two reasons for this. Firstly, it[154] may involve determining whether the *lex causae* accepts the doctrine of *renvoi*.[155] Secondly, some foreign

149 Indeed, with total *renvoi* it is impossible to reach any decision if both countries accept the doctrine. This is the so-called *circulus inextricabilis*. This problem might be largely academic since most civil law countries do not have *renvoi* and most common law countries use the same connecting factors as each other.
150 See ch 4 II B 3, *infra*.
151 At least the doctrine of total *renvoi*.
152 For more detailed discussion of why there are choice rules see ch 2, *infra*.
153 As Collier (n 145, *supra*) says, at p 25, "This process is undertaken only because our Courts wish to undertake it".
154 Only the doctrine of total *renvoi*.
155 See *Re Duke of Wellington* [1947] Ch 506 at 515. Collier (n 145, *supra*) at p 25 argues that this objection is "either misguided or exaggerated".

connecting factors may be problematic to apply. For example, it is not clear which domestic law represents the "law of the nationality" of a British subject.[156]

It is suggested that these difficulties can be exaggerated. In particular, the second problem is one with which countries who use nationality as a connecting factor have to contend anyway. Where the *lex causae*'s nationality rule is applicable then the *lex causae*'s method of applying that rule to those whose nationality is in a composite or federal state should be adopted by the forum.

5. Renvoi is Inappropriate in Some Areas of Law

It has been judicially stated that *renvoi* should not apply in the law of contract[157] or tort.[158] It is of interest that it has been mainly used in relation to succession, property and marriage. It is precisely these areas in which the "conflict of rules" is most likely to arise.

Thus, it can be seen that the criticisms of the use of *renvoi* generally do not apply to its use in the "conflict of rules" scenario. Analysis of the case law shows that the doctrine of *renvoi* has usually been invoked in order to produce the desired result. We shall suggest below that the choice between the choice rule and the recognition rule or the choice between two choice rules should be made expressly in order to achieve the result which is consistent with the policy of the forum. It is submitted that the use of *renvoi*, where it is required for this purpose, would be appropriate and in keeping with the development of that doctrine.

Indeed, Gottlieb[159] concludes that in relation to both *renvoi* and the incidental question:

> "All mechanical solutions of the problem must fail, simply because they will not serve the function of helping to fulfil the purpose of each rule. Only individualization of each rule will bring to light what we are trying to achieve by its application."

Before moving on to advocate a method which does take into account the purpose of the rules, we shall in the next chapter examine the validity of Gottlieb's conclusion about mechanical solutions and, in particular, whether the "conflict of rules" analysis can cast any new light on the traditional models.

156 See *Re O'Keefe* [1940] Ch 124.
157 *Re United Railways of Havana and Regla Warehouses Ltd* [1960] Ch 52 and *Amin Rasheed Shipping Corp v Kuwait Insurance Co* [1984] AC 50.
158 *McElroy v McAllister* (1949) SC 110.
159 Gottlieb (1955) 33 Can BRev 523 at p 543.

Chapter 2

Global Solutions

I. THE CONCEPT OF A GLOBAL SOLUTION

In our discussion of the traditional approach to the incidental question, we saw that modern authors do not support an automatic preference for application of either the private international law rules of the *lex fori* or of the *lex causae*. However, there has been no discussion of whether some other global rule might be appropriate.[1] The "conflict of rules" analysis provides the possibility of an automatic preference in favour of either the choice of law rule or the recognition rule in cases involving a foreign judgment or decree. Whilst a preference for the choice rule corresponds to the *lex causae* approach and preference for the recognition rule corresponds to the *lex fori* approach, it may be possible to justify a preference for one "type" of rule over the other because of the inherent nature of the type of rule, which can be understood by considering the theoretical basis of each type of rule.

An additional option, which could be applicable whether or not a foreign judgment is involved, is to give automatic preference to a statutory rule over a common law rule. In order to assess the viability of such a preference rule it will be necessary to examine the results which would be achieved as well as considering the theoretical rationale.

Thus, before rejecting completely the possibility of a global solution, we shall examine the merits of each of these possible preference rules in turn. For reasons which will be explained below, we shall distinguish between situations where recognition rules result in the recognition of foreign judgments and those where they lead to denial of recognition. To promote clarity, in the latter case the rules will be referred to as "non-recognition rules".

A major deficiency with any global rule is that it is applied "blindly" without any attention being paid to the result of the application in each particular case. This has been one of the main criticisms of traditional mechanical jurisdiction choice of law rules. However, it is clear that courts sometimes use "transparent devices" or "escape routes"[2] in order to ensure that the desired result is reached rather than that which would be achieved by "blind" application of the mechanical rule. Such methods might also be used together with one of the global preference rules. Probably the most familiar "escape route" is public

1 However, the views of Ehrenzweig (*supra*, ch 1, n 4) and Gottlieb (*supra*, ch 1, n 140) would suggest the rejection of all global solutions.

2 Carter (1993) 42 ICLQ 1 at 1.

policy. Thus, in the final section of this chapter, we will show how public policy might be used in the "conflict of rules" context as a method of "escaping" from an undesirable result produced by a global principle in favour of the recognition rule.

II. GIVING PREFERENCE TO CHOICE OF LAW RULES

A. Introduction

A considerable amount of academic ink has been spilled in considering the fundamental question of why we have choice of law rules. Since we are primarily concerned with the "conflict of rules" situation in England and the Commonwealth, where choice of law rules are still basically jurisdiction selecting, we shall only be concerned at this stage with theories which explain such traditional rules.[3] During the present century, three main theories have been advocated: comity, vested rights and justice. Since comity provides a stronger basis for recognition rules than for choice rules, this theory will be discussed in section III, below. Since the vested rights theory has been widely discredited,[4] it would be inappropriate to base a preference rule on the doctrine. However, a brief analysis of the theory can help us to understand the relationship between choice rules and recognition rules, which is at the crux of the "conflict of rules" problem presently under discussion.

B. Vested Rights

Under this theory,[5] which was espoused by Dicey in England and Beale in the USA,[6] the purpose of the conflict of laws is to recognise and enforce rights which have been duly acquired in foreign countries. It assumes that only one law has "jurisdiction"[7] to determine what legal consequences attach to a given situation.

Where this law confers rights upon a person, that person should not be deprived of those rights simply because (s)he moves to another country. Thus, the validity of properly created vested rights should not be called into question anywhere. Conversely, rights conferred by laws other than that with "jurisdiction" are not recognised or enforced.

If the vested rights theory were universally recognised, then all countries would decide all conflict cases in the same way, in which case it would be theoretically impossible for there to be a conflict between choice rules and recognition rules. Clearly, this is not the case and, as we have seen, such conflicts do arise.

3 There will be some discussion of result selecting approaches in ch 3.
4 Morris (ch 1, n 6 *supra*) at p 510 says, "We may as well admit it: the vested rights theory is dead" and see references in Kegel *International Encyclopedia of Comparative Law*, vol III, at p 10, nn 69, 72 and 76.
5 For brief history of the doctrine see Kegel *ibid*, ch 3 at pp 9-10. For judicial approval in England see *Re Askew* [1930] 2 Ch 259 at 267.
6 Who made it the basis of the First Restatement of the Conflict of Laws, American Law Institute, of which he was the Reporter.
7 "Jurisdiction" is not used here in its usual meaning of having the right to hear a case.

The vested rights theory would seem to require a global preference in favour of the choice rule, which gives effect to vested rights, because, *ex hypothesi*, the foreign judgment must have been wrong in giving effect to rights which were not properly created or refusing recognition to rights which were properly created.

It may therefore seem somewhat surprising that some writers[8] have regarded the theory of vested rights as being the basis of the doctrine of "obligation"[9] which has been used to justify the recognition of foreign judgments.[10] The paradox of the incompatibility of the two doctrines and whether the doctrine of obligation, which has been described as "alive and well",[11] can support an automatic preference in favour of the recognition rule will be discussed below.[12]

C. Justice to the Parties

This theory rests on the premise that it is often not just to the parties to apply the *lex fori* to cases with a foreign element[13] and that the purpose of choice of law rules, like that of domestic rules, should be to do justice to the parties.[14] This approach is supported by many modern writers. For example, Cheshire and North[15] write:

> "... [W]hen the circumstances indicate that the internal law of a foreign country will provide a solution more just, more convenient and more in accord with the expectations of the parties than the internal law of England, the English judge does not hesitate to give effect to the foreign rules."

Jaffey[16] claims:

> "The most important factor underlying choice of law rules must be the desire to achieve justice between the parties."

McLeod[17] opines:

> "[A] theory of relative justice which attempts to balance the expectations of the individuals and the interests of the country and the administration of justice provides the best vehicle for the development of positive law."

8 See, for example, Collier (ch 1, n 145 *supra*) at p 380.
9 Discussed in section III D, *infra*.
10 Other writers, however, strongly deny that there is any connection between the two doctrines. See, for example, Morris (ch 1, n 6, *supra*) at p 105.
11 See Morris (ch 1, n 6, *supra*) p 107 and Cheshire and North (ch 1, n 6, *supra*) p 346.
12 At III D 2.
13 See Wolff, *Private International Law* (2nd edn, 1950) pp 1-2 and Carswell (1959) 8 ICLQ 268 at 277.
14 Jaffey (1982) 2 OJLS 368 at 377.
15 Cheshire and North (ch 1, n 6, *supra*) at p 39.
16 Jaffey, *Introduction to the Conflict of Laws* (1988) p 275.
17 McLeod, *The Conflict of Laws* (1983) at p 21, approved in *Vladi v Vladi* (1987) 39 DLR 4th 563 at 570.

Graveson[18] seeks to maintain that–

> "[T]he basis and the guiding principle on which conflict of laws in the common law is being built up is that of doing justice in cases involving a foreign element, in which the court would fall short of achieving justice if it were to ignore the significance of such foreign elements in the case before it as are relevant."

In order to determine whether the fact that choice of law rules do justice between the parties is sufficient to justify giving them preference, we need to isolate the essence of the concept of justice in this context. As there is no clear consensus among writers that a given principle embodies justice, it will be necessary to make a number of assumptions. Firstly, it will be assumed that justice here refers to justice in determining which system of law should determine the outcome of a case (referred to as "conflicts justice") rather than the justice of substantive law (referred to as "substantive justice").[19] Secondly, it will be assumed that the various principles of "conflicts justice" which have been proposed in the literature[20] are to a large extent[21] manifestations of the concept of giving effect to the reasonable expectations [22] of the parties.[23]

Thus, it can be argued that if choice of law rules are carefully designed to do justice by protecting the reasonable expectations of the parties, then they should take precedence over recognition rules which simply require that a foreign judgment be applied "blindly", without examining the merits and checking that the judgment has done justice in the above sense.

The counter-argument in favour of giving precedence to recognition rules is that where parties have gone to the trouble and expense of litigating in a forum which has jurisdiction in the international sense, they should reasonably expect that the judgment will be recognised and enforced in other countries, even where its result is different from that which would have been obtained had the case been decided in those other countries.

The conflicting arguments can best be illustrated by referring to example M6 above.[24] Up until the time of the nullity proceedings in Portugal, the parties" reasonable expectations would have been that the validity and continued subsistence of their marriage should be determined by New York law because all the connections deemed relevant to validity of marriage both by New York

18 Graveson, "Judicial Justice as a Contemporary Basis of the English Conflict of Laws," in Graveson (ed), *Comparative Conflict of Laws*, vol I (1977) at p 51.

19 See Kegel (n 4, *supra*) at pp 15 and 44 and Cavers, *The Choice of Law Process* (1965) at pp 130 *et seq*.

20 See, in particular, Jaffey (n 16, *supra*) at pp 275-278 and at (1982) 2 OJLS 368.

21 Jaffey himself, (n 16, *supra*) at p 276 recognises that expectation is relevant to a number of the principles, although he maintains that it does not fully explain them.

22 Sometimes also referred to as "legitimate" or "justified" expectations.

23 The "reasonable expectation" principle is part of most modern approaches to choice of law. For example, it is one of the Restatement Second's choice-influencing factors. The same basic concept has been expressed slightly differently by some writers. For example, Shapira, *The Interest Approach to Choice of Law* (1970) ch 3 refers to the question of whether or not a party has fair notice of the applicability of a particular law. The principle is also consistent with the theory of substantive justice propounded by philosopher Rawls and quoted in Cavers (n 20, *supra*) at p 130.

24 At ch 1, IV B, *supra*.

law and by English law were with New York. However, once the decree has been pronounced, it can be argued that the parties should now reasonably expect that a decree pronounced by a court of competent jurisdiction[25] is to be recognised throughout the world, even though it is not recognised by the law of their domicile. Does justice require that the "new" expectations arising out of the Portugese proceedings override the original expectations?

One of the criticisms of excessive reliance on the parties' expectations has been that, often, parties do not actually address their minds to the question of which law governs the transaction or relationship into which they are entering. Thus, the law simply imputes expectations to them. It might be argued that where parties have gone to the trouble of litigating, they are more likely to have thought about and relied upon the fact that the judgment will be recognised in other countries. Thus, greater weight should be accorded to their expectations.

However, it is suggested that it is impossible to generalise about parties' actual expectations, either in connection with the applicability of a particular law or the recognition of a judgment abroad. Sometimes parties give very careful thought to the legal consequences of their actions. This thought must be based on an expectation that a particular legal system is to govern. Conversely, when commencing litigation there may be no reason to think about recognition/ enforcement abroad because at that time they are only concerned with recognition/ enforcement in the forum where they are litigating. Only because of later unforeseen events does recognition/enforcement abroad become an issue.

Thus, whether parties' expectations about the applicability of the choice rule or their expectations over the enforceability of a judgment should prevail would have to be decided in each case or at least in each category of case.

III. GIVING PREFERENCE TO RECOGNITION RULES

A. Introduction

In order to seek justification for preferring the recognition rule where the result of recognising the foreign judgment conflicts with the result of applying the choice of law rule, it is necessary to examine the various theories[26] put forward to explain recognition rules.[27] In order to come to the conclusion that one of the rationales for recognising judgments does justify a global preference in favour of recognition rules, we would have to find that that rationale prevails over the need to do "justice" to the parties by application of the choice of law rule, as discussed above.[28]

25 This assumes that competence is looked at through the eyes of English law.

26 Whilst Von Mehren and Trautman (1968) 81 Harv LR 1601 at 1603 claim that traditional theories "contribute little to any real understanding" of recognition practice, English and Commonwealth courts and writers still rely on them. In fact, Von Mehren's five policies and the principle of justice which they advocate (*ibid*) are all embodied in the theories discussed. There does not seem to be academic agreement as to which theories are separate. For example, Patchett, *Recognition of Commercial Judgments and Awards in the Commonwealth* (1984) treats reciprocity as separate from comity.

27 The Court of Appeal has recently stated that the "cases give virtually no guidance on this essential issue" in *Cape v Adams Industries* [1991] 1 All ER 929 at 1037.

28 At section II C of this chapter.

When discussing the rationale behind choice of law rules, it was not necessary to distinguish between different areas of law. However, in relation to recognition of judgments, matrimonial causes must be distinguished from *in personam* judgments[29] *inter alia* for the following reasons:

(i) Business efficacy is not relevant.
(ii) Such decrees operate as *in rem* judgments and may be challenged by third parties.[30]
(iii) Non-judicial divorces and annulments may be recognised.
(iv) A matrimonial decree does not require a sum of money to be paid.

Thus, specific reference[31] will be made as to the applicability of each theory to matrimonial causes and one theory advanced which is only applicable to matrimonial causes.[32]

Consideration of the theories behind recognition rules usually concentrate on the reasons why certain judgments *should* be recognised. However, in dealing with the "conflict of rules" scenario, we also need to consider the situation where the recognition rules do *not* provide for recognition (to be referred to as non-recognition rules), but application of the choice of law rule would produce the same result as recognition. In order to decide whether there is any justification for a global preference for the non-recognition rule, we need to understand the bases and reasons for non-recognition.

B. Estoppel *Per Rem Judicatam*[33]

This is a rule of evidence which has been summarised as follows:

> "Where a final judicial decision has been pronounced by either an English or (with certain exceptions) a foreign tribunal of competent jurisdiction over the parties to, and the subject matter of the litigation any party or parties to such litigation, as against any other party or privy thereto and in the case of decisions *in rem*, as against any other person, is estopped in any subsequent litigation from disputing or questioning such decision on the merits."[34]

It is now beyond doubt that this doctrine, which is frequently referred to as *res judicata*,[35] applies to foreign judgments.[36]

29 We will not be dealing with non-matrimonial judgments *in rem*.
30 See, for example, *Pemberton v Hughes* [1899] 1 Ch 781 and *Powell v Cockburn* (1976) 68 DLR (3d) 700.
31 See at n 36, text accompanying n 67 and text accompanying n 93, *infra*.
32 See section F, *infra*.
33 See Spencer Bower and Turner, *The Doctrine of Res Judicata* (2nd edn, 1969) ch 1.
34 *Ibid* at p 9. This definition (which was contained in the first edition of Spencer Bower) was cited with approval in *Carl Zeiss Stifung v Rayner and Keeler Ltd (No 2)* [1967] 1 AC 853 at 933.
35 This term covers both cause of action and issue estoppel.
36 See House of Lords decisions in *Carl Zeiss Stiftung v Rayner and Keeler Ltd (No 2)* [1967] 1 AC 853 and *The Sennar (No 2)* [1985] 1 WLR 490. Whilst the doctrine of *res judicata* may be used in respect of matrimonial decrees (see *Vervaeke v Smith* [1983] 1 AC 145 and Family Law Act 1986, s 51(1), it does not help much in the "conflict of rules" context, since it begs the question as to whether recognition of the change in matrimonial status, which is the *res judicata* of the foreign decree, necessarily requires recognition of resulting changes in rights and obligations. See section II B 1 in each of chs 4 and 6, *infra*.

However, the doctrine of *res judicata* does not itself provide a *reason* for recognising foreign judgments. Rather it would seem that the effect of the recognition rules is to apply this domestic doctrine to those foreign judgments which are required to be recognised.[37] Therefore, we need to identify one or more modern rationale(s) of the *res judicata* rule to see if it/they can equally support recognition of foreign judgments.

1. Finality of Litigation

There is said to be a general community interest in the termination of disputes and in the finality and conclusiveness of judicial decisions.[38] This requires that parties should not be allowed to litigate in this country a dispute which has been decided by judicial decision elsewhere.

Can this interest supersede the interest in "justice"? In the domestic context, once a party's rights of appeal are exhausted then it is assumed that justice has been done.[39] Thus, there can be no conflict between the requirements of justice and that of finality. In the conflict of laws context, this is not the case. The foreign decision may not be in conformity with "conflicts justice" and/or "substantive justice". To allow review of the merits of foreign decisions to test for "substantive" justice would completely undermine the idea of finality of judicial decisions in the international context.

However, it is suggested that to allow review of the "conflicts justice" of foreign decisions in the few cases where the result of recognition is incompatible with the application of the forum's choice of law rules could be allowed as an exception without detracting from the finality objective to any great extent.[40] Thus, it may be concluded that the need for finality cannot justify giving precedence to the recognition rule in the "conflict of rules" scenario.

2. Protection of Individuals

There is said to be a right for an individual to be protected from vexatious multiplication of suits.[41] Without this protection, a party who has greater resources is given an unfair advantage. A financially weaker party may be

37 Von Mehren and Trautman (1968) 81 Harv LR 1601 at 1606 suggest that "treating recognition problems as an aspect of *res judicata* tends to lead to a confusion of concepts which should be kept separate" because of differences between the policies relating to domestic and foreign judgments.

38 Spencer Bower and Turner (n 33, *supra*) at p 10 and Read, *Recognition and Enforcement of Foreign Judgments* (1938) pp 111-122. The finality point is summed up by the Latin phrase "*interest rei publicae ut sit finis litum*", and was one of the bases of the recent Court of Appeal decision in *Hewitson v Hewitson* [1995] 1 FLR 241 in which leave to apply for financial relief after a foreign divorce under the Matrimonial and Family Proceedings Act 1984, Pt III was refused.

39 Unless public policy requires otherwise. In the case of *Man (Sugar) v Haryanto* [1991] 1 Lloyds 429 at 436, an English decision upholding the contract was followed by an Indonesian decision declaring it unenforceable for illegality. The court asked whether, "as a matter of English law the public policy in favour of finality is overridden by some more important public policy based on the unenforceability of illegal contracts?" In this case the answer was in the negative.

40 It will be suggested below that this is in fact already done under the guise of public policy. See discussion of *Gray v Formosa* [1963] P 259 and *Vervaeke v Smith* [1983] 1 AC 145 at section VI, *infra*.

41 Spencer *Bower and Turner* (n 33, *supra*) at p 10. Von Mehren and Trautman (1968) 81 Harv LR 1061 refer to protection against harassing or evasive tactics.

unable to afford to defend numerous actions on the same issue that he has already won in another court.

It is suggested that this rationale is part of the "justice" theory elaborated above.[42] Thus, it can be understood in terms of fulfilling the parties" reasonable expectations, which are assumed to be that the decision of a competent court is binding and cannot be challenged in other jurisdictions. However, as explained there, these reasonable expectations have to be weighed against reasonable expectations of having a particular law applied, where these exist and there can be no single definitive rule as to which of these expectations should prevail. As stated earlier,[43] the requirements of "conflicts justice" will have to be determined in each case or category of case.

C. Comity

1. Introduction

The idea that private international law is based on comity dates back to Huber and was adopted by Story. The latter wrote:

> "The true foundation on which the subject rests is that rules which are to govern are those which arise from mutual interest and utility; from the sense of the inconveniences which would arise from a contrary doctrine; and from a sort of moral necessity to do justice in order that justice may be done to us in return."[44]

It can be seen that Story's concept of comity includes a number of different elements. It is therefore not surprising that the notion of comity has been understood differently by different writers and judges.[45] It is submitted that the label "comity" has been applied to cover three distinct doctrines,[46] which can be called reciprocity, judicial courtesy and business efficacy respectively. Whilst Story seems to be talking generally about the whole of the conflicts of law, it has long been realised that comity cannot serve as an adequate basis for choice of law rules.[47] Thus, comity has been far more widely used to explain

42 At section II C, *supra*.

43 *Ibid*.

44 Story, *Commentaries on the Conflicts of Law* (1834) s 35.

45 For a detailed judicial analysis of the history and meaning of the concept of comity in relation to the recognition of foreign judgments, see (1990) 76 DLR (4th) 256, per La Forest J at 262 *et seq*. See also *Cape v Adams Industries* [1991] 1 All ER 929 at 1037.

46 The fact that comity has different meanings has been recognised by judges in connection with recognition of foreign judgments. In *Wood v Wood* [1957] P 254, Evershed MR said that "questions of reciprocity must always be relevant upon the matter of comity". This suggests that reciprocity is just one element of comity. He does not specify what the other elements are.

47 Thus, it is quite clear that the court's willingness to apply a foreign rule does not in any way depend on any evidence that there would be reciprocity by the courts of that foreign country. Comity in the sense of judicial courtesy is impractical because *inter alia* it would not provide an answer where the law of more than one other country wished to apply; it is dependent on other countries" conflict rules and it would lead to inconsistent decisions in similar cases depending on the view of the foreign court. Comity in the sense of business efficacy, as will argued below, is better understood as part of the theory of justice.

recognition of foreign judgments[48] and if comity can support any global preference rule, it would be one in favour of the recognition rule. Thus, each of the three meanings of comity will be examined in turn to see if any of them can support such a global preference rule.

2. Reciprocity

The concept of reciprocity in relation to the regulation of foreign judgments itself is used in different senses in the case law and literature. Firstly, it means that a court will recognise a foreign judgment provided that the courts of that foreign country would recognise such a decision of the forum. Reciprocity in this sense either requires a bilateral or multilateral treaty in which both countries agree to recognise judgments of the other on certain conditions or evidence of the practice of the foreign court in relation to judgments of the forum.

Secondly, reciprocity may mean that the forum will recognise a foreign judgment if there exists in relation to the foreign court a connection[49] which would have given the forum jurisdiction *mutatis mutandis*. It is reciprocity in this second sense which was used in the case of *Travers v Holley*.[50] McClean points out that the rule does not strictly involve reciprocity at all because it is not necessary to establish that the foreign country has a rule corresponding to that in *Travers v Holley*.[51]

Patchett[52] calls the second category "judicially determined reciprocity" and contrasts this with "legislatively determined reciprocity". It is suggested that this division is theoretically unsound because it confuses two issues. The real distinction is between *reciprocity in relation to recognition of judgments* ("recognition reciprocity") and *reciprocity founded on jurisdictional bases* ("jurisdictional reciprocity"). "Recognition reciprocity" could be determined legislatively or judicially.[53] However, in England[54] there is in fact no judicial determination of reciprocity in this sense. Thus, for *practical* purposes, Patchett's labelling is accurate.

48 Early judicial pronouncements on the question of recognition of foreign judgments clearly based such recognition on "comity" (see, for example, cases quoted by Patchett (n 26, *supra*) p 47 and by Piggott, *Foreign Judgments* (1908) Part I at p 11). Comity is still mentioned loosely by judges in relation to the recognition of foreign judgments (see, for example, *Macaulay v Macaulay* [1991] 1 FLR 235 at 241 and *Wood v Wood* [1954] P 254, where the Court of Appeal suggested that comity did not require giving exaggerated respect to the judgments of other states).

49 Whether or not this is actually the jurisdictional base relied on by the foreign court: cf *Robinson-Scott v Robinson-Scott* [1957] 3 All ER 473. Under some Commonwealth statutes, such as the New Zealand Family Proceedings Act 1980, the foreign courts must *actually have exercised jurisdiction* on one of the bases on which the forum would take jurisdiction.

50 [1953] P 246.

51 McClean, *Recognition of Family Judgments in the Commonwealth* (1983) at p 40. Von Mehren and Trautman (1968) 81 Harv LR 1601 at 1617, n 53 suggest that the term "equivalence" is preferable to avoid confusion with reciprocity in the first sense.

52 *Op cit* (n 26, *supra*) at p 52. See also Khan-Freund (ch 1, n 26, *supra*) at p 29 and Russell (1952) 1 ICLQ 181.

53 Khan-Freund (*ibid*, at p 23) points out that the significance of this distinction is that legislation determines *ex ante* whether there is reciprocity; whereas Courts can only decided *ex post*.

54 Cf in the US *Hilton v Guyot* (1895) 159 US 113.

In England,[55] "jurisdictional reciprocity" cannot be considered as a basis for recognising foreign judgments. The rule in *Travers v Holley* has been held to be "limited to a judgment *in rem* in a matter affecting matrimonial status"[56] and was repealed in relation to divorces and legal separations by the Recognition of Divorces and Legal Separation Act 1971 and in relation to nullity decrees by the Family Law Act 1986. Thus, we shall be using reciprocity exclusively in the "recognition reciprocity" sense.

Whilst the common law rules for recognition of foreign judgments do not involve any requirement of reciprocity,[57] it has been suggested[58] that the real reason that judges enforce foreign judgments is the hope that their judgments would be recognised and enforced abroad.[59] This "self-interest"[60] theory might be seen to be borne out by the fact that most of the later statutory recognition rules do require reciprocity. Thus, the Administration of Justice Act 1920 and the Foreign Judgments (Reciprocal Enforcement) Act 1933[61] both provide for registration of foreign judgments *only* where there is reciprocity.[62] However, Khan-Freund[63] points out that here reciprocity is a condition for the use of a simplified enforcement procedure rather than for enforcement *per se*.

More recent developments would seem further to endorse the reciprocity theory. The whole basis of the Brussels and Lugano Conventions,[64] which provide for virtually automatic recognition of judgments, is that of reciprocity between member states. Thus, states are prepared to increase their obligation to recognise foreign judgments[65] in return for the same treatment for their own judgments.

Nonetheless, so long as a good many judgments[66] are still recognised or refused recognition without any regard to reciprocity, this cannot be a complete explanation. In particular, it is worth noting that the rules for recognising matrimonial decrees,[67] whilst originally enacted[68] in pursuance of ratification

55 Cf in Canada, following the decision of the Supreme Court of Canada in *Morguard Investments Ltd v De Savoye* (1990) 76 DLR (4th) 256, jurisdictional reciprocity is now a basis of recognition of *in personam* judgments, at least in relation to judgments of sister provinces.

56 *Re Trepca Mines* [1960] 1 WLR 1273 at 1280-1282, per Hodson LJ.

57 See, for example, *Adams v Cape Industries* [1991] 1 All ER 929 at 1037.

58 See, for example Patchett (n 26, *supra*) at p 41.

59 See, for example, per Lord Hardwick in *Omychund v Barker* (1777) 1 Ak 21 at 50, 26 ER 15 at 33.

60 This term is used by Patchett (n 26, *supra*).

61 See ch 1, section IV A 1, *supra*.

62 An Order in Council is required to extend the Act to a particular country. Such an order may only be made where there are reciprocal provisions for recognition of UK judgments by that country. See the 1920 Act, s 14 (as amended by the Civil Jurisdiction and Judgments Act 1982, s 35(3)) and the Foreign Judgments (Reciprocal Enforcement) Act 1933, s 1 (as amended by the Civil Jurisdiction and Judgments Act 1982, s 35(1) and Sch 10).

63 Khan-Freund (ch 1, n 26, *supra*) at p 24.

64 Discussed at ch 1, IV A 1, *supra*. See also the Maintenance Orders (Reciprocal Enforcement) Act 1972.

65 For example, the defences available against recognition are narrower under the Brussels and Lugano Conventions than at common law.

66 Ie all judgments of states which are not parties to a multilateral or bilateral recognition treaty with the UK.

67 See ch 1, IV A 2, *supra*.

68 In the Recognition of Divorces and Legal Separations Act 1971.

of the Hague Convention on Recognition of Divorces and Legal Separations, do not involve any element of reciprocity.

It is suggested that the importance of legislatively determined reciprocity is that it may allow the recognition of judgments which would not otherwise be recognised.[69] Thus, whatever is the rationale for common law recognition of judgments has to be supplemented by legislatively determined reciprocity. In relation to those cases where there is recognition *only*[70] because one of the Conventions applies, reciprocity is the basis for recognition and we must decide whether reciprocity can support the automatic preference of the recognition rule.

It is suggested that the decisive factor here is that the conflict of laws is essentially concerned with the private law rights of individuals.[71] Legislatively determined reciprocity is based on the state's political and economic considerations. Thus, in so far as recognition rules are based on reciprocity they should not take precedence over choice rules which we are assuming to be based on "justice" between the parties.

3. *Judicial Courtesy*

It seems that this is the sense in which the word comity was originally used[72] when justifying the application of foreign law. In other words, foreign laws are applied in order to show courtesy to other sovereign states[73] and foreign judgments are recognised in order to show respect to the decisions of other judges.[74] However, whilst many of the problems raised in relation to the applicability of this theory to choice of law rules do not apply to recognition,[75]

69 Although not matrimonial decrees, as "status and legal capacity of natural persons" are expressly excluded from the scope of the Brussels and Lugano Conventions (Art 1) and the Foreign Judgments (Reciprocal Enforcement) Act 1933 seems not to apply to matrimonial decrees (see *Maples v Maples* [1988] Fam 14 and *Vervaeke v Smith* [1981] 1 All ER 55 at 90, per Cumming-Bruce and Everleigh J, but cf per Arnold P at 87 and Law Com No 137 at para 2.31).

70 This cannot apply to recognition of judgments under the Foreign Judgments (Reciprocal Enforcement) Act 1933 Act, since the Act primarily affected the *method* of recognition and made no fundamental change to *entitlement* thereto (although it has been held not to have been purely a codification of the common law: see *Societe Cooperative Sidmetal v Titan International Ltd* [1966] 1 QB 828).

71 Patchett (n 26, *supra*) at p 61 expresses this idea as, "[T]he *res litigiosa* being considered by the enforcing forum is a matter of private dispute rather than being a matter of international *casus belli*".

72 See, for example, *Hughes v Cornelius* (1680) 2 Shaw 232 and *Dicey's Conflict of Laws* (4th edn, 1927) at p 9. Llewelyn Davies (1937) 18 BYBIL 49 at 57 alleges that "courtesy" is a misunderstanding of Huber's use of the term "comity".

73 Cheshire and North (ch 1, n 6, *supra*) at p 5 point out that this theory can hardly explain the readiness of the English courts to apply enemy law in time of war.

74 See *Re E* [1967] Ch 287 at 301, where Cross J said that he was sending a copy of his judgment to the American judge whose child custody order he was not following. La Forest J in *Morguard Investments Ltd v De Savoye* (1990) 76 DLR 256, per La Forest J at 268 commented that states will show respect "to the actions of a state legitimately taken within its territory".

75 See n 47, *supra*. (i) There are less likely to be conflicting foreign judgments than conflicting foreign laws (cf the recent case of *Showlag v Mansour* [1994] 2 All ER 129, where the Privy Council stated that as a general rule the first judgment in time should take precedence: see also the Brussels Convention, Art 27(5)); (ii) the theory does not depend on other countries having conflicts rules; (iii) inconsistency of forum judicial decisions is not an issue.

the fundamental problem that recognition would be based on judicial discretion[76] as opposed to rights of the parties remains.[77] Thus, comity in the sense of judicial courtesy cannot support any global preference rule.

4. Business Efficacy

Huber wrote:

> "Although the laws of one country can have no direct force in another country, yet nothing could be more inconvenient to the commerce and general intercourse of nations than that transactions valid by the law of one place should be rendered of no effect elsewhere owing to a difference in the law."[78]

Recently, a Canadian judge has described the doctrine of comity in modern times as follows:

> "[T]he rules of private international law are grounded in the need in modern times to facilitate the flow of wealth, skills and people across state lines in a fair and orderly manner."[79]

Thus, comity is understood as meaning protecting the interest of the commercial world. The role of choice of law rules is to promote certainty. Thus, when people are involved in transactions, which they reasonably expect to be governed by the law of a particular country, they should be able to rely on the fact that the law of that country will be applied throughout the world.

The idea that certainty in international commerce requires recognition of foreign judgments[80] is summed up by Jones LJ in *Re Davidson's STs*:[81]

> "It would be impossible to carry on the business of the world if Courts refused to act upon what had been done by other Courts of competent jurisdiction."

More recently, Slade LJ's "working of the society of nations"[82] must be referring mainly to the functioning of international trade and commerce. However, as his Lordship recognises, this reasoning "tells one nothing of

76 Patchett (n 26, *supra*) at p 50 suggests that the uncertainty and vagueness of the doctrine of comity was part of its strength because it enabled changes to be made in the light of socio-economic development.
77 See Cheshire and North (ch 1, n 6, *supra*) at p 4, who claim that courtesy is therefore a matter for sovereigns and not judges.
78 *De Conflictu Legum*. See translation in Llewellyn Davies (1937) 18 BYBIL 49 at 65.
79 In *Morguard Investments Ltd v Savoye* (1990) 76 DLR (4th) 256 at 269, per La Forest J. In support, he cites *inter alia* the following quotation from Yntema (1957) 35 Can Bar Rev: ". . . the function of conflict rules is to select, interpret and apply in each case the particular local law that will best promote suitable conditions of interstate and international commerce . . ."
80 See Von Mehren and Trautman, (1968) 81 Harv LR 1601 at 1603.
81 (1873) 15 Eq 383. See also Patchett (n 26, *supra*) at p 48.
82 *Adams v Cape Industries* [1991] 1 All ER 929 at 1037. Slade LJ says that the principle of recognition of foreign judgments ". . . must stem from an acknowledgment that the society of nations will work better if some foreign judgments are taken to create rights which supersede the underlying cause of action, and which may be directly enforced in countries where the defendant or his assets are to be found".

practical value about how to identify" which foreign judgments should be recognised.[83]

Whilst the idea of business efficacy in the above sense may be viewed as part of the doctrine of comity[84] in the rather loose sense that the aim is to protect the international community as a whole, it is suggested that the need to protect the parties" expectations is more appropriately understood as part of the theory of "justice"[85] for two reasons. Firstly, the doctrine of comity is concerned with the interests of nations, whereas "justice" emphasises the interests of the parties.[86] The latter is more appropriate, since we are essentially concerned with private law, which is designed to protect the interests of individuals. Secondly, the business efficacy concept can only apply in the commercial context, whereas "justice" is equally relevant in the non-commercial context.

We have already[87] discussed the potential conflict between fulfilling parties' reasonable expectations about applicable law and their expectations about the enforceability of judgments and concluded that therefore "conflicts justice" cannot support a global preference for either type of rule. Rather, the requirements of "conflicts justice" have to be determined in each category of case.

D. The Doctrine of Obligation

1. The Doctrine

The doctrine of obligation, which can be traced back[88] to the 1830s was summed up in the classic words of Blackburn J in *Schisby v Westenholz*:[89]

> "The judgment of a court of competent jurisdiction over the defendant imposes a duty or obligation on him to pay the sum for which judgment is given, which the courts in this country are bound to enforce."

This doctrine, which was enthusiastically espoused[90] in the common law world, has recently been reiterated in modern terms by the House of Lords:

> "A foreign judgment given by a court of competent jurisdiction over the defendant is treated by the common law as imposing a legal obligation on the judgment debtor which will be enforced in an action on the judgment by an English court

83 *Ibid.*
84 Cf the comment of Meredith CJCP that "it is not the comity of nations, it is the needs of mercantile and other intercourses the world over that must govern" in *Maguire v Maguire* (1921) 50 Ont LR 100 at 111.
85 See at section II C, *supra*.
86 See Jaffey (1982) 2 OJLS 368.
87 At section II C, *supra*.
88 See *Warrender v Warrender* (1835) 2 Cl and Fin 401, when Lord Brougham suggested that foreign judgments were not recognised *ex comitatae* but rather *ex debito justiciae* and the more explicit enunciation of the doctrine by Parke B in *Russell v Smyth* (1842) 9 M & W 810 and *Williams v Jones* (1845) 13 M & W 628.
89 (1870) LR 6 QB 155 at 159. See also *Goddard v Gray* (1870) 27 LR 6 QB 139.
90 The only opponent seems to be Piggott (n 48, *supra*) at p 13. His argument that the obligation arising from a judgment is only enforceable in the state which calls it into being is unconvincing. If this were correct then we would not enforce any foreign created rights and private international law would not exist. Piggott does not explain why what he calls inchoate obligations arising abroad should be recognised and *choses jugees* should not.

in which the defendant will not be permitted to reopen issues of either fact or law which have been decided against him by the foreign court."[91]

Moreover, the Court of Appeal in *Adams v Cape Industries*[92] has sought to explain the doctrine in relationship to the foreign court's territorial jurisdiction on the basis of the presence of the defendant as follows:

> ". . . [B]y making himself present he contracts-in to a network of obligations created by the local law and the local courts."

It should be noted that the doctrine has not been considered to be applicable to matrimonial or other status determining decrees because there is no obligation to pay any sum of money and thus no judgment debtor.[93] Moreover, whilst Slade LJ's "contracting-in" approach may be appropriate where the party in question has a relevant connection to the judgment-giving state, it is difficult to apply to the situation where jurisdiction is taken on the basis of the other party's connection only. However, it might simply be argued that the judgment of a jurisdictionally competent court imposes an obligation on both parties[94] to act in accordance with the judgment. A foreign court in recognising the foreign decree is enforcing this obligation.

Thus, it might be claimed that a global preference in favour of the recognition rule can be justified on the basis of the enforcement of the obligation created by the foreign judgment. Before accepting this apparently attractive contention, it is necessary to examine more carefully the basis of the doctrine of obligation.

2. *The Basis of the Doctrine*

In particular, as mentioned above,[95] there is a view that the doctrine of obligation is based on the vested rights the theory. If this is correct, then we might ask why was the vested rights theory itself not used to explain recognition of foreign judgments? Why was it necessary to create a new doctrine?

The first answer which suggests itself is that the vested rights theory was not adopted in relation to recognition of foreign judgments for the same reasons that it was discredited in relation to choice of law. However, most of the objections[96] to the theory in the choice of law context do not apply in respect of recognition of foreign judgments.[97] Thus, this explanation is not adequate.

91 *Owens Bank Ltd v Bracco* [1992] 2 WLR 621, per Lord Bridge at 627.
92 [1991] 1 All ER 929 at 1038-1041, per Slade LJ.
93 See p 36, *supra*.
94 And in the case of a judgment *in rem*, the whole world.
95 At section II B, *supra*.
96 See generally Morris (ch 1, n 6, *supra*) at pp 443-444; Collier (ch 1, n 145, *supra*) at pp 380-382; Wolff, *Private International Law* (2nd edn, 1950) at p 3; Cook, *The Logical and Legal Bases of the Conflict of Laws* (1942) ch 1 and Llwellyn Davies (1957) 18 BYBIL 49.
97 For example: (i) there *are* rules telling us which courts have jurisdiction to decide cases (cf there are no rules telling us which country has "jurisdiction" to vest particular types of rights; (ii) the problem of *renvoi* does not arise in relation to recognition of judgments because it is clear how the foreign court has decided the case; (iii) there is no need to provide for cases dealing with capacities and disabilities, since a judgment *ex hypothesi* creates rights.

The real difficulty, it is suggested, is that under the doctrine of vested rights itself, it is theoretically indefensible to distinguish between foreign laws and foreign judgments. It has been pointed out[98] that to recognise a foreign judgment is in fact to recognise the law[99] of the foreign country. Therefore, the vested rights doctrine cannot logically support the enforcement of rights acquired under the law applied by a foreign Court in preference to vested rights acquired under other relevant laws.[100]

Thus, it was necessary for a different doctrine to be developed which would only apply to foreign judgments. The doctrine of obligation met this need. Yet it must be recognised that this doctrine is in fact merely a corollary[101] of the vested rights doctrine. Instead of focusing on the right of the judgment creditor created by the judgment, this doctrine focuses on the obligation or duty of the judgment debtor. The question of applying the doctrine to enforce rights which have not yet crystallised into a judgment debt does not arise. By creating a new doctrine, the unjustifiable preference for the law of the judgment-giving state over the laws of other relevant states seems to have been legitimised.

Once it is appreciated that the doctrine of obligation is merely a selective application of the doctrine of vested rights to certain types of vested rights (ie those that have been confirmed by a judgment), it will be seen that this doctrine cannot be used to support a global preference for recognition rules over choice of law rules.

Even if the view[102] that the two doctrines are quite independent is accepted, there is no escape from the fact that, conceptually, the two doctrines are simply different manifestations of a single jurisprudential principle that rights created by jurisdictionally competent laws or courts will be enforced.[103] To reiterate the point made by Patchett,[104] recognition of a foreign judgment is in fact recognition of the law of the country of the court rendering that judgment. Thus, the doctrine of obligation cannot support a global preference in favour of the recognition rule.

E. Implied Contract

It has been suggested that the basis of recognition of foreign judgments is that there has been an implied contract by the judgment debtor to pay the sum of

98 See Patchett (n 26, *supra*) at p 54 and Slade LJ, who refers to the "obligations created by the local *law* and by the local courts" (my emphasis) in *Cape v Adams Industries* [1991] 1 All ER 929 at 1038.

99 "[i.e.] the 'law' as represented in the document called the judgment in which the foreign country has set out the respective rights of the parties involved in the dispute." (Patchett, *ibid*).

100 Or vice versa, see section II B, *supra*.

101 See Read (n 38, *supra*) at pp 84-85.

102 See, for example, Morris (ch 1, n 6, *supra*) at p 105.

103 This can be seen more clearly when the theories are described as follows. The theory of vested rights states that an English court must recognise rights created by foreign law where English law considers that the foreign law in question has "jurisdiction" to vest those rights. The doctrine of obligation states that an English court must recognise the rights of the judgment creditor as adjudged by a foreign court where English law considers that the foreign court has jurisdiction to decide the case.

104 See n 99, *supra*.

money which the court has decided is due.[105] In *Grant v Easton*,[106] Lord Esher said that –

> "the liability of the defendant arises upon an implied contract to pay the amount of the foreign judgment."

Read,[107] however, claims that implied contract is not a separate theory from the doctrine of obligation. He postulates that the implied contract theory was created so that the action of assumpsit, which was only available in relation to a contractual debt, could be used to enforce foreign judgments. Accordingly, he explains the words of Lord Esher and Brett MR in *Grant v Easton*[108] as meaning that, for procedural purposes, the court must treat a foreign judgment as though it were enforcing an implied contract. This point has been illustrated[109] by the fact that the creditor's action on a foreign judgment is barred after six years like contract claims; whereas a claim on an English judgment is only barred after 12 years.

If "implied contract" were a separate theory, could it support a preference for the recognition rule? The theory is based on the enforcement of foreign contractual rights. Yet it provides for the selective enforcement of one particular type of contractual right, ie the right to have the judgment satisfied. Surely, it would be anomalous to recognise a right based on an implied contract to satisfy the foreign judgment in preference to a right based on an express contract which had not yet been litigated. Thus, it is submitted that the implied contract theory cannot support giving precedence to recognition rules.

F. Avoidance of Limping Marriages[110]

It is clear from perusal of the legislative history of the rules governing recognition of foreign matrimonial decrees that the main rationale behind those rules is to avoid limping marriages.[111] In order to achieve this aim, the traditional jurisdictional links were widened.

However, it is crucial to appreciate that preference for the recognition rule may not necessarily prevent limping marriages where there is a third country involved which does not recognise the decree.[112] Thus, whilst avoidance of limping marriages may be the rationale for liberal recognition rules, it cannot support a global preference for the recognition rule in the "conflict of rules" situation.[113]

105 Read (n 38, *supra*) at p 112. See also *Halsburys, Laws of England* (4th edn, 1975) vol 8 (Conflict of Laws), section 715.
106 (1883) LR 13 QBD 302.
107 Read (n 38, *supra*) at pp 112-113.
108 (1883) LR 13 QBD 302 at 303.
109 Cheshire and North (ch 1, n 6, *supra*) at p 346.
110 Jaffey calls this "uniformity of status in different countries", (1982) 2 OJLS 368 at 369.
111 See eg 315 HL Debs (16.2.71) at cols 483-486 per Lord Hailsham; Law Com. 34; Bellet and Goldman's Explanatory Document, Actes et Documents De La Haye, Onzieme Tome (translation at (1971) 5 Fam LQ 303, 321-367) paras 9, 47 and 48 and Anton (1969) 18 ICLQ 61.
112 See ch 4, II B 3, *infra*.
113 It should also be pointed out that avoidance of limping marriages requires recognition of a change in status, but does not necessarily require acknowledgment of consequences of that change other than the right to remarry.

IV. "NON-RECOGNITION RULES"

A. Introduction

A judgment may be refused recognition because of lack of jurisdiction or because one of a number of defences applies. In both situations, the rule which bars recognition will be referred to as a "non-recognition rule". In the first type, the non-recognition rule is simply the reverse of part of the recognition rule; ie the judgment is not recognised because there is no recognised jurisdictional link. In the second type, the defences act as non-recognition rules. The orthodox approach is to treat jurisdictional requirements as recognition rules rather than non-recognition rules[114] and thus the two types of rules now under consideration are treated as conceptually different and not categorised together as non-recognition rules. The justification for this approach is presumably that if the foreign court does not have jurisdiction, the judgment is seen to be made without competent authority and thus there is no basis on which to recognise it. In contrast, the defences are literally reasons not to recognise a judgment which has been made by a competent tribunal and appears to be *prima facie* effective.

However, it is suggested that as both types of rule reflect a policy reason for non-recognition of the judgment, they should be considered together in examining the conflict between non-recognition rules and choice of law rules. We will have to consider the various policy reasons behind the different rules in more depth before determining whether or not a global preference in favour of the non-recognition rule is appropriate in the case of either or both types of non-recognition rule.

In most situations, non-recognition of a foreign judgment means that the issue can be litigated *ab initio* in the English court, which is free to apply its own choice of law rules. These may happen to produce the same result as the foreign judgment, but since the foreign judgment is not effective there is no actual conflict between the non-recognition rule and the choice of law rules. However, there are a few situations in which, although a foreign judgment is not entitled to recognition, *application of choice of law rules to a subsequent transaction has the result of giving effect to the foreign judgment*[115] *and thus is inconsistent with the non-recognition rule.* We will examine whether non-recognition rules in such cases should take precedence over choice of law rules.

The non-recognition rules, like the recognition rules, are different in the case of matrimonial decrees. In particular, the defences in the case of matrimonial decrees, which are now statutory, are discretionary whereas in non-matrimonial cases the defences are mandatory.[116] Thus, it will be appropriate to look at the two categories separately.

114 Jurisdiction is generally treated as different from defences in the textbooks, but cf the Administration of Justice Act 1920 and the Foreign Judgments (Reciprocal Enforcement) Act 1933, where lack of jurisdiction is listed together with defences as grounds for non-registration (see ch 1, IV A 1, *supra*).

115 This may be referred to as "incidental recognition", see Gordon (ch 1, n 39, *supra*) ch 9.

116 Because they negative the existence of the obligation for which recognition/enforcement is sought.

B. Non-Matrimonial Cases

1. The Problem Explained

The problem can be illustrated by examples P3 and P4.[117] In the former, if we recognise Zeldon's title in accordance with the choice rule we are indirectly recognising the Ruritanian judgment, which is not entitled to recognition. In the latter, if we refuse to recognise Zeldon's title we are indirectly enforcing the judgment of the Ruritanian court. Without this judgment,[118] title would remain in Yves, who would be able to pass it on to Zeldon.

The crucial point in both situations is that the judgment of the Ruritanian court changes the title, while the painting is physically in Ruritania. If this change in title is recognised in accordance with the *situs* rule, then indirectly the judgment is being recognised and the choice rule prevails. If, however, the non-recognition rule prevails, it would have to be held that no effect can be given to the vesting of title in Winkworth by that judgment. This could perhaps be done by way of public policy exception to the *lex situs* rule.[119]

2. Analysis of the Non-Recognition Rules

In order to decide whether there should be a global preference for the non-recognition rule we need to consider the possible bases for non-recognition and the rationale for each basis. Before looking at each basis individually, we will consider the theory that all defences are simply circumstances which negative the obligation. It is suggested that absence of obligation alone cannot provide a good reason to override the choice of law rule. Although no obligation is created by English law which necessitates direct recognition or enforcement of the judgment, this does not mean that the judgment should not give rise to rights and obligations in Ruritanian law, which would be given effect to by application of our choice of law rules.

Thus, we can only justify giving preference to non-recognition rules if there is some stronger policy reason for non-recognition than simply negativing the obligation which would otherwise be created. We will consider the policy behind the common law defences to recognition of a foreign judgment[120] with reference to example P3:[121]

(A) FRAUD

Assume that Winkworth brings fraudulent evidence to show that Yves did not buy in market overt in Italy.

The application of the fraud defence so as to allow the English Court to rehear the issue of fraud,[122] even where there is no new evidence, has been criticised

117 Chapter 1, IV B, *supra*.
118 Since nothing else happens in Ruritania to divest Yves of the title he had acquired while the painting was in Italy, prior to its entry into Ruritania.
119 See the "third exception" referred to by Slade J in *Winkworth v Christie* [1980] Ch 496 at 501.
120 See ch 1, n 55, *supra*.
121 Chapter 1, IV B, *supra*.
122 See *Abuloff v Oppenheimer* (1882) 10 QBD 295; *Vadala v Lawes* (1890) 25 QBD 310 and *Jet Holdings v Patel* [1990] 1 QB 355.

by academics.[123] The House of Lords in the recent decision of *Owens v Bracco*[124] also indicated that the rule may not be defensible. However, they were unable to change it in that case because they were dealing with the Administration of Justice Act 1920 and thus had to construe the fraud defence contained therein on the basis of the common law in 1920.

It is suggested that the reason that courts have been prepared to make what seems to be an anomalous exception in the case of fraud is because of the fundamental nature of fraud.[125] Where a judgment has been obtained by fraud it is considered to be contrary to basic standards of justice to recognise or enforce it. Thus, even where the question of fraud has been considered and rejected by a foreign court, an English court will not ignore a plea of fraud. *The policy seems to be that the risk of allowing multiplication of suits and preventing finality of litigation is less serious than the risk of enforcing a judgment obtained by fraud.*[126]

Given this approach to fraud, which it is submitted is correct, no rights should be recognised which were obtained by virtue of the fraudulent Ruritanian judgment. It would not, it is suggested, be difficult to apply the public policy exception to the *situs* rule where the *lex situs* gives effect to a fraudulent judgment.

(B) BREACH OF NATURAL JUSTICE

Assume that Yves was not given notice or the opportunity to be heard and so cannot bring evidence of the Italian market overt rule.

Breach of natural justice has in the past been limited to cases of lack of notice or lack of opportunity to be heard and these criteria were strictly interpreted.[127] In *Jet Holdings Inc v Patel*[128] the Court of Appeal suggested that just as with fraud, so with breach of natural justice it should not be necessary to have raised the defence in the foreign proceedings. It is suggested that the analogy between the two defences can be extended for our purposes. Thus, breach of natural justice should be considered fundamental in the same way as fraud and there should be no recognition of any change in title based on a judgment, which has

123 See, for example, Cheshire and North (ch 1, n 6, *supra*) p 380; Collier [1992] CLJ 439 and Read (n 38, *supra*) at p 279. Von Mehren and Trautman (1968) 81 Harv LR 1601 at 1667 claim that the English approach is out of line with international practice and it has recently been rejected in Australia (see Sykes and Pryles (n 246, *infra*) at p ix of the preface).

124 [1992] 2 All ER 193.

125 Levontin (1967) 2 Isr LR 197 at 207 suggests that it is the domestic rule not allowing review where fraud is alleged which is anomalous, but required for reasons of "sovereignty"; whereas "our treatment of foreign judgments fraudulently obtained is unmarred by considerations of respect for authority and is therefore more consonant with the dictates of pure justice and with the animus of the common law against fraud".

126 Cf the dictum of Beatty CJ in the Californian case of *Pico v Cohn* (1891) 25 P 970 at 971 that "Endless litigation, in which nothing was ever finally determined . . . would be worse than the occasional miscarriage of justice".

127 For example, *Jacobson v Frachon* (1928) 138 LT 386, where a biased expert's report was not sufficient to make out the defence because the court was not bound to accept the report and the parties had availed themselves of the opportunity to attack the report in court.

128 [1990] 1 QB 335 at 345.

been obtained in breach of the rules of natural justice, even where choice of law rules would normally require this.

This suggestion can more easily be accepted if the defence of natural justice is kept within strict limits. However, the recent case of *Adams v Cape Industries*[129] seems to have opened up the definition of this defence to include matters other than lack of notice or opportunity to be heard. With respect, Cheshire and North's suggestion[130] that cases of other kinds of procedural unfairness should be dealt with under public policy is to be preferred.

(C) CONTRARY TO PUBLIC POLICY

The public policy defence has been so limited that it is difficult to construct a potential public policy defence in the context of the example being used here. For completeness, the situation will be examined, even though it is unlikely to arise.

The main difference between the public policy defence and the two defences already discussed is that the public policy defence will not succeed where the defence was available to the defendant in the foreign proceedings but was not raised there.[131] However, where this hurdle is overcome and the defence is made out, it seems almost obvious that no title derived from such a judgment should be recognised and that therefore the non-recognition rule should prevail. Again, there would be no difficulty in achieving such a result by use of the public policy exception to the *lex situs* rule.

(D) WANT OF JURISDICTION

Assume, for example, that Yves is not resident in Ruritania and does not submit to the Ruritanian court.

The policy basis of the jurisdictional requirements in relation to recognition of *in personam* judgments is that it is not fair for the defendant to be bound by a decision of a foreign court unless he is either resident in the foreign jurisdiction or submits. The question arises whether this policy is sufficiently fundamental to override the choice of law rules where the effect of the application of these would be indirectly to recognise the foreign judgment.

Whilst there is no clear answer to this question as a whole, it is difficult to see how the policy of the non-recognition rule can be considered fundamental in any situation where an English court could have taken jurisdiction *mutatis mutandis*.[132] Thus, without further discussion, we can conclude that an automatic preference for the "lack of jurisdiction rule" cannot be supported.

This means that a global preference for non-recognition rules in non-matrimonial cases cannot be justified. Perhaps, though, a global rule in favour of those non-recognition rules which are defences could be supported.

129 [1990] Ch 433.
130 *Op cit* (ch 1, n 6, *supra*) at p 386.
131 See *Israel Discount Bank v Hadjipateras* [1984] 1 WLR 137 and discussion in Cheshire and North (ch 1, n 6, *supra*) at pp 371-372 and p 381 and Collier [1984] CLJ 47.
132 On the facts of example P3, the English court would have discretion to take jurisdiction under RSC Order 11, r 1(1)(i).

It is suggested that the above conclusions can also be supported by an analysis based on "conflicts justice". The parties should reasonably expect that a judgment obtained by fraud or in breach of natural justice[133] should not be either directly or indirectly recognised in other places. However, they might also reasonably expect that a judgment should be recognised if there is some real and substantial connection between the issue to be tried and the court, even if that connection does not satisfy the relatively narrow English rules for determining the international jurisdiction of foreign tribunals.

C. Matrimonial Causes

1. The Problem Explained

The question as to whether "non recognition rules" should take precedence arises in the classic *Schwebel v Ungar* incidental question situation, illustrated by example M1.[134] If the non-recognition rule takes precedence, the remarriage will not be recognised and the first wife will retain all marital rights. Some commentators take the view that the non-recognition rule should always take precedence as a matter of common sense[135] or because it is based on public policy.[136] There have also been suggestions[137] that a distinction might be drawn between non-recognition for want of jurisdiction and non-recognition because one of the defences is successfully invoked. In order to determine whether either of these approaches can be supported, we need to consider the policy behind the various non-recognition rules and to analyse whether all or any of these policies require an automatic preference for the non-recognition rule.

2. Protection of the Respondent

When we examine each non-recognition rule in turn, we will find that one of the rationales for a number of the rules is protection of the respondent. Thus, it will be helpful at the outset to consider whether this policy requires giving precedence to the non-recognition rule. The first question to ask is how non-recognition of the divorce protects the respondent, who is usually the wife. Non-recognition cannot force her husband to return to her and, indeed, where the divorce is a religious one, she will be considered by her community as divorced.

Perusal of the parliamentary debates suggests that it is primarily financial protection which is envisaged.[138] However, this seems to ignore the fact that since 1984, the English court has jurisdiction to make an order for financial

133 Although the parties" expectations about the procedure alleged to be in breach of natural justice is not conclusive as to whether there has been such a breach or not: *Adams v Cape Industries* [1991] 1 All ER 929 at 1050.

134 Chapter 1, IV B, *supra*.

135 See Law Commission Consultation Paper on "Recognition of Foreign Nullity Decrees and Related Matters" (1983) at para 6.50. This Consultation Paper was not published (for explanation see Law Com No 137 at para 1.8), but a copy is available from the Commission on request.

136 For example, Gordon (ch 1, n 39, *supra*) at p 151.

137 By consultees of the Law Commission (see Law Com No 137 at para 6.60).

138 See, for example, per the Lord Chancellor at 473 HL Debs col 1082 (22.4.86). See also per Lord Simon at 343 HL Debs col 320 (8.6.73) in a debate on s 16 of the Domicile and Matrimonial Proceedings Act 1973, which instituted the restrictions, which were extended by the Family Law Act 1986.

provision following a recognised *formal* divorce on the same basis as it may do after an English divorce.[139] The reason that the wife who is divorced informally may be in need of financial protection if the divorce were recognised is that Parliament has decided to deny her the opportunity to claim financial relief. In any event, not all wives need financial protection. In some cases, the husband has no available assets and in others the wife has more assets than the husband.

Even more crucially, the non-recognition rule, far from protecting the respondent, may actually be prejudicial to him/her,[140] if (s)he wishes to remarry.[141] Thus, we may conclude that the policy of protecting the respondent cannot justify an automatic preference for the non-recognition rule.

3. Analysis of the Non-Recognition Rules

We will now examine the various non-recognition rules, which will be illustrated by reference to the examples set out in Chapter 1, above,[142] to discover whether they are based on any other policies which can support such a preference.

(A) NOT EFFECTIVE UNDER THE LAW OF THE COUNTRY WHERE OBTAINED

In example M1, assume that Natasha and Alexander were in Vienna long enough to acquire a habitual residence there. The *get* would still not be recognised because it was not effective under the law of Austria, even if was recognised by the law of the Russian domicile.

It may seem obvious that a judgment should not be given greater effect abroad than it has in the jurisdiction in which it was granted.[143] However, at common law, a divorce could be recognised, even though it was of no effect whatsoever in the country where it was obtained, provided that it was recognised by the law of the domicile of the parties under the rule in *Armitage v Attorney-General.*[144]

In addition, a foreign decree could be recognised even though, because of procedural irregularities,[145] it was a "mere scrap of paper"[146] in the country where it was given.[147] Levontin explains this apparent paradox on the basis that:

> "It is no concern of ours to discipline the officers, judicial or others, of foreign States, to make them abide within the limits of their respective stations. It is

139 Under the Matrimonial and Family Proceedings Act 1984, Pt III.

140 This situation is only likely to arise where there is want of jurisdiction because the defences are discretionary.

141 See comment of Anton in relation to informal divorces in the Hague Conference Proceedings, Actes et Documents De La Haye, Onzieme Tome, p 100.

142 At section IV B.

143 See Levontin (1967) 2 Isr LR 197 at 201-202.

144 [1906] P 135.

145 Cf internal incompetence by the municipal law of the judgment granting state will prevent its recognition, see *Adams v Adams* [1971] P 206 and *Papdopoulos v Papadopoulos* [1930] P. 55.

146 Levontin (1967) 2 Isr LR 197 at 203.

147 *Pemberton v Hughes* [1899] 1 Ch 781, *Merker v Merker.* [1962] 3 All ER 928 and *Vanquelin v Bouard* (1863) 15 CBNS 341.

certainly not our concern to the extent of making us sacrifice substantive justice."[148]

So, why was the requirement of effectiveness introduced? Under the Recognition of Legal Divorces and Separations Act 1971, the requirement of effectiveness applied only to "overseas divorces" recognised under s 2. Thus, whilst the rule on procedural irregularities was probably reversed,[149] the rule in *Armitage v Attorney-General* was saved by s 6 of the Act. There was no discussion by the Law Commission or in Parliament about the effectiveness requirement. It appears that the wording simply followed that of the Hague Convention[150] which was being implemented,[151] although it was clearly not necessary to adopt this restriction.[152]

In 1984 the Law Commission[153] recommended extending the effectiveness requirement to divorces and annulments obtained on the basis of domicile. In their view, the statutory reversal of a few decisions was "a small price to pay" for the increased simplicity and certainty which will result from having uniform requirements for all the jurisdictional bases of recognition. With respect, this approach evades the real issue as to why it is not sufficient that the divorce is recognised by the law of the domicile, when this had been sufficient since 1906. There is no discussion of the policy basis of the requirement of effectiveness.[154]

Moreover, the uniformity argument put forward by the Commission is not convincing. The distinction between domicile and the other jurisdictional bases can be justified both on historical[155] and rational grounds.[156] If uniformity is so precious, it could equally have been achieved by extending the other jurisdictional bases to include decrees recognised by the law of the nationality and the law of the habitual residence.[157] Furthermore, whilst the Law Commission's approach might have been justifiable in the context of their proposals under which there would only be one set of jurisdictional bases, it

148 (1967) 2 Isr LR 197 at 298. This rationale seems wide enough to cover cases of lack of internal competence, but see n 145, *supra*.

149 Cheshire and North (ch 1, n 6, *supra*) at p 660 n 8 suggest that in the case of procedural irregularities, the decree should be recognised if it is effective in the country unless and until it is set aside.

150 Article 1 specifies that the Convention applies to divorces ". . . which follow judicial or other proceedings officially recognised in that State and which *are legally effective there*" (emphasis supplied). The effectiveness requirement was not in the preliminary draft. Bellet and Goldman (n 111, *supra*) suggest that the requirement was probably already implicit from the word "obtained", but "it seemed preferable to spell it out in some many words". There is no discussion of the rationale behind the requirement.

151 Law Com No 137 (1984) at para 6.12.

152 The Convention provides the minimum requirements for recognition and contracting states are allowed to be more generous (art 17).

153 Law Com No 137, paras 6.13 *et seq.*

154 Von Mehren and Trautman (1968) 81 Harv LR 1601 do present such a discussion and conclude (at 1660) that "there are situations in which a judgment void where rendered can properly be treated as valid, particularly, when it becomes incidentally relevant in litigation in another jurisdiction".

155 That domicile has traditionally governed matters of personal status at common law.

156 Since capacity to remarry is governed by the law of the domicile, the "conflict of rules" problem will be less likely to arise if recognition by the law of the domicile is sufficient. This argument is restricted to domicile in the English sense.

157 As in Australia, see Family Law Act 1975, s 104(8).

cannot be supported in the context of the actual legislation which retained the differential jurisdictional bases.[158]

Thus, so far we have not discovered the rationale behind the effectiveness requirement. Two suggested explanations are: (i) that the requirement is based on respect for the policy of the state where the divorce or annulment is obtained, which may be seen as an aspect of comity;[159] and (ii) that the requirement is designed to reduce limping marriages.

In relation to the former, we have already seen that comity cannot support a preference for recognition rules[160] and there seems to be no reason why this conclusion should not apply equally to non-recognition rules. In respect of the latter, if the decree is recognised by a third jurisdiction, there will in any event be a limping marriage.[161]

(B) WANT OF JURISDICTION IN FORMAL JUDICIAL DIVORCES

Assume the facts of example M4. The Mexican divorce is not recognised because neither party has a relevant connection with Mexico.

Two reasons may be identified for requiring a relevant jurisdictional link. Firstly, it is unfair to the respondent to allow the petitioner to litigate in a forum with which neither spouse has any real connection.[162] Secondly, parties should not be allowed to evade the law of the countries to which they belong. It is suggested that the second reason is weak because there is no general concept of "fraud *a la loi*" in English law[163] and because the wide jurisdictional requirements themselves allow evasion.[164] In any event, the forum only has a real interest in preventing evasion of its own law. Thus, protection of the respondent[165] can be seen as the main purpose.

158 See ch 1, IV A 2, *supra.*

159 Cf Levontin (1967) 2 Isr LR 197, who claims that comity does not generally extend to "enforcing administrative or public or fiscal laws of other countries" and thus substantive justice should not be sacrificed in order to enforce internal regulation of the administration of justice in a foreign state. Although the reference is to procedural irregularities, this point might equally apply to the foreign's country's insistence that divorces, etc, take place in a civil court.

160 Section II B, *supra.*

161 See at section III F, *supra.*

162 The concept of requiring a real connection was made explicit in the common law rules: see *Indyka v Indyka* [1969] 1 AC 33 (which was followed in relation to nullity decrees in *Law v Gustin* [1976] Fam 155). The Law Commission has expressed the view that the policy behind the statutory bases of recognition contained in the Recognition of Legal Divorces and Separations Act 1971 "is very close to *Indyka v Indyka,* though stated with the greater precision of a statute" (Law Com No 137 at para 5.14). It should be noted that whilst this comment might hold true of the Family Law Act 1986 in relation to formal divorces, it does not hold true in relation to informal divorces.

163 See Kahn-Freud (ch 1, n 24, *supra*) at p 284.

164 For example, where one party obtains a divorce in the country of his/her nationality, with which (s)he retains a purely nominal link and the other spouse has no connection at all or where one party obtains a "domicile" in a country like Nevada after a very short period of residence (as, for example, in *Lawrence v Lawrence* [1985] Fam 106).

165 See at section 2, *supra.*

(C) WANT OF JURISDICTION IN FORMAL TRANSNATIONAL DIVORCES

Assume in example M8 that the trans-national *get* is not recognised because s 46 of the Family Law Act 1986 requires all the proceedings to be in the same overseas jurisdiction.[166]

No good reason has been put forward for denying recognition to such a divorce on jurisdictional grounds. Provided that a relevant jurisdictional link exists with the place where the divorce is obtained *at the time of the institution of the proceedings*, it should be irrelevant if the proceedings are instituted in a third country. So long as the divorce is effective in the country where it is obtained, why should the forum impose an additional requirement relating to the place of initiation of proceedings, when it does not interfere in any other aspect of the foreign divorce procedure? Whilst the drafting of the 1971 Act may have made such an interpretation of the law inevitable,[167] the change in drafting in the 1986 Act left the position open to recognise such divorces.[168] It is, with respect, most unfortunate that the High Court, which admitted that there was no good policy reason not to recognise the divorce, was not prepared to admit that the new wording was ambiguous. This would have allowed them to conclude that, as the mischief which the legislation was intended to remedy was the creation of limping marriages, the divorce should be recognised.[169]

Perhaps one saving grace of the decision in *Grinburg* case is the court's recognition that the fact that part of the divorce proceedings were carried out on English soil was not in itself[170] a policy reason for denying recognition.

(D) LACK OF NOTICE OR OPPORTUNITY TO PARTICIPATE

Assume that in example M4 above, Evita is a citizen of Mexico and thus the divorce is *prima facie* entitled to recognition under s 46(1) of the Family Law Act 1986. However, assume that no notice is given to Pedro of the divorce hearing or that he is not afforded an opportunity to take part in the proceedings.

166 See *Berkovits v A-G, ex p Grinburg* [1995] 2 All ER 683, discussed at ch I, IV A 2, *supra*.

167 As in *R v Secretary of State for the Home Office, ex p Ghulam Fatima* [1986] AC 527.

168 With respect, the arguments which lead to Wall J's conclusion that his interpretation gives the words of their statute their natural meaning are flawed. *Inter alia*: 1. His argument that because the phrases "obtained by means of proceedings" and "obtained in a country outside the British Island" appear in the same sentence they must mean "obtained by means of proceedings in a country outside the British Islands" is not convincing. If that is what Parliament intended why did they not say so without the superfluous words? 2. His view that the section refers to "one set of proceedings" is problematic. Subsection (1) merely requires that the divorce was obtained by means of "proceedings". There is no requirement that the various steps involved have to be part of a single set of proceedings. 3. His finding that "it cannot have been the intention of Parliament to have legislated for the recognition of transnational divorce" whilst, at the same time, denying the right of a spouse so divorced to seek relief under Pt II of the 1984 Act is inconsistent with the fact that Parliament legislated for recognition of informal divorces, and yet s 12 of the 1984 provides no right to a spouse divorced in such a way to seek relief. Thus, it is submitted that his Lordship's construction is a gloss on the statute and not the natural meaning.

169 This reasoning was used by Lord Diplock in *Quazi v Quazi* [1979] 3 All ER 897 at 900.

170 Of course, in a different situation, where there was seen to be a deliberate evasion of English law, public policy might require refusal of recognition. In this case, both parties were Israeli and the wife was now living in Israel. Divorce by means of *get* in accordance with Jewish law was the only method of divorce which would be recognised in Israel.

The English court has discretion to refuse recognition under the Family Law Act 1986, s 51(3)(a). Case law[171] shows that recognition is usually only refused where it would cause hardship to the respondent.[172] Thus, the policy behind this non-recognition rule is also primarily to protect the respondent.[173]

(E) WANT OF JURISDICTION IN INFORMAL DIVORCES (THE DOMICILE REQUIREMENT)

Assume the facts of M7.

It appears that the considerably more restrictive jurisdictional requirements in relation to informal divorces reflect a policy of minimising the recognition of such divorces because of their "uncivilised" nature[174] and because they discriminate against[175] and do insufficient to protect women.[176] There also seems to be an element of protection of the taxpayer because if the divorced wife is not provided for by her husband, the state will have to support her.[177] However, again it seems that the element of protecting the wife is dominant.[178]

(F) WANT OF JURISDICTION IN INFORMAL DIVORCES (HABITUAL RESIDENCE IN ENGLAND)

Assume in example M7 that both parties are domiciled in India and that the talaq is recognised in India. However, at the relevant time, Ahmed has been habitually resident in England for more than 12 months.

Again, the "jurisdictional requirements" in s 46(2) of the Family Law Act 1986 are not met and the *talaq* will not be recognised. Whilst the habitual residence provision may be understood as part of the policy of minimising recognition of informal divorces, it is more difficult to explain the actual restriction itself in terms of protection of the wife, especially where the wife has remained resident in India throughout. Why should the wife need more protection just because the husband has been living in England?[179]

171 For example, *Newmarch v Newmarch* [1978] Fam 79, and see Dickson (1979) 28 ICLQ 132.

172 As in *Joyce v Joyce* [1979] Fam 93. The enactment of Pt III of the Matrimonial and Family Proceedings Act 1984, which allows financial provision to be awarded by an English court after an overseas divorce has been granted, reduces the likelihood of recognition causing hardship. See the recent Scottish case of *Tahir v Tahir* [1993] SLT 194.

173 See section 2, *supra*.

174 See per Lord Hailsham in 473 HL Debs Cols 1081-1082 (22.4.86) and per Cumming-Bruce LJ in *Chaudhary* [1985] 2 WLR 350 at 359F-G.

175 If this policy was taken to its logical conclusion no unilateral divorce would be recognised, whether formal or informal, if that form of divorce was only available to men.

176 See per Lord Hailsham at n 169, *supra*, and 102 HC Debs, Family Law Bill 24/10/86 per Mr Brown at col 1443 and per Solicitor-General at col 1444. Cf Young [1987] LS 78 at 82, who points out that certain types of formal divorces may be just as prejudicial to women and that in some societies women may be protected by community practice rather than legal provisions.

177 See per Lord Simon 343 HL Debs col 320 (8.6.73).

178 Ie the reason that the divorces are regarded as uncivilised and that their discriminatory nature is disliked is because they appear to prejudice the wife.

179 Lord Hailsham in 473 HL Debs col 1082 (22.4.86) said that the aim was to give greater protection to wives resident in the UK because it would be wrong to deny a wife living here the protection of our courts. Whilst this may have been a sound explanation of the position between 1974 and 1986, where a foreign informal divorce was only refused recognition where *both* parties had been habitually resident in England (see per Lord Simon 343 HL Debs col. 321 (8.6.73)) it does not explain the increased restrictiveness of the 1986 Act.

At least one of the rationales for the requirement appears to be to prevent "evasion" of the English divorce law, which can be resorted to wherever one party has been habitually resident in England for one year immediately preceding institution of the proceedings.

Does this selective application of an anti-evasion policy[180] justify a global preference for the non-recognition rule? Two questions must be considered. Firstly, is it in fact evasion to obtain a divorce in the country of domicile rather than in place of the habitual residence?[181] Secondly, how does non-recognition further the anti-evasion policy? As we have seen,[182] the main concern in Parliament seems to have been about evasion of financial obligations. Non-recognition might be a deterrent. It is not worthwhile for the English domiciled Indian Muslim to go back to India to divorce his wife by *talaq* because he will still be bound to support her in England and the new wife he marries in India will not be able to enter the country.[183] However, the deterrent argument is not applicable if it is the wife who wishes to remarry. Thus, at least in this situation, the non-recognition rule should not take precedence and therefore the anti-evasion policy cannot support a global preference for the non-recognition rule.

(G) LACK OF CERTIFICATION

Assume in example M7 that both parties are domiciled in India and neither has been habitually resident in England for 12 months. However, for bureaucratic reasons a certificate confirming the effectiveness of the divorce under Indian law cannot be obtained.

The English court may refuse recognition under the Family Law Act 1986, s 51(3)(b). There is no reported case law yet on this provision and it is not known what approach the courts will take in lack of certification cases.[184]

If, as with lack of notice in judicial proceedings, the discretion to refuse recognition is only exercised where recognition would cause hardship to the respondent, then it will be clear that the purpose of this non recognition rule is also protection of the respondent. If discretion is exercised more widely, it may seem that the purpose is generally to minimise recognition of informal divorces. However, as seen above,[185] the reason for this policy is also primarily to protect wives.

(H) CONTRARY TO PUBLIC POLICY

The public policy exception could be invoked in many different situations. We will give two examples:

180 See text accompanying to n 163, *supra*.

181 See Young [1987] LS 78 at 86. It is particularly difficult to justify a positive answer to the question if the petitioner has not been habitually resident in the UK for one year.

182 See n 138 and accompanying text, *supra*.

183 Cf if he is domiciled in India, the remarriage may be a valid polygamous marriage even if the divorce is not recognised. However, the second wife may not be able to enter the UK because of the restrictions of the Immigration Act 1988, s 2.

184 In the House of Commons, the Solicitor General 102 HC Deb at col 1444 (24/10/86) said that the policy was "the necessity and desirability to have some objective certification or assurance of the validity of the relevant divorce". With respect, this adds little to the legislation itself.

185 At (C), *supra*.

(i) Assume in example M7 that neither party has been habitually resident in the UK for 12 months. However, both parties have been habitually resident in New York for a number of years. Although the requirements of s 46(2) are met, the court decides that recognition would be contrary to public policy because the only purpose of the husband returning to India to pronounce the *talaq* was to attempt to evade his financial responsibilities to his wife[186] under the law of New York.[187]

Here, the non-recognition rule performs the dual purpose of protecting the wife[188] and preventing evasion of New York law. However, again, it is suggested that the second purpose is subsidiary to the first. We are only concerned with evasion of New York law because it causes prejudice to the wife.[189] Thus, in this example, it is suggested that the purpose of the public policy non recognition rule would also be protection of the wife.

(ii) In example M5, assume that the decree is refused recognition on public policy grounds on the basis that recognition is inconsistent with the English policy of validation of sham marriages.

Presumably, one of the purposes of this policy is to deter sham marriages. If remarriage after the decree is recognised, the effectiveness of the deterrence is substantially impaired.

We may conclude from the above survey of non recognition rules in relation to matrimonial decrees that there is no clear distinction between the policy objectives of the jurisdictional requirements and the "defences". A better distinction is between non-recognition rules which are primarily designed to protect the respondent and those which are designed to prevent evasion of either English law or some other domestic system of law or to deter a particular type of undesirable behaviour *per se*.[190] However, even in relation to the second category it may not always be possible to justify preferring the non-recognition rule if this prejudices the respondent. In any event, it is clear that the a global rule in favour of non-recognition rules in matrimonial cases cannot be supported.

186 See, for example, *Joyce v Joyce* [1979] Fam 93.

187 Assume that a *talaq* pronounced in New York would not be valid there (*Shikoh v Murff* 257 F 2d 306 (2 Cir 1958) and that the New York court would not award financial provision in this case (cf *Chaudhary v Chaudhary* 159 NJ Super 566, 388 A 2d 1000 (1978)).

188 See also *Zaal v Zaal* (1983) 4 FLR 284, where the bare *talaq* was held to fulfil the jurisdictional requirements under the 1971 Act, but was refused recognition on grounds of public policy and in particular that the wife was not informed that she had been divorced until some time afterwards.

189 In *Eroglu v Eroglu* [1994] 2 FLR 287, the fact that the parties" divorce had been a fraud on the Turkish court did not make recognition contrary to public policy. The court emphasised that the there was no deception of the wife as she had co-operated in obtaining the divorce and distinguished *Kendall v Kendall* [1977] Fam 208.

190 The effectiveness requirements seems to be *sui generis*.

V. GIVING PREFERENCE TO THE RULE WHICH IS STATUTORY

A. Introduction

In this section, we shall be seeking justification for preferring the statutory rule, where one of the rules is statutory and the other is not. This would be a global rule applicable in all cases where one of the relevant rules was not statutory. Clearly, such a rule would not be of any use to a country where the whole of the conflicts of law is codified or where none of it is enacted in statutory form. However, in England and other common law countries, where there has been piecemeal statutory reform of the conflict of laws, it is now not unusual for the recognition rule in question to be statutory and the choice of law rule common law or vice versa. It is also possible, although less likely, in the case of a conflict between two choice of law rules for one of them to be statutory and the other common law.

A problem of definition may arise in relation to common law rules which are saved by statute. Are such rules now to be considered as common law or statutory for the purposes of the suggested rule? It is suggested that this may depend on the form of the statute. If the rules are actually set out in the legislation, they would now derive their force from the statute;[191] whereas, if the legislation is simply clarifying the fact that the common law rules have not been changed,[192] then the rules can arguably still be regarded as part of the common law.

Table 1[193] shows which recognition rules and choice rules have been enacted in England. It can be seen that recognition rules have been codified more than choice of law rules. Thus, in England a rule giving preference to the statutory rule would in most cases be identical[194] in practice to a rule giving preference to the recognition rule. In contrast, in Israel, as can be seen from Table 2,[195] choice rules have been put into statutory form more than recognition rules. Thus, in the recognition situation it will be instructive to compare the operation of the proposed preference in favour of the statutory rule in England and Israel.

Particular reference will be made to the classic example of the "conflict of rules" situation involving capacity to remarry after a foreign divorce which is recognised by the law governing remarriage and not by the forum or vice versa.[196] We have already examined the English recognition rules.[196a] The

191 This would seem to be the case with s 6 of the Recognition of Divorces and Legal Separations Act 1971 (as amended by the Domicile and Matrimonial Proceedings Act 1973), which defined and extended the common law rules.

192 For example, the Canadian Divorce Act 1985, s 22(3) provides: "Nothing in this section abrogates or derogates from any other rule of law respecting the recognition of divorces granted otherwise than under this Act." See also the Australian Family Law Act 1975, s 104(5).

193 In the Appendix, *infra*.

194 The difference would be in the rationale. The applicability of the recognition rule would be being justified by virtue of its statutory form rather than because of the nature of the rule.

195 In the Appendix, *infra*.

196 As in examples M1 to M4 in ch 1, IV B, *supra*.

196a At ch 1, IV A 2, *supra*.

English choice of law rule is assumed to be the dual domicile test.[197] In Israel, art 64(2) of the Palestine Order in Council 1922 provides that capacity to marry is governed by the law of the nationality of the parties.[198] In contrast, there are no local provisions governing recognition of foreign matrimonial decrees. Article 46 of that Order,[199] provides that the English common law should fill any gaps in local law and thus the common law recognition rules would seem to be applicable.[200]

To illustrate the situation where there is a conflict between two choice of law rules of the forum we will consider two examples from English law: firstly, the situation where there is a conflict between the statutory rule governing recognition of foreign legitimations by subsequent marriage and the common law rule choice rule governing succession and secondly, the situation where there is a conflict between the statutory choice of law rules governing formal validity of certain foreign marriages and the choice of law rule governing capacity to marry.[201]

B. Theoretical Basis

It is suggested that three rationales can be given for preferring the statutory rule.

1. Statutory Rules are Invariably More Certain than Common Law Rules

This point can be illustrated in a number of ways. Codifications of recognition rules[202] in England do not suffer from the same ambiguities as the common law recognition rules.[203] The potential uncertainty of common law choice rules can be seen from the debate surrounding the English choice of law rule governing capacity to marry.[204] In Israel, it is not clear how the old English common law rules for recognition of divorces would apply in practice because of certain important differences between the two systems.[205]

197 Cf ch 4, I C, *infra*.

198 There is express provision for *renvoi* where the law of the nationality applies the law of the domicile.

199 This has, in fact, now been repealed by the Foundations of Law 1980, s 2(a). However, s 2(b) of that Law saves all English law which had already been adopted in Israel before the coming into force of that Law.

200 In the case of *Kaba v Saikaly CA* 189/4546 ALR 270, discussed in Levontin (1954) 3 Am J Comp Law 199 at 203, the Supreme Court of Israel refused to recognise a divorce obtained in a Syrian court in respect of parties domiciled in Israel, even though they were nationals of Syria. Levontin argues that it is illogical to have a choice rule based on nationality and not to respect a determination of status made by the court of the nationality.

201 See ch 1, III B 2, *supra* for discussion of classification of all of these rules as choice of law rules.

202 Whether the codification of the contract choice of law rules has lead to greater certainty is a matter of dispute. See Cheshire and North (ch 1, n 6, *supra*) pp 460-461 and references cited there.

203 For example, it is still not clear whether presence in the foreign country is sufficient jurisdictional basis for recognition of an *in personam* judgment (see ch 1, n 50, *supra*). The uncertainty of the "real and substantial" connection test, introduced in *Indyka v Indyka* [1969] 1 AC 33, was one of the motivations for the speedy enactment of the Recognition of Divorces and Legal Separations Act 1971 (see per Lord Hailsham 315 HL Debs col 485 (16.2.71).

204 See at ch 4, I C, *infra*.

205 Firstly, domicile in Israel is more like the Continental than the common law concept. See the definition in Succession Law 1965, s 135 as "the place in which his life is centred" and articles by Shaki (1966) 16 Scripta Hierosolymitana 163 and Shava (1983) 5 Tel Aviv Studies in Law 144). Secondly, the rule in *Travers v Holley* is difficult to apply because the divorce jurisdiction in Israel is very broad. When the divorce jurisdiction of the religious courts is combined with the divorce jurisdiction of the civil courts under the 1969 Dissolution of Marriages (Special Cases) Law, the only marriages which there is not jurisdiction to dissolve are those where both parties belong to one of the recognised religions (see 1969 Law, s 2) but do

2. Statutory Rules Have Usually Been Enacted to Further a Clearly Defined Policy Whereas the Policy Behind Common Law Rules may be Obscure and Outdated

This can be illustrated by the English recognition codes, which were enacted to implement International Conventions. The policy behind the 1971 enactment of the recognition rules for divorces was to reduce limping marriages.[206] The policy behind the Civil Jurisdiction and Judgments Act was to facilitate free flow of judgments within the European Community.[207]

In contrast, the policy behind common law choice of law rules cannot always be stated definitively. The rationale for the dual domicile test would seem to be that the country of the domicile has the most interest in the status of its domiciliaries.[208] The criticisms of the domicile rule stem from the argument that the interest of the domicile is weak, or non-existent, where the parties no longer have any connection with that country. Of course, if the choice rule is a more flexible rule, as advocated by various writers,[209] the policy behind it may be clearer and stronger.

In Israel, the position is more obscure. It is not clear whether there was any policy rationale behind the deliberate preference by the mandatory legislature of the nationality choice rule[210] over the common law domicile rule. Vitta[211] claims that it was simply a retention from the old Ottoman Law; whereas Silburg[212] suggests that the preference for nationality stems from the fact that most foreign nationals during the period of the Mandate were immigrants from Europe, where their status was governed by the *lex patriae*. In any event, since 1959 domicile has been preferred in choice of law provisions in statute.[213] Thus, there seems to be no sound policy reason behind the nationality rule today.

The application of the old English common law recognition rules is simply a leftover from the period of the Mandate and is only applicable by virtue of a residual provision of the Palestine Order in Council.[214] However, the first two

not fall within the jurisdiction of the appropriate religious court (eg Jews who are neither resident nor nationals of Israel). However, under the latter Act, the President of the Supreme Court does have discretion not to grant relief wherever this is not appropriate and it is expected that he would exercise this discretion in a case which had no connection with Israel (Shava (1970) 26 Hapraklit 302 at p 304) (Hebrew). However, a literal application of the rule in *Travers v Holley* would seem to mean that almost all foreign divorce decrees should be recognised. Levontin (1954) 3 Am Comp Law 199 argues that the common law recognition rules are completely inappropriate because nationality and not domicile governs issues of personal status in Israel. It should be noted that Levontin was writing before the decisions in *Travers v Holley* and *Indyka v Indyka*.

206 See references at n 111, *supra*.

207 See the Preamble to the Brussels Convention.

208 See Law Com W P No 89, para 3.27.

209 See Jaffey (1978) 41 MLR 38 (discussed at ch 3, III B 3, *infra*) and (1982) 2 OJLS 368, and Fentiman [1985] CLJ 256.

210 Enacted in the Palestine Order in Council 1922, art 46(2).

211 (1977) 12 Isr LR 129.

212 Silberg, *Personal Status in Israel* (1958, Hebrew) at p 335.

213 For example, in s 17 of the Family Law Amendment (Maintenance Law) 1959, ss 76 and 77 of the Capacity and Guardianship Law 1962 and ss 136, 137 and 139 of the Succession Law 1965. See Shaki (1966) Scripta Hierosolymitana 163 and Shava (1983) 5 Tel Aviv University Studies in Law 144.

214 Art 46 (see n 199, *supra*).

common law rules of recognition[215] are consistent with the trend in Israeli private international law of the increasing use of domicile as a connecting factor.[216] The reciprocity rule would not be easy to apply in Israel.[217] It is difficult to believe that the *Indyka* "real and substantial connection test", which was abrogated in England shortly after its creation,[218] is intended to further any Israeli policy. Although, curiously, it may well be that taking into account the President of the Supreme Court's discretion[219] to determine jurisdiction under the 1969 Dissolution of Marriage (Special Cases) Law, the Israeli position on jurisdiction in divorce cases is similar to the *Indyka* test.

Furthermore, even in England, the argument would not seem to hold good in relation to all choice of law rules. Thus, for example, it is not clear that the policy behind the rule that intestate succession is governed by the domicile of the deceased is any less clear than that behind the rule that foreign legitimations by subsequent marriage are to be governed by the domicile of the father at the date of the marriage.[220] Both involve the assumption that the law of the domicile has the most interest in relation to matters of personal status. Moreover, as shown by the Law Commission,[221] the Foreign Marriage Act statutory choice rules for formal validity of marriage were in need of reform.

3. Rules of Statutory Interpretation Require That a Statutory Provision Overrules Any Pre-Existing Inconsistent Common Law Rule[222]

In English law, the statutory recognition rule is not directly inconsistent with the common law rule because they are different types of rules. However, it might be argued that since the result of the application of the common law choice rule is inconsistent with that of the statutory rule, the latter should prevail.

Similarly, the statutory choice rule governing legitimation by subsequent marriage is hardly inconsistent *per se* with the common law succession rule. However, again it might be argued that where the two rules will give conflicting results, the statutory rule should prevail.

In relation to Israel, there is a stronger argument that the statutory rule should take precedence because English common law is only to be introduced into Israel where local law does not extend or apply and "so far only as the circumstances of Israel

215 Which depend on domicile (see ch 4, I B 1, *infra*).

216 See references at n 213, *supra*.

217 See n 205, *supra*.

218 By the Recognition of Divorces and Legal Separations Act 1971, although it is still applied in some Commonwealth jurisdictions (see ch 4, I B 1, *infra*).

219 Note 205, *supra*.

220 The latter rule was clearly originally enacted in the Legitimacy Act 1926, s 8(1) to bring the conflicts rule in to line with domestic rule. At common law, the conflicts rule required that the father be domiciled in the country providing for legitimation both at the date of the birth of the child and at the date of the marriage.

221 WP No 89 para 6.1(A)(7)-(10) and Rept No 165. Their recommendations have been enacted in the Foreign Marriages (Amendment) Act 1988 and SI 1990/598.

222 Edgar, *Craies on Statute Law* (7th edn, 1971) pp 338 *et seq*.

and its inhabitants . . . permit and subject to such qualification as local circumstances render necessary".[223]

C. Non-Recognition Rules

It may be argued that statute need not be preferred in the case of non-recognition because the statute only states the circumstances when recognition is accorded. It does not, with the exception of non-judicial divorces obtained within the British Isles,[224] provide that divorces which do not meet the jurisdiction requirements should not be recognised, although this is the way the statute is applied.[225] Further, as we have seen, the defences merely provide the court with the opportunity to refuse recognition of the matrimonial decree. The court is not mandated to refuse recognition where one of the defences is made out.

This argument would lead to the result that a statutory recognition rule should be preferred where it results in recognition, but not necessarily where it results in non-recognition.[226] The difficulty with this is that it would be necessary to find another rule to deal with the non-recognition situation and thus the preference for the statutory rule would no longer be a global rule.[227]

D. Results

1. Conflict Between Recognition Rule and Choice Rule

We will consider how examples M2 and M4[228] would be decided in England and Israel using the preference for the statutory rule approach. In example M2, the remarriage will be valid in England because the divorce is recognised under the statutory recognition code. Conversely, in Israel, whilst the divorce should be recognised on the basis of the *Indyka* test,[229] the remarriage will be invalid because there is no capacity under the Argentinian law of the nationality.[230]

However, the opposite results will be achieved where the divorce is not recognised by the forum. Thus, in example M4, the English court will not recognise the remarriage. Conversely, in Israel, preference for the statutory rule would mean applying the nationality choice rule. Thus, the remarriage will be

223 Palestine Order in Council 1922, art 46. Levontin (1954) Am J Comp Law 199 at 206 argues that as the local choice rule makes provision for determining the status of a foreigner, there is no need to have recourse to the common law recognition rules.

224 Family Law Act 1986, s 44(1).

225 For example, informal divorces have not been recognised where one of the parties is domiciled in England, as in *Chaudhary v Chaudhary* [1985] Fam 19.

226 This can also be supported by the presumption (see Craies, n 30, *supra*) that statute invades common law rights as little as possible; ie the statutory non-recognition rule should not remove from the "spouse" the common law capacity to remarry where (s)he has such capacity by the law of his/her domicile, unless the statute clearly requires this result.

227 However, a specific rule will be constructed which reflects this point (see ch 4, II 3, *infra*).

228 Chapter 1, IV B, *supra*.

229 The decision in *Kaba v Saikaly* (n 200, *supra*) might have been different today on the basis that the Syrian court was a court with a real and substantial connection, although it is significant that nationality alone will not necessarily be sufficient under the *Indyka* rule (see eg *Keresztessy v Keresztessy* (1976) 73 DLR (3d) 347).

230 Unless renvoi applies (n 198, *supra*): ie Argentina refers the issue of capacity to the law of the domicile which it considers is Mexico.

recognised because the divorce is recognised by Argentinian law, which is the *lex patriae*.

2. Conflict Between Two Choice of Law Rules

Preference for the statutory choice rule will result in Cuthbert's sharing in the intestacy in example L1, but not in L2.

E. Conclusion

Whilst there may be some merit in the rationales put forward in favour of the statutory rule, they fail to explain the difference between the results in England and those in Israel in the above examples. Similarly, in the case of a conflict between two choice rules, the results are only justifiable if the fact that one rule has been enacted means that it is based on a stronger policy than a rule which has been enacted. This may not always be the case.

Thus, the fortuitous element in whether a choice rule or recognition rule is enacted increases the risk of arbitrary results, which is inherent in all mechanical global rules.

In Parts II and III of this book, we will be constructing specific preference rules to overcome this problem. From the discussion in the current section, it can be concluded that, whilst specific rules should be formulated without reference to whether they result in giving precedence to the statutory rule over the common law rule, the fact that a proposed preference rule has such an effect will provide it with additional support.

VI. PUBLIC POLICY AS AN ESCAPE ROUTE

Public policy has been chosen for more detailed examination because it is easy to show how it could apply in the "conflict of rules" context as a method of "escaping" from an undesirable result produced by a global principle in favour of the recognition rule. Two cases, *Gray v Formosa*[231] and *Vervaeke v Smith*,[232] concerning recognition of foreign nullity decrees[233] will illustrate this point. Although they are not strictly "conflict of rules" cases because recognition was the only issue in the case before the court,[234] each case could have arisen in a choice of rule context.[235] In example M9, the "conflict of rules" does arise in a similar fact situation.[236]

231 [1963] P 259 (followed reluctantly in *Lepre* v *Lepre* [1969] P 52).

232 [1983] 2 All ER 144.

233 The fact that the cases are matrimonial decrees is not in itself important here, because the public policy defence relied on applies equally in relation to other judgments.

234 They belong to the category of "pure recognition cases" (see ch 1, III C, *supra*).

235 *Vervaeke v Smith* could easily have presented a choice of rule problem if the issue of recognition had arisen in the course of litigation about the succession to the estate of the second husband and such succession had been governed by a foreign law. *Gray v Formosa* could have arisen in a choice of rule context if, for example, the parties had remarried and the decrees were not recognised by the law governing the validity of the remarriages. In such a case, the court could (prior to s 50 of the Family Law Act 1986) have openly applied the choice of law rule in preference to the recognition rule or achieved the same result by refusing to recognise the judgments on public policy grounds. Following s 50, only the latter course would be available.

236 See ch 1, IV B, *supra*.

In these two cases, nullity decrees were granted by Maltese and Belgian courts, respectively, in relation to marriages which had been celebrated in England. The ground for the decree in the first case was lack of celebration in Roman Catholic form as required by Maltese law[237] and in the second that the marriage was a sham as the parties never intended to live together as husband and wife. In *Gray v Formosa* the application of English choice of law rules to the question of the validity of the marriage would have led to the application of English law as the *lex loci celebrationis* and the marriage would have been held valid. The position in *Vervaeke v Smith* is slightly more complicated. The Court of Appeal found that the validity of the marriage fell to be determined by English law under the exception in *Sottomeyer v De Barros (No 2)*.[238] Thus, the petitioner's foreign incapacity, which was unknown to English law, would be ignored because she married an English domiciliary in England. In the House of Lords, only Lord Simon considered the choice of law issue. He found that the question of the validity of a sham marriage was a question of quintessential validity and should be governed either by the *lex loci celebrationis* or, alternatively, by the country with which the marriage has the most real and substantial connection. Either way, English law governed and the marriage was valid.

The English courts refused to recognise both of these nullity decrees.[239] In *Gray v Formosa* the court found that recognition would constitute a denial of "substantial justice". It has been suggested that this concept coincides with that of public policy.[240] In *Vervaeke v Smith* the House of Lords[241] concluded *inter alia*[242] that recognition of the decree was precluded by public policy.

Carter[243] includes both of the above cases in his third category of public policy, ie application of a foreign rule or recognition of a foreign judgment would "lead to an unacceptably unjust result in the particular circumstances of the instant case". The injustice in *Gray v Formosa* is that the wife would have been deprived of financial relief if the foreign decree had been recognised.[244] It is more difficult[245] to pinpoint the injustice in *Vervaeke v Smith.* Carter suggests that, although the petitioner's unsavoury background was said not to

237 The husband was Maltese.

238 (1879) 5 PD 94.

239 Cf *Merker v Merker* [1963] P 283, *Galene v Galene* [1939] P 237 and *De Massa v De Massa* [1939] 2 All ER 150n, where nullity decrees were recognised even though the marriages would have been valid by English choice of law rules. See also the Australian case of *Vasallo v Vasallo* [1952] SASR 129 and the South African case of *De Bono v De Bono* 1948 (2) SA 802, where Maltese nullity decrees were recognised on similar facts to *Gray v Formosa*.

240 Carter (1993) 42 ICLQ 1 at 5. According to Sir John Arnold P in *Armitage v Nanchen* (1983) 4 FLR 293 at 298, it is "very much like public policy".

241 The Court of Appeal, [1981] 1 All ER 55, had held that recognition was not contrary to public policy, but refused recognition on other grounds.

242 Arguably the ratio (or at least the main ratio) of the case was the narrower ground that the Belgian judgment was inconsistent with an earlier English judgment on the same issue, which should therefore have been treated as *res judicata* by the Belgian court. Non-recognition of foreign matrimonial decrees in such circumstances is now provided for by the Family Law Act 1986, s 51(1).

243 (1993) 42 ICLQ 1.

244 Whereas, because the decree was not recognised, the English court was able to grant a divorce itself and the wife could then claim financial relief.

245 Jaffey (1983) 32 ICLQ 500 at 503 claims that there was no question of any injustice to the respondent.

be relevant, in fact this, combined with her behaviour in the course of litigation, led to the unarticulated feeling that it would be unjust for her to win and succeed to the estate of the man she alleged to be her husband by virtue of the second marriage.

It is suggested that the idea that the courts refused to recognise the judgments because the result was unjust can be refined by postulating that what the courts were really doing was preferring the "just" result of the application of choice of law[246] rules to the "unjust" result of the application of the recognition rule.[247] A hint that this thinking underlay the decision in *Vervaeke v Smith* can be seen from the judgment of Lord Simon.[248] He expressly states that the fact that the choice of law rule provides for English law to determine the validity of the marriage is a reason for preferring English policy in relation to sham marriages and for refusing recognition of the Belgian decree, which is contrary to public policy.

In *Gray v Formosa* Lord Denning said "the marriage was lawful in England, as lawful as any marriage would be".[249] Since the marriage took place in England and at the time both parties were domiciled there, the court was no doubt thinking about English domestic law. However, it is clear that applying choice of law rules, English domestic law was the relevant law to determine formal validity of the marriage and that it was because the Maltese decision was inconsistent with English law that it offended English ideas of justice.[250] Donovan LJ said:[251]

> "It ill accords with present day notions of tolerance and justice that a wife validly married *according to our law* should be told by a foreign court that she is a mere cohabitant and her children bastards simply on the ground that her husband did not marry her in the church of a particular religious denomination." (emphasis supplied)

In *Lepre v Lepre*,[252] the facts of which were virtually identical with those of *Gray v Formosa*, Sir Jocelyn Simon P referred to the fact that the marriage was valid by the English choice of law rule. He followed *Gray v Formosa* in refusing to recognise the Maltese decree because it offended against English concepts of justice.

246 See Sykes and Pryles, *Australian Private International Law* (3rd edn, 1991) p 475.

247 *Ogden v Ogden* [1908] P 46 might also be seen as an example of preferring the English choice of law rule (under which the marriage was formally valid by the English *lex loci celebrationis*) to the recognition rule which would have required recognition of the nullity decree granted by the French court of domicile on the basis that the parties lacked capacity due to absence of parental consent. However, it can hardly be said that the result of the application of the choice rule was more just in this case because the effect was that the wife was unable to obtain a divorce.

248 [1983] 2 All ER 144 at 159.

249 [1965] P 259 at 367.

250 This conclusion has been widely criticised by commentators. See, for example, Lipstein [1972B] CLJ 67 at p 89.

251 [1963] P 259 at 270.

252 [1969] P 52.

Thus, in all three cases public policy was a "transparent device"[253] used to escape from the result of applying the recognition rule blindly when the result of the application of the choice of law rule was preferred. If this approach can be found in a case where the choice of law rule did not strictly come into play, *a fortiori* we would expect to find it in a real "conflict of rules" case.

Carter[254] suggests that the need to resort to an escape route indicates that there are shortcomings in the rules themselves and that the ultimate method of eliminating reliance on public policy is

> "improvement in the detail of, the sophistication of, and not least the realism of, choice of law rules and rules governing the recognition and enforcement of foreign judgments."

In other words, so long as we have rigid mechanical and global principles we will need to rely on the unruly horse of public policy. The alternative, at least in the "conflict of rules" context, is result-selection.

253 This may account for the criticism, which has been levelled at the use of public policy in these cases. See, for example, Carter (1962) 38 BYIL 497 and (1978) 49 BYIL.

254 Carter (1993) 42 ICLQ 1

Chapter 3

Specific Result-Orientated Rules

I. INTRODUCTION

The impetus for the result selection movement seems to have been disillusionment with some of the results[1] produced by mechanical jurisdiction selecting rules, which paid no attention to the content of the rules to be applied[2] or to the result of the application[3] of those rules. The criticism of the traditional rules is summarised by Collier:[4]

> "[T]he concepts of choice of law are too rigid and artificial and cause the courts to reach decisions repugnant to common sense and ideas of justice or to use transparent devices to arrive at a more satisfactory result, by avoiding their application."

The global preference rules which we considered in Chapter 2, are analogous to jurisdiction selecting rules because they are applied "blindly", without any attention being paid to the result of their application in each particular case. We have already seen that relying on escape routes is not a satisfactory solution. Thus, in Parts II and III of the book, we will be applying a result selecting approach to determine which of the two conflicting rules should prevail in the "conflict of rules" scenario.

In this chapter, we will be developing a result-selection methodology which is appropriate for our purposes. Firstly, the result-orientated approach, which it is proposed to adopt, will be illustrated by reference to choice of law examples in the literature and analysed critically. Some of the problems with result-orientation in relation to pure choice of law will be found not to be relevant in the "conflict of rules" context. Solutions to the remaining difficulties will be sought. Finally, the conclusions of this analysis will be converted into a practical methodology for use in subsequent chapters.

1 See, eg, Cook, *Logical and Legal Basis of the Conflict of Laws*, ch 1; Cavers (1933) 47 Harv LR 173; and Currie, *Selected Essays on the Conflict of Laws* (1963).

2 Cavers, *ibid*, refers to "an austere unconcern for the consequences".

3 In particular, whether the result was in accordance with the social policies behind the rules. See, eg, Hancock "Three Approaches to the Choice of Law Problem", in Nadelman *et al* (eds) *Legal Essays in Honour of HE Yntema* (1961).

4 Collier (ch 1, n 145, *supra*) at p 384. See also Shapira *The Interest Approach to Choice of Law* (1970) pp 20-24.

II. RESULT ORIENTATION

A. The Difference Between Ad Hoc Result Selection and Result-Orientation

A number of different result selecting techniques have been advocated by various writers,[5] mainly from North America. Some critics have lumped them altogether.[6] However, in fact, two main categories may be distinguished:

1. Methods which require judges to select the appropriate result *ad hoc* on the basis of, for example, which of the conflicting laws is "better";[7] which government has an interest in application of its own law[8] or which country's interest will be less seriously impaired[9] if its law is not applied.
2. Methods which create *rules* designed to achieve the desired result in each particular category of case. These techniques, which we shall call collectively result-orientation, can be said to be a *via media* between traditional jurisdiction selection[10] and the case by case *ad hoc* result selection discussed above. It involves the construction of choice of law rules for particular categories of case to ensure that the desired result is reached.

Most of the criticism by English writers[11] has been directed against the first category. Whilst some of their objections are not applicable in the "conflict of rules" scenario,[12] the fundamental defects of lack of certainty, predictability and consistency are fatal to the acceptance of such an approach in England.[13] Thus, we may reject the *ad hoc* result selection approach[14] and concentrate on result-orientation.

B. Examples of Result-Orientated Rules

1. Cavers' Principles of Preference

Cavers, who seems to have been the founder[15] of this approach, advocates "a selection between individual substantive rules of private international law"[16]

5 See summaries of the various theories in Kegel (ch 2, n 4, *supra*).
6 See, eg, Collier (ch 1, n 145, *supra*) pp 383-386.
7 Ehrenzweig (ch 1, n 4, *supra*), who uses the term *lex potior*, cites American judicial support for this approach (at p 229).
8 Currie, *Selected Essays on the Conflict of Laws* (1963). According to this approach, where there is a "true conflict" between the interests of different governments, the *lex fori* should apply.
9 Baxter (1963) 16 Stan LR 1. This approach has been adopted by the Supreme Court of California *inter alia* in *Bernard v Harrah's Club* 546 P 2d 719 (1976).
10 As Morris (ch 1, n 6) at p 450, points out, some of our apparently mechanical choice rules can be seen as "a synthesis" of a number of result orientated rules.
11 See, eg, Jaffey (1982) 2 OJLS 368 at 378 and Fawcett (1982) 31 ICLQ 150.
12 Eg, the objection to over-emphasis on the *lex fori* because it negates the whole purpose of the conflict of laws is not applicable in a situation where *ex hypothesi* the conflict is between the choice rules of the *forum* and the recognition rule of the *forum* (see ch 1, III A, *supra*).
13 The only part of the approach which might be acceptable is the identification of false conflicts. See Morris (ch 1, n 6, *supra*) pp 461 *et seq.*
14 Gottlieb (1977) 26 ICLQ 734 at 782-795 seems to be adopting an *ad hoc* approach to the incidental question when he attempts to isolate the prime consideration in each of his model problems. He admits that his solutions involve value judgments which may not be universally accepted.
15 He first advocated it in (1933) 47 Harv LR 173. See also his book, *The Choice of Law Process* (1965).
16 Kegel (ch 2, n 4 *supra*) at p 39.

by means of principles of preference. This means that in each area of law there are a number of possible jurisdiction selecting rules. The principles of preference provide which of those rules should apply to a particular law-fact pattern.[17] The principles are designed to ensure that the result produced in each law-fact category will be just between the parties.

2. *Morris*

Morris uses a result-orientated approach to recommend a choice of law rule for capacity to enter into a contract.[18]

He starts by identifying the two most likely choice of law rules as being the proper law of the contract and the law of the domicile of the party alleged to be incapable. He then distinguishes two law-fact situations:

(i) The party in question has capacity by the law of the domicile but not by the proper law.
(ii) The party in question has capacity by the proper law but not by the law of his domicile.

He concludes that the first category results in a false conflict.[19] In order to come to this conclusion he has to rely on two hypotheses: firstly, that the purpose of the invalidating rule is to protect the minor from his own immaturity; and secondly, that a country only has an interest in protection of minors who are its own domiciliaries. Thus, reasons Morris, neither country has any interest in invalidating this contract; whereas the proper law, which has other connections with the contract, has an interest in upholding contracts.

The second category produces a real conflict. The law of the domicile does have an interest in protecting the minor. The proper law has an interest in upholding contracts. The latter should generally be preferred because of commercial convenience.

Accordingly, Morris produces a result orientated rule[20] that a contract will be valid if there is capacity by either the law of the domicile or the proper law. It can be seen that Morris has used a *generalised* governmental interest analysis approach to determine whether a particular law should apply in a particular law-fact situation. The conclusion of the analysis is used to create a rule which applies to all similar law-fact situations.

3. *Jaffey*[21]

Jaffey adopts a similar approach in relation to essential validity of marriage. He identifies the two most likely choice of law rules as being the domicile of each

17 Eg, in Cavers' five principles applicable to torts, depending on the law-fact situation, one of the following rules will apply: (i) the law of the place of acting; (ii) the law of the parties' home state; (iii) where the parties have different home states, the law of that which affords the lower degree of protection; (iv) the law of the state in which a relationship between two parties has its seat.
18 Morris (ch 1, n 6, *supra*) at pp 269-271.
19 The idea of the false conflict originates from Currie (n 8, *supra*).
20 See Dicey and Morris (ch 1, n 6, *supra*) rule 181(1).
21 (1978) 41 MLR 38.

party and the intended matrimonial home. He then investigates each different type of incapacity to determine what interest each of these laws has in relation to each reason for invalidity. On this basis he proposes a rule which will produce the desired result in each law-fact situation.

In relation to polygamy, Jaffey concludes that it is the society in which the couple are living which is most affected by polygamy. However he adds that:

> "English law can tolerate the validity of a polygamous marriage between foreigners who come to live in England after the marriage . . . when polygamy is in accordance with the religious belief of the community or communities to which the parties belong at the time of the marriage."[22]

Thus, he concludes that:

> "a polygamous marriage should only be invalid if, and only if, it is invalid by the law of either party's domicile time of the marriage, provided that it is not invalid if, within a reasonable time of the celebration of the marriage, the parties establish a matrimonial home in a country by the law of which the marriage is valid." [23]

The same conclusion is reached in relation to prohibited degrees of relationship because the matrimonial home has most interest.[24] Whereas in relation to non-age, it is claimed that the law of the domicile of the "under-age" party has an interest in protecting its domiciliaries from premature marriage and should therefore govern.

C. Critique of Result-Orientated Rules

1. Basis of Construction of Rules

Morris alleges that Cavers' approach would not work any better than Currie's interest analysis approach in an international situation[25] because a judge cannot express a preference for rules adopted by one sovereign state over those of another. This criticism seems to be based on Cavers' own admission that his principles are "value judgments", but it is suggested that it is misconceived. Surely, the difficulty is not in expressing preference for the laws of one state over that of another because the whole basis of choice of law rules is to express such a preference. Rather, the objection is to using *subjective* criteria to exercise this preference.[26] Whilst the description of Cavers' principles as value judgments

22 *Ibid* at 40.

23 *Ibid* at 42.

24 Because "[t]he purpose of such rules is to prevent marriage relationships which are offensive to the morality or religion prevailing in the country concerned". *(ibid)*. It is not expressly stated that marriages which are allowed by the spouses' domicile can be tolerated by the matrimonial home. It is suggested that there must be limits to such tolerance. For example, it must be doubtful whether a marriage between a brother and sister would be recognised in England, even if valid by the law of the domicile.

25 As opposed to an inter-state case.

26 This was one of the main problems with both the "better law" approach and Currie's governmental interest analysis (see n 8, *supra*).

may suggest that they are subjective, it is submitted that there is a significant difference between Cavers and Currie. The criteria used in Cavers' principles can be objectively ascertained and applied by anyone. They do not depend on the court's views as to what is "better" or whether a state has an interest in the application of its law to a particular situations. True, subjective notions have to be taken into account in formulating the principles. But this is equally so with all choice of law rules. For example, the rule that the *lex domicilii* applies to determine the essential validity of a marriage involves the subjective notion that the domicile is the most appropriate law to govern. Furthermore, as with traditional choice rules, Cavers' principles are the result of reasoned analysis.[27] The fact that not everyone will agree with that analysis does not make his principles subjective any more than the fact that not everyone agrees that the law of the domicile is the most appropriate choice of law rule for marriage.

Indeed, Morris and Jaffey's approach of basing their rules on governmental interest analysis is no less problematic from this point of view. Whilst result-orientation overcomes the difficulty of actually determining the interests of each particular government in each particular case, it does not solve the problem of identifying governmental interest in the first place. Whilst this might be relatively easy in Morris's contract example, it is more speculative in relation to a potentially controversial issue like marriage and the analysis of the author of the rule may not command general acceptance.

It may be concluded that, *in the choice of law context*, the problem of the basis on which to select the result for each category of case can only be solved by the development of a set of objective criteria[28] and principles to inform the categorisation of law-fact patterns and the construction of the result-orientated rules.

However, it is submitted that the absence of objective criteria is not a problem in the context of our search for a preference rule in the "*conflict of rules*" situation. We are using principles of preference to decide between *English* choice rules and *English* recognition rules. The appropriate objective criteria should already have been taken into account in formulating the choice of law and recognition rules. Where there is a conflict between those rules, then the policy of the forum must determine which prevails and thus it is appropriate to base the principles of preference on *English* value-judgments as reflected in domestic policy. We will deal with the problem of ascertainment of domestic policy below.[29]

2. *Self-Sufficiency and Complexity*

Cavers' approach is not, nor does it purport to be, self-sufficient and it is potentially excessively complex. In a sense, these two points may be two sides of the same coin. It may be that Cavers has not attempted to formulate a

27 See p 133 of Cavers' book (n 1, *supra*). Analysis behind the principles of preference can be seen in the specific chapters of the book (eg torts in ch VI).

28 Such as Jaffey's principles of justice (see ch 2, II C, *supra*).

29 See section D, *infra*.

complete system to cover every conceivable law-fact pattern because to do so would be excessively complex. In any event, since it is beyond the realms of human ability to foresee every possibility, some provision must be made for the unforeseen case.

These criticisms do not seem applicable to Morris and Jaffey because they are both attempting to deal only with a specific issue which has only a limited number of variables. Thus, it is possible to create a non-complex self-sufficient rule. Similarly, the variables in the "*conflict of rules*" situation are limited. Thus, it should be possible to formulate principles to cover all likely situations without undue complexity and the likelihood of an unforeseen situation arising is substantially reduced.

3. Certainty

It has been suggested that if the task of formulating the principles of preference is left to the courts, there would be considerable uncertainty during the development period.[30]

Again, this criticism is not pertinent in the present context. The outcome of cases where the "conflict of rules" arises is at present uncertain apart from where statute[31] applies. Thus, the adoption of a result-orientated approach would not create any further uncertainty.

D. Ascertainment of Policy

The need to determine the policy behind substantive laws has been one of the most criticised aspects[32] of result selection. Whilst the criticism is generally made with reference to *ad hoc* result selection, most of it is equally pertinent to the search for policy in order to construct result-orientated rules, especially where it is envisaged that the courts themselves will have to develop the rules.

North, like other writers, emphasises that the search for the policy of a particular rule is "immeasurably more difficult"[33] in the international, rather than the inter-state, context, in which the approach has been applied in the USA. Even then, judicial attempts at analysis of the policy of the rules of sister-states have been exposed as "forum oriented assessment".[34] This is exactly what is required for our purposes!

Nonetheless, it must be appreciated that even assessment of forum policy is not free from problems. Firstly, we must guard against the idea that an English judge or any other English lawyer can instinctively divine what domestic policy is on any issue. In order to ascertain policy, proper research of the domestic law

30 The Law Commission (WP No 89, p 28 at fn 104) suggest "50 years is too long for most people to wait for the establishment of rules to determine whether their marriage is valid".
31 Ie Family Law Act 1986, s 50 (see ch 4, II B 2, *infra*).
32 North, *Essays in Private International Law* (1993) at p 114, claims that the "difficulties are legion".
33 *Ibid* at p 116.
34 Cheshire and North (ch 1, n 6, *supra*) at p 33.

and its basis must be undertaken. Reference should be made, where appropriate, to the legislative history of statutes.[35]

Secondly, as North points out,[36] considerable care has to be taken when dealing with older statutes and cases, which may no longer reflect domestic policy. It is suggested that this problem can be solved to a large extent by reference to the reports of the Law Commission or other bodies. In fact, there are relevant reports relating to all the topics covered in this Part of this book.

Thirdly, we should remember that, whilst we refer to forum policy, the state itself rarely has an interest in disputes between individuals other than the pervasive interest of ensuring that justice is done between the parties. Thus, the search for the policy of the forum is really a search for the forum's idea of what constitutes justice[37] between the parties in each case. For convenience, we will continue to refer to this as the forum's policy, but the justice point should be borne in mind.

E. Conclusion in Relation to Result Orientation

As with choice of law rules, a result selecting approach, as opposed to a global or mechanical rule, can ensure that results are reached which are consistent with the forum's policy.

The fundamental distinction between the two situations is that in the pure choice of law context, there may be a legitimate concern for the policies behind foreign laws; whereas in the "conflict of rules" context, these policies if appropriate have already been taken into account in formulating the choice of law and recognition rules. Thus, where there is a conflict between those rules, it is justifiable to determine which prevails on the basis solely of the policy of the forum.

Provided that clear result-orientated rules are constructed to give effect to forum policy, the approach advocated will not cause uncertainty or unpredictability. Since the "conflict of rules" only arises in limited circumstances, it should be possible to create rules which are easily understood and not over-complex.

III. METHODOLOGY

A. Introduction

In the next eight chapters we will be constructing result-orientated rules, which will be called preference rules, to solve the conflict between two conflicts rules and in relation to particular topics. Our aim is to produce results which are in

35 Cf North (n 33, *supra*) at p 115. English courts will now refer to Hansard in certain situations (see *Pepper v Hart* [1993] AC 593). In any event, we are not expecting courts to ascertain forum policy in each case.

36 *Ibid* at p 115.

37 In this connection, justice means "substantive justice" between the parties. Assuming that our conflicts rules are based on justice (see ch 2, II C, *supra*), then *either* solution to the problem should be in conformity with conflicts justice because either the choice of law rule or the recognition rule will be applied.

conformity with the policy of the forum. Whilst we are mainly concerned with result, it will be more intellectually satisfying and easier to justify the proposed rule if an acceptable theoretical basis can be found for the proposed rule.

B. Identification of the Conflict

In order to understand the scope of the problem, an assessment will be undertaken of when the "conflict of rules" is likely to arise in relation to each topic. This will involve a consideration of the relevant choice of law rules and a brief survey of the recognition rules of other countries[38] to indicate when a decree will be recognised abroad and not in the forum and vice versa.

C. Possible Solutions

Four possible preference rules will be considered in relation to each issue. These are:

1. Always prefer the choice rule.
2. Always prefer the recognition rule.
3. Prefer the choice rule for some purposes and the recognition rule for others (a "differential rule").
4. Prefer the rule which upholds the validity of the marriage, the succession claim, matrimonial property rights or the tort claim, as the case may be.

It will be seen that the first two rules are identical with the global rules, which have already been rejected.[39] Whilst these rules cannot be supported as global rules, they may produce the appropriate result in a particular category of case. Where the desired result can be achieved either by application of one of the global rules or by means of an expressly result selecting rule, the former may be preferred as being more consistent with orthodox theory.
There are number of possible differentiations which may serve as the basis for the differential approach in the third preference rule. Differential rules appropriate for each subject will be considered, as required, in each chapter.

D. Construction of the Result-Orientated Rule[40]

1. For each of the four possible preference rules in turn:
   (a) The *theoretical basis* for the rule in relation to the particular topic will be sought.

38 The English recognition rules are outlined in ch 1. The survey of foreign recognition rules for matrimonial decrees in ch 4 at I B is equally relevant to chs 5, 6 and 7.

39 We saw in ch 2, *supra*, that the third global rule, preference for the statutory rule, in English law would always result in a preference, if at all, for the recognition rule. Thus, it is not helpful to consider it as a separate preference rule. However, we should bear in mind our conclusion that, where the recognition rule is favoured, then the fact that it is statutory (if that is the case) may add extra weight to its selection as the preference rule.

40 The structure of the chapters in Part III of this book (ie chs 9, 10 and 11) is slightly different. Instead of stage 1, there will be a discussion of whether there are any considerations which require distinctions to be made with the analogous subjects in Part II.

(b) Any case law and statutory *authority* for each rule will be reviewed.
(c) The *results* produced by the rule in relation to each of the possible law-fact patterns will be demonstrated and illustrated in tabular form.

2. Forum policy will be ascertained by examination and analysis of legislation, case law and reports of law reform bodies.
3. Forum policy will be applied to determine by analogous reasoning what result is required by such policy in the "conflict of rules" situation in relation to each law-fact category.
4. The rule(s) which produce(s) the desired result for each law-fact category will be recommended as the appropriate preference rule(s) for that situation.

PART II

SPECIFIC SOLUTIONS IN CASES WHERE THERE IS A CONFLICT BETWEEN A CHOICE OF LAW RULE AND A RECOGNITION RULE

Chapter 4

Capacity to Remarry

I. SCOPE OF THE PROBLEM

A. Introduction

The likelihood of a conflict arising between the choice rule and the recognition rule in relation to remarriage after a matrimonial decree has increased substantially over the last 50 years. Until 1953, foreign divorces and nullity decrees were only recognised in England when they were granted by or recognised in the country of domicile. As the choice rule for capacity to marry was the law of the domicile, a conflict between the choice rules and the recognition rules could only arise where the party in question had changed his/her domicile between the date of the divorce or nullity decree and the date of the remarriage. The widening of the grounds of recognition of foreign divorces and nullity decrees at common law meant that the conflict could arise even without a change of domicile where the decree was recognised by the widened rules.

As we have seen,[1] recognition of divorce and nullity decrees are now governed by statute. In order to identify the scope for the "conflict of rules" arising, we need to examine the rules for recognition of matrimonial decrees in other countries.

B. Recognition of Decrees in Other Countries

A brief survey of some foreign recognition rules will be sufficient to indicate in what sort of situation divorces will be recognised in England and not in the country of domicile and vice versa. It will be convenient to consider the position in Commonwealth countries, the USA and civil law countries separately.

1. Commonwealth Countries[2]

(A) RECOGNITION RULES IN COMMONWEALTH COUNTRIES

In general, Commonwealth countries still adhere to the common law recognition rules.[3] Thus a foreign divorce will be recognised in the following four situations:

1 At ch 1, IV A 2, *supra*.
2 See generally McClean (ch 2, n 51, *supra*).
3 Often, these have been codified or expressly saved by statute. See McClean, *ibid*, ch 2, the Canadian Divorce and Corollary Relief Act 1985, s 22(3) and the Australian Family Law Act 1975, s 104(5).

(i) Where it is obtained in the country of the parties' domicile.[4]
(ii) Where it is recognised by the law of the parties' domicile.[5]
(iii) Where the recognising court would *mutatis mutandis* have jurisdiction on the basis of the facts existing in relation to the foreign court.[6]
(iv) Where it is obtained in a country with which one of the parties had a "real and substantial connection".[7]

Some countries have added to those rules by statute either to promote certainty,[8] or in order to enable them to ratify the Hague Convention on Divorce and Legal Separations.[9]

(B) COMPARISON WITH ENGLISH RECOGNITION RULES

In relation to *formal* divorces, the English statutory jurisdictional bases will generally produce more liberal results than the common law rules. For example, nationality alone[10] or domicile in the sense of the decree granting state after a period of short temporary residence[11], will not constitute a "real and substantial connection".[12] The reciprocity principle will only lead to more generous results in the rare situation[13] that the recognising country has jurisdiction rules wider than habitual residence, nationality or domicile.

4 Rule in *Le Mesurier* [1895] AC 517. Where the wife has a separate domicile, statute will usually provide that it is sufficient if the divorce is granted in the domicile of either parties (eg Australian Family Law Act 1975, s 104(3)). Even where the wife's domicile is dependent on the husband, statute may provide that a divorce granted on the basis of the wife's domicile, determined as if she were unmarried, will be recognised (eg Canadian Divorce Act 1968, s 6(2)).

5 Rule in *Armitage v A-G* [1906] P 135.

6 *Travers v Holley* [1953] P 246 (for application in Australia see Sykes and Pryles (ch 2, n 246, supra) at p 466 and in Canada see Allerie and Director of Vital Statistics (1963) 41 DLR (2d) 553). It is not sufficient that the divorce would be recognised in such a country; ie it is not possible to combine the rule in Armitage with that in *Travers v Holley, Mountbatten v Mountbatten* [1959] P 43.

7 *Indyka v Indyka* [1969] 1 AC 33 (for application in Australia see *Nicholson v Nicholson* [1971] 1 NSWLR 1 and *In the Marriage of Dornom*, Australian Digest, 3rd edn (1992) 35-417 para 18.68, and in Canada see *Kish v Director of Vital Statistics* (1973) 35 DLR (3d) 530). It seems to be sufficient that the divorce was recognised in the country with which there is a real and substantial connection, *Mahoney v Mahoney* [1968] 1 WLR 1773 (ie it is possible to combine the *Indyka* rule with the *Armitage* rule), although this result has been criticised. For analysis of the development of the *Indyka* rule see McClean (ch 2, n 51, supra) at pp 43 *et seq.*

8 Eg, in Canada, there is statutory provision for recognition of a divorce granted on the basis of the domicile of the wife (determined as if she were unmarried) and for a divorce granted in a country where either party was ordinarily resident for more than one year before commencement of the proceedings (Divorce Act 1986, s 22).

9 Eg, in Australia.

10 *Keresztessy v Keresztessy* (1976) 73 DLR (3d) 347. Although, in Australia, such a divorce would be recognised under the reciprocity principle because jurisdiction is taken on the basis of nationality alone (Family Law Act 1975, s 39(3)(a)).

11 As in Nevada. See *Suko v Suko* [1971] VR 28 and compare *Lawrence v Lawrence* [1985] Fam 106.

12 *A fortiori*, connections other than nationality, habitual residence or domicile will not be sufficient (eg the place where the marriage was celebrated and the parties were previously domiciled, *Peters v Peters* [1968] P 275). The possibility of residence which is not yet habitual being sufficient is unlikely, given the liberal interpretation of habitual residence in England, (see *R v London Borough of Brent, ex p Shah* [1983] 2 AC 309) and the fact that periods of residence of less than a year have been held not to evidence a real and substantial connection (see eg *Re Darling* [1975] 1 NZLR 382 and other cases cited by McClean (ch 2, n 51, *supra*) at p 48).

13 Eg, in Australia, nullity jurisdiction may be founded on mere presence (Family Law Act 1975, s 39(4)(b)).

However, the effectiveness requirement in the English statute may restrict recognition of divorces which would be recognised under the common law rules[14] or under a foreign statute. For example, in Australia it is sufficient that the divorce is "*effected in accordance* with the law of an overseas jurisdiction";[15] whereas, as we saw above, the English statute requires that the divorce is effective in the jurisdiction *in which* it was obtained. Thus, for example, a *talaq* pronounced in Australia would be recognised[16] there provided that it was done so in accordance with the law of a foreign country, such as Pakistan or India, with which one of the required connecting factors existed.

In relation to *informal* divorces, the scope for discrepancy is much wider because of the English legislation which was designed to be more restrictive than the common law.[17] There is no evidence that foreign courts will refuse to recognise informal divorces on public policy grounds.

2. *The United States*

(A) US RECOGNITION RULES

The position in relation to recognition of foreign divorces in the USA is not entirely clear. Scoles and Hay[18] discern the following general rules from the case law:

(i) A foreign divorce of foreign nationals obtained in a country with which one party has a close relationship[19] will be recognised provided that it is valid in that country. This will include extra-judicial divorces obtained abroad.[20] The fact that the parties are domiciliaries of a US state would not seem to prevent recognition.[21]

(ii) A foreign divorce of US nationals obtained in the country of domicile[22] will be recognised provided that it is valid there.

14 It has been held in Australia that under the statute, as at common law, it is sufficient that the tribunal has general competence to hear the type of action involved and that it is not relevant that the jurisdiction was exercised irregularly, see *Norman v Norman (No 3)* (1970) 16 FLR 231. (For discussion of the effectiveness requirement in England see ch 2, IV C 3, *supra*.)

15 Section 104(8) makes clear that the phrase "effected in accordance with the law of an overseas jurisdiction" includes all situations where the *overseas jurisdiction* recognises a divorce obtained in a third country. It is arguable that this provision only applies to the statutory bases of recognition and so does not overrule *Mountbatten v Mountbatten* [1959] P 43 (see Sykes and Pryles (ch 2, n 246, *supra*) at p 470).

16 Sykes and Pryles, *ibid*; cf English Family Law Act 1986, s 44(2) (discussed in ch 1, IV A 2, *supra*).

17 See the leading pre-1973 English case of *Qureshi v Qureshi* [1972] Fam 173. The Australian legislation specifically provides that all the recognition provisions apply "in relation to dissolutions and annulments effected whether by decree, legislation or otherwise" (Family Law Act 1985, s 104(10). The word "decree" has been removed in the recognition provisions of the Canadian Divorce and Corollary Relief Act 1985 to remove any ambiguity (see Castel, Canadian Conflict of Laws (2nd edn, 1986) at p 315).

18 Scoles and Hay, Conflict of Laws (1982) at pp 495 et seq. See also Baade (1972) 72 Col LR 329 at 334 *et seq* and Comment (1969) 35 Minn LR 612.

19 Based on US Restatment (2nd) para 72 which provides for divorce jurisdiction "if either spouse has such a relationship to the state as would make it reasonable for the state to dissolve the marriage".

20 Eg, *Machransky v Machransky* 31 Ohio App 482, 166 NE 423 (1927) and see *Chaudry v Chaudry* 159 NJ Super 566, 388 A 2d 1000 (1978), discussed at text accompanying n 28, *infra*.

21 *Sherif v Sherif* 76 Misc 2d 905, 352 NYS 2d 781 (1974) (*talaq* obtained in Pakistan).

22 Domicile of one party is probably sufficient. See Comment (1969) 53 Minn Law Rev 612 at 619-620.

(iii) A foreign *inter partes* divorce of US domiciliaries who travel abroad for the purposes of obtaining the divorce will be recognised, even if the jurisdiction of the foreign court is based on short residence or mere appearance.[23] However, *ex parte* divorces obtained in such circumstances will not be recognised[24] nor will "mail-order" divorces obtained whilst remaining in the USA.[25]

(iv) Extra-judicial divorces obtained in the USA will not be recognised.[26] The key distinction is whether the divorce authority originates from abroad and not whether the parties were physically present in the USA or not.[27] Thus, in *Chaudry v Chaudry*[28] a trans-national *talaq* pronounced at the Pakistani Consulate in New York and later confirmed by a court in Pakistan, where the wife was resident at the time, was treated as obtained in Pakistan and recognised.[29]

(B) COMPARISON WITH ENGLISH RECOGNITION RULES

There would seem to be little scope[30] for discrepancy between principle (i) and English law in relation to formal divorces. However, informal divorces may be recognised in situations where they would not be recognised in England.[31]

Principle (ii) would seem to yield similar results to the English rules both in relation to formal[32] and informal divorces.[33]

The divorces recognised under principle (iii) will only be recognised in England where one party is a national of, domiciled in or habitually resident in the foreign country. Thus, usually vacation divorces will not be recognised[34] unless one party has become domiciled in the "divorce haven" within the meaning of the concept in that country.[35]

23 Thus, easy "vacation" divorces obtained in Mexico, Haiti and the Dominican Republic have been recognised. See, eg, leading New York case of *Rosentiel v Rosentiel* 16 N.Y. 2d 64, 73, 262 NYS 2d 86, 209 NE 2d 709, 712 (1965). Provided that such a divorce is recognised in one state, a declaratory judgment obtained therein will be recognised in all other states of the Union under the "Full-Faith-and-Credit" principles of the US Constitution.

24 Scoles and Hay (n 18, *supra*) p 501.

25 See *Rosenbaum v Rosenbaum* 309 NY 371, 130 NE 2d 902 (1955).

26 See *Shikoh v Murff* 257 F 2d 306 (2d Cir 1958) and *Chertok v Chertok* 208 App Div 161, 203 NYS 163 (1924) and Comment (1969) 53 Minn LR 612 at 627 *et seq.*

27 Comment, *ibid*, at 635.

28 159 NJ Super 566, 388 A 2d 1000 (1978).

29 Under the principle in (i) above. It was held that "principles of comity" required recognition.

30 Although *ex parte* divorces obtained in the country of nationality of one party might not be recognised, at least where the parties are US domiciliaries.

31 Eg, a bare *talaq* pronounced in the circumstances of *Sherif v Sherif* 76 Misc 3d 905, 352 NYS 2d 781 (1974), would not be recognised in England because it was not obtained in the domicile of either party.

32 Habitual residence under English law may well amount to domicile in the US sense.

33 Except perhaps in relation to a divorce where one party has been habitually resident in England for 12 months.

34 Mere residence or appearance will not suffice. Thus, a decree obtained in Mexico after two days' residence there, would still not be recognised in England, even if recognised in the New York residence of the wife (as in *Mountbatten v Mountbatten* [1959] P 43).

35 See eg *Lawrence v Lawrence* [1985] Fam 106, discussed in section II B 2, *infra.*

36 159 NJ Super 566, 388 A 2d 1000 *(1978)*.

Divorces refused recognition under principle (iv) will not be recognised in England because they are not effective in the place where they are obtained. However, a trans-national *talaq* or *get* originating in the USA but obtained in a third country as in *Chaudry v Chaudry*[36] will apparently not be recognised in England[37] because the proceedings did not all take place in the same overseas country.[38]

3. Civil Law Countries[38a]

A distinction must be drawn between those countries which have adopted the Hague Convention[39] and those which have not. In the former, the only scope for discrepancy in relation to formal divorces and legal separations covered by the Convention,[40] will be where the English rules or the foreign rules[41] are more generous[41a] than those of the Convention or where a reservation has been entered under art 19 or 24 of the Convention.[42] Informal divorces are not covered by the Convention.

In relation to divorces not covered by the Convention, civil law countries tend to combine jurisdictional and choice-of-law considerations to determine whether to recognise a divorce.[43] In general, a foreign divorce of a home national will not be recognised unless it is consistent with the substantive law of the nationality. This may result in refusal to recognise divorces[44] which would be recognised in England, where recognition does not depend on what substantive law was applied.

No distinction seems to be made between formal and informal divorces, although extra-judicial proceedings in the forum may well not be recognised.[45]

37 See discussion in ch 1, IV A 2, *supra.*

38 See *Berkovits v A-G, ex p Grinburg* [1995] 2 All ER 683, discussed in ch 1, IV A 2, *supra.*

38a See generally the relevant parts of each chapter in Hamilton and Standley, *Family Law in Europe* (1995).

39 Czechoslovkia, Cyprus, Denmark, Egypt, Finland, Italy, The Netherlands, Norway, Slovak Republic, Sweden and Switzerland (written communication from Secretariat Hague Conference dated 28 July 1994).

40 The Convention only requires recognition of divorces obtained in contracting states (art 1).

41 Apparently, under reforms in the Italian Private International Law of 1995, foreign court orders relating to family matters are automatically recognised unless they are contrary to Italian principles of public order or the rights to bring a defence have not been respected. See Hamilton and Standley (n 38a, *supra*), in Addendum following the Preface.

41a Eg, under the Hague Convention, the nationality of the petitioner is only a sufficient jurisdictional base if s/he is or has been (for at least one year in the previous two) habitually resident in the country of nationality (art 2(4)). Alternatively, where the country of last habitual residence does not provide for divorce, it will be sufficient if the petitioner was present in the country of his/her nationality at the date of the institution of proceedings (art 2(5)). Similarly the habitual residence of the petitioner alone is not sufficient unless the habitual residence has lasted for at least one year or the spouses last habitually resided there together (art 2(2)).

42 Czechoslovakia, Italy, Luxemburg and the Slovak Republic entered reservations under art 19, para 1. Switzerland and Czechoslovakia have entered reservations under art 24 (see Information Concerning Hague Convention on Private International Law (1993) XL Netherlands Int Law Review 278-279).

43 Eg, France. See Rabel, The Conflict of Laws: A Comparative Study, vol 1 (1958) at p 509 and Hamilton and Standley (n 38a, *supra* at p 151).

44 The likelihood of this will decrease as grounds for divorce are liberalised (see Scoles and Hay, n 18, *supra*, at p 506, para 15.27, n 2).

45 Eg, in Germany: see decision in BGH [1982] NJW 517, cited in Scoles and Hay, Conflict of Laws 1989-1990 Supplement, para 15.24.

4. Countries not Providing for Divorce

The "conflict of rules" will arise wherever one of the parties is domiciled in a country which does not allow divorce at all.[46] Most of the relevant English decisions concerned Italian domiciliaries at a time when Italian law did not provide for divorce and would not recognise the foreign divorces of their nationals.[47] In recent years, Italy and various other countries which did not make provision for divorce have now done so.[48] Thus, the scope for conflict where the *lex causae* is a country which does not recognise divorce at all is relatively small[49] in practical terms.

C. Choice of Law Rule for Capacity to Marry

There has long been a dispute between leading English academics as to whether capacity to marry is governed by the dual domicile test[50] or the intended matrimonial home test.[51] Whilst the decisions in most of the old case law were equivocal, there was little express judicial preference[52] for the intended matrimonial home test. More recently, some judges have favoured a real and substantial connection test,[53] which seems to be a modern version of the intended matrimonial home test, or a rule of alternative reference.[54] Thus, the law may be said to be in a state of flux[55] in England.

In general, it will make little difference to the "conflict of rules" analysis which rule is used. However, in some cases, applying a law other than the domicile may make it possible to avoid the "conflict of rules" problem completely where there is no dispute between the law to be applied and the forum about the recognition of the decree.[56] It must be borne in mind, though,

46 Article 20 of the Hague Convention on Legal Separations and Divorce allows a contracting state to reserve the right not to recognise a divorce if it does not provide for divorce and both parties are nationals of that country. This reservation has not been used (see reference in n 40, *supra*).

47 Eg, *Perrini v Perrini* [1979] Fam 84, *R v Brentwood Marriage Registrar, ex p Arias* [1968] QB 956 and *Padolecchia v Padolecchia* [1968] P 314.

48 Eg, Argentina (Law No 23.515, which came into effect on 21 June 1987), Brazil (Amendment XI to Constitution in 1977) and Spain (Law No. 30/1981 of 7 July 1981).

49 Divorce is still not available in the Republic of Ireland following the success of the opponents of divorce in the referendum of 26 June 1986. However, foreign divorces granted by the court of the domicile or recognised by the law of the domicile will be recognised. See Hamilton and Standley (n 38a *supra*) at p 247.

50 Supported in successive editions of Dicey and Morris (ch 1, n 6, *supra*) and Morris (ch 1, n 144, *supra*).

51 Supported in early editions of Cheshire's *Private International Law*, eg 7th edn (1965) pp 276 *et seq.*

52 Cf *Radwan v Radwan (No 2)* [1973] Fam 35. However, Cumming-Bruce J specifically limited his decision to capacity to enter into a polygamous marriage and the decision has been trenchantly criticised. See, eg, Karsten (1973) 36 MLR 291 and Pearl [1973] CLJ 143.

53 See Lincoln J in *Lawrence v Lawrence* [1985] Fam 106 and Lord Simon in *Vervaeke v Smith* [1983] AC 145. See also Fentiman [1985] CLJ 256.

54 See Cairns LJ in *Lawrence v Lawrence* [1985] Fam 106.

55 According to the Law Commission, WP No 89 at p 60, "there is no decision which prevents the Court of Appeal or the House of Lords from adopting either test". Furthermore, one of the reasons that they did not make any recommendations for statutory reform of the choice of law rule for essential validity of marriage in Rept No 165 was to allow the courts to continue to develop the law themselves.

56 As was done by Anthony Lincoln J at first instance in *Lawrence v Lawrence* [1985] Fam 106. Here, the forum itself was held to be the country with the most real and substantial connection and thus no conflict could arise.

that it will not always be possible to show that another law has a closer connection than the law of the domicile.[57]

For ease of exposition, we will continue with the assumption that the choice rule for capacity to marry is the *lex domicilii*, unless otherwise stated.

II. POSSIBLE SOLUTIONS[58]

A. Prefer the Choice Rule

1. Theoretical Basis

This approach, under which the validity of the remarriage is determined solely according to the choice of law rule governing capacity and the forum's recognition rules are ignored can be supported by the following alternative theories.

(A) "THE STATUS THEORY"

The concept that status is governed by domicile is fundamental[59] and takes precedence over other competing rules.[60] This idea can be illustrated by the fact that, historically, the English rule for recognising foreign divorce and nullity decrees was simply an application of the domicile choice rule. However, even then it was possible for a conflict to arise where there was a change of domicile. The question of recognition would be governed by the law of the domicile at the time of the decree whilst the capacity would be governed by the law of domicile at the time of remarriage. In such a case, the "status theory" would seem to favour the domicile at the time of remarriage because, in determining the party's present status, the deciding factor is whether the remarriage is valid.[61]

(B) "THE CAPACITY THEORY"

This theory is based on the premise that the validity of the remarriage depends upon the capacity of the parties and that capacity is separate from status. Thus, capacity is governed by the law indicated by the choice of law rule and does not

57 In *R v Immigration Appeal Tribunal, ex p Rafika Bibi* [1989] Imm AR 1, it was held that the real and substantial connection test was inappropriate because the marriage had connection with two legal systems. The husband was a British citizen, domiciled in England, who married a Bangladeshi domiciliary in Bangladesh in 1969. As the wife remained in Bangladesh and the husband lived in England, there was found to be no matrimonial home.

58 For tabular illustration of results of applying each preference rule, see Table 3 in the Appendix, *infra*.

59 See *Udny v Udny* (1869) LR 1 Sc and Div 441 at p 457, per Lord Westbury, Dicey and Morris (9th edn, 1973) Rule 31 and Graveson, *The Conflict of Laws* (7th edn, 1974) at p 226. Levontin (1953) 3 Am J Comp Law 199 at 202 writes, "Anglo-American law . . . considers the community of a person's domicile as the one most intimately connected with his status and with the legal, social and economic consequences flowing therefrom". The Law Commission (Rept No 137 para 6.59) refers to "the tradition of the common law that status is exclusively to be determined by the law of the domicile".

60 See *Gottlieb (1977) 26 ICLQ* 734 at 778.

61 In *Padolecchia v Padolecchia* [1968] P 314, the court favoured the domicile at the time of the remarriage because otherwise the propositus would be denied the power "to cha*nge* his capacity by changing his domicile or nationality". Palsson (ch 1, n 42) cites a German case (at p 223) supporting application of the national law at the time of the remarriage and an Italian case (at p 222, n 706) supporting application of the national law at the time of the divorce. Gottlieb (1977) 26 ICLQ 734 at 777 suggests that it might be sufficient if either domicile recognises the divorce.

flow directly from status as determined by the foreign decree. Allen distinguishes between status, capacity and rights as follows:

> "Status, the condition which gives rise to certain capacities or incapacities or both; Capacity, the power to acquire and exercise rights; and the Rights themselves which are acquired by the exercise of capacity." [62]

One advantage of the "capacity theory" over the "status theory" is that it does not depend on the choice of law rule for the essential validity of marriage being the domicile.

2. *Authority*

Support for the "status theory" can be found in the two classic common law cases[63] where the "conflict of rules" arose, the Ontario case of *Schwebel v Ungar*[64] and the English case of *R v Brentwood Superintendant Registrar of Marriages, ex p Arias*.[65] It will be helpful to give a summary of the facts of these cases.

In *Schwebel v Ungar* the defendant, W, married her first husband, H1, in Hungary in 1945. Shortly after their marriage they decided to emigrate to Israel. In a transit camp in Italy H1 gave W a *get,* an extra-judicial Jewish divorce. The defendant then continued to Israel, where she acquired a domicile of choice and lived for a number of years before coming to Ontario, where she met and married the Ontario domiciled plaintiff. The Jewish divorce was not recognised either by the law of Hungary or Italy and was thus not eligible for recognition under the recognition rules of Ontario. However, the *get* was recognised in Israel, the domicile of W. It was held that since by her domicile W was single and had capacity to remarry, the second marriage was valid.

In the *Brentwood Marriage* case H was an Italian national domiciled in Switzerland. His first marriage had been dissolved in Switzerland and his first wife had remarried. However, under the law of H's nationality the divorce was not recognised and he did not have capacity to remarry. Since the Swiss law referred capacity to marry to the law of the nationality he was unable to remarry in Switzerland and thus came with his intended second wife to England, hoping to remarry. The Swiss divorce was eligible for recognition under English recognition rules. The Brentwood Marriage Registrar refused to marry them because H lacked capacity. This decision was upheld by the Divisional Court on the ground that capacity to marry is governed by the law of the domicile and that by Swiss law H did not have such capacity.

In the *Brentwood Marriage* case the problem was not expressed by the court as being a conflict between choice rules and recognition rules. However, in line with the "status theory", the court emphasised the importance of status being

62 (1930) 46 LQR 277 at 279. Engdahl (1969) 55 Iowa LR 56 at 65 contrasts this approach with Austin, who would say that "the rights, duties, capacities or incapacities . . . *constitute* the status".

63 Palsson (ch 1, n 42, *supra*) pp 229-239 brings many examples of the supremacy of the *lex patriae* in Continental decisions.

64 (1963) 42 DLR (2d) 622; affd (1964) 48 DLR (2d) 644.

65 [1968] 2 QB 596 (hereinafter "the *Brentwood Marriage* case").

governed by the law of the domicile. In the words of Sachs LJ, "status is particularly a matter for the law of the country in which the parties are domiciled".[66]

In *Schwebel v Ungar*, where there does seem to have been an awareness of the conflict between Ontario recognition rules and Ontario choice rules, it was stated that:

> "to hold otherwise would be to determine the personal status of a person not domiciled in Ontario by the law of Ontario instead of by the law of that person's country of domicile."

and:

> "for the limited purpose of resolving the difficulty created by the peculiar facts of the case, the governing consideration is the status of the Respondent under the law of her domicile at the time of her second marriage and not the means whereby she secured the status."

Again, the supremacy of the domicile seems to have been the main concern[67] in line with the "status theory".

3. Results

(A) WHERE THE *LEX CAUSAE* RECOGNISES THE DECREE

This is the situation in example M1.[68] We saw that application of the choice rule will lead to the validity of the remarriage between Alexander and Bella.

This may lead to absurdity[69] if the forum is called upon to determine the validity of the matrimonial decree in a different context. For example, suppose that Natasha, the first wife, becomes domiciled in England. It would seem that she would not have capacity to remarry because the *get* is not recognised. If she died intestate domiciled in England, Alexander would seem to have the right to claim the surviving spouse's share as he would seem to be recognised as Natasha's husband by the law of her domicile at the date of her death.[70] Similarly, if Alexander were to become domiciled in England and to die intestate, he might be considered to leave two widows. It is thus possible that Alexander might be considered as married to Bella for some purposes and to

66 [1968] 2 QB 956 at 967-968.

67 An alternative explanation of *Schwebel v Ungar* is that the case extended the Ontario recognition rules so that a divorce would be recognised if it was recognised by a domicile subsequently acquired by one of the parties, see Gottlieb (1977) 26 ICLQ 734 at 776 and Webb (1965) 14 ICLQ 659.

68 Chapter 1, IV B, *supra*.

69 See Jaffey (1975) 91 LQR 320, 322 and Gordon (ch 1, n 39, *supra*) pp 151-152.

70 Cf the approach in the German decision, KG 13 Jan 1925, JW 1925, 2146, brought by Palsson (ch 1, n 42, *supra*) at p 223, where it was held that whilst the original divorce decree was not recognised, the celebration of a valid remarriage by one of the parties had the effect of ending the first marriage from the date of the remarriage. Gordon (ch 1, n 39, *supra*) at pp 151-153 supports such an approach.

Natasha for other purposes. This has been referred to as "legal bigamy"[71] and "internal disharmony".[72]

Engdahl argues that such disharmony is not problematic[73] because the notion of universality of marriage[74] is misconceived. Whether or not Engdahl's view is accepted, the fact that the result creates disharmony cannot be considered separately from the other aspects of the result. As Clark[75] says, "Logical inconsistency need not bother us if a valid social policy is served."

We shall examine below[76] forum policy in relation to remarriage following divorce.

We should also point out that in many cases inconsistency of status within the forum will be an entirely theoretical problem because the party's status will not in fact become an issue in the different circumstances postulated. Usually the parties to the first marriage which has been purported to be dissolved will not wish to assert that their marriage continues. Any claim, relying on the continued subsistence of that marriage, can be barred by the doctrine of preclusion[77] where appropriate.

(B) WHERE THE *LEX CAUSAE* DOES NOT RECOGNISE THE DECREE

In this situation too, there will be internal disharmony. As we saw in the *Brentwood Marriage* case, whilst the first marriage was no longer considered to be subsisting for any purposes as between the parties to it, in relation to the proposed remarriage the husband was still considered to be a married person. This inconsistency created by the English decision simply mimics the inconsistency[78] of the Swiss position.

A similar phenomenon can be seen from example M2.[79] Evita is considered as a divorced person in England because the divorce is recognised. However, she cannot validly remarry whilst she retains her Argentinian domicile.

This practical problem is the converse of "legal bigamy". Thus, one[80] or both[81] parties are in a state of "enforced legal celibacy". The spouse in question is no longer married to his/her first spouse and cannot remarry.[82] (S)he is thus

71 Palsson *ibid* at pp 216 and 225.
72 See ch 1, n 24, *supra*.
73 (1969) 55 Iowa LR 56. At p 101 he gives other examples of where marriages are recognised for some purposes and not others.
74 See Graveson (n 59, *supra)* at pp 234-238.
75 *The Law of Domestic Relations* (2nd edn, 1987) para 13.4.
76 At section III, *infra*.
77 Discussed in detail at ch 5, II A 4, *infra*.
78 It may be argued that this position contains no inconsistency but merely distinguishes between the effect of a divorce decree in ending the legal relationship between the parties to the first marriage and the effect of a divorce decree as a licence to remarry. See Palsson (ch 1, n 42, *supra*) at p 240 and discussion at section B 1, *infra*.
79 Chapter 1, IV B, *supra*.
80 In the *Brentwood Marriage* case, it was only the husband who could not remarry because of his Italian nationality.
81 In example M2, Pedro also cannot remarry whilst he retains his Brazilian domicile.
82 This has been called "legal schizophrenia", Palsson (ch 1, n 42, *supra*) at p 256.

being denied the fundamental right of marriage.[83] The unfairness of this situation is exacerbated where the other party to the first marriage is free to remarry, as in the *Brentwood Marriage* case.

B. Prefer the Recognition Rule

1. Theoretical Basis

It may be argued that, where the foreign decree is recognised, the recognition policy of the forum should be applied to its logical conclusion by giving "full effect" to the foreign divorce decree. Ackner LJ expresses the logic as follows:

> "I consider that it is plainly inconsistent with recognising a divorce to say in the same breath that the marriage which it purported to dissolve still continues in existence. Such a recognition would be a hollow and empty gesture."[84]

This rationale assumes that it is necessary to allow remarriage in order to give "full effect" to a matrimonial decree.

The basis for preferring the recognition rule where the decree is not recognised is much less clear.[85] It has been suggested that the basis is the forum's interest in monogamy.[86] Thus, whilst the forum still considers the first marriage to be subsisting it cannot recognise the validity of the second marriage, even if it is valid by the law of the domicile.[87] Nott[88] suggests that a distinction might be drawn in this situation between allowing remarriage in the forum, which would be tantamount to authorising bigamy and recognition of a foreign remarriage in which the forum has less interest.

2. Authority

(A) WHERE THE DECREE IS RECOGNISED

Support for the "full effect" or "logical conclusion" approach can be found in recent English case law and statute.

In the Court of Appeal case of *Lawrence v Lawrence*,[89] H1 and W were at all material times domiciled in Brazil. W obtained a divorce from H1 in Nevada. This divorce was not recognised in Brazil, but did satisfy the English recognition rules because of W's domicile in Nevada in the Nevada sense. The case concerned the validity of W's

83 Khan Freund (ch 1, n 103, supra) at p 293 writes: "The revulsion which one feels against this decision is not, however, caused by its treatment of the incidental question, but by its result which is inimical to the freedom of marriage."
84 [1985] Fam 106 at 123. The same idea has been expressed variously as "the obvious consequences" (per Anthony Lincoln J in *Lawrence v Lawrence* [1985] Fam 106 at 112) and "the tail must go with the hide" (per Douglas J in *Estin v Estin* 334 US 541, 68 SCt 1213 (1948)).
85 We have already seen that the policy behind the non-recognition rule does not necessarily require invalidation of the remarriage (ch 2 IV C, *supra*).
86 See Palsson (ch 1, n 42, *supra*) at p 216.
87 See Jaffey (1979) 91 LQR 320 at 322.
88 (1985) 15 Fam Law 199 at 202.
89 [1985] Fam 106.

remarriage to H2, an English domiciliary. A majority of the Court of Appeal held that the recognition of the divorce by virtue of the 1971 Recognition of Divorce and Legal Separations Act 1971 carried with it the right to remarry and thus the second marriage was valid. The minority in the Court of Appeal and the first instance judge came to the same conclusion on different grounds.[90]

Whether or not this approach in fact represented English law at the time of the decision in *Lawrence* is open to doubt. In particular, it will be noted that the decision appears to be irreconcilable with that in the *Brentwood Marriage* case. There are, however, two possible ways in which the cases might be distinguished.

Firstly, it might be argued that it is the wording of the 1971 Act[91] which requires the conclusion that recognition of the divorce automatically confers freedom to remarry. This seems to be the basis of Sir David Cairn's judgment,[92] which is narrower on this point than Ackner LJ's. Since the divorce in the *Brentwood Marriage* case was recognised under common law prior to the 1971 Act, this conclusion did not follow there.

Secondly, the *Brentwood* case concerned the question of *a priori* permission to remarry, whereas *Lawrence* concerned the *ex post facto* recognition of a second marriage which had already taken place. It might be argued that the policy of giving "full effect" to the foreign divorce is more important where the parties have already relied on that divorce in order to effect a second marriage.[93] However, it is clear that neither of the majority in *Lawrence* purported to make such a distinction.

It is therefore submitted that both of these apparent distinctions merely attempt to disguise the fact that the policy in the two cases is diametrically opposed. In the *Brentwood* case, precedence was accorded to the domicile choice rule; whereas in *Lawrence* precedence was accorded to the recognition rule. This conclusion can be supported by reference to the case of *Perrini.*[94]

In this case, W1, an American domiciled in New Jersey obtained a nullity decree from H, an Italian national, in the New Jersey courts. This decree was entitled to recognition in England on the basis of W1's residence in New Jersey for more than three years, but was not recognised in Italy. H subsequently remarried W2, an English domiciliary, in England. It was held at first instance that the second marriage was valid.

90 Ie that the essential validity of the second marriage was governed by English law as the law of the intended matrimonial home or the law with the most real and substantial connection to the marriage (see section I C, *supra*).

91 Ie that in s 3 of the 1971 Act (now s 46 of the Family Law Act 1986) where it is stated that, "the validity of an overseas divorce . . . shall be recognised", the word divorce must be taken to have the same meaning as divorce in English domestic law unless the contrary is stated, ie dissolution with the consequential right to remarry.

92 See [1985] Fam 106 at 135C-D.

93 This view was taken by German courts prior to 1971 (see Palsson, ch 1, n 42, *supra*, at p 232). But cf Clarkson (1990) 10 Legal Studies 80 at 82, who claims that there is no justification for applying more lenient rules to the *ex post facto* situation, because, taken to its logical conclusion, this approach would require recognition of all marriages.

94 [1979] Fam 84.

The main problem with this decision is that the conflict between the recognition rule and the choice rule does not seem to have been perceived by the judge who does not mention the *Brentwood* case. However, the mere fact that Sir George Baker P simply treated the case as a recognition case suggests that he agreed with the conclusion later reached by Ackner LJ that recognition of a foreign divorce or nullity decree confers capacity to remarry. Since the case concerned common law recognition rules, Sir David Cairns' "*via media*" could not apply.

Whether or not *Lawrence* and *Perrini* were correctly decided at the time, the enactment of s 50 of the Family Law Act 1986 has ensured that the decisions would today be correct. However, these pre-s 50 decisions are not only of historical interest for two reasons. Firstly, as already seen they give us some insight into the basis for giving precedence to the recognition rule and, secondly, they may be relevant where the case falls outside s 50 as explained below.

Section 50 of the Family Law Act 1986 states:

> "Where in any part of the United Kingdom—
> (a) a divorce or annulment has been granted by a court of civil jurisdiction, or
> (b) the validity of a divorce or annulment is recognised by virtue of this Part[95]
> the fact that the divorce or annulment would not be recognised elsewhere shall not preclude either party to the marriage from re-marrying in that part of the United Kingdom or cause the remarriage of either party (wherever the re-marriage takes place) to be treated as invalid in that part."

This provision replaces s 7 of the Recognition of Divorces and Legal Separations Act 1971, which was limited to persons re-marrying in the United Kingdom after a foreign divorce. The anomalies caused by this limitation[96] can be seen by the fact that that section would have applied to the facts of the *Brentwood* case, but did not apply in *Lawrence*. Indeed, this discrepancy may help to explain the attitude of the Court of Appeal in the latter case.[97]

Thus, in searching for the policy behind s 50, it is helpful first to consider the history of s 7. The 1971 Act was enacted to give effect to the 1970 Hague Convention on Recognition of Divorces and Legal Separations, the objective of which was to increase recognition of divorces and legal separations in the member states and thus to reduce limping marriages. Article 11 of the Convention provides:

> "A State which is obliged to recognize a divorce under this Convention may not preclude either spouse from remarrying on the ground that the law of another State does not recognize that divorce."

95 Ie Part II of the Family Law Act 1986.
96 Discussed in more detail at section C, *infra*.
97 Sir David Cairns ([1985] Fam 106 at 135) claims that it would be absurd if the divorce enabled the wife to remarry in England but not in Nevada. However, the ratio of the majority in the Court of Appeal in *Lawrence* appears to render s 7 of the 1971 Act redundant. Sir David Cairns overcomes this difficulty by suggesting that s 7 was strictly unnecessary and was enacted to avoid any doubt for the benefit of Marriage Registrars requested to celebrate marriages after foreign divorces. Cf Purchas LJ (at 131).

This seems to have been understood by the United Kingdom[98] as only requiring a state to allow remarriage in that state following a recognised foreign decree. But, as the Law Commission points out,[99] the article is ambiguously phrased and could be interpreted as precluding a state from not recognising the validity of a foreign remarriage following a recognised decree. Thus, it is suggested that the Law Commission could have based its recommendation to extend s 7 to cover all remarriages on this ambiguity[100] and on the anomalies caused by the limitations in s 7. Nonetheless, the Law Commission went further and clearly supported –

> "the policy that where a divorce or annulment is recognised in this country, the parties should be free to remarry, whether here or abroad, even though regarded as incapable by the law of their domicile because of non-recognition there of the divorce or annulment."

What is perhaps strange is that the Commission do not attempt to justify their support for this policy other than by asserting, without proffering any evidence, that there would seem to have been general agreement as to this policy. With respect, the *Brentwood Marriage* case itself together with the fact that in 1971 the Bill submitted to Parliament included the limited s 7 instead of the wider version suggested at that time by the Law Commission[101] contradict this assertion. What is clear is that s 50, which enacted the Law Commission's 1984 recommendation on widening s 7, is based on a policy of giving precedence to the recognition rule.

(B) WHERE THE DECREE IS NOT RECOGNISED

The only English case which might appear to support application of the recognition rule in the situation where the foreign decree is not recognised by the forum is *Shaw v Gould*.[102] In this case, the Scottish divorce decree was not recognised in England. However, the "conflict of rules" problem did not in fact arise in that case for two reasons. Firstly, the real issue was one of succession and the succession in question was governed by English law.[103] Secondly, even if the real issue had been one of capacity to marry, the wife's capacity to remarry

98 Most of the other contracting states apparently did not find it necessary to make any special provision to comply with art 11 because their law already preferred the recognition rule. See Palsson (ch 1, n 42, *supra*) at p 254. Cf the Australian Family Law Act 1975, s 104(9). It is also of interest that none of the pre-1970 Commonwealth legislation has any provision regulating the validity of remarriages. See McClean (ch 2, n 51, *supra*) at pp 61 *et seq*.

99 Law Com 137 at para 6.55.

100 Although art 11 clearly does not apply to remarriages after English divorces, the inclusion of such cases within s 50 could have been explained on the basis of the limited policy of giving full effect to decrees of the forum (but cf section C 2, *infra*).

101 Clause 7 of the Draft Bill (Law Com 34 at p 40) simply states that "neither spouse should be precluded from remarrying". Whilst there is no geographical limitation in the clause, it does not expressly state that foreign remarriages will be recognised, as does s 50 Family Law Act 1976. Thus, its meaning was ambiguous.

102 (1868) LR 3 H L 55.

103 The testator died domiciled in England and the succession was in relation to movables.

was in fact governed by English law. She could not obtain a domicile of choice in Scotland because, according to English law, she still had a domicile dependent on her first husband.

However, Palsson's survey[104] among European countries reveals that in general the recognition rule has been preferred and the re-marriage not recognised.[105] The Law Commission in their Consultation Paper[106] had recommended that this rule should be adopted. However, because of opposition at the consultation stage, this recommendation was not contained in the report. Thus, section 50 only covers cases of recognition of foreign decrees and leaves unclear what would be the result in a *Schwebel* type cases.

3. Results

(A) WHERE THE DECREE IS RECOGNISED

The remarriage will be recognised and will therefore limp between the forum and the law of the domicile, which does not recognise its validity. Thus, in example M2[107] the marriage limps between England and Argentina.

It might be argued that in many cases the remarriage will limp already if the decree-granting jurisdiction recognises the remarriage. Thus, in example M3,[108] the marriage already limps between Israel and Russia. However, this result will not follow if the decree granting jurisdiction itself prefers the choice rule to its own decree.[109] Thus, in example M2, if Mexico applies the law of the nationality to determine the validity of the marriage there will be no limp.

Where the marriage does already limp, the decision of the forum will determine whether the marriage limps between the forum and the domicile or between the forum and the decree-granting jurisdiction. On one view, once the marriage limps the harm is already done and whatever the forum decides will not make any difference. On the other hand, it might be crucial which way the marriage limps because the limp will only cause actual hardship if the parties have a real interest in the views of both of those jurisdictions as to the validity of their marriage. Thus, where they no longer have a connection with the decree-granting jurisdiction, as in example M2, it can be argued that a limp with that country does not matter as much as a limp with the domicile which will continue to have an interest in the status of the parties. On the other hand, where the parties retain a strong connection with the decree-granting jurisdiction a limp between the forum and that jurisdiction may be more serious than a limp with the domicile.

Also, the degree of hardship caused by the limp depends on the circumstances in which the validity of the marriage is called into question. One major problem

104 *Op cit* (ch 1, n 42) at pp 213-216.

105 Although he does point out that, in most of the cases, the capacity of the other party to the second marriage was governed by the *lex fori* as either the *lex domicilii* or *lex patriae*. So the decisions could be explained on the basis that the impediment of the prior marriage was treated as bilateral and rendered the other party incapable by his/her personal law.

106 Unpublished (1983) (see ch 2, n 127, *supra)* at para 6.50.

107 At ch 1, IV B, *supra*.

108 *Ibid.*

109 This was the position of Swiss law in the *Brentwood Marriage* case.

is that it is impossible to foresee the future and so it is not known when the question of validity in a particular jurisdiction will arise. If the second marriage limps there would always seem to be the potential for abuse by one party. For example, on the breakdown of the second marriage, a deserting husband might choose to move to a country where the second marriage is not recognised because his financial obligations to his second wife cannot be enforced against him there.

(B) WHERE THE DECREE IS NOT RECOGNISED

The effect of applying the recognition rule would be that the remarriage is invalid, with the result that the second marriage limps as between the forum and the domicile. In example M1,[110] the remarriage would limp as between Israel and England.

The Law Commission in their report dismiss this problem by explaining that it is very unlikely to arise for two reasons.[111] Firstly, the United Kingdom's liberal recognition laws mean that few foreign divorces are not recognised. Secondly, where the remarriage takes place in the United Kingdom, capacity by the *lex loci celebrationis* is required in addition to capacity by the domicile. The Commission further justifies its inaction by reference to the Australian legislation,[112] which is in similar terms to what is now the Family Law Act 1986, s 50. With respect, the Law Commission's reasons are not convincing. We have already seen that the English rules for recognition of divorces are significantly more restrictive than their Australian counterparts,[113] in particular with respect to informal divorces. Secondly, there is no clear authority that capacity by the *lex loci celebrationis* (even where it is part of the United Kingdom) is required.[114] Apart from this, the question of validity of a second marriage contracted abroad after a non-recognised decree is just as likely, if not more so,[115] to arise.

We have already demonstrated that the policy behind "non-recognition rules"[116] does not necessarily require invalidation of the second marriage and that, on the contrary, invalidation may harm the "victim" whom the non-recognition rule is designed to protect. Everything will depend on the circumstances and who is denying the validity of the decree. Thus, automatic preference for the recognition rule could lead to hardship. Maybe this was why, at the end of the day, the Law Commission left the problem to the courts.

C. A "Differential Rule"

1. Introduction

Under a differential approach, the choice of rule is preferred in some fact situations and in others the recognition rule prevails. English law

110 Chapter 1, IV B, *supra*.
111 Law Com No 137 at para 6.60.
112 Family Law Act 1975, s 104(9).
113 Section I B 1, *supra*.
114 Law Com WP 89, para 3.8 and Clarkson (1990) 10 Legal Studies 80.
115 The very fact that the decree is not recognised in England means that the parties are likely to remarry in a country where it is recognised.
116 Chapter 2, IV C.

probably[117] did, and possibly still does,[118] adopt such an approach to the "conflict of rules" problem in relation to capacity to remarry.

The clearest example of a differential approach is s 7 of the Recognition of Divorces and Legal Separations Act 1971. This purports to apply the recognition rule where the remarriage takes place in England after a foreign decree. Thus, the common law preference for the choice rule[119] would have remained applicable where (a) the remarriage was abroad or (b) the remarriage followed an English decree or (c) the remarriage followed a foreign nullity (as opposed to divorce) decree.

It has already been seen that whilst s 50 of the Family Law Act 1986 removes the above distinctions in respect of marriage following divorces which are recognised, it maintains the silence of s 7 of the 1971 Act in respect of decrees which are not recognised. Thus, we are again left with a differential approach. Where the divorce is recognised, the recognition rule is applied. Where the divorce is not recognised by the forum, the choice rule is applied. We shall call this differentiation (d).

2. The Possible Bases for Differentiation

We now will examine these four bases for differentiation in turn.

(A) THE PLACE OF THE REMARRIAGE

The apparent[120] discrepancy between the treatment of remarriages in the United Kingdom[121] and those abroad under s 7 of the Recognition of Divorces and Legal Separations Act 1971 was perceived by many[122] including the Law Commission[123] as anomalous. The differential approach of s 7 is, however, supported by Carter.[124] Whilst in general denigrating any rule which accords preference for the recognition rule, he suggests that such preference can be justified in the narrow circumstances provided for by s 7. He argues that the marriage is only likely to be celebrated in England if at least one party is domiciled and the marriage has a real and substantial connection with England. Hence, application of the forum's recognition rules is justifiable.

With respect, the first part of Carter's explanation is difficult to accept. In the situation which he envisages, s 7 is not needed to validate the remarriage in England. The party whose incapacity is in doubt cannot be domiciled in England because then there would not be any discrepancy between the choice rule and the recognition rule. Where the party whose incapacity is not in doubt

117 The doubt is caused by the decision in *Lawrence v Lawrence* [1985] Fam 106, which seems to treat s 7 of the Recognition of Divorces and Legal Separations Act 1971 as redundant or merely declaratory.
118 If the choice rule is preferred in the *Schwebel v Ungar* situation (see example M1 at ch 1, IV B, *supra*).
119 See A2, *supra*.
120 See n 117, *supra*.
121 For convenience we will refer below to celebration in England.
122 See, eg, the concluding comment of Sir David Cairns in *Lawrence v Lawrence* [1985] Fam 106 at 135E.
123 Law Com No 137, para 6.56.
124 (1985) 101 LQR 496 at 505.

is domiciled in the United Kingdom, the marriage will in any event be valid under the rule in *Sottomeyer v De Barros (No 2).*[125]

The second part of his explanation might however provide a sound policy base for the differential approach in s 7, which could then be justified as follows. In cases where there is no prior connection between the parties and the forum, the supremacy of the domicile principle applies to the question of the validity of the remarriage; whereas if the remarriage takes place in the United Kingdom, this provides sufficient connection with the forum for it to prefer its own recognition rules to that of the domicile. Academic[126] and judicial[127] support for the interest of the forum in the capacity of the parties where it is also the *lex loci celebrationis* can be found. On the other hand, this justification of the rule almost encourages forum shopping. Where parties know that a marriage will not be recognised by the law of the domicile because of non-recognition of a foreign decree, they can come to England to get remarried even if they had no prior connection with England provided that the foreign decree is recognised by the relatively liberal English recognition rules. It would seem that discouragement of such forum shopping was one of the reasons why the Court in the *Brentwood Marriage* case[128] refused to allow the parties to remarry in England.

With respect, the *Brentwood* approach is to be preferred. The mere fact that the marriage is celebrated in England should not in itself affect whether precedence is given to choice of law rules or recognition rules. However, a different view may be taken where the fact of the celebration of the marriage in England is indicative of a real and substantial connection with the country. An appropriate test might be either that England is the intended matrimonial home of the parties or that one of them has been habitually resident in England for one year.

Thus, it is suggested that a differential approach cannot be justified if it depends entirely on whether the remarriage was celebrated in the forum. Only where there is some further connection with the forum, as suggested above, could the displacement of the choice rule in favour of the recognition rule be justified.[129] It might be noted that this idea is really a rejection of the domicile rule where the forum is seen to be more closely connected with the issue.[130] Thus, a similar result might be achieved by replacing the domicile choice rule with a real and substantial connection[131] rule. There would then be no need for this differential approach because the choice rules would in any case require that English law is to be applied in the circumstances in which it is envisaged above that the recognition rule should displace the choice rule.

125 (1879) 5 PD 94.
126 See Clarkson [1990] 10 Legal Studies 80 and references therein at p 83.
127 *Sottomeyer v De Barros (No 2)* (1879) 5 PD 94.
128 [1968] 2 QB 956.
129 This idea of displacing a foreign governing law in favour of the law of the forum where the latter is more closely connected to the issue can be found in relation to the choice of law rule for torts in the House of Lords' decision in *Boys v Chaplin* [1971] AC 356.
130 Just as the *Boys v Chaplin* "exception" is a rejection of the *lex loci delicti* where the forum (or in theory some other law) is more closely connected.
131 See section I C, *supra*.

(B) THE PLACE OF THE DECREE[132]

Although the question has never directly arisen, there are weak dicta in *Breen v Breen*[133] which may indicate that the choice rule should apply to a foreign remarriage following an English decree. Nonetheless, commentators[134] seem to have assumed that, notwithstanding the wording of s 7, where a remarriage followed an English divorce or nullity decree the parties would automatically be accorded capacity to remarry, regardless of the choice of law rules, without any better justification than that it would "seem right" to do so.[135] This seems to be an assertion of the "full effect" or "logical conclusion" argument which is the basis of giving precedence to the recognition rule in all cases.[136] The question here is whether, if that argument is not accepted generally, there is any particular reason why, on a differential approach, it should apply to remarriages following English decrees. Two possible reasons might be suggested for treating remarriages following English decrees differently. The first is that such decrees are intrinsically in some way of greater weight than foreign decrees and the second is that as matter of policy a court should give "full effect" to its own decrees even if it does not give "full effect" to foreign decrees which it recognises.

(i) "English Decrees are of Greater Weight"

If the jurisdiction rules for granting decrees are narrower than those for recognising decrees, it could be argued that an English decree involves a stronger connection with the parties than a foreign decree, which therefore justifies the decree overriding the law of the domicile. In fact, as we have seen, recognition rules in respect of formal divorces are more liberal in that decrees granted in the country of nationality, habitual residence for less than one year and domicile in the sense of the decree-granting jurisdiction will be recognised, although none of these bases is sufficient for jurisdiction in England and Wales.

However, the argument is defective, partly because of the artificial nature of domicile. Whilst domicile in the English sense may involve a greater connection than domicile in the foreign sense,[137] the converse might equally be true.[138] Moreover, it does not seem possible to differentiate between those foreign decrees where jurisdiction is based on domicile or habitual residence for one year and English decrees.

132 See ch 1, V, *supra*.

133 [1964] P 144.

134 Law Com No 137, para 6.*56;* Cheshire and North (ch 1, n 6, *supra*) p 592 and Lipstein [1972B] CLJ 67 at 95. This problem has caused much difficulty in various European countries, in particular Germany and Switzerland. See Palsson (ch 1, n 42, *supra*) at pp 229 *et seq*.

135 See Cheshire and North *ibid* at p 592. According to Schmidt (ch 1, n 1, *supra* at p 359), Lagarde holds that the incidental question should be governed by the *lex fori* in such a case because the fact that the authorities of the forum have taken part in the creation of the legal situation (here the divorce) which is the subject of the incidental question means that this question "is so closely inserted in the legal system of the forum that this has a predominant interest in it".

136 See section B 1, *supra*.

137 See, eg, in *Lawrence v Lawrence* [1985] Fam 106, where domicile in Nevada was acquired after six weeks' residence, which was only intended to be temporary.

138 Eg, where a domicile of origin has revived.

(ii) Policy

It is clearly undesirable that a legal system should in one breath grant a person a divorce and in the next refuse to allow him/her to remarry because such a divorce is not recognised by the law of the domicile. However, it might be argued that this phenomenon is no more than a manifestation of the general "internal disharmony" problem which, as we have seen,[139] arises from according precedence to the choice rules. In which case, if, despite the inconsistency problem, the choice rule is preferred, there is no reason to distinguish between forum decrees and foreign decrees.

On the other hand, the view might be taken that inconsistency between the forum's decree and the party's status is more serious than where the inconsistency arises from the recognition of a foreign decree. In particular, parties will invariably expect that a divorce in England will allow them to remarry or have a remarriage recognised in England; whereas they might not automatically assume that a divorce abroad will enable them to remarry or have their remarriage recognised in England.

Thus, it may be possible to justify a preference for the forum's domestic law over the choice rule on the basis of "conflicts justice",[140] even if the choice rule takes precedence over recognition rules in relation to foreign decrees.

(C) TYPE OF DECREE

It is clear that the reason that s 7 only applied to divorce and not nullity decrees is because the 1971 Act itself did not deal with nullity decrees, rather than because of any deliberate policy to distinguish between the effects of the two types of decree on capacity to remarry. However, the decision in *Perrini*[141] was justified by some commentators[142] on the basis that it concerned a nullity decree rather than a divorce decree as in the *Brentwood Marriage* case.[143] But there is no explanation as to *why* there should be any difference between the two types of decree.

From a private international law perspective, the main difference between divorce and nullity is that nowadays the *lex fori* frequently governs the former,[144] whereas the personal law at the time of the first marriage, at least where the marriage is alleged to be void as opposed to voidable, usually governs the latter. It might be argued that where the foreign court has applied the parties' personal law rather than its own law *qua lex fori*, the decree somehow has greater weight, which justifies giving precedence to the recognition rules. However, this argument is anathema to the general principle of not examining the intrinsic merits of foreign judgments.

139 See at A 3, *supra*.
140 See ch 2, II C, *supra*.
141 [1979] Fam 84 (discussed at B 2, *supra*).
142 See, eg, Young (1980) 24 ICLQ 515 at 518.
143 [1968] 2 QB 596 (discussed at A2, *supra*).
144 Palsson *International Encyclopedia of Comparative Law*, vol III, ch 16 at para 16-125 *et seq*, explains that many Continental jurisdictions have modified the nationality choice rule to such an extent that the law of the forum usually applies.

Application of the personal law rather than the *lex fori* by the decree granting court reduces the likelihood of conflict between choice and recognition rules. In any event, there are far fewer nullity decrees than divorces granted. However, it is not clear why the reduced likelihood of the "conflict of rules" situation arising indicates that a different principle should govern when it does.[145]

(D) WHETHER OR NOT THE DECREE IS RECOGNISED BY THE FORUM

We will assume that the result of the enactment of s 50 of the Family Law Act 1986 is that the recognition rule applies where the decree is recognised and that the choice rule applies where the decree is not recognised.[146]

This differential rule may be justified on the basis that the "full effect" doctrine only applies when the decree is recognised. We have seen that whilst the policy of recognising a decree may require that capacity to remarry is conferred,[147] the converse is not true.[148]

3. Conclusion about "Differential Rules"

It may be concluded that the first and third bases of differentiation cannot be supported. The second basis might be supportable, but as it merely enables differentiation between forum decrees and foreign decrees, it assumes a preference for the choice of law rule in respect of the latter. Thus, for our purposes, it is identical with the first preference rule. However, the fourth basis, which reflects the assumed consequences of s 50 of the Family Law Act 1986, could provide a sound preference rule. Thus, throughout this thesis "the differential rule" will mean according precedence to the recognition rule where it leads to recognition and otherwise to the choice rule.

D. Prefer the Rule which Upholds the Validity of the Marriage

The principle of upholding the validity of the marriage has been supported by a number of writers.[149] The reason given is because of the general social policy in favour of marriage. The presumption in favour of validity is usually considered to apply once a marriage has already been celebrated rather than when the parties are seeking permission to celebrate a marriage.[150]

It may, however, be argued that the presumption should apply equally to the first marriage. Thus, it does not help us to decide which marriage should be

145 On the contrary, the Family Law Act 1986 deliberately places recognition of foreign nullity decrees and foreign divorce decrees on the same footing, despite the differences mentioned above (see discussion at Law Com 137 paras 5.12-5.13).

146 See C 1, *supra*.

147 At B 1, *supra*.

148 At ch 2, IV, *supra*.

149 Law Com WP 89, para 2.35(e); Hartley (1972) 35 MLR 571; Jaffey (1978) 41 MLR 38; Scoles and Hay (n 18, *supra*) at p 416 and Palsson (ch 1, n 42, *supra*) at p 18. The decision in the German case mentioned at n 70, *supra*, would seem to be based on the policy of upholding the validity of the remarriage. See also the American Uniform Marriage and Divorce Act, s 210, providing that a marriage should be recognised if valid by either the place of celebration or the law of the domicile.

150 Law Commission, *ibid.*

upheld. It is suggested that this argument is fallacious for the following reasons. Firstly, the presumption relates to the validity *ab initio* of the marriage and therefore does not have any relevance in relation to whether a valid marriage has been terminated.[151] Secondly, in so far as there is a presumption of the continued validity of the first marriage, it may be countered by a presumption of the validity of the foreign divorce.[152] Thirdly, the recognition of the second marriage does not necessarily mean that the first marriage should be considered as terminated for all purposes. Once it is recognised that marriage and divorce need not be universal,[153] it is possible to allow the continuation of marital rights arising from the first marriage where it is just to do so,[154] whilst also recognising the second marriage. Thirdly, to the extent that the recognition of the second marriage is inconsistent with the continued subsistence of the first,[155] there may be policy reasons for preferring the second marriage,[155a] to which the presumption would give effect.

III. POLICY

A. The Present Law[156]

The sole ground for divorce is irretrievable breakdown of marriage. This can be proved by five alternative facts of which three are virtually identical to the old matrimonial offences[157] and two involve periods of separation. The substitution of the breakdown principle for the doctrine of the matrimonial offence was recommended by the Law Commission to enable "the empty legal shell" of broken marriages "to be destroyed with the maximum fairness, and the minimum bitterness, distress and humiliation".[158]

It is clear, both from the Law Commission's Report[159] and from the Parliamentary debates[160] on the Bill that one of the motivating factors behind the reform was to enable those whose marriages had broken down to be able to remarry. In particular, there was concern about the number of illicit stable

151 In *Hussain v Rahman,* 10 October 1980 (Lexis), the court clearly wished to uphold the validity of the second marriage, despite the lack of any clear evidence that the first marriage had been dissolved.
152 See *Powell v Cockburn* (1976) 68 DLR 3d 700 at 706. Clark (n 75, *supra*) at p 136 states that the presumption that the latest of successive marriage is valid prevails over the other presumptions of validation of marriage. See also Swisher and Jones (1995) 29 Fam Law Q 409.
153 See North (ch 3, n 32, *supra*) at pp 132-133.
154 Below, we will be seeking to construct result-orientated preference rules for this purposes in relation to succession, matrimonial property and claims in tort in chs 5, 6 and 7 respectively.
155 Eg, a court would not be able to order the spouse who has remarried to cohabit with the first spouse.
155a See Swisher and Jones (n 152, *supra*).
156 The Family Law Act 1996 is not expected to be implemented for about two years. Until then the relevant provisions of the Matrimonial Causes Act 1973 (which re-enacted the Divorce Reform Act 1969) continue to apply.
157 Adultery, cruelty (now behaviour) and desertion.
158 The Field of Choice, Law Com No 6 at para 14.
159 *Ibid*, para 33 *et seq.*
160 See, eg, 775 HC Debs, Divorce Reform Bill (17.12.68) at col 1062, per Mr D Weitzman and at col 1091, per Mr D Awdry. Also, 784 HC Debs Divorce Reform Bill (12.6.69) at col 203, per Mr D Awdry and at col 207, per Mr L Abse.

unions, which were thought[161] to be a result of the restrictive divorce law, and the resultant illegitimate offspring. Thus, one of the main reasons for enabling dead marriages to be buried was in order to facilitate remarriage. In other words, the focus of divorce law had started to shift from concern about the reason for the breakdown of the first marriage to concern about second relationships.

The main[162] limitation to the "burying dead marriages" policy is the "hardship bar". The court may refuse to grant a decree on the basis of five years separation where it would cause grave financial or other hardship to the respondent and it would in all the circumstances be wrong to dissolve the marriage.[163] This provision prefers the interests of the "innocent" respondent to the general policy. However, apart from the fact that only a small percentage of decrees are based on five years separation,[164] the provision has been interpreted very restrictively[165] and in practice is only likely[166] to be successfully invoked where the parties are middle aged and there is the loss[167] of the expectation of a widow's occupational pension[168] for which the husband is unable to compensate by other means.[169] Otherwise, it has been recognised that it is the separation which causes the hardship and not the divorce itself.

Thus, it can be seen that the present law gives precedence to second marriages, subject to limited protection for first spouses. Only in exceptional circumstances should the first spouse be protected by keeping the dead marriage alive.

B. The New Law

In 1990 the Law Commission put forward proposals for a new ground for divorce.[170] Their scheme was adopted with only minor modification by the government[171] and after more substantial amendment in Parliament was enacted in the Family Law Act 1996.

161 The fact that non-marital cohabitation continued to increase after the liberalisation of the divorce law (see Social Trends 18 (1988), Central Statistical Office) suggests that this assumption was not correct.
162 In addition, the grant of the decree absolute could be delayed in two situations: (a) Where the divorce is on the basis of two years or five years separation and the respondent shows that insufficient financial provision has been made for him/her by the petitioner (Matrimonial Causes Act 1973, s 10). Since usually the petitioner can obtain proper provision through an application for financial provision, this section is rarely used. (b) In exceptional circumstances where it is desirable in the interests of the child for the decree to be delayed (Matrimonial Causes Act 1973, s 41(2), as amended by the Children Act 1989, Sched 12, para 31).
163 Matrimonial Causes Act 1973, s 5.
164 The figure has gradually dropped from 11.6% in 1971 to 5.5% in 1989. The statistics do not show fact relied on after 1989.
165 The fact that divorce has been contrary to the respondent's religious beliefs has not been sufficient hardship. See *Rukat v Rukat* [1975] Fam 63 and *Banik v Banik [1973]* 1 WLR 860.
166 Even if grave financial hardship is made out it may still not be "wrong" to dissolve the marriage. See, eg, *Brickell v Brickell* [1974] Fam 31 and *Matthias v Matthias* [1972] Fam 287 at 299 *et seq.*
167 The loss must be a net loss to the wife. Thus, there will not be considered to be a loss where any payments to the wife would result in a *pro tanto* loss of social security benefits: *Reiterbund v Reiterbund* [1975] Fam 99 and *Jackson v Jackson* [1993] 2 FLR 848.
168 As in *Julian v Julian* (1972) 116 SJ 763.
169 Eg, taking out an annuity as in *Le Marchant v Le Marchant* [1977] 1 WLR 559.
170 Law Com No 192 (1990).
171 In "Looking to the Future: Mediation and the Ground for Divorce – The Government's Proposals" (Lord Chancellor's Dept, April 1995) Cmnd 2799 (hereinafter "the White Paper").

Under the new regime, divorce will be granted on the petition of either or both parties after a set period of reflection and consideration.[172] The period starts to run after a statement of marital breakdown is made,[172a] but the divorce is only granted after a statement of *irretrievable* marital breakdown has been made by one or both parties.

The Law Commission's work and the new Act confirm the shift away from the question as to whether or not a marriage can be terminated. However, "illicit stable unions" are no longer seen as a social problem in the same way as in 1966. Rather, it has been realised that the process of divorce[173] can have long-term effects on the parties and their children. Thus, today[174] the emphasis is placed on the *method* of burying dead marriages, ie ensuring that the burial[175] is as humane as possible so that the parties can get on to make a new start in life after their failed marriage. Thus, it is taken for granted that the central concern is about future relationships. It is not sufficient simply to validate second marriages, but also to put the parties in the right frame of mind to maximise their chance of success. The title of the Government Consultation[176] and White Papers,[177] "Looking to the Future" aptly describes this policy.

It might be thought that a number of aspects of the new scheme detract from the principle of burying dead marriages. Firstly, the introduction of the waiting period means that some spouses would have to wait longer to get a divorce.[178] Secondly, under the new scheme, the divorce will not be granted until all the ancillary matters have been settled.[179] Thirdly, the existing hardship bar is retained and will become available in relation to all divorces.[180]

However, it is suggested that while the new Act evidences a greater concern to save marriages[180a] it does not indicate any change in the policy of giving precedence to second marriages. One of the reasons that the parties may be

172 The normal period will be nine months, but will be extended to 15 months if one party applies for such an extension or there are minor children (s 7 Family Law Act 1996).

172a This statement can only be made three months after an information meeting has been attended (s 8(2) Family Law Act 1996).

173 Divorce is seen as part of a massive transition, which divorce law should make as smooth as possible for the parties and their children (Law Com No 170, para 3.50).

174 The Field of Choice (n 158, *supra*) also called for marriages to be dissolved with the maximum fairness and minimum bitterness. However, the retention of the fault-based grounds meant that this aim was not realised. See Law Com No 170, paras 3.13-3.27.

175 The "burial" involves not only obtaining a decree but also sorting out all the ancillary matters, such as children and property.

176 "Looking to the Future: Mediation and the Ground for Divorce – A Consultation Paper", Cmnd 2424 (Lord Chancellor's Dept 1993), (hereinafter the "Consultation Paper").

177 *Supra*, n 171.

178 At present fault-based divorces may be obtained in a few months (See the Consultation Paper n 176, *supra* at para 5.2).

179 But a court has the power to dispense with this precondition where there are special circumstances justifying the grant of the divorce at the end of the waiting period, notwithstanding that arrangments have not been finalised (s 9(7) Family Law Act 1996).

180 Section 10 Family Law Act 1996. There is provision for the bar to be cancelled if circumstances change.

180a See the statement of general principles in s 1 of the Family Law Act 1996. See also ss 22, 23 8(9)(a), 8(2) and 12(2).

required to wait a little longer is so that the second marriage is more likely to start out on the right footing.[181]

IV. APPLICATION OF POLICY

It is submitted that the "bury dead marriages" and "looking to the future" policies outlined above both require that, where the first marriage has in fact broken down and a second marriage has been entered into after a dissolution (whether that dissolution is in fact recognised in English law or not), it is the second marriage (the "alive" marriage) which should be recognised in preference to the first (the "dead" marriage).

Whilst it is more than possible that by the time the issue reaches court, the second marriage may also be "dead",[182] policy would seem to dictate that the one which has been "dead" the longest should be buried first. Alternatively, it might be considered that the relevant time for deciding which marriage is to be preferred is at the date of the second marriage.[183]

Forum policy can be implemented by adoption of either "the differential rule"[184] or the express result selection rule of upholding the validity of the marriage.[185] The former is tentatively preferred because the rule itself may be supported independently of the result.

It must be stressed that the rule recommended here only applies to the conflict between choice rules and recognition rules in relation to *the validity of the remarriage*. It does not attempt to solve this conflict, for example, in relation to succession or financial or property issues. Thus, whilst deciding that the remarriage is a valid monogamous marriage, this does not mean that the first spouse might not retain entitlement to some rights from the first marriage, for example in relation to succession, maintenance and pension rights. Where entitlement to these rights is governed by the law of a foreign country, a "conflict of rules" may arise, which will have to be solved by a preference rule which reflects the policy in relation to that particular issue.[186] Where entitlement to these rights is governed by the law of the forum,[187] then there is no "conflict of rules" and if the forum does not recognise the decree, the first wife should retain her marital rights.[188] It is suggested that the possibility of the first spouse retaining rights, despite the validity of the remarriage, reflects the policy of domestic law of giving precedence to second marriages and,

181 See Consultation Paper (n 176, *supra*). This consideration might seem to justify the requirement of finalising all the ancillary matters before the decree is granted.

182 Frequently, the issue of the validity of the second marriage comes to light because one party wants a decree of nullity on the ground of bigamy. See, eg, *Schwebel v Unger* (1964) 48 DLR (2d) 644 and *Lawrence v Lawrence* [1985] Fam 106.

183 This seems to be the approach taken by the putative marriage doctrine applied in some countries. For example, in *Stephens v Falchi* [1938] 3 DLR 590, the second husband could succeed to the estate by virtue of the doctrine even though the divorce was not recognised and the second marriage was therefore void. The second marriage had also broken down before the death of the wife.

184 Section C *3, supra.*

185 Section D, *supra.*

186 See chs 5, 6 and 7, *infra.*

187 Either *qua lex fori* or because the relevant choice rule points to the forum.

188 Unless the doctrine of preclusion is applied to such cases. See ch 5, II A 3, *infra*. The problem of two "spouses" sharing rights is discussed in relation to specific issues at ch 5, I C, and ch 6, I E, *infra*.

wherever possible, providing protection for the first spouse by means other than keeping alive a dead marriage.

Thus, the preference rule recommended is the differential rule, under which the recognition rule prevails where the decree is recognised and the choice rule prevails where the decree is not recognised. It will be noticed that this solution is consistent with s 50 of the Family Law Act 1986, but goes further than that section by providing for cases which fall outside it.[189]

189 See Briggs (1989) 9 OJLS 251 at 258 and Jaffey (1985) 48 MLR 465 at 469.

Chapter 5

Succession by Spouses

I. SCOPE OF THE PROBLEM

A. Introduction

Where there is disagreement between the *lex fori* and the *lex successionis* as to whether a matrimonial decree[1] made in respect of a marriage of the deceased should be recognised, there will be a conflict as to whether the "spouse" may succeed as a spouse. In example M1,[2] if the choice of law rules are followed, Israeli law will apply as the law of the domicile of the deceased in relation to the devolution of movables on his intestacy. Thus, the divorce is recognised and the first "spouse", Natasha, will not receive the share of Alexander's estate which is due to a spouse under a will or intestacy since under that law (s)he is no longer married to the deceased at the date of death. Whereas if the forum's recognition rules are applied, Natasha will take, as (s)he is still considered as married to the deceased.

As with the case of remarriage, this problem has traditionally been analysed as an example of the incidental question. The question posed is whether the incidental or preliminary question of the recognition of the decree is governed by the conflicts rules of the *lex fori* or the conflicts rules of the *lex causae*. However, as in the case of validity of remarriages, it is suggested that it is more helpful to treat the problem as a single question: in this case, whether the "spouse" is to be treated as a spouse for the purposes of succession. The issue is whether this question should be governed by the forum's choice rules including renvoi[3] (ie the whole of the *lex successionis*) or by the forum's recognition rules. The scope for discrepancy between the latter and the foreign recognition rules has been examined.[4]

B. Choice of Law Rules

It is well established that the law of the domicile at the date of death applies in relation to movables[5] and that the *lex situs* applies in relation to immovables[6] both in intestate succession and in determining devolution of the property under

1 A judicial separation would also be relevant here because in many systems, including English domestic law, such a decree terminates the rights of the parties to inherit from each other on intestacy.
2 Chapter 1, IV B, *supra*.
3 See ch 1, VI, *supra*.
4 Chapter 4, I B, *supra*.
5 Dicey and Morris (ch 1, n 6, *supra*) Rules 134 and 139.
6 *Ibid*, Rules 135 and 140.

a will. In relation to wills, questions of formal validity may be governed by a number of alternative laws (of which the domicile at death is one) and questions of construction are governed by the law intended by the testator,[7] which is presumed to be governed by the law of the domicile at the date the will is made. It is not clear whether the question of whether a person is a spouse of the deceased should be regarded as a question of construction of the will or of devolution of the property.

The scission between movables and immovables and the application of the *lex situs* to intestate succession have been subject to severe academic[8] and judicial[9] criticism. The Hague Conference on Private International Law's Convention on Succession, to which the United Kingdom is a party, provides for unity of succession with habitual residence and nationality at the date of death being the main connecting factors. However, the United Kingdom has not ratified this Convention and thus we must work on the basis that scission will remain for the foreseeable future.

Thus, where the law of the *situs* of the immovables is different from the domicile at death, or indeed where there are immovables situated in more than one jurisdiction, the devolution of each type of property will be governed by its own *lex successionis*. If the question of whether a persons is a spouse is a question of devolution of the property, a person who is considered to be a spouse for the purposes of succession to movables may not be considered to be a spouse for the purposes of succession to immovables and a person who succeeds as spouse to immovables in one jurisdiction may not be so entitled in another jurisdiction.

This anomaly may be considered to be a good reason for preferring to apply the law governing the interpretation of the will to determine whether an alleged spouse can inherit as a spouse.

C. Discretionary Family Provision Schemes

The "conflict of rules" can only arise where the English court applies foreign rules of succession. Thus, it is clear that the problem can occur in relation to testate succession, intestate succession and fixed inheritance rights. However, there is no authority on whether an English court would be prepared to apply a discretionary family provision statute of a foreign *lex successionis*. The English texts do not discuss this point,[10] but there is some pertinent Commonwealth case law.[11]

7 *Ibid*, Rule 141.

8 See Morris (1969) 85 LQR 339 at 348-352; Cohn (1956) 5 ICLQ 395; Wolff, *Private International Law* (2nd edn, 1950) p 567 *et seq*.

9 See comments of Sir Nicholas Brown-Wilkinson V-C in *Re Collens* [1986] Ch 505 at 512-513.

10 Dicey and Morris (ch 1, n 6, *supra*, at pp 1035-1038) talk only about the jurisdiction of the English court to make an order under the Inheritance (Provision for Family and Dependants) Act 1975 and the jurisdiction of other courts to make orders under *their own* similar legislation.

11 In addition to cases discussed below, see also *Re Corlet* [1942] 3 DLR 271 where the Alberta court held that its family provision legislation did not apply because the deceased died domiciled in the Isle of Man. It did not consider it necessary to examine whether similar provision was available under Isle of Man law. See also *Re Terry* [1951] NZLR 30.

In *Re Paulin*,[12] Sholl J in the Supreme Court of Victoria refused to apply the New South Wales statute on the basis that under that statute, discretion to make orders was granted *only* to the New South Wales Court. In *Re Bailey*,[13] the New Zealand High Court held that it was unable to apply the English discretionary scheme in respect of immovables in England because the testator did not die domiciled in England as required by the legislation. The very fact that the court considered the terms of the English legislation might suggest that in principle they would have been prepared to apply it if it did not contain the limiting requirement. However, Prichard J went on to consider the Australian courts' refusal to make orders affecting foreign immovables even where both jurisdictions had discretionary schemes. He commented:

> "This attitude, if not strictly logical, is eminently reasonable because the remedy is, from its nature, a discretionary one – from which it follows that the Court in which the proceedings are brought can afford relief affecting immovables in another Sate in accordance with the *lex situs* only by purporting to exercise a discretion which is in fact reposed in the Judges of the Courts of the *lex situs.*"

With respect, it is submitted that the reasoning of both Prichard J and Sholl J pays insufficient attention to the policy behind the legislation. The prime motivation[14] for the enactment of family provision statutes was to protect family members to whom a legal duty of support, or at least a moral duty, was owed by the deceased during his lifetime. No doubt, the legislature had in mind the exercise of the discretion by their own courts. However, this is true of any domestic statute. There is nothing inherent in the discretion which requires it to be exercised by the home courts only.

As Sholl J himself pointed out,[15] where the foreign law provides for fixed succession rights for dependents, it would enforce those rights, as in *Re Ross.*[16] With respect, it is anomalous to treat fixed rights differently from discretionary schemes, as the purpose behind the two is the same.[17] The reason that some systems have preferred discretionary schemes is in order to preserve flexibility.[18] Application of the scheme by a foreign court does not impinge on flexibility.

The result of a refusal to apply foreign discretionary schemes is to leave a gap in the protection accorded. This is particularly apparent in a case like *Re Paulin*,[19] where the forum itself has similar legislation. In that case, the fact that part of the estate consisted of immovables in another state reduced the amount of the order in favour of the widow. The widow could only recover this amount by taking out a second application in the state where the immovables were

12 [1950] VLR 462. See also *Heuston v Barber* (1990) 19 NSWLR 354.
13 [1985] 2 NZLR 656.
14 See III 2 (c), *infra*.
15 [1950] VLR 462 at 466-467.
16 [1930] 1 Ch 377.
17 See III 2 (d), *infra*.
18 Law Com No 52, para 34. Cf Scottish Law Commission Report No 124 in which retention of fixed shares is recommended to preserve certainty.
19 [1950] VLR 462.

situated.[20] One of the aims of the conflict of laws is to enable the same result to be reached whichever forum is chosen and to avoid unnecessary multiplicity of litigation. Refusal to apply foreign discretionary schemes is inconsistent with this objective.

The Victoria court did try to prevent the need for a second application. In determining how much to order under the Victoria Act, the court calculated the amount that would be due if an order were made for the whole estate, including the immovable property in New South Wales. Sholl J then apportioned the order in proportion to the value of the property in the respective countries. He said that the purpose of spelling out how much would be ordered by the New South Wales Court was –

> "in order that the parties may consider the possibility of agreement hereafter in order to avoid an application to the New South Wales Court."[21]

Thus, ironically, by indirect means the Victoria court achieved a result virtually identical with that which would have been achieved if it had been prepared to apply the New South Wales legislation. With respect, it would have been preferable to have reached this result directly and to have avoided the need for the widow to have the continued aggravation of negotiation and the likelihood of having to accept a smaller sum to avoid the need for further litigation.

For present purposes, we shall assume that the English court would be prepared to apply a foreign discretionary scheme.

D. Second Marriages

It should be reiterated that each particular instance of conflict between choice rules and recognition rules is being treated as a separate problem. Thus, the fact that the second marriage is regarded as valid under the proposed preference rule for the validity of remarriages, set out in Chapter 4 above, should not necessarily mean that the first marriage be treated as no longer valid for the purposes of succession.

However, a further more difficult question arises. Should the validity of the *second* marriage for the purposes of *succession* be governed by the principles suggested in Chapter 4, above, or by the principles which are considered appropriate for succession cases.

It is suggested that the policy[22] behind the preference rule recommended in Chapter 4 requires that where the second marriage is upheld under that rule, it should be upheld for all purposes. Thus, the second spouse should be entitled to a spouse's rights to succession. Therefore, if the preference rule to be constructed for succession results in the first spouse retaining succession rights,

20 If the immovables had been situated in England, the English court would not have had jurisdiction under its discretionary scheme because the deceased died domiciled in Victoria. Thus the gap would have been greater (see *Re Bailey* [1985] 2 NZLR 656, discussed in the text at n 13, *supra*).

21 [1950] VLR 462 at 468.

22 See ch 4, III and IV, *supra*.

the first and second spouses will *both* be entitled to succeed as spouses, unless the first spouse is estopped from claiming under the doctrine of preclusion.[23] In this situation, legal bigamy is not just a theoretical problem, but a practical reality. However, according to Palsson,[24] legal bigamy is least problematic where the bigamous marriages have in any event been dissolved by death. Presumably this is because the policy of the law which prohibits bigamy is not actually infringed by a decision that a marriage which has now been terminated by death was bigamous.

The practical difficulty of two spouses sharing succession rights can be solved relatively simply by dividing the spouse's share whether in a will or on intestacy between the two "spouses" equally. This is already necessary in the case of valid actually polygamous marriages.[25] The Law Commission[26] envisages the possibility of a bigamist being held liable to make provision for two wives under the family provision legislation where the "wife" in the void marriage *bona fide* believes it is valid.[27]

The difficulty with this pragmatic approach is that it may involve selective application[28] of two laws. Thus, in example M2[29] above, the preference rule recommended in Chapter 4 would lead to the validity of the second marriage by application of the recognition rule. Thus, Juan may succeed as Evita's husband. If we decide that in succession the choice rule should be preferred, Argentinian law will be applied as the *lex successionis* and Pedro will be able to claim as Evita's husband. The solution suggested here is that they should share the husband's portion. However, this result does not accord either with the recognition rules of the forum, which would only allow Juan to take or with the Argentinian *lex successionis,* which would only allow Pedro to take.

A similar problem could arise if we were to assume that we decide that recognition rules should be preferred for the purposes of succession. In example M1,[30] as the divorce is not recognised, Natasha would be able to claim the wife's share.[31] However, as the remarriage will be recognised under the preference rule for remarriages, Bella can also succeed as Alexander's wife. The solution under which they share the wife's portion does not accord with either the recognition rules of the forum, which would only allow Natasha to succeed, or the Israeli *lex successionis*, which would only allow Bella to succeed.

23 See II A 4, *infra*.

24 *Op cit* (ch 1, n 42) at p 225. He is commenting on the German case RG 24 Jan 1941 RGZ 165, 398, where both "widows" were held to be entitled to a widow's pension.

25 In *Re Sehota* [1978] 3 All ER 385 everything was left to one of the wives. The other claimed successfully under the Inheritance Provision for Family and Dependents) Act 1975. However, it has not yet been judicially decided whether each wife should be entitled to a surviving spouse's statutory legacy or whether this amount should be shared between them.

26 Law Com No 61, para 29.

27 See definition of spouse under the Inheritance (Provision for Family and Dependants) Act 1975, s 25(4).

28 This is known as "depecage" or "picking and choosing": see Morris (ch 1, n 144, *supra*) at p 463.

29 At ch 1, IV B, *supra*.

30 *Ibid.*

31 This would also be the case where English law is the *lex successionis*, as for example in relation to immovables situation in England.

Morris[32] suggests that "picking and choosing" is not a problem where "the issues are unrelated except by the circumstances that they both arise in the same case". In the present situation, are the claims of the two widow(er)s related? In one sense they are both claiming in the same succession. On the other hand, the key question in each case is the relationship of the claimant with the deceased. It is suggested that there is no reason why different laws should not apply in relation to the two claimants if this is necessary in order to produce a result which accords with the policy of the forum. Even though the forum only recognises one spouse as the valid spouse, making provision for both spouses might actually be in accordance with its policy[33] on what might loosely be called "family provision on death".

II. POSSIBLE SOLUTIONS[34]

A. Prefer the Choice Rule

1. Theoretical Basis

The main argument for preferring the choice rule in relation to succession cases is the fundamental nature of the rules that succession to movables is governed by the domicile and succession to immovables by the *lex situs*.

The former seems to flow from the "status theory" discussed above.[35] In both testate and intestate succession to movables, whether and how much a surviving spouse is to receive is governed by the law of the domicile at death. Thus, it is logical[36] that this law should also determine whether an alleged surviving spouse is in fact a surviving spouse or an ex-spouse whose marriage has been terminated by a divorce or nullity decree.

Whilst the application of the *lex situs* to immovables has been criticised,[37] there is force in the underlying rationale that only the *lex situs* can control the ownership of immovables within its territory. Thus, any determination of ownership which is inconsistent with the *lex situs* may be ineffective, a mere *brutum fulmen*.[38] Regardless of the arguments for and against the application of the *lex situs*, so long as that law does govern both testate and intestate succession to immovables it is only logical that it should also govern whether an alleged surviving spouse is in fact a surviving spouse or not.

If the question of whether the "spouse" is to be treated as a spouse is really a question of interpretation which is presumed to be governed by the law of the domicile at the time of making of the will,[39] the above reasoning is inapplicable.

32 Morris (ch 1, n 6) at p 463.
33 See III and IV, *infra*.
34 For tabular illustration of the results of applying the different preference rules see Table 4 in Appendix, *infra*.
35 At ch 4, II A 1, *supra*.
36 Ehrenzweig (ch 1, n 4, *supra*, at p 170) suggests that "foreign rules of succession may well be inseparable from the family law to which they refer".
37 See references at n 8, *supra*.
38 Morris (ch 1, n 6, *supra*) p 345.
39 See n 7, *supra*.

However, the preference for the choice rule could then be supported on the basis of the rationale for that rule, ie giving effect to the intentions of the testator.

2. Authority

There is no direct English authority on the "conflict of rules" in succession cases. However, it has been suggested[40] that the Australian case of *Haque v Haque*[41] is authority in support of applying the conflicts rules of the *lex successionis*.[42] The material facts were as follows:

The husband, who was domiciled in India, although resident in Western Australia, divorced his second polygamous wife, Azra, by talaq. He later remarried her, but the remarriage was irregular by Muslim law. The High Court of Australia held that Azra could not succeed as according to Muslim law, which was applicable under the law of the deceased's domicile, she was not his wife. Thus, the first wife and the children of the two marriages took the movable estate[43] in the shares prescribed by Muslim law.

It may be argued that the case is not strong authority because it was not clear that the result would have been any different if the recognition rule had been applied. Firstly, it would seem that the second marriage, which took place in Western Australia, was not recognised as valid in that jurisdiction because it was a polygamous marriage. Secondly, if the marriage was valid, it would seem that the divorce would have been recognised under the common law rules because it was "obtained" in India, the place of the couple's domicile. Nonetheless, the court clearly preferred the choice rule as they did not discuss the issue of recognition.

There is English authority that where there is a conflict between a *choice rule* of the forum and the application of the *lex successionis* concerning the right of a beneficiary to succeed, the *lex successionis* prevails over the choice rules of the forum.[44]

Ehrenzweig[45] suggests that the real rationale for application of the *lex successionis* in cases like this is that the forum considers that unity of distribution of the estate is more important than unity of family relationships. This rationale would apply equally to the cases where there is a conflict between the *recognition* rule of the forum and the application of the *lex successionis*. Ehrenzweig's explanation may seem flawed in relation to those systems[46]

40 See Gottlieb (1977) 26 ICLQ 734 at 774.

41 (1962) 108 CLR 230.

42 The case might also be understood as relating to matrimonial property because a deed was entered into between the parties on marriage. This aspect is discussed at ch 6, II A 2, *infra*.

43 In *Haque v Haque (No 2)* (1964) 114 CLR 98 it was held by a majority of the High Court of Australia that all the property was movables. Thus, the issue of succession to immovables did not arise. However, Barwick J, dissenting in relation to some of the assets, held that succession to the immovables was governed by the law of Western Australia as the *lex situs* and that the immovables would pass under the will of the deceased, which was valid under that law, although not recognised by Muslim law.

44 *Re Johnson* [1903] 1 Ch 821, discussed in detail at ch 10, II B, *infra*.

45 *Op cit* (ch 1, n 4, *supra*).

46 Including English law and US law, about which he was primarily writing.

whose choice of law rules for succession allow for disunity between succession to movables and immovables and between succession to immovables situated in different jurisdictions.[47] However, it may be argued that this possibility of disunity may make it more important that there should not be further disunity in relation to recognition of status.

Finally, it should be mentioned that the Hague Succession Convention of 1988 does not contain an express provision dealing with the incidental question.[48] However, art 7(2)(a) provides that the applicable law shall govern *inter alia* "the determination of the heirs, devisees and legatees". Whilst this may simply refer to determination of the categories of persons who may inherit, it could also be interpreted to include determination of which persons fit into those categories. It is suggested that the latter approach is preferable in order to reach international uniformity of decisions, which is the purpose of such a harmonisation Convention.[49]

3. *Results*

(A) WHERE THE *LEX CAUSAE* RECOGNISES THE DECREE

In this situation, the first spouse will not be able to take. Thus, in example M1,[50] Israeli law will apply to succession to movables and Natasha will not be able to claim as she is no longer considered to be Alexander's spouse.

If Alexander leaves immovables, whether Natasha can claim will depend on whether the *lex situs* recognises the *get*. Where the immovables are situated in England, there can be no "conflict of rules" because English law will be the *lex situs* as well as the *lex fori*.

The barring of the first wife from succession may not be a just result. In particular, the reason that the divorce is not recognised by the forum may be because of some unfairness in the acquisition or effect of the divorce. This problem would have to be dealt with by judicious use of the doctrine of public policy. In other words, the *lex successionis* will not be applied where its application would lead to a manifestly unjust result.

(B) WHERE THE *LEX SUCCESSIONIS* DOES NOT RECOGNISE THE DECREE

In this situation, the first spouse will be able to succeed. Thus, in example M2,[51] Juan can succeed because under Argentinian law he is still married to Evita. This result occurs irrespective of the merits of the "spouse", whether or not (s)he instituted the divorce and whether or not (s)he has remarried. This problem may be alleviated by use of the doctrine of preclusion. Since this doctrine is most likely to operate in relation to succession it will be convenient to consider it in detail at this point.

47 In *Re Johnson* [1903] 1 Ch 821, the estate consisted only of movables.
48 Cf the Marriage Convention discussed at ch 8, *infra*.
49 See Schmidt (ch 1, n 1, *supra*) at p 392.
50 Chapter 1, IV B, *supra*.
51 *Ibid*.

4. The Doctrine of Preclusion

(A) THE OPERATION OF THE DOCTRINE

This doctrine, which is a form of estoppel,[52] has been applied in Canada and the United States,[53] although not yet in England. It has been criticised, particularly by British commentators. Thus, it is necessary to examine the operation of the doctrine in North America, its basis and the criticisms levied against it in order to assess whether it would be appropriate to incorporate it in some form into the preference rules which we are seeking to construct.

The American Restatement[54] provides the most helpful description of the doctrine. This states:

> "A person may be precluded from attacking the validity of a foreign divorce decree if, under the circumstances, it would be inequitable for him to do so."

The subsequent comments on the scope of the rule include the following passage:

> "The rule is not limited to situations of what might be termed 'true estoppel' where one party induces another to rely to his damage upon certain representations as to the facts of the case. The rule may be applied whenever, under all the circumstances, it would be inequitable to permit a particular person to challenge the validity of a divorce decree. Such inequity may exist when action has been taken in reliance on the divorce or expectations are based on it or when the attack on the divorce is inconsistent with the earlier conduct of the attacking party."

Thus, if the doctrine were applied in the situation under discussion, even where the *lex successionis* holds that the decree is not recognised and thus the "spouse" can take by way of succession, (s)he would be precluded from doing so where it would be inequitable to allow reliance by the "spouse" on the invalidity of the decree. Whilst this is clearly a very broad definition, in practice the doctrine is only likely to operate in the following circumstances:

(i) the claimant "spouse" initiated the matrimonial proceedings;[55]
(ii) the claimant "spouse" participated[56] in the proceedings unless there is some alleviating explanation;[57]

52 The doctrine is referred to as preclusion here rather than estoppel to emphasise that it need not be limited by the constraints of the latter doctrine, as for example in the dicta in *Gaffney v Gaffney* [1975] IR 133, discussed in detail below.

53 Where it is sometimes referred to as quasi-estoppel. See, eg, *Krause v Krause* 282 NY 355, 26 NE 2d 290 (1940).

54 American Law Institute, Restatement of the Law, Second, Conflict of Laws, 2d (1971), section 74. This was cited with approval by the Supreme Court of Canada in *Downton v Royal Trust Co* (1973) 34 DLR (3d) 403.

55 As in *Re Jones* (1961) 25 DLR 595.

56 See *Stephens v Falchi* [1938] 3 DLR 590 at 595. Cf *Caldwell v Caldwell* 298 NY 146, 81 NE 2d 60, where the New York courts would not apply the doctrine in relation to Mexican "mail order" divorces. The reason seems to be that they did not want to accord any effects at all to such divorces on public policy grounds.

57 See *Downton v Royal Trust Co* (1973) 43 DLR (3d) 403, where the wife's submission to the Nevada court would have precluded her from later claiming under the Family Relief Act in Newfoundland where the decree was not recognised, but for the fact that her submission was only in order to protect existing benefits under a separation agreement and did not confer on her any further benefits.

(iii) the claimant "spouse" has obtained some benefit from the proceedings. This might include claiming and being awarded alimony or other financial provision only obtainable on termination of the marriage;[58]
(iv) the claimant "spouse" has relied on the validity of the proceedings by remarrying.[59]

Potentially the doctrine of preclusion might be applied in any case where a "spouse"[60] was seeking to deny the validity of a divorce in order to obtain a pecuniary benefit.[61] For the present we are only concerned with its application where the "spouse" is seeking to claim to succeed to the deceased's estate. The doctrine has been held to apply to inheritance on intestacy[62] and under will.[63] By analogy it ought also to apply to fixed rights of inheritance.[64]

(B) RATIONALE OF THE DOCTRINE

The rationale for the doctrine is set out by Laskin CJ, giving the judgment of the court in *Downton v Royal Trust Co*:[65]

> "The doctrine has an ethical basis: a refusal to permit a person to insist, to his or her pecuniary advantage, on a relationship which that person has previously deliberately sought to terminate."

In one case, a Canadian judge said that to allow the "spouse" to rely on the invalidity of the decree in order to claim benefits out of the estate of the deceased spouse would be a "parody of justice".[66]

(C) CRITICISM OF THE DOCTRINE

Battersby[67] claims that the problems resulting from the application of the doctrine are such that the doctrine cannot be justified. His main criticisms are:

(i) If the forum does not recognise the decree, it is illogical that it should give the decree some validity through the doctrine of preclusion.
(ii) The doctrine creates problems for personal representatives.
(iii) The doctrine creates anomalous distinctions because there are other situations in which it is inequitable for one spouse (eg estrangement or misconduct) to claim against the other's estate and yet there is no preclusion.

58 See dicta in *Downton v Royal Trust Co* (1973) 34 DLR (3d) 403.
59 *Ibid.*
60 In *Fromowitz v Fromovitz* (1977) 79 DLR (3d) 148 it was held that the doctrine could only apply against a party to an invalid decree and that a third party could not be precluded from relying on the invalidity of the decree. In this case, a man was not precluded from relying on the invalidity of his "wife's" Mexican divorce from her first husband in order to deny any obligation to maintain her.
61 Such as claims under insurance policies, fatal accidents Acts, or workmen's compensation legislation. See Battersby (1977) 16 UWOnt LR 163.
62 See *Re Capon* (1965) 49 DLR (2d) 675 and authorities quoted there.
63 *Re Jones* (1961) 25 DLR 595, but see criticism by Battersby (1977) 16 UWOnt LR 163 at 176-177.
64 See Battersby, *ibid*, at p 190.
65 (1973) 43 DLR (3d) 403 at 412.
66 Per Schroeder JA in *Re Capon* [1956] 49 ROD 2d at 576.
67 (1977) 16 UWOnt LR 163.

(iv) The doctrine is crude in that it cannot balance the merits of the "spouse" against the merits of the beneficiaries who will take in his/her place.
(v) The doctrine may not operate fairly to the extent that it puts emphasis on who actually applied for the foreign decree. Where both parties have agreed to obtain a decree, it may be purely arbitrary who actually petitions for it and whether the other party participates in the proceedings.
(vi) To allow the "spouse" to claim is not a "parody of justice" because to attempt to do something (in this case terminate the marriage) is not the same as succeeding in doing it.

It must immediately be pointed out that Battersby is concerned with the situation where both the *lex fori* and the *lex successionis* agree that the decree should not be recognised. In other words, there is no conflict of conflicts rules. In the context with which we are concerned, the forum does recognise the decree. Once this is borne in mind it can be seen that most of Battersby's arguments are either inapplicable or of less force. Using the same numbered paragraphs:

(i) This point is inapplicable because the forum does recognise the decree although the *lex successionis* does not. Thus, the application of the doctrine actually gives effect to the law of the forum by way of an exception to the application of the *lex successionis*.
(ii) Since there is already a dispute about the validity of the decree, the personal representatives are already in a difficult situation. Application of the doctrine of preclusion will not make things worse and may be a just solution to the conflict.
(iii) The situation is not comparable with other domestic situations. Here the doctrine is applied to solve a particular problem arising in the conflicts of law.
(iv) If the doctrine is treated as discretionary, the relative merits could be considered.
(v) The problem of the emphasis on who is the petitioner can be resolved either by treating the doctrine as discretionary or restricting the operation of the doctrine to cases where the "spouse" has obtained benefits as a result of the decree, irrespective of who actually applied for it.
(vi) The fact that the foreign decree is not only valid by the law of the place where it was obtained but also by the law of the forum, although not by the *lex successionis*, removes the force of this point.

(D) APPLICATION OF THE DOCTRINE IN ENGLAND

There is little English case law on the question. Dicey and Morris claim that "all of it is hostile to the adoption of a doctrine of preclusion or estoppel".[68]

68 Dicey and Morris (ch 1, n 6, *supra*) at p 760. The case of *Palmer v Palmer* (1859) 1 Sw & Tr 551 is quoted by Sykes and Pryles (ch 2, n 246) at p 481. In this case, it was held *obiter* that even if the foreign decree which the wife had obtained was invalid, she could not complain of her husband's adultery with his second wife. It seems that this case is probably better explained on the basis that the wife could be seen as responsible for the adultery and therefore could not rely on it rather than on the basis of the doctrine of preclusion. No doubt this is why the case is not quoted by the English textwriters.

However, closer examination of the cases will reveal that there is nothing in them to deny the application of the doctrine of preclusion in an appropriate case,[69] at least not in the "conflict of rules" context.

Two of the cases involved what have been referred to as "strictly matrimonial causes".[70] In *Bonaparte v Bonaparte*,[71] the wife contended, on her second husband's petition for nullity, that he was estopped from questioning the validity of the foreign divorce decree in relation to her first marriage because it was obtained by his fraud and misrepresentation. It is hardly surprising that her contention was not accepted because if the doctrine of estoppel had been applied, the parties' status would have been left uncertain. In any event, even in North America, the doctrine cannot be applied against a third party.[72]

In *Hornett v Hornett*,[73] the husband sought a declaration that the foreign decree of divorce was valid. It was held that the fact that the parties had continued to cohabit for 11 years after the valid foreign decree did not estop him from later asserting the validity of that decree. Again, if the doctrine had been applied the parties' status would have been uncertain. Cumming-Bruce J said:

> ". . . there are great difficulties about applying a doctrine of estoppel to a legal decree affecting status."

As has been pointed out,[74] this comment must be viewed in the context in which it was made.[75] The rejection of the doctrine of preclusion as against a party seeking a nullity decree or a declaration of status does not necessarily imply its rejection in other contexts.[76]

However, there are also two cases, one English and one Irish, which seem to suggest that the doctrine does not apply even in cases which are not "strictly matrimonial causes".

In *Papadopolous v Papadopolous*,[77] the decision of a magistrate awarding maintenance to a wife who had obtained a decree of nullity from a Maltese court which was not recognised here, was upheld. It was assumed that because the parties were still man and wife there was no alternative[78] but to award maintenance. Although counsel for the husband claimed that the magistrate was wrong in holding that the wife was not estopped from alleging that she was a

69 Dicey and Morris, *ibid*, admit that "the English Courts have not yet been confronted with such starkly unmeritorious claims as the American and Canadian courts have sometimes been".

70 *Downton v Royal Trust* (1972) 34 DLR (3d) 403 at 413.

71 [1892] P 402, followed in the Australian decision of *Alexandrov v Alexandrov* [1967] SASR 303.

72 See *Fromovitz v Fromovitz* (1977) 79 DLR (3d) 148.

73 [1971] P 255.

74 Carter (1971) 45 BYBIL 410 at 412.

75 Eg, it is clear that estoppel *per rem judicatam* and promissory estoppel may operate to prevent a party attacking a forum decree. See *King v Kureishy* (1982) 13 Fam Law 1982 and Lexis (23.11.82).

76 Indeed in *Downton v Royal Trust Co* (1972) 34 DLR (3d) 403 at 413, it seems to have been accepted that the doctrine could not apply in "strictly matrimonial causes" because "marital status *per se* cannot be altered or perpetuated by a preclusion doctrine".

77 [1935] P 55.

78 *Ibid*, at 68.

wife, this point is not considered in any of the judgments.[79] Thus, while on the merits this might have been a case where the doctrine could have applied, the lack of discussion of the issue makes it a weak precedent. In the Irish case of *Gaffney v Gaffney*[80] both parties were domiciled in the Republic of Ireland. Under duress by the husband, the wife obtained[81] a divorce in England by stating falsely that she and her husband were domiciled in England. The wife later claimed in the husband's intestacy. It was held that the English decree was not valid because of the lack of jurisdiction and that the wife was not estopped from claiming. The latter can clearly be supported on the basis that the estoppel should not operate against a spouse who had obtained a divorce under duress. However, the court went on to state that even if the plaintiff had been a free agent there could not be any estoppel in relation to the question of whether a marriage had been dissolved.[82]

The main basis for this assertion was that the decree in England could not support an estoppel because the court did not have jurisdiction. It is suggested that this decision is not good authority against the use of the doctrine of preclusion in the context under discussion for the following reasons. Firstly, for our purposes, the disputed decree is assumed to be valid and made with jurisdiction in the country where it is obtained and is also recognised by the law of the forum, although not the *lex successionis*. Secondly, at least two[83] of the four judges in the *Gaffney* case were concerned with the technicalities of estoppel by record. The doctrine advocated here is a flexible equitable doctrine which does not depend on the record, but on the injustice of allowing a party to obtain a pecuniary advantage because of the fortuitous fact that the decree is not recognised by the *lex successionis*.

It should be reiterated that in all four of the cases discussed above, the decree was not recognised by the law of the forum. Whereas in the "conflict of rules" situation presently under discussion, the decree is recognised by the form, not by the *lex successionis*.

The main English textwriters oppose the application of the doctrine.[84] Dicey and Morris[85] claim that the doctrine leads to the loss of "all certainty in question of matrimonial status". Cheshire and North explain that estoppel is inappropriate in the present context because –

> "the paramount issue from which all else flows is the marital status of the parties at the time of the [deceased]'s death, and of that there can be no doubt."[85a]

79 Cf Lord Merrivale's interruption (*ibid* at 58) referring to *Jenkins v Robertson* (1867) LR 1 HL Sc 117, 121. This seems to relate to the issue of whether the parties' consent to the foreign judgment created an estoppel rather than to the equitable doctrine being discussed here.

80 [1975] IR 133.

81 In fact, the husband made all the arrangements and the wife simply signed the documents as requested and attended court on the husband's instructions.

82 [1975] IR 125 at 143, per Kenny J at first instance. In the Supreme Court at 152, per Walsh J; at 154, per Henchy J and at 157, per Griffin J.

83 Griffin and Henchy JJ.

84 Cf Carter, who suggests that the use of the doctrine of estoppel "seems attractive" in the context presently under discussion in (1971) 45 BYBIL 410 at 412.

85 *Op cit* (ch 1, n 6, *supra*) at p 759.

85a *Op cit* (ch 1, n 6, *supra*) at p 688.

With respect, it is submitted that this statement oversimplifies the issue. In the present context, we already have a conflict between the recognition rules of the forum and the *lex successionis* as to the marital status of the parties at the date of death and thus it cannot be said that there is no doubt as to the marital status for the purpose of succession. That is the very matter which is in dispute. Instead we should focus on the single question of whether the "surviving spouse" should inherit. This will involve looking at the policy of the forum on this matter. If that policy dictates that the "spouse" should not inherit despite the fact that (s)he can take under the *lex successionis*,[86] there seems no reason why a discretionary doctrine of preclusion should not operate as a rule of the forum's public policy. Use of preclusion in this way does not prevent the "surviving spouse" from claiming the validity of the marriage in other contexts and therefore should not be seen as incompatible with the general principle that the existence of a matrimonial decree does not prevent either party from claiming the continued subsistence of the marriage.

B. Apply the Recognition Rule

1. Theoretical Basis

Application of the recognition rule where the decree is recognised is based on the "full effect" doctrine, in the same way as in relation to remarriage. The hypothesis is that the recognition of a decree annulling or dissolving marriage logically requires full recognition of all the consequences thereof. Thus, once a decree is recognised, the "spouse" must cease to be the spouse for all purposes,[87] including succession. However, this interpretation is open to challenge by the argument that recognition of a divorce decree is simply an acknowledgment of the change of status and does not necessarily involve acceptance that there has been any variation in the rights and obligations flowing from status.[88]

It is much more difficult to justify application of the recognition rule where it will result in non-recognition. It may be suggested that the very fact that the decree has not been recognised suggests that there has been some "unfairness" in the process of obtaining the decree[89] or in its effect.[90] Thus, it would be unfair to debar the "spouse" from inheriting as a result of that decree, even where the *lex successionis* would recognise the decree. The forum's interest is in preventing the loss of rights by means of the unfair decree.

86 Assumed here to be the applicable rule.

87 This argument is expressed in *Estin v Estin* 334 US 541, 68 S Ct 1231 (1948) as "once a divorce is granted, the whole marriage relation is dissolved, leaving no roots or tendrils of any kind".

88 See Engdahl (1969) Iowa LR 56 at 111-114. Dicey and Morris (9th edn, 1973) rule 31 distinguish between status and the results of status. See also Graveson (ch 4, n 59, *supra*).

89 Either because an unconnected forum has been chosen (ie forum shopping) or because of lack of notice or opportunity to participate.

90 Ie because its effect is manifestly contrary to public policy.

2. Authority

The New York decision in *Re Degramo's Estate* [91] has been cited[92] as authority for preferring the forum's non-recognition rule in a succession case. However, since it was held that the damages received by the deceased's estate from the railroad company responsible for her death should be distributed according to the "wrongful death" statute of the *lex loci delicti* and not according to the law governing the succession, the case should be treated as authority in relation to wrongful death claims rather than succession and will be discussed in that context below.[93]

No other authority has been found which supports preference for the recognition rule in a succession case.

3. Results

(A) WHERE THE DECREE IS RECOGNISED

The spouse will not be able to take irrespective of the circumstances surrounding the divorce and his/her connection with the forum. Thus, even a spouse who has been divorced against his/her will and perhaps without his/her knowledge in a forum with which (s)he has no connection may be prevented from receiving any share in the estate of his/her "spouse" because of the liberal recognition rules of the forum, even though the law governing the succession would award him/her such. The hardship would seem to be particularly apparent where the "spouse" is closely connected to the *lex successionis* and not at all connected to the forum.[94]

Can we assume that this problem would not arise because recognition would be refused in such a case? A formal divorce will be recognised if a relevant connection exists between *either* spouse and the country where the divorce is obtained.[95] Thus, lack of consent or connection would only seem to be relevant where they result in lack of notice or opportunity to participate. However, even these grounds are limited because the question as to whether it would have been reasonable to take steps to notify a party of the proceedings or to give a party opportunity to participate is assessed in the light of the nature of the proceedings. Thus, if a foreign system allows unilateral divorce by court order *ex parte* it is difficult to see how recognition can be refused under s 51(3)(a).[96]

Recognition may also be refused under s 51(3)(c) where recognition would be manifestly contrary to public policy. Would the fact that one party did not consent to the divorce and/or that one spouse had no connection with the jurisdiction where the divorce was obtained render recognition contrary to

91 33 New York Supplement 502 (1895).
92 Gottlieb (1977) 6 ICLQ 743 at 770.
93 At ch 7, II B 2, *infra*.
94 The case may be being heard in the forum because, for example, the executors are resident here or movables are situated here.
95 See ch 1, IV A 2, *supra*.
96 And the better view seems to be that in such cases, lack of notice should not be a ground for refusal of recognition on the ground of public policy. See Gordon (ch 1, n 39, *supra*) at pp 134-135 and *D v D (Recognition of Foreign Divorce)* [1994] 1 FLR 38 at 52.

public policy? In *Chaudhary v Chaudhary*,[97] Ormrod LJ said that it was against public policy in a case where both parties were domiciled in England to allow one to avoid the incidents of his/her domiciliary law by travelling abroad to a country whose laws appeared to be more favourable to him/her. It is far from clear that this would be the case where the parties were domiciled abroad as there would be no "evasion" of English law. Also, the concern here was that the husband would be avoiding his financial obligations by obtaining a divorce in a particular jurisdiction. In the case of succession, the deprivation of the surviving spouse's inheritance rights occurs as a result of the divorce *per se* and not as a result of the divorce in a particular jurisdiction. However, where the surviving "spouse" has not obtained any financial relief following divorce because it was obtained in an inappropriate jurisdiction, it may be against public policy now to deprive him/her also of any rights to succession on death.

In deciding whether to exercise their discretion to refuse recognition where the grounds under s 51(3)(a) or (c) are satisfied, the courts take into account all the surrounding circumstances including –

> "an assessment of what the legitimate objectives of the petitioning spouse are, and to what extent those objectives can be achieved if the foreign decree remains valid."[98]

In two cases,[99] recognition has been refused where it would prevent the petitioner from obtaining financial relief. By analogy, "unfair"[100] deprivation of the wife of inheritance from an estate would be a factor in favour of exercising the discretion to refuse recognition. However, as against this, courts also have to consider other aspects[101] of the effects of non-recognition, including "the likely consequences to the spouses and any children of the family . . . if recognition would be refused".[102]

Since one of the spouses is dead and the other relies on the lack of validity of the decree, there should not be any adverse consequences to the spouses provided that the validity of a subsequent remarriage of the deceased can be recognised in accordance with the rule recommended in Chapter 4. Where the

97 [1985] Fam 19.

98 *Newmarch v Newmarch* [1978] Fam 79 at 95.

99 *Joyce v Joyce* [1979] Fam 93 and *Mamdani v Mamdani* [1984] FLR 699. These cases both involved lack of opportunity to participate. They would probably be decided differently today because even if the foreign decree where recognised the wife could claim financial provision in England under the Matrimonial and Family Proceedings Act 1984 (see ch 6, I A, *infra*).

100 Because no other provision had been made in circumstances where it was reasonable for such provision to be made. Sometimes it may still be possible to claim financial provision ancillary to the matrimonial decree from the estate in the country where the divorce was obtained. In English law, an application for financial relief is not a cause of action which survives for or against a party's estate. See Bromley and Lowe, *Bromley's Family Law* (8th edn, 1992) p 652. Thus no order could be made for relief after a foreign divorce under the Matrimonial and Family Proceedings Act 1984, Part III after the death of either party.

101 The courts seem reluctant to exercise their discretion to refuse recognition because of concerns about comity. See, eg, *Newmarch v Newmarch* [1978] Fam 79.

102 *Ibid* at 95.

refusal of recognition would affect the validity of the subsequent marriage,[103] the situation may be more problematic.[104] The children may, of course, be affected if their share of the estate will decrease if the first spouse can claim, but this is not a factor of any weight.

In conclusion, whilst one of the "non-recognition" rules may operate where recognition would result in "unfair" disinheritance, this result cannot be guaranteed.

(B) WHERE THE DECREE IS NOT RECOGNISED

If the recognition rule is preferred, non-recognition by the forum will allow the "spouse" to inherit. However, as we have seen, the policy behind the non-recognition rule may not require that both spouses should retain succession rights. A divorce will usually be refused recognition in order to protect the respondent.[105] Thus, whilst it might[106] be unfair to debar the respondent from succeeding to the deceased petitioner's estate, it is less likely to be unfair to debar the petitioner from succeeding to the respondent's estate. On the contrary, it might seem unfair to allow the petitioner to inherit in this situation.

Again, the doctrine of preclusion might be used here in order to prevent succession by the unmeritorious by preventing the claimant spouse from attacking the decree. The use of the doctrine is more difficult to justify in this context than previously because here it is the forum which refuses recognition. The effect of application of the doctrine is to give some validity to the decree in direct conflict with the non-recognition by the forum.[107] However, it is submitted that the situation can still be distinguished from the cases in which the use of the doctrine has been expressly or impliedly rejected, because there is already a dispute as to the validity of the decree. The effect of the operation of the doctrine is in fact to prefer the choice of law rule by way of exception to a principle of preference in favour of the recognition rule of the forum.

C. The "Differential Rule"

1. Theoretical Basis

In relation to validity of remarriage, the theoretical basis of the "differential rule" was stated to be that the "full effect" doctrine only applies where the decree is recognised and that otherwise the arguments in favour of application of the choice of law rule prevail.[108] The same basis is applicable here with the

103 Where the decree is not recognised by the *lex domicilli*, non-recognition by the forum will result in invalidation of the second marriage (there is no "conflict of rules" and s 50 of the Family Law Act 1986 does not apply).

104 Although in *Joyce v Joyce* [1979] Fam 93 Lane J held that the disadvantage to the wife of not having any share in the matrimonial home outweighed the disadvantage to the husband of non-recognition, despite the fact that the husband had remarried on the strength of the decree.

105 See ch 2, IV C, *supra*.

106 But not if the respondent has already received adequate provision.

107 See Battersby's first criticism at text accompanying n 67, *supra*.

108 Chapter 4, II C 2(D) and 3, *supra*.

caveat that the application of the "full effect" doctrine is more controversial in relation to termination of the first spouse's succession rights.[109]

2. *Result*

Since the divorce is always recognised, the "spouse" will be debarred from inheritance in every case.

D. Upholding Succession Rights

It has already been submitted that the key issue in relation to succession should not be seen as the continued validity of the first marriage, but rather whether the "former spouse" should inherit. Thus, a principle based upon the presumption of validity of marriage[110] is not appropriate to decide this question.

Here, it is suggested that a similar approach of validating rights would lead to a presumption of upholding succession rights for "spouses", where it would not be unfair to do so. Such an expressly result selecting preference rule could take the form of a presumption in favour of the application of whichever law resulted in succession by the "spouse". The presumption might be rebutted in circumstances where the doctrine of preclusion would estop the claimant from relying on the invalidity of the decree.

III. POLICY

An examination of the English domestic rules relating to succession by spouses under will, on intestacy and by court-ordered family provision is required in order to ascertain the relevant forum policy.

A. Wills

In interpreting a will, the policy of the law is to give effect to the intention of the testator.[111] This can be illustrated by s 18A of the Wills Act 1837 (as amended by the Family Law Act 1986), which provides that where a marriage has been terminated by a divorce or annulment which is entitled to recognition in England and Wales under the Family Law Act 1986: (i) an appointment of the former spouse as an executor is deemed to be omitted; and (ii) any devise/bequest to a former spouse lapses except in so far as contrary intention appears from the will.

The rationale behind this provision must be that a former spouse should not benefit from a will made before divorce[112] because it is assumed[113] that the

109 See at B 1, *supra*.
110 See ch 4, II D, *supra*.
111 See Clark and Ross Martyn, *Theobald on Wills* (15th edn, 1993) at p 199.
112 See Law Reform Committee's 22nd Report, "Making and Revocation of Wills" (1980) Cmnd 7902 and the Law Commission Consultation Paper, "The effect of Divorce on Wills" (1992), which recommends changing the method of giving effect to this policy.
113 The exceptional case is covered by the proviso that the provision does not apply where a contrary intention appears.

testator did not wish to benefit the former spouse, but simply forgot to change his will.[114]

It is not entirely clear when this provision of domestic English law will be applicable in a case involving a foreign element. If the provision is considered to relate to a question of interpretation, then it will apply if it was the law which the testator intended to govern the will. This would be presumed to be English law where the testator was domiciled in England *at the time of making of the will.*[115] If it is regarded as an issue of essential validity, then the provision will be applied in relation to immovables situated in England and in relation to movables where the testator died domiciled in England.

B. Provision for Dependants

1. The Scheme of the 1975 Act

Under the Inheritance (Provision for Family and Dependants) Act 1975, the court has discretion to award financial provision from a deceased's estate in favour of a spouse or former spouse where the effect of the deceased's will and/or the laws of intestacy is such that reasonable financial provision has not been made for the claimant. In the case of a former spouse, the reasonable financial provision is restricted to such financial provision as "it would be reasonable in all the circumstances of the case for the applicant to receive for his maintenance".[116] In the case of a surviving spouse,[117] reasonable financial provision is such provision as "it would be reasonable in all the circumstances of the case for a husband or wife to receive, whether or not that provision is required for his or her maintenance".[118]

In the latter case, in deciding whether provision is reasonable, the court must take into account how much the applicant might have expected to receive if the marriage had been terminated by divorce instead of by death.[119]

Where the deceased died within 12 months of the matrimonial decree and the application for financial provision has not been made or has not been determined by the date of death, the court may, if it thinks it just to do so, treat the former spouse as a surviving spouse for the purpose of determining reasonable financial provision under the Act.[120] The Act applies wherever the deceased died domiciled in England and Wales.[121] However, in applying the Act, the

114 In Parliament, the Lord Chancellor said, "At present, divorce has no effect on a will and thus there can be unintended results where a testator who does not remarry fails to make a new will". (428 HL Debs Administration of Justice Bill, 8 March 1982, col 31).

115 See n 7, *supra*.

116 Inheritance (Provision for Family and Dependants) Act 1975, s 1(2)(b).

117 Unless there was a decree of judicial separation in force.

118 Inheritance (Provision for Family and Dependants) Act 1975, s 1(2)(a).

119 *Ibid*, s 3(2).

120 *Ibid*, s 14.

121 *Ibid*, s 1.

court is applying domestic English law rules as the *lex fori*.[122] Thus, no "conflict of rules" problem can arise.

2. Former Spouses

"Former spouse" was originally defined to include only those whose marriages have been dissolved or annulled under the Matrimonial Causes Act 1973. Thus, those who had obtained a matrimonial decree abroad which was recognised in England and Wales could not claim under the category of former spouse. Three reasons were given for this exclusion in the Law Commission Report[123] which preceded the 1975 Act:

(i) It is not appropriate for English courts to interfere where a foreign law has decided financial provision.
(ii) Where the former spouse is still dependent on the deceased (s)he can claim as a dependent under s 1(1)(e) of the 1975 Act.
(iii) In order to extend the definition it would have been necessary to cover the whole question of financial provision in England after the dissolution or annulment of a marriage abroad.

The first and third reasons could no longer be sustained once legislation to provide financial provision after a foreign matrimonial decree was proposed by the Law Commission. Thus, it was recommended[124] that the definition of "former" spouse be widened to include those whose divorce or annulment was recognised. This recommendation was implemented in the Matrimonial and Family Proceedings Act 1984.[125]

Perhaps the most interesting aspect of this legislation for our purposes is the recognition that a former spouse, wherever the decree was obtained, may have a legitimate claim for maintenance from the estate of the testator.[126] Thus, the legislature has made it plain that there is a continuing obligation to provide for a former spouse unless there is a court order made at the time of the financial provision order on divorce barring an order on death.[127]

It was made clear by the Court of Appeal in *Re Fullard*[128] that there would be few situations in which a successful claim could be made by a former spouse, since in most cases, (s)he will have already received all that (s)he is entitled to

122 In relation to movables, English law will also be the *lex successionis*. The issue of whether an order can be made in respect of immovables situated abroad has not come before the English courts. It would appear that there would be jurisdiction to hear the case under the 1975 Act provided that the deceased died domiciled in England and Wales. The first exception to the *Mocambique* Rule (see Cheshire and North (ch 1, n 6, *supra*) at pp 255-256) should be applicable as the action is founded on the obligation of the deceased. However, Commonwealth courts have consistently refused to make such orders under similar family provision legislation. See cases cited by Miller (1990) 39 ICLQ 261 at 271.

123 Law Comm No 61, para 45 *et seq*.

124 Law Comm WP 77 and Rept No 117.

125 Section 25(2), amending the Inheritance (Provision for Family and Dependants) Act 1975, s 25(1).

126 Provided, of course, that the testator dies domiciled in England and Wales.

127 Inheritance (Provision for Family and Dependants) Act 1975, s 15. Following the substitution of this section by the Matrimonial and Family Proceedings Act 1984, s 8, such an order can be made without the consent of the parties.

128 [1981] 2 All ER 796.

at the time of the decree. This would not be the case, however, where there have been insufficient assets at the time to provide adequately for the claimant and following death a capital sum has been released,[129] which will enable the claimant to be maintained. Alternatively, if the claimant is dependent on unsecured maintenance which ends on death, if there is sufficient capital in the estate this can be used to ensure continuation of the maintenance. It is also possible to envisage cases where the claimant was badly advised and did not pursue his/her right to maintenance at the time of the decree. Depending on the other claims on the estate, it might be appropriate for maintenance to be paid to the former spouse out of the estate.

3. The Rationale Behind Discretionary Family Provision for Spouses and Former Spouses

The rationale behind the present discretionary family provision for spouses and former spouses can be seen to be twofold. Firstly, a person's obligation to his/her spouse does not end on death. The family is still treated as the main support unit even once a provider has died. Thus, where (s)he is able, a testator should make provision for the other family members and should not leave his/her dependants, including spouses and, where appropriate, ex-spouses to rely upon the state for support. Where (s)he has failed to do so, the law will do so for him/her.

Secondly, in relation to spouses, discretionary family provision is needed to enable the inequities caused by the system of separation of property to be counter-balanced.[130] Where spouses have both contributed in different ways to the acquisition of assets, their respective contributions may well not be properly reflected in the legal and beneficial ownership of those assets. Typically, men who earn outside the home tend to own more of the assets, whereas women who have contributed to the family in the home whether financially or otherwise tend to own fewer of the assets. Discretionary family provision on death, just like property adjustment on divorce,[131] enables a court to make provision for the survivor[132] which will reflect these contributions.[133]

The second reason explains why the level of provision which may be made for a wife is higher than for other dependents. This reason does not apply to a former spouse because it is assumed that there will have been financial provision at the time of the decree.[134] Where for some reason adequate provision

129 Eg, under life insurance or pension policies.

130 See Miller (1986) 102 LQR 445.

131 See *Wachtel v Wachtel* [1973] 2 WLR 366. The Law Commission decided that the widening of family provision on death for a spouse to be akin to that on divorce made it unnecessary to introduce fixed rights of inheritance for a spouse. The *Wachtel* approach meant that the wife would usually get one third, which was what they had suggested would be the appropriate fixed share: Law Com No 52, para 44

132 Usually the wife, but cf *Re Moody* [1992] 2 All ER 524, where a widower successfully claimed under the Act against his deceased wife's estate. He was allowed to continue to live in the matrimonial home which had belonged to the deceased.

133 Cf *Stead v Stead* [1985] FLR 16, where the award was small and did not reflect the contributions. See criticism by Miller (1986) 102 LQR 445 at 467.

134 That this is so is apparent from the s 14 of the 1975 Act (see text at n 120, *supra*).

has not been made at the time of a decree, an award restricted[135] to maintenance may still be available on death.

4. *Fixed Share Schemes*

Some laws[136] ensure proper provision for dependents by setting down fixed amounts or fixed shares[137] which have to be bequeathed to each category of relative on death.[138] If a will fails to make the required provision, it will automatically be varied so as to do so.

The Law Commission[139] considered the possibility of introducing a fixed share scheme in England. However, they preferred to extend the discretionary scheme because of its flexibility.[140] However, it is clear that the two alternative schemes were simply treated as different methods of implementing the policy of making provision for dependants and thus the rationale for making such provision in relation to spouses should be the same as that identified above.

C. Intestacy

1. *The Present Scheme*

At present, on intestacy the surviving spouse receives:

(i) all the chattels; and
(ii) if there are no surviving issue, parents or siblings of the whole blood, the whole estate; or
(iii) if there are issue, a statutory legacy of £125,000 and life interest in half of the rest of the deceased's property; or
(iv) if there are no issue, but parents or siblings (or their issue), a statutory legacy of £200,000 and half of the rest absolutely.[141]

Under the Matrimonial Homes Act 1952 a surviving spouse is entitled to insist that the matrimonial home is appropriated to him/her towards any absolute interest which (s)he has in the estate. Where the value of the matrimonial home is more than the surviving spouse's absolute interest in the estate, (s)he can make up the difference from his/her own resources. In many cases, the matrimonial home will be held in joint names and therefore will pass to the surviving spouse under the principle of survivorship.

135 Unless the case comes within s 14 of the Act (see text at n 120, *supra*).
136 Eg, in Scotland, the surviving spouse has a right to one third of the deceased's movable estate if there are issue of the deceased surviving and otherwise to one half (see Scottish Law Com No 124, para 3.1), In the United States, most separate property states give the surviving spouse a fixed share or fixed sum (see Miller (1990) 39 ICLQ 261).
137 Sometimes referred to as "forced shares" or "non-barrable interests".
138 In community systems, there are usually fixed shares for descendents. See, eg, French Civil Code, art 913, which reserves two-thirds of the estate for the children where there are two children. For Italian law see *Re Ross* [1930] 1 Ch 377; for Swiss law see *Re Trufort* (1887) 36 Ch D 600.
139 Law Com No 52, paras 31-45.
140 Cf Scottish Law Com No 124 at paras 3.3 *et seq*, where the Scottish Law Commission considered the same issue and came to the opposite conclusion.
141 Both of the sums were increased by SI 1993/2906, which came into effect from 1 December 1993.

The Law Commission of England and Wales has recently produced a working paper[142] and report[143] considering reform of the intestacy rules. They recommended *inter alia* that on intestacy a surviving spouse should receive the whole estate.[144]

2. The Policy Behind Intestacy Provision for Spouses

Whilst the Law Commission's main proposals have not been adopted by the government, their discussion forms a useful basis for the consideration of the policy behind the present law. In the Working Paper,[145] four possible bases on which intestacy law might be based are mooted. These are:

(i) presumed wishes of the deceased deduced from the provisions that the average testator makes in his will;
(ii) provision to those who are most likely to have the greatest need;
(iii) provision according to desert;
(iv) provision according to length of the cohabitation during the marriage.

In their Report,[146] the Commission state that their proposed reforms are based on two "considerations". The first is the need for certain, clear and simple rules. The second, which is more relevant for our purposes and upon which it is claimed consultees agreed, is the "need to ensure that the surviving spouse receives adequate provision". This can be seen to correspond roughly to the second of the bases in the Working Paper. Thus, it is submitted that whilst it is alleged[147] that consultation produced "no agreement upon the single most appropriate principle to be applied", the Commission itself has chosen provision for the surviving spouse to be the most important policy objective of intestacy law. This conclusion is clearly supported by the recommendation in the Report that the surviving spouse should take the whole estate. For what it is worth, over 70% of the respondents in the Law Commission's public opinion survey supported the surviving spouse receiving all, even where there were children.[148]

Whilst the Law Commission's views cannot be regarded as representing domestic policy as they have not been adopted, it is suggested that in fact the present law to a large extent supports their view that the most important purpose of the law of intestacy is to make adequate provision for a surviving spouse. Whilst the Law Commission argue that the present law does not actually do this at the moment in all cases,[149] it is still clear that in the majority of cases the

142 Law Com WP No 108.
143 Law Com No 187.
144 Cf Scottish Law Com No 124, in which the continuation of the scheme of a statutory legacy for the spouse was recommended.
145 Law Com WP No 108, Part IV.
146 Law Com No 187, paras 24-26.
147 *Ibid*, para 24.
148 Law Com No 187, Appendix C, para 2.8.
149 Where the matrimonial home is not jointly owned, the rules on intestacy will often result in a surviving wife receiving less than (s)he would on divorce.

surviving spouse will receive the whole of or at least a very substantial proportion of the estate.[150]

It is suggested that the reasons for the policy of giving priority to the surviving spouse are the same as the reasons put forward above[151] for the court's discretion to award financial provision to a surviving spouse where reasonable provision has not been made. It should be remembered that that discretion extends to cases where the rules of intestacy do not make adequate provision for the surviving spouse.

IV. APPLICATION OF POLICY

Having identified the policy of English law in relation to inheritance by spouses in purely domestic cases, we need to see how this policy applies in relation to cases which have a foreign element and where there is a dispute about the validity of the decree between the forum and the *lex successionis*.

A. Wills

We have seen that it is axiomatic that in interpreting a will the aim is to uphold the wishes of the testator. Thus, it could be argued that where there is a will, whether a "spouse" should be considered to be a spouse should be decided in the way in which the testator would have wished.

1. Where the Testator is the Other "Spouse"

Where there has been a divorce, judicial separation or nullity decree pronounced, unless there was evidence that the testator did not accept the validity of the decree, it must be presumed that (s)he did not intend the person whom (s)he considered to be his/her "former spouse" to inherit. This seems to be the assumption behind the Wills Act 1837, s 18A, as amended.

The policy behind this statutory provision can be achieved for cases where English law is not the *lex causae* by selecting a preference rule which will result in disinheritance. Thus, the "differential rule"[152] is appropriate.

2. The Testator is a Third Party

What happens where the will of a third party confers a benefit on the spouse of X and there has been a matrimonial decree between X and his/her spouse the validity of which is in dispute between the *lex causae* and the forum? It is not quite so clear that the testator did not intend the "spouse" to take. The existence of an invalid decree might not affect his/her wish to benefit the "spouse". But which law should decide whether the decree is valid? It is suggested that the

150 The recent increase in the size of the statutory legacy from £85,000 to £125,000 may be thought to reflect the Law Commission's favoured policy, especially in view of the fact that house prices have not risen at all, and in many cases have fallen, in England in recent years.

151 At B 3, *supra*.

152 See at II C, *supra*.

issue of validity should so far as possible be seen through the eyes of the testator.

In this situation, it would seem that application of the law of the testator's domicile at the time of making the will, as the law governing interpretation, is more likely to reflect the testator's intention than his domicile at the date of death. Against this, it might be argued that the reason that the testator desisted in changing his/her will before death was because (s)he relied on the view taken by the law of his/her domicile at that time as to the validity of the decree. Both positions involve an element of speculation. It is suggested that since the choice of law rule for interpretation of a will is the same for movables and immovables it will be convenient to apply that rule.

Should the doctrine of preclusion apply in this situation? In *Re Jones*,[153] it was held *obiter* that it should. Battersby[154] disagrees on the basis that the doctrine is too blunt an instrument to produce rational results in the context of wills. He suggests that problems in relation to wills can be solved as questions of construction. This might help in determining whether a gift to "the spouse of X" was meant to refer to the first spouse in relation to whom there had been an invalid decree or the second spouse where the validity of the marriage was in doubt. However, it would not help if X had not remarried. There is only one possible "spouse" of X and yet if the decree is valid, the gift lapses. However, the writer agrees with Battersby that preclusion is inappropriate here because the testator's intention is not known.

Therefore, it is submitted that the best alternative is to assume that the testator's definition of spouse is the same as the *lex causae*, which should be treated as being the law governing interpretation of the will.

B. Provision for Dependents

1. Discretionary Schemes[155]

It will usually be necessary to determine whether the first marriage has been terminated either because the foreign scheme does not provide for ex-spouses or because there is a different level of provision for spouses and ex-spouses, as in the English scheme.

We saw above that English policy requires that proper provision should be made for both spouses and former spouses. Thus, we should apply whichever rule will enable the "spouse" to obtain the higher level of provision. We saw above that this would be achieved by a presumption in favour of upholding succession rights of spouses. Since the provision is discretionary, the court will only make an order in favour of a "spouse" who is meritorious. Thus, for example, no order will be made where the "spouse" has already been adequately provided for in divorce proceedings.

153 (1961) 25 DLR (2d) (BC Sup Ct) 595 upheld (1962) 31 DLR (2d) 292 (Sup Ct Canada).
154 (1977) 16 UWOnt 163 at 177.
155 It will be remembered that we are assuming that an English court would be prepared to apply a foreign discretionary scheme: see I C, *supra*.

2. *Fixed Share Schemes*[156]

It is quite conceivable that an English court would be faced with a case where a foreign will fails to provide the fixed amount specified by the *lex succesionis* for a "spouse". The personal representatives argue that there has been a divorce and so the "spouse" is not entitled to the fixed share and the "spouse" argues that the divorce is not valid.

Since the rationale behind such fixed shares is assumed to be the same as that behind the discretionary system,[157] the same policy should in principle be applicable. Thus, the preference rule would be the presumption in favour of upholding succession rights of spouses.

The main problems with this solution is that the fixed share system does not have the same safeguards against abuse as the English law discretionary system. The latter can ensure that unmeritorious claimants do not succeed and that, for example, a spouse who has obtained financial provision following a matrimonial decree cannot have a "second bite of the cherry";[158] whereas under the fixed share system the "spouse" would take automatically under the proposed preference rule.

It is suggested that to some extent these safeguards might be provided by a limited use of the doctrine of preclusion, under which a "spouse" who had already received financial provision could not rely on the invalidity of the decree in order to claim a fixed share on death. It will be seen that such a limited use of the doctrine of preclusion avoids the main criticisms of that doctrine.[159] In particular, it is irrelevant whether the claimant petitioned for the decree or participated in the proceedings. The operation of the doctrine is not based on a vague notion that the "spouse's" involvement in the proceedings is inconsistent with claiming a pecuniary benefit, but on the specific principle that since the "spouse" has obtained adequate provision on an alleged termination of the marriage, (s)he cannot now claim more provision on the real termination of the marriage by death.

This solution would also deal with the difficulty which may arise where the parties were subject to a community of property regime, but the *lex successionis* is a separate property system. Thus, where the community property has already been divided on termination of the marriage by matrimonial decree, the "surviving spouse" should be precluded from relying on the invalidity of the decree in order to claim a fixed share in the succession, because (s)he has already had the benefit of the operation of the marital property regime.[160]

156 See II B 4, *supra*.
157 *Ibid*.
158 See *Re Fullard* [1982] Fam 42.
159 See at II A 4 (C), *supra*.
160 The purpose of community property interests and fixed shares are essentially the same (see Marsh, *Marital Property in the Conflict of Laws* (1952) at p 245). The problem of "over-protection" or "under-protection" as a result of migration from a community state to a separate property state or vice versa is well documented (see, eg Marsh, *ibid*; McClanahan, *Community Property Law in the United States* (1982) at ch 13; and Miller (1990) 39 ICLQ 261, 263-267).

Thus it is suggested that in relation to fixed shares, the presumption of upholding succession rights of spouses should apply subject to the limited operation of preclusion doctrine. Whilst this will clearly not provide the same flexibility as the discretionary system, it is suggested that it is the preference rule which most closely reflects domestic policy.

C. Intestacy

We saw above that the rationale behind the law in respect of spouses on intestacy was in reality the same as that for the discretionary family provision. Thus, we would expect that the same preference rule would be appropriate. Two particular points should be made to support this hypothesis.

Firstly, the policy of providing for spouses is not limited to spouses who are still living in marital harmony. Thus, the mere fact of separation without any decree does not prevent a spouse claiming the full share on intestacy. This approach was endorsed by the Law Commission.[161] Secondly, the policy of providing for spouses on intestacy should apply to all spouses who have not been provided for at the time of a matrimonial decree. This result can be ensured by applying the doctrine of preclusion to those for whom adequate provision has already been made. The comments about this doctrine[162] made in relation to fixed shares are equally applicable here.

161 Law Com No 187, para 39.
162 At text accompanying n 159, *supra*.

Chapter 6

Matrimonial Property

I. THE SCOPE OF THE PROBLEM

A. Introduction

Where there is a disagreement between the *lex fori* and the law governing the matrimonial property relations of the party as to whether a matrimonial decree should be recognised, there may be a conflict about the matrimonial property rights of the parties. The recognition or otherwise of the decree may affect the question of whether property acquired after the decree falls within the matrimonial regime and who has control over the property included within the regime.

At the outset, we should emphasise that the English court will generally not be concerned with establishing the spouses' respective rights under a foreign matrimonial property regime if it has jurisdiction to make a financial provision order under the English discretionary distribution scheme. Such jurisdiction will exist automatically where the English court has granted the matrimonial decree.[1] Applications for financial relief following a recognised foreign formal divorce may be made with the leave of the court where the jurisdictional requirements of s 15 of the Matrimonial and Family Proceedings Act 1984 are satisfied.[2] In this situation, the "conflict of rules" problem will not arise because it is clear that the scheme only applies where English law recognises the foreign divorce. Thus, the court is only likely to be concerned with determining rights under foreign matrimonial property regimes on death, on bankruptcy of one of the parties or on marriage breakdown where the English scheme is not applicable.[3]

We will have to spend more time than in previous chapters defining the scope of the problem for two reasons. Firstly, the choice of law rule is not clearly established. Secondly, there has been little discussion of the conflict of laws treatment of deferred community of property regimes and equitable distribution schemes.

1 Unless the application for financial relief is made after the petitioner has remarried.

2 Where either party was domiciled or habitually resident in England for one year at the time of the application or at the time when the foreign divorce was obtained or either has a beneficial interest in possession in a dwelling-house in England and Wales.

3 Eg, where the parties do not wish to take matrimonial proceedings; after a foreign decree which is not recognised or where the applicant spouse has remarried before applying for financial provision.

B. The Choice of Law Rule

Traditionally, choice of law rules in respect of matrimonial property have been classified into cases where there is a marriage contract and where there is none. However, this distinction has been criticised by a number of writers who claim that all matrimonial property regimes are contractual. Upon marriage, they are either expressly or impliedly agreed by the parties or are presumed by law. According to the proponents[4] of this contractual analysis, there is a presumption, in the absence of an express or implied contract, that the parties have agreed on the application of the basic regime imposed by the law of the husband's domicile.[5] This presumed contract, like express and implied contracts, is governed by its proper law.[6]

The contractual analysis has a number of attractions. Firstly, it protects the justified expectations of the spouses.[7] Secondly, it avoids the problems of devising an appropriate choice of law rule. Thirdly, the use of the proper law provides flexibility.[8] Fourthly, it would seem that the proper law applies to both movables and immovables. Finally, as we shall see, it can be applied more easily to diverse types of matrimonial property regimes.

However, the dual classification is too entrenched to be ignored. The choice of law rule in cases where there is no express or implied contract would seem to be the law of the matrimonial domicile, at least in relation to movables. Ownership of immovables would seem to be governed by the *lex situs*.[9]

According to case law, the matrimonial domicile is presumed to be the husband's domicile at the date of the marriage.[10] The problem of ascertaining the matrimonial domicile following the abolition of the wife's dependent domicile has not been judicially considered. The Hague Convention on the Law Applicable to Matrimonial Property Regimes (1978) attempts to solve the problem by providing the law of the common habitual residence[11] of the parties after marriage[12] as the governing law, in the absence of designation by the

4 Goldberg (1970) 19 ICLQ 557 and Castel, *Canadian Conflict of Laws* vol 2 (1977) at p 422 and (1982) 60 Can Bar Rev 180.

5 In the recent British Columbian case of *Tezcan v Tezcan* (1992) 87 DLR (4th) 503, it was held that whether there was a contract or not was a question for the law which would be the proper law if there were a contract. In this case, Turkish law held there was no contract.

6 Where there is such an agreement, the rights of the parties are governed by the proper law of such agreement (as determined at common law because the Rome Convention is inapplicable (art. 1(2)(b))).

7 Castel, *Canadian Conflict of Laws* vol 2 (1977) at p 422.

8 Eg, where the spouses have separate domiciles.

9 *Welsh v Tennant* [1891] AC 639; *Tezcan v Tezcan* (1992) 87 DLR (4th) 503. This would seem to be unsatisfactory for the same reasons that the scission between movables and immovables for succession is unsatisfactory (see ch 5, n 8, *supra)*. In particular, the spouses' property relationship could be governed by a number of different regimes if they own immovable property in several different jurisdictions. On the other hand, at least the *lex situs* is always certain. Maybe this is why it has been adopted statutorily as the choice of law rule in, eg, Nova Scotia (Matrimonial Property Act 1980, s 22) and New Zealand (Matrimonial Property Act 1976, s 7).

10 *Re Egerton's Will Trusts* [1956] Ch 593. As we have seen, the proponents of the contractual analysis take a different view about the nature of the presumption referred to here.

11 Article 4.

12 See also the Ontario Family Law Act 1986, s 15 and the Nova Scotia Matrimonial Property Act, s 22, which prescribe the last common habitual residence of the spouses.

spouses. However, as this Convention has not been signed by the United Kingdom, it is necessary to find a solution based on the traditional domicile rule.

Two suggestions have appeared in recent publications. The editors of the latest edition of *Dicey and Morris* have proposed that where the spouses have separate domiciles –

> "the applicable law should be that of the country with which the parties and the marriage have the closest connection, equal weight being given to connections with each party." [13]

Davie[14] suggests adopting the United States approach, under which the law of the domicile of the person who acquired the property applies.

With respect, the former is to be preferred. One of the rationales for matrimonial property regimes is that the spouses' rights should not depend on acquisition. If the assets acquired by each party are subject to different regimes, anomalous results may be produced. The main defect in Dicey and Morris's formulation is the lack of certainty of the unstructured proper law test. It is suggested that this may be alleviated by the use of presumptions.[15]

English case law has not finally established[16] whether the governing law changes with a change of domicile by one or both parties. However, the majority of academic opinion[17] seems to favour the North American[18] system of partial mutability under which the law of the new domicile will govern subject to vested rights which have already been acquired under the law of the previous domicile.

The problem of change of domicile is made considerably more complicated by the wife's independent domicile. Most writers point out that one spouse should not be able to upset the whole matrimonial property regime by a unilateral change of domicile.[19] The proper law formula suggested by Dicey and Morris should avoid such difficulties. Whilst change of domicile of one of the

13 Dicey and Morris (ch 1, n 6, *supra*) at p 1069.
14 (1993) 42 ICLQ 855 at 875.
15 Analogous to those in the Rome Convention, art 4. For example, there could be a presumption that the marriage is most closely connected to the country where the parties have or had their last matrimonial home.
16 For discussion of the apparently conflicting case law see Davie (1993) 42 ICLQ 855 at 876-880 and Dicey and Morris (ch 1, n 6, *supra*) at pp 1082-1086.
17 Cheshire and North (ch 1, n 6, *supra*) at p 871; Morris (ch 1, n 6, *supra*) at p 370; Dicey and Morris, *The Conflict of Laws* (11th edn, 1987) rule 156 supported by Collier (ch 1, n 145, *supra*) pp. 283-284. (However, in the 12th edn (1993), Dicey and Morris have adopted the immutability rule in rule 152.) Under the contractual analysis, the spouses can change the matrimonial regime by express agreement.
18 Scoles and Hay (ch 4, n 18, *supra*) write at p 461: "The cases in the United States are quite uniform in applying the law of the marital domicile at the time the property is acquired, but respect the continued existence of marital rights acquired during an earlier domicile elsewhere." For Canada, see *Re Heung Won Lee* (1963) 36 DLR (2d) 177 at 183-184.
19 Eg, Cheshire and North (ch 1, n 6, *supra*) at p 872. It might be noted that under English law, the spouses could acquire different domiciles while still living happily together, if upon losing their common domicile of choice, they did not acquire a new domicile of choice but both reverted to their respective domiciles of origin.

parties will clearly be relevant, if the other spouse has no connection with the new domicile it will be unlikely to be the most connected law.

Whilst we should bear in mind the difficulties with the choice of law rule, in order to concentrate on the problems with which we are dealing, we will assume that the spouses have a common domicile at all relevant times, unless the contrary is stated.

C. Different Types of Matrimonial Regime

We will now examine how, if at all, the "conflict of rules" problem may arise in respect of different types of matrimonial property regime. We shall use the traditional division into three basic types of regimes: separate property regimes, immediate community regimes and deferred community regimes. We shall also consider whether discretionary distribution[20] schemes operating on divorce can be considered as a fourth type of regime. However, we should be aware of the limitations of this classification. Firstly, there are so many variations in individual regimes that, as Wolff[21] said, "a general survey can do no more than describe the fundamental types ignoring the deviations between them".

Secondly, reforms in recent years have to a large extent blurred the distinctions between separate and community schemes.[22]

1. Separate Property Regimes

Under separate property systems,[23] neither party has any rights in the property of the other by virtue of the marriage. The rules to be used to determine their respective beneficial interests in property where the legal title is vested in one or both spouses are the same[24] before, during and after their marriage. Thus the recognition or otherwise of the decree is irrelevant to the ownership of property and the "conflict of rules" problem cannot arise. We shall consider below to what extent if at all the introduction of a scheme for apportioning the assets on termination of the marriage affects this conclusion.

2. Immediate Community Regimes

(A) THE VARIOUS SCHEMES

Common to all types of immediate community regime is the fact that during the marriage the property which is included within the scheme is owned jointly by the spouses.

20 These are generally called "equitable" distribution schemes in the US, but the adjective "discretionary", which is used in England is more appropriate (see Glendon, *New Family and New Property* (1981) at p 64).

21 Wolff, *Private International Law* (2nd edn, 1950) at p 353.

22 See Glendon (n 20, *supra*) at p 58 and Rheinstein and Glendon *International Encyclopedia of Comparative Law* (1980), vol iv, ch 4 at p 170.

23 Examples of completely separate property states are Muslim countries such as Turkey (see *Tezcan v Tezcan* (1992) 87 DLR (4th) 503) and Iran (see *Vladi v Vladi* (1987) 39 DLR (4th) 563).

24 Although certain presumptions may apply during the marriage, such as the presumption of advancement. It is suggested that the fact that there has been a divorce or nullity decree, whether recognised or not, would usually be sufficient to rebut the presumption. Thus, the issue of recognition would not of itself be decisive as to ownership.

The differences lie in three main aspects of the regimes. Firstly, which property[25] is subject to the regime? In particular, pre-marital property and post-marital gifts and inheritances are excluded from "acquests" regimes. But there are a number of different permutations. Secondly, who has the right to deal with the community during the continuation of the marriage? Traditionally, the husband had sole control, but this power has been substantially eroded in many community systems.[26]

Thirdly, how are the assets divided on divorce?[27] Originally, each spouse simply retained his/her undivided half share in each asset. Where possible, the assets were physically divided and otherwise they could be sold and the proceeds divided. This is called the "item theory". In modern times, the assets are usually divided between the parties by agreement or, failing consensus, by a court. Some systems,[28] still clinging to the philosophy of the "item theory", provide that this partition has retroactive effect to the date of divorce. Other systems[29] have abandoned the "item theory" in favour of the "aggregate theory", in which they work out an equal division of all the assets. Ownership changes from the date of the division. Some community states[30] have gone a step further and moved from equal division to equitable division. Others[31] have simply given the court power to depart from equal division where this would lead to injustice.

(B) THE "CONFLICT OF RULES" SCENARIO

Assume that the foreign matrimonial decree is not recognised by the forum but is recognised by the *lex causae*, as in example M10.[32] If the recognition rule is applied, the marriage still subsists and Theresa may[33] be able to share in property acquired after the alleged divorce. Also, until a valid divorce is pronounced the community regime for management will continue and neither spouse will be able to realise his/her share in the asset or request partition.

25 It is possible to have a community limited to particular types of assets. For example, the Law Commission recommended joint ownership of the matrimonial home (Law Com No 86) and later of chattels bought for joint use (Law Com No 175). If these suggestions had been taken up, there would have been a Statutory Community scheme in relation to the specified type of property.

26 Since the French reform of 1966, the wife's co-operation is now required in transactions of major significance (see Rheinstein and Glendon (n 22, *supra*) at para 11 *et seq*). Some of the American Community States have introduced "joint management" (see Glendon, n 20, *supra*, at pp 147-148).

27 See McClanahan (ch 5, n 160, *supra*) at pp 531 *et seq*.

28 Eg, France and Holland. In Puerto Rico each spouse becomes immediately entitled on divorce to one half of the property. From that time onwards "the spouses may sell, assign or convey their rights in the conjugal property, subject to the final liquidation". See McClanahan (ch 5, n 160, *supra*) at p 539.

29 Eg, California, Lousiana (from 1981).

30 Eg, Arizona, Idaho, Nevada, Texas and Washington.

31 Eg, France and Holland. Cf, California, Nevada and New Mexico, where equal division is only to be departed from in specified circumstances (see Rheinstein and Glendon, n 22, *supra*, at para 99).

32 At ch 1, IV B, *supra*.

33 In some countries, property acquired after separation is the separate property of the acquiring spouse (eg California Civil Code, s 5118). In the jurisdictions where there is a discretion to vary the 50/50 split of assets, this discretion may be used to exclude post-separation acquisitions from the community, where inclusion of them would be inequitable.

34 In those systems which give retrospective effect to the final division, the ownership is treated as changing at the date of divorce.

Conversely, if the choice rule is applied, the marriage no longer subsists and the community is dissolved. Thus, post-decree acquisitions are the separate property of the "acquirer". In example M10, Theresa will be able to realise her share immediately.[34]

3. Deferred Community Regimes[35]

(A) THE VARIOUS SCHEMES

Under these regimes, property is owned separately during the marriage and each party has full powers to deal with his or her own property. However, on termination by divorce,[36] and in most systems also by death,[37] the property included within the regime is shared equally between the parties. Again, there are differences as to which property comes within the regime. In some countries all the property of both spouses is included,[38] subject to mutual agreement to the contrary. In other jurisdictions, only the gains made during the marriage are included.[39] However, it must be pointed out that under most modern schemes, a court has discretion to deviate from equal sharing of the community assets.[40]

A second important difference is the method of distribution. In some systems,[41] each spouse acquires a right to share in the property of the other on dissolution of the community. Whereas in other systems,[42] the "loser" spouse simply has a right to claim an equalising "compensation" payment from the "gainer" spouse. Thus, it has been suggested[43] that the labelling of the West German scheme as a deferred community scheme is misleading. Nevertheless, in order to be consistent with most of the literature, we will include what might be called "fixed distribution" or "compensation" schemes under the heading of deferred regimes, whilst bearing in mind the important differences.

35 Sometimes also called "participation schemes". Friedmann *Matrimonial Property Law* (1955) uses the term "intermediate schemes".

36 A different regime usually applies where the marriage is annulled.

37 Cf the Israeli scheme. Also in some systems, such as Germany, the rules on death are different and the surviving spouse may elect between taking under the inheritance or the "community" rules.

38 Eg, Scandinavian countries and Holland. This may be called a deferred universal community.

39 This may be called a deferred community of acquests. Such a regime operates in Israel and in Germany. Under the Reunification Treaty, West German family law applies throughout Germany from 3 October 1990. However, in the case of spouses married in East Germany before that date, either may elect that the old GDR regime still applies (see Frank (1991) 30 J Fam Law 335 at 341-343).

40 Eg, under the Swedish Marriage Act 1987 uneven division is allowed where the relevant circumstances indicate that equal division would be unreasonable. Similarly, in British Columbia, the court may vary the equal division where it would be unfair having regard to the various circumstances set out therein (Family Relations Act 1979, s 43).

41 Such as the Danish, Dutch and British Columbian schemes.

42 Such as the German and Ontario regimes. For discussion of the difference between the British Columbia and Ontario schemes see *Tezcan v Tezcan* (1992) 87 DLR (4th) 503 at 512 and Raffery (1982) 20 UWOL Rev 177 at 197.

43 Voegeli and Wilenbacher "Property Division and Pension-Splitting in FRG" in Weitzmann and Maclean (eds) *Economic Consequences of Divorce, The International Perspective* (1992).

44 However, courts and legislatures in other jurisdictions have recognised the issues. For example, in *Vladi v Vladi* (1987) 39 DLR (4th) 563 (discussed further below), the Nova Scotia Supreme Court

(B) CONFLICTS TREATMENT OF DEFERRED SCHEMES

The standard English conflicts of law texts do not discuss the conflictual aspects of deferred schemes[44] because they treat them as separate property schemes,[45] under which property rights are not affected by marriage. Thus, where the community crystallises on divorce, the issue will be seen as one of financial relief on divorce, which is governed by the *lex fori*. If this is correct, the "conflict of rules" problem cannot arise because *ex hypothesi* there can be no conflict where the choice of law rule is the *lex fori*. Where the English court has no jurisdiction to deal with financial relief on divorce, it would presumably have to decide any issue regarding ownership of the matrimonial property on the basis of separate property principles,[46] under which the termination is irrelevant.

Where the community crystallises on death, the issue is likely to be treated as one of succession. Thus, if the law governing the deferred community is the *lex successionis,* it will be applied. Otherwise, the appropriate *lex successionis* will be applied.

It is respectfully suggested that the assumption of the textwriters should be challenged and that foreign deferred community schemes should come within the matrimonial property choice of law rules and therefore be capable of being given effect to by the English court on divorce, where there is no jurisdiction under the English discretionary distribution scheme, and on death. The desirability of such an approach can best be illustrated by means of an example.

Suppose that Marguerita and Hans are Danish domiciliaries who marry in Denmark. In the absence of contrary agreement, their matrimonial property is subject to the Danish deferred regime. Hans acquires substantial property in England. The marriage breaks down. The parties leave Denmark and have no remaining assets there. Hans goes to live in Japan and Marguerita goes to live in France. Hans obtains a divorce in Japan. He is currently working in England for a few months and Marguerita wishes to claim title to half of Hans' property in England, to which she is entitled under Danish law, on the dissolution of the deferred community.

If the court is not prepared to give effect to the Danish deferred regime, it would have to declare that all the property is Hans's separate property.[47] It is suggested that such a result is not consistent with conflicts' justice because it does not accord with the parties' legitimate expectations. It is distortionary because it

applied the West German (fixed right distribution) scheme as the law of the last common habitual residence of the parties. The New Zealand Matrimonial Property Act 1976, s 7 provides a choice of law rule for application of its fixed right distribution regime.

45 See, eg, Dicey and Morris (ch 1, n 6, *supra*) at p 1068 and Morris (ch 1, n 6, *supra*) at p 366.

46 The procedure under the Married Women's Property Act 1882, s 17 can be used in respect of foreign property provided that there is jurisdiction over the defendant: *Razelos v Razelos* [1969] 3 All ER 929.

47 This is the same problem as that experienced when spouses migrate from a separate property state to a community state. This problem has been dealt with in the United States, *inter alia*, by treating some property as quasi-community property. See McClanahan (ch 5, n 160, *supra*) ch 13 and Schreter (1962) 50 Calif LR 206.

48 Both England and Denmark provide for sharing of assets on divorce.

accords neither with the domestic policy of the forum nor with that of the law governing the parties' matrimonial property relationship.[48]

As there is no jurisdiction under the Matrimonial and Family Proceedings Act 1984, it would seem that Marguerita's only recourse is to obtain a judgment in Denmark granting her a half share which can be recognised in England. This would seem to be virtually impossible, without Hans's co-operation.[49] Even if it is possible, surely it will be fairer and more convenient for the English court[50] to apply the Danish regime directly.[51] In particular, it should be noted that if the couple came from Belgium or some other immediate community state, the court would clearly be prepared to enforce Marguerita's title to half the property.

(C) BASIS FOR APPLYING FOREIGN DEFERRED SCHEMES

Whether or not the contractual analysis is accepted, the English court will only enforce the foreign scheme if it classifies it as a matrimonial property regime rather than ancillary relief on divorce. There is some Canadian authority for such a characterisation. In *Tezcan v Tezcan*[52], the British Columbia Court of Appeal characterised the claim before them as a property[53] matter because it would be so under both of the competing jurisdictions, Turkey and British Columbia. They found that the deferred regime contained in their own Family Relations Act was a property matter because "its true nature and character is to regulate the right to the beneficial use of property and its revenues and the disposition thereof".[54]

Nova Scotia seems to have avoided the problem of classification, at least in respect of movables,[55] by providing the same choice of law rule (ie the last common habitual residence) in relation to "the division of matrimonial assets and the ownership of movable property as between the spouses". In *Vladi v Vladi*[56] this provision was used in order to apply the West German deferred scheme.

49 A foreign judgment will only be recognised if Hans is resident in the relevant foreign country or submits to the jurisdiction of the foreign court. It should be noted that as the issue is a right in property arising out of a matrimonial relationship, it is excluded from the scope of the Brussels Convention.

50 Which would seem to be the *forum conveniens*. In both *Tezcan v Tezcan* (1987) 46 DLR (4th) 176 and *Vladi v Vladi* (1986) 73 NSR (2d) 418, the respective Canadian courts were prepared to take jurisdiction because otherwise the wife would not obtain any share in the husband's property.

51 It may be argued that the English court cannot calculate the shares of the parties in specific items of property if other items of property are not within its jurisdiction. However, account can be taken of the value of the foreign properties. In *Tezcan v Tezcan* (1992) 87 DLR (4th) 503, the court took into account the value of Turkish properties in ascertaining how to divide the British Columbian properties. It should also be noted that the English court, in deciding whether and how much financial relief to grant after a foreign divorce, has to take into account foreign financial provision which has already or is likely to be made (MFPA 1984, ss 16(2) and 18(6)).

52 (1992) 87 DLR (4th) 503.

53 It was common ground that the *lex situs* was the common law choice of law rule applicable to proprietary claims arising from marriage in respect of immovable property.

54 This definition was adopted from the case of *Derrickson v Derrickson* (1986) 26 DLR (4th) 175.

55 Section 22(2) of the Matrimonial Property Act 1980 (NS) provides that "The ownership of immovable property as between spouses is governed by the law of the place where that property is situated". Thus, in relation to immovables it would seem necessary to determine whether the issue was one of division of assets or ownership of the property.

56 (1987) 39 DLR (4th) 563.

57 See Gray, *Reallocation of Property on Divorce* (1977) ch 2.

It is suggested that the classification of deferred schemes as issues of matrimonial property, rather than divorce, can be supported on a number of grounds.

(i) In most systems the deferred regime was not introduced in order to provide a solution on divorce. It was introduced in order to give effect to the matrimonial partnership[57] concept whilst allowing women more independence during marriage[58].
(ii) As we have seen, in practice there is often little difference between immediate and deferred regimes in the divorce situation.
(iii) It is incorrect to say that ownership of marital acquisitions is totally unaffected by the existence of the marriage.[59] This is reflected by the common anti-avoidance provisions, under which one spouse is either prohibited from dealing with certain types of property[60] or can be restrained[61] from dealing with his own property in a specific way if this would defeat the rights of the other under the deferred community. Under some regimes,[62] one party can ask for dissolution of the community if the other has abused his powers under the community, even whilst the marriage still subsists.

However, even if the issue is classified as one of matrimonial property, it is not clear whether an English court would be prepared to do any more than simply declare the property rights which have been vested by the foreign scheme.[63] In which case a distinction would have to be made between those regimes under which rights in the property are acquired and those where only a right to compensation is acquired.[64] It is suggested that such differential treatment would be unfortunate and that the court should take the view that it can enforce a foreign matrimonial property regime even where the rights are not yet vested.

(D) APPLICATION OF THE CHOICE RULE

Under the contractual analysis, the English court would enforce the terms of the implied/presumed contract, which are supplied by the provisions of the foreign deferred regime. The foreign law, in the above example Danish, will govern as the proper law of the contract.

The situation is more complicated if the contractual analysis is rejected. How would the English matrimonial domicile rule work in relation to deferred

58 In some systems, such as Quebec, traditional community regimes have been reformed into deferred regimes for this reason.
59 Although the Israeli Spouses' Property Relations Law, s 4 specifically states this.
60 Eg, under the Danish regime, the matrimonial home cannot be sold or mortgaged without both spouses' consent (see Pederson (1965) 28 MLR 137 at 140). There is a similar provision in the German Family Code, art 15: see Forder (1987) 1 Int J of Law and the Family 47 at 61.
61 By court order. Note that under English law, a restraining order can only be sought once matrimonial proceedings have been commenced: Matrimonial Causes Act 1973, s 37.
62 Eg, the Danish regime para 38 and Dutch regime para 180. See Pederson (1965) 28 MLR 137 at 141.
63 It might take the view that it has no power to redistribute assets other than that accorded to it by statute. See *Pettit v Pettit* [1970] AC 777.
64 See text at nn 41-43, *supra*.
65 (1987) 39 DLR (4th) 563.
66 (1992) 87 DLR (4th) 503.

schemes? The particular difficulty with deferred schemes is one of timing. This problem did not arise in the two Canadian cases discussed above. In *Vladi v Vladi*[65] the choice of law rule, the last common habitual residence, specifies the appropriate time. In *Tezcan v Tezcan*,[66] the property concerned was immovable and thus subject to the *lex situs* which is unaffected by time.

However, under the domicile rule, we need to know at what point in time the parties have to be domiciled in the deferred regime country in order for that scheme to be applied. It is suggested that as a matter of *principle* the most appropriate option[67] is to apply the domicile at the date of the acquisition of each item of property, as this corresponds to the partial mutability approach advocated above.[68] The very essence of the deferred regime is that the actual realisation of rights is deferred. This assumes that inchoate and largely unenforcable[69] rights are actually acquired during the marriage, presumably at the time of acquisition. The parties' legitimate expectations as to their rights in acquests during the marriage will presumably reflect the matrimonial property regime in the country of domicile at the time of acquisition. Thus, that regime should be applied on later termination in relation to those acquests. The problem of the non-vesting of rights could be solved by saying that on the subsequent termination of the marriage, the rights are retrospectively vested according to the law of the domicile at the time of acquisition.

The main drawback with this proposal is the *practical* complexity of determining the domicile at the time of the acquisition of each asset. It is suggested that this problem should not be exaggerated. It is unusual for couples to change domicile more than once during their marriage. In any event, the administrative difficulties are no greater than in applying the partial mutability approach to immediate community schemes.

It should be reiterated that application of the deferred regime by the English court would not affect the English court's jurisdiction to apply its own discretionary scheme, where available,[70] at the date of divorce. The English[71] discretionary scheme allows for the variation of all rights in the property, whether or not vested under any previous scheme. Nonetheless, the legitimate

67 The other two options are: (i) The date of the marriage. This approach is subject to the same defects as the immutablity principle. Whilst it has been adopted in Israel, it has been criticised (Shava (1982) 31 ICLQ 307 and Goldwater (1981) 16 Isr LR 368) and an amendment proposed (Fasberg (1990) 39 ICLQ 856 at 858). (ii) The date of the termination of the marriage. This corresponds to full mutability and treats the scheme as if it is a pure distribution rather than a community regime at all. (An even more extreme form of mutability can be found in the New Zealand Matrimonial Property Act 1976, s 7, which provides that the New Zealand deferred regime applies wherever either spouse is domiciled in New Zealand *at the date of the application*. This is criticised by Forsyth (1977) 7 NZULR 397 at 399).

68 See text accompanying n 18, *supra*.

69 Until termination of the marriage, the only method of enforcement is usually by means of anti-avoidance devices (see n 62, *supra*).

70 See text accompanying nn 1 and 2, *supra*.

71 Although some discretionary distribution schemes are limited to property acquired during the marriage.

72 The court is obliged "to have regard to all the circumstances of the case" (Matrimonial Causes Act 1973, s 25(1), as amended by the Matrimonial and Family Proceedings Act 1984). For discussion of

expectations of the parties at the time of acquisition should at least be a relevant[72] factor.

(E) CONCLUSION

If the above hypothesis is correct, then the "conflict of rules" problem will arise in relation to deferred regimes,[73] where there is a dispute as to whether the foreign decree is recognised or not. The recognition or otherwise of the decree may[74] affect both the *quantum* of the property to be included within the deferred community and whether or not the rights thereunder can yet be realised.[75] Thus, in the example given above, the problem would arise if the Japanese decree was recognised by Danish law[76] and not English law or *vice versa*. This could affect Marguerita's rights to property acquired by Hans after the decree or her right to claim at all.[77]

4. Discretionary Distribution Schemes

(A) INTRODUCTION

In modern times, most Western separate property systems[78] have introduced discretionary schemes for reallocation of matrimonial property on divorce, similar to the English scheme. Can the "conflict of rules" problem arise in relation to such regimes?

At first sight, the answer would seem to be in the negative because the English court always applies English law to the question of redistribution of property on divorce, even where the divorce was obtained abroad.[79] However,

then effect of a matrimonial property contract, see Cretney and Masson, *The Principles of Family Law* (5th edn, 1990) ch 21 and Law Society, *Maintenance and Capital Provision on Divorce* (1991).

73 At least those under which rights in property are vested automatically on termination.

74 As with immediate community schemes, some systems exclude from the community property acquired after separation. See eg, New Zealand, where property acquired after the parties have ceased to live together normally constitutes separate property as distinct from matrimonial property (Matrimonial Property Act 1976, s 9(4)). In Germany, the court may prevent a party from sharing in post-separation acquisitions of the other where separation follows from the deliberate choice of the former (see Gray, n 57, *supra*) at p 253.

75 Although under some regimes the community can be dissolved otherwise than on divorce or death. For example, under the Ontario Family Law Act 1986 a claim for division can be made where there is separation with no reasonable prospect of resumed cohabitation (see Baxter (1987) 35 Am J Comp Law 801 at 804). In Denmark, one party may apply to dissolve the community where the other has abused the assets (para 38 of the Danish Matrimonial Property Act 1925).

76 Under all the versions of the choice of law rules discussed above, Danish law would still apply even if one or both spouses has lost their Danish domicile since they have not acquired a new common domicile and there does not seem to be any other country which is now more closely connected with the marriage.

77 Although no doubt she could in any event request dissolution of the community.

78 Eg, in Australia, Canada and the separate property states of the USA. According to Bala (1987) 1 Int J Law and Family 1 at 16, by 1984 all 42 common law property states had adopted some form of discretionary distribution law, although in three the reform was judicial rather than legislative.

79 The Law Commission expressly preferred English law to govern financial relief following a foreign divorce because: (i) the foreign law may not give effective relief which is exactly the mischief aimed at; (ii) it is not easy to think of an appropriate choice of law rule; and (iii) it would be expensive and difficult to get expert evidence about foreign law (Law Com WP No 77 (1980), para 56).

80 See pp 276-277, *supra*.

81 Eg, under s 17 of the Married Woman's Property Act 1882.

this does not cover the situation where the English court does *not* have jurisdiction to exercise its powers of property adjustment following an overseas divorce,[80] but simply has to determine who has ownership of property situated in England.[81] The orthodox approach would be to apply the foreign law's separate property system, ignoring its distribution scheme. It is submitted that this approach should not be accepted without further analysis.

(B) SHOULD FOREIGN DISCRETIONARY SCHEMES BE APPLIED?

It is suggested, that as a matter of *principle*, an English court should be prepared to apply a foreign equitable distribution scheme, where it cannot apply its own,[82] for the same reasons as those advocated above in relation to deferred community schemes.[83] In particular:

(i) Statutory redistributive powers were created in order to reflect the real value of the non-economic contributions of the wife, which cannot otherwise be recognised under a separate property system,[84] and the modern concept of matrimonial partnership.[85] Thus, discretionary distribution schemes in separate property systems should not create substantive rights any less than deferred community systems.[86] The main reason[87] for preferring discretionary regimes seems to be the desire for flexibility[88] to take into account variation between the circumstances, including the length and financial circumstances[89] of specific marriages. This demonstrates the difficulty of finding an appropriate fixed formula for such rights rather than any inconsistency with the conferring of substantive rights which crystallise when their quantum is fixed by a court.

The fact that under discretionary distribution systems one spouse has rights in the property of the other prior to divorce has been recognised by

82 This deals with the Law Commission's first objection, n 79, *supra*.

83 The arguments are also similar to those put forward in relation to discretionary financial provision on death, see ch 5, I C, *supra*.

84 See ch 5, III B 3, *supra*.

85 See n 57, *supra* and Law Com No 25.

86 See Gray (n 57, *supra*) at p 336. Waters (1970) 22 McGill LJ 315 at 318 writes: "Community of acquests is a deliberate modern attempt to place the parties in a fair and equitable position; separation as to property, accompanied by a statutory judicial discretion to allocate assets between the parties on the termination of marriage, is another. The second deserves as much respect as the first." A number of English writers have commented on the similarity of the results obtained under the English discretionary system and deferred community of acquests regimes. See, eg, Freedman *et al*, "Property and Marriage: An Integrated Approach" Institute of Fiscal Studies Reports Series No 29 (1988) and Forder (1987) 1 Int J of Law and the Family 47 at 48.

87 See Law Com No 52.

88 It is significant that in recent years there has been increasing disillusionment with discretionary systems. In New Zealand the discretionary system introduced in 1963 was replaced by a deferred community system in 1976. In England there is now a fixed formula system in relation to child support under the Child Support Act 1991. It has also been suggested that the use of computerisation may enable the creation of formulae which are sufficiently sophisticated to take into account all relevant factors. See Green, *Maintenance and capital provision on divorce: A need for precision?* (1987).

89 Eg, under the 1973 Act, early case law showed the need for a different approach in high, middle and low income cases, see Bromley and Lowe (ch 5, n 100, *supra*) at pp 767-768.

90 Sampson; "Common Law Property in a Texas Divorce" (1979) 42 Tex BJ 131, quoted in Scoles and Hay at p 466 writes: "It is true that 'common law separate property' assets or rights brought into Texas

a number of American writers[90] and courts[91] in US community states when considering the nature of property brought in by migrants from separate property states.

(ii) Applying the foreign law's separate property system without its discretionary distribution scheme may produce results which are not consistent with conflicts' justice and are distortionary.[92] However, it may be argued that there is a significant distinction between deferred community and discretionary schemes because of the *practical* difficulty of ascertaining how the foreign court would have exercised its discretion in any particular case. It is suggested that this difficulty is largely illusory. After examining case law, a foreign court is in almost as good a position as a domestic court[93] to exercise the discretionary powers. Also as we have seen, modern immediate and deferred community schemes usually allow for court discretion to vary the equal shares[94] or in some cases[95] for equitable distribution *ab initio*. It would seem that, today, in order to apply most immediate or deferred community schemes, a court will have to consider whether to exercise such a discretion.[96]

(C) BASIS FOR APPLICATION OF FOREIGN DISCRETIONARY SCHEMES

Under the contractual analysis, it could be held that where parties are domiciled in an equitable distribution regime at the date of the marriage, the provisions of the discretionary scheme form the terms of an implied or presumed contract. In other words, the parties are deemed to agree that on termination of the marriage their property rights are to be determined by a court in accordance with the statutory regime. The English court should be able to enforce the terms of that contract. Such contract might be varied by express or implied agreement, where the parties' domicile changes. If the contractual analysis is rejected, the choice

by a husband come with legal title vested in him. However, it follows logically that the property also must come to the state attached with whatever equitable claims the wife has under the statutes and caselaw of the common law jurisdiction. Thus, if the husband's separate property is subject to equitable division in the state of origin, it must be similarly subject to such treatment in Texas."

91 Eg, in *Hughes v Hughes* 91 NM 339, 573 P2d 1194, 1201 (1978), the New Mexico court held that the characterisation of the property as separate must be made under the applicable laws of the State of Iowa from where the parties had migrated. Thus, "the property is subject to all the wife's incidents of ownership, claims, rights and legal relations provided in any and all of the law of the State of Iowa that affect marital property". See also *Rau v Rau* 432 P 2d 910 (Arizona 1967); *Burton v Burton* 531 P 2d 204 (Arizona 1975); *Berle v Berle* 546 P 2d 407 (Idaho 1976).

92 See text accompanying n 48, *supra*.

93 One of the reasons for the disillusionment with discretionary scheme is the evidence of inconsistency between decisions of different courts. See Eekelaar, *Regulating Divorce* (1991) pp 61 *et seq*. There is no reason why this should be any worse where a foreign court is involved. There is also no reason why there should be any more difficulty in bringing evidence of the foreign law than in any other type of case. This answers the Law Commission's third objection (n 79, *supra*).

94 Eg, in Germany and Nova Scotia.

95 Arizona, Texas, Idaho, Nevada and Washington.

96 In *Vladi v Vladi* (1987) 39 DLR (4th) 563, the trial judge expressly found that there was no case for invoking the West German provision for unequal division where equal division would be grossly unfair.

97 See text accompanying n 67, *supra*. This answers the Law Commission's second objection (n 79, *supra*).

of law rule would be the domicile of the parties at the date of the acquisition of the asset in question.[97]

However, as we saw in relation to deferred community schemes, whichever analysis is adopted, an English court can only apply a foreign regime if it can classify it as relating to matrimonial property rather than to financial relief on divorce. It is reluctantly conceded that the classification problem seems to be insurmountable in relation to discretionary distribution schemes. In this situation, the forum has a domestic scheme of its own. Thus, its classification will be heavily influenced by its own scheme, which is treated as relief ancillary to divorce.[98] Whilst there are cogent arguments[99] in favour of classification as a matrimonial property regime, it is unlikely that these would be accepted in England.[100]

(D) CONCLUSION

Despite the real similarities in the rationale behind discretionary distribution schemes and community schemes, it is unlikely that an English court would be prepared to give effect to a foreign discretionary scheme. Thus, it is more realistic to proceed on the basis that the "conflict of rules" situation could not arise in relation to such schemes.

D. Matrimonial Property and Succession

The interrelationship between matrimonial property and succession is complex.[101] In the situation of a disputed decree followed by death of one of the parties, there may well not have been any division of the matrimonial property on divorce.

If the relevant regime only provides for realisation on termination by divorce,[102] then if the decree is not recognised, the divorce regime will not apply at all and the only issue will be as to succession. If the decree is recognised, the regime will have to determine whether rights to division of assets on divorce can be claimed by or against the estate of one of the spouses.[103]

98 Even where financial provision is awarded under the Matrimonial and Family Proceedings Act 1984 it is clearly regarded as being ancillary to the foreign divorce.

99 (i) Division of property between the parties is basically a private law issue *inter se*, as distinct from the issue of whether a divorce should be granted or recognised, which is a matter for the policy of the forum. (ii) Parties may rely on the financial provision law in their place of domicile in organising their financial affairs, in much the same way as they may rely on a traditional matrimonial property regime For example, they may take much less care about who has legal title to investments and household durables. Thus, it is not only on divorce that the scheme is relevant. Acknowledgment of this fact led most of the community states in the USA to treat property brought in by migrants from separate property states as "quasi-community" property which is available for distribution on divorce (see references at n 47, *supra*).

100 There is also the problem of whether an English court has power to order redistribution of assets at all (n 63, *supra* and accompanying text).

101 For some aspects of this see references in ch 5, at n 160, *supra*.

102 This is the position with all discretionary distribution regimes and some deferred community regimes eg, Israel.

103 In English law, no order for financial relief can be made after the death of either party. See Bromley and Lowe (ch 5, n 100, *supra*) at p 725, citing *Dipple v Dipple* [1942] P 65.

104 See ch 5, I D, *supra*.

Where the community or deferred community regime applies on death as well as divorce, whether or not the decree is recognised may affect the question whether post-decree acquisitions are part of the community property to be distributed on death. If the divorce is not recognised, the distribution on death will be as normal. If the divorce is recognised, then in theory the community is dissolved by the divorce and division should take place under the divorce rules in favour of or against the deceased's estate. This will clearly be the case where the effect of divorce is to impose an automatic division of assets. It is less clear what will be the position where partition requires agreement or court order and neither has been obtained before the date of death.

E. Second Marriages

We must consider how the matrimonial property rights of the first spouse should be affected where there has been a second marriage which is valid under the preference rule recommended in Chapter 4. As with succession, the validity of the second marriage should not necessarily mean that the first marriage has ceased to subsist for all purposes. However, the possibility of the two wives sharing the rights is more problematic than in relation to succession,[104] both as a matter of principle and from the practical point of view.

As a matter of principle, the difference is that it is more objectionable to enforce the marital rights of the concurrent marriages by affording property rights to both wives during the lifetime of the "bigamist". From a practical point of view, how can property acquired by one spouse (we will assume the husband) after the disputed decree form part of the community of property or deferred community regime[105] of two different spouses?

It is suggested that the best solution, where the first marriage ought to be upheld for the purposes of matrimonial property rights, is to limit the matrimonial property rights of the second spouse. Her property rights would be considered to be subject to those of the first spouse. In other words, the husband's half share in his post-decree acquisitions under the community regime with the first wife would belong to the community with the second wife.

II. POSSIBLE SOLUTIONS[106]

A. Apply the Choice Rule

1. Theoretical Basis

Since the choice rule depends on whether there is a contract governing the matrimonial property, we will have to consider the contractual situation

105 In some regimes, the assets will not be included in the first regime because they have been acquired after separation. Otherwise, depending on the circumstances, it may be appropriate to invoke the unfairness exception to equal sharing (where there is such an exception, in relation to these assets.)

106 For tabular illustration of results of applying different preference rules, see Tables 5A and 5B in the Appendix, *infra*.

separately. Under the "contractual analysis",[107] all situations would fall within this category, including deferred community regimes.

(A) WHERE THERE IS A CONTRACT

The question as to whether particular property has been acquired during the continuation of the marriage would seem to be a pure question of construction of the contract, which should be governed by its proper law. It would seem anomalous if the proper law were to determine the existence of all the requirements necessary for the creation of a right under the marriage settlement except for the question of the continued existence of the marriage.

It will be remembered that application of the choice rule in the "conflict of rules" scenario involves use of the doctrine of *renvoi* in the broad sense that we are using the conflicts rules (the type known as recognition rules) of the *lex causae*.[108] It has been judicially stated[109] and is generally accepted[110] that *renvoi* does not apply in relation to contract. Does this cause any problems for the above view that the choice rule should apply where there is a marriage settlement?

There would seem to be two main reasons why *renvoi* is thought inappropriate in contract cases. Firstly, the doctrine of unity requires that, unless the parties provide otherwise, all contractual issues should be decided by the same law to avoid distortions which can occur from the interrelationship between two systems with different rules. In our context, there is no breach of unity because we are not remitting a contractual issue for determination by another domestic system. We are simply using the recognition rules of the proper law to determine the validity of the decree. Indeed, the rationale behind the doctrine of unity would seem to require that the validity of the decree should be tested by the proper law rather than by the forum. Otherwise, a distortionary result could occur under which rights would be conferred on a spouse under the marriage contract even though such rights would not be conferred either under the proper law[111] or under the forum.[112]

A second reason for rejecting *renvoi* in relation to contract is that when parties choose a law to govern their contract, they are assumed to refer to the domestic law of that legal system only and not to its conflicts provisions. Again, this argument has no real relevance to our problem. If we are concerned with the parties' intention at the time of contracting, it would seem more likely that they would envisage the issue of continued subsistence being determined by their chosen[113] proper law than by a forum whose identity is not yet known to them.

107 See text accompanying n 4 *et seq, supra*.
108 See ch 1, VI, *supra*.
109 *Re United Railways of Havana and Regla Warehouses Ltd* [1960] Ch 52; *Amin Rasheed Shipping Corporation v Kuwait Insurance Co Ltd* [1984] AC 50.
110 Article 15 of the Rome Convention expressly excludes *renvoi*.
111 Because it considers the marriage to have been previously dissolved.
112 Because, eg, it did not recognise the validity of the marriage contract.
113 Whether expressly, impliedly or by presumption.

Thus, it is suggested that arguments of principle point to application of the choice rule in all cases where there is a marriage settlement, although these would seem to be considerably weaker in the case of implied and presumed contracts.

(B) WHERE THERE IS NO CONTRACT

There would seem to be two main arguments in favour of the choice rule. The first is the familiar one that the domicile is dominant in relation to all matters relating to status. The second is the internal consistency of the regime itself. Even if the regime is not treated as being contractual, it is designed to be a complete scheme for determining the rights of the parties in respect of matrimonial property. It should define itself all the various requirements which have to be fulfilled in order for certain rights to be created. One of the most fundamental requirements will be the formation and *continuation* of a valid marriage. The law governing the regime should determine whether this requirement is met. Otherwise, as we have seen, we may end up with distortionary results which are consistent with neither the *lex causae* nor the *lex fori*.

One practical difficulty with applying the choice rule is that, under the principle of partial mutability, there may be several different systems applying to different items of property where there has been a change in domicile. This creates the potential for considerable complexity, if the divorce is recognised by some of the systems and not others. However, it would seem wrong to reject the choice rule for all cases just because there may be cases where there are two or more successive domiciles.

2. Authority

The Australian case of *Haque v Haque*,[114] which we discussed above in relation to succession,[115] may also be cited in support of the application of the law governing the marital property settlement. In this case, the settlement was governed by Muslim law and the court applied Muslim law to determine if Azra was the deceased's wife. The limitations of the case as authority in relation to the "conflict of rules", explained in chapter 7,[116] are equally applicable here.

3. Results

It will be helpful to examine how the choice rule would work in practice by reference to a hypothetical example. We will assume that the contract or the regime provide that:

(i) the contract/regime applies to all property acquired during subsistence of the marriage; and
(ii) some rights under the contract or regime are only realisable on termination.

114 (1962) 108 CLR 230.
115 At ch 5, II A 2, *supra*.
116 *Ibid.*

(A) WHERE THE *LEX CAUSAE* RECOGNISES THE DECREE

This will lead to exclusion from a share in post-decree acquisitions, but will allow immediate realisation where this is an issue. One spouse may use the decree[117] in order to exclude unfairly the other from sharing in post-decree acquisitions. As with succession, the reason that the decree is not recognised by the forum may be that there has been some element of unfairness about the way in which it was obtained or its effect.[118] The unfairness may be exacerbated where the parties no longer have any real connection with the country whose law governs the contract or the matrimonial regime applicable to the assets in question. Again, it seems that this problem would have to be dealt with by judicious use of the doctrine of public policy. In other words, the recognition rules of the proper law of the contract or of the matrimonial domicile would not apply where their application would lead to a manifestly unjust result.

(B) WHERE THE *LEX CAUSAE* DOES NOT RECOGNISE THE DECREE

This would result in the potential sharing of post-decree acquisitions, but may prevent immediate realisation. This gives rise to two possible difficulties.

The first is legal bigamy. We have already seen that this concept *per se* is not a fatal objection to the application of the choice rule,[119] although it is more problematic in relation to matrimonial property than succession.[120] Furthermore, we have already suggested a solution to the practical problem of one party being subject to matrimonial property regimes with two successive spouses at the same time.[121]

The second is the possibility of abuse whereby a spouse relies on the fortuitous fact of non-recognition by the *lex causae* in order to obtain a pecuniary benefit. This argument seems to have less validity here than in relation to succession[122] because the *lex causae* will have or have had a real connection with both spouses. Under the contractual analysis it is a law chosen either expressly, impliedly or by reference to objective factors pertaining at the time of the creation of the contract. Otherwise, it is the law of the matrimonial domicile at the relevant time. Thus, it is not simply fortuitous that this law applies to determine the continued subsistence of the marriage. This can be compared with the situation on succession where the law governing the distribution may be a law which has no connection with the marriage between the parties.[123] If, however, there were a situation in which one party's reliance on non-recognition was abusive, the doctrine of preclusion[124] could be used to prevent denial of the validity of the decree.

117 The decree may have been obtained specifically for this purpose.
118 See ch 5, II A 3(a), *supra*.
119 See ch 4, II A 3(a), *supra*.
120 See I E, *supra*. It is arguable that the contractual situation is less problematic because the marriage is being treated as still subsisting only for the purposes of the contract, which can be considered as legally isolated from the provisions of general law rules.
121 At I E, *supra*.
122 See ch 5, II A 3(B), *supra*.
123 Either the *lex situs* in the case of immovables or the domicile at death, which was acquired by the deceased after the separation of the parties.
124 Discussed in detail in ch 5, II A 4, *supra*.

It may be argued that the delay in realisation is not a problem because it is appropriate for the law governing the regime to specify when realisation is possible.

B. Apply the Recognition Rule

1. Theoretical Basis

It is suggested that the "logical consequences" argument is weaker here than in relation to remarriage or succession. In particular, courts have shown a willingness to ignore the financial and proprietary effects of a foreign decree even though they recognise the decree.

For example, under the doctrine of divisible divorce, the New York courts[125] have been prepared to continue and even to grant a spousal maintenance order,[126] even though they were obliged to recognise a decree of divorce obtained in a sister state. The English Court of Appeal in *Wood v Wood*[127] in effect[128] applied this doctrine when they allowed an English maintenance order granted in favour of a married woman to continue[129] despite the fact that the subsequent Nevada divorce was required to be recognised.[130] The following comment by Goodhart, in a note on the first instance decision is apt in our context:

> "There is much to be said for the American doctrine of divisible divorce, as it provides that a marriage which has been terminated by the Courts of one State, having proper jurisdiction, must be regarded as terminated in all other states, so that no problems of bigamy or illegitimacy can arise in the case of subsequent marriage, but it does not follow from this that a husband should be enabled, by obtaining such an *ex parte* divorce to avoid all the financial obligations which he may owe to his wife." [131]

Furthermore, s 51(5) of the Family Law Act 1986 specifically provides[132] that there is no requirement to recognise any maintenance or other ancillary order made in the foreign matrimonial proceedings.

2. Results

(A) WHERE THE DECREE IS RECOGNISED

Application of the recognition rule will prevent sharing of post-decree acquisitions, but allow immediate realisation. The former may be unjust where

125 *Estin v Estin (1948)* 334 US 541 and *Vanderbilt v Vanderbilt* (1956) 1 NY 2d 342.
126 As opposed to an order of alimony between ex-spouses.
127 [1957] P 254.
128 Lord Evershed MR preferred to reach the same result by different means.
129 There was no jurisdiction to grant post-divorce maintenance.
130 Cf the opposite situation arose in *Macaulay v Macaulay* [1991] 1 FLR 235. The English court refused to recognise the Irish maintenance order because it was irreconcilable with the English divorce decree.
131 (1957) LQR 29 at 32.
132 This replaces s 8(3) of the 1971 Recognition of Divorces and Legal Separations Act 1971. See *Sabbagh v Sabbagh* [1985] FLR 29, where the court recognised the Brazilian judicial separation, but did not recognise its effect of freezing the proprietary rights of the parties.

a divorce has been obtained *ex parte*, or in some other way unfairly, and the respondent is the one deprived of the share. As we have seen, whilst deprivation of financial provision on divorce is a factor to be taken into consideration in exercising the discretion to refuse to recognise a decree under the Family Law Act 1986, s 51, there is no guarantee that recognition will be refused in every case where it would be unjust to deprive the "spouse" of a share in post-decree acquisitions under a foreign matrimonial property regime. In particular, it should be pointed out that here, as in relation to succession, the deprivation occurs as a result of the divorce *per se* and not as a result of the fact that the divorce was obtained abroad.[133]

(B) WHERE THE DECREE IS NOT RECOGNISED

The "spouse" will be allowed to share in post-decree acquisitions, but may not be able to claim immediate realisation. Any unfairness caused by one spouse relying on the fortuitous fact of non-recognition by the forum in order to obtain a benefit can be dealt with by the doctrine of preclusion.[134]

The inability to realise may be more of a problem here. The spouses have obtained a decree which is recognised by the law governing their matrimonial property regime. And yet they cannot realise their rights under that regime because the forum does not recognise the decree.

They would seem to have two options. The first is to litigate in the country of the *lex causae* where they will be able to obtain an order for immediate realisation. However, this may not be practicable where one or both parties have severed all connection with that country. Even if a judgment is obtained in the foreign country, it will not be recognised in England unless the defendant is resident there or submitted to the foreign court.[135] The second option is for them to obtain a fresh divorce either in the forum or which will be recognised by the forum. This can only be done if the relevant jurisdictional base[136] and grounds exist.[137]

C. The "Differential Rule"

Application of the "differential rule"[138] leads to recognition of the decree in all cases and therefore would produce the result that there would be no sharing in post-decree acquisitions, but there could be immediate realisation.

133 As in *Joyce v Joyce* [1979] Fam 93 and *Mamdani v Mamdani* [1984] FLR 699.

134 Discussed in detail at ch 5, II A 4, *supra*.

135 Even if it is a judgment of the court which granted the matrimonial decree. Whilst the case of *Philips v Batho* [1913] 3 KB 25 suggests that an *in personam* judgment which is ancillary to an *in rem* judgment (in this case the matrimonial decree) will be recognised, the decision has been severely criticised and is generally considered to be incorrect. See, eg, Cheshire and North (ch 1, n 6, *supra*) at p 363.

136 If England is the forum, one party must be domiciled or have been habitually resident for one year in the jurisdiction.

137 In relation to a divorce in England, the latter will not generally be a problem where a divorce has already been obtained, although it is not recognised.

138 See ch 4, II C 3, *supra*.

D. Upholding Matrimonial Property Rights

It will be remembered that in the preceding two chapters, we mooted express result selection preference rules in favour of upholding the remarriage and succession rights respectively. By analogy, it might be suggested here that an appropriate preference rule would be to apply the rule which would uphold matrimonial property rights.

The difficulty is in defining what we mean by upholding matrimonial property rights. It is suggested that this has to be understood in the context of the purpose of the scheme in question. Since all types of community scheme are primarily designed to promote sharing, it might seem that rights are best upheld by including post-decree acquisitions in the scheme to maximise sharing. Where actual sharing depends on realisation it might seem that upholding rights also requires allowing the parties access to their shares. However, we have seen that in the case of a disputed decree, sharing in post-decree acquisitions and immediate realisation will often[139] be mutually exclusive objectives.

Thus, it seems that a preference rule based on upholding matrimonial property rights is not practicable.

III. POLICY

A. Overview of English Domestic Law

In order to determine the policy of English law, we will have to give a brief summary of domestic matrimonial property law. The separate property system introduced by the Married Women's Property Act 1882 still applies in principle to determine ownership of the matrimonial property, subject to a number of limited specific exceptions.[140]

However, the importance of the separate property system has been considerably diminished by the introduction in 1970 of extensive property adjustment powers exercisable by a court on termination of a marriage by a divorce or nullity decree and on the granting of a decree of judicial separation. The 1970 provisions were consolidated in 1973 and have since been amended by the Matrimonial Property and Family Proceedings Act 1984. Courts have made clear that wherever possible in disputes about ownership of matrimonial property following breakdown of marriage, parties should rely on these wide redistributive powers rather than ask the courts to settle the issue of beneficial ownership.[141] However, there will still be situations in which ownership may have to be ascertained. These include on succession,[142] the insolvency of one spouse or if there is no jurisdiction to apply the statutory regime.[143]

139 Unless realisation may take place other than on divorce or annulment.

140 The common law presumption of advancement and statutory provision for sharing of the unused part of housekeeping allowances (Married Women's Property Act 1964) and acquisition of a share in property by making improvements thereto (Matrimonial and Family Proceedings Act 1970, s 37).

141 See *Wachtel v Wachtel* [1973] Fam 70 at 92 and *Kowalczuk v Kowalczuk* [1973] 1 WLR 930 at 934.

142 Although there is discretion to provide provision for a spouse out of the estate under the Inheritance (Provision for Family and Dependants) Act 1975, this will not be exercised until the exact respective shares of the deceased and the surviving spouse have been established.

143 Notes 1 and 2, *supra* and accompanying text.

Indeed, the Law Commission[144] in 1973 considered that, despite the width of the property adjustment powers, there was a need to provide automatic statutory co-ownership of the matrimonial home, which in most marriages is the most valuable asset. In 1988 they made a further recommendation[145] that in relation to pure personalty, goods intended wholly or mainly for the use or benefit of both spouses should vest in them both jointly.[146] The implementation of these proposals would be tantamount to introducing a system of community of property for couples who do not have investments other than the matrimonial home. However, there is no indication that they are likely to be implemented. This is no doubt, partly because in most cases the difficulties of ownership only arise on divorce[147] and because in any event spouses are increasingly putting assets into joint names.[148]

Given the above state of affairs, it might be difficult to state the policy of English law in relation to matrimonial property prior to breakdown. However, the policy of providing for sharing of matrimonial property on termination by divorce or annulment is clear.

B. English Law Approach to the Issues in Question

How does English law deal with the two issues which are of concern in relation to the "conflict of rules" situation?

1. Sharing of Post-Decree Acquisitions

Under the English discretionary distribution scheme, all property belonging to either spouse, whenever acquired, is susceptible to redistribution.[149] Whilst the fact that property was acquired after the cessation of cohabitation[150] or divorce will be relevant in determining to what extent such property should be shared, it is only one factor in the exercise of the discretion as a whole. Thus, domestic policy in relation to sharing of post-decree assets is part of the overall policy in relation to financial provision on divorce.

The search for such policy must start with a brief examination of the statutory guidelines, provided in the Matrimonial Causes Act 1973, as amended by the Matrimonial and Family Proceedings Act 1984. It should be borne in mind that whilst the 1984 reform seems to have been primarily concerned with

144 Law Com No 52. They reiterated this proposal in 1982 in Law Com No 115 at para 112.

145 Law Com No 175. It is interesting to note that the Commission preferred this limited proposal to complete introduction of community of property largely for pragmatic reasons. See paras 3.3-3.6.

146 The Family Law (Scotland) Act 1985 provides *inter alia* for a presumption that household goods are owned in equal shares.

147 In relation to unmarried cohabitees, ownership has to be determined on breakdown of their relationship. However, the proposals for joint ownership would not apply to cohabitees.

148 See Bromley and Lowe (ch 5, n 100, *supra*) at p 564, n 2.

149 Moreover, the courts take into account resources which the parties are likely to have available in the future (MCA 1973, s 25(2)(a), as amended).

150 In *Krystman v Krystman* [1973] 3 All ER 247 no order was made in respect of a marriage of 26 years during which the parties had only cohabited for the first two weeks. See Deech (1982) 98 LQR 621 at 630-632.

redistribution of income, in the form of maintenance, the same principles apply to property adjustment.[151]

(A) THE STATUTORY GUIDELINES[152]

The court is mandated to take into account all the criteria set out in the Matrimonial Causes Act s 25(2), with first consideration being given to the welfare of any children of the family.[153] The court must also consider whether it is possible to make an order which will terminate any further support obligations between the parties or, alternatively, to make a fixed period maintenance order after which there would be such termination of support.[154]

(B) THE POLICY OBJECTIVES

Little help can be gleaned from case law because, as empirical evidence shows,[155] the discretion is still largely unstructured and there is inconsistency in the application of the criteria. Thus, the policy objectives must be deduced from the statutory provisions themselves, viewed in the light of their legislative history.

It is suggested that the three main objectives are:

(i) To Guarantee that Needs Are Met[156]

Property adjustment should, so far as possible, provide for the present and future reasonable needs of the children of the family[157] and the parties.

(ii) To Facilitate a Clean Break[158]

Property adjustment should, so far as possible, ensure that the parties can be self-sufficient following divorce and there should not be any further financial interdependence between them.[159]

(iii) To Reflect Contributions[160]

Property adjustment should enable non-economic contributions and the concept of the matrimonial partnership to be recognised in money's worth.

151 Dewar, *Law and the Family* (2nd edn 1992) at p 297; Hoggett and Pearl, *The Family Law and Society: Cases and Materials* (3rd edn, 1991) pp 254-255.
152 For detailed discussion of the guidelines and their application, see Bromley and Lowe (ch 5, n 100, *supra*) at ch 21 and Dewar *ibid* at ch 6.
153 Matrimonial Causes Act 1973, s 25(1) (as substituted by the Matrimonial and Family Proceedings Act 1984).
154 Matrimonial Causes Act 1973, s 25A (introduced by the Matrimonial and Family Proceedings Act 1984).
155 Eekelaar (n 93, *supra*) at pp 60 *et seq*.
156 See Law Com No 103 at para 70 *et seq*; Law Com No 112 at paras 24-25; and Matrimonial Causes Act 1973, s 25(2)(b) (as substituted by Matrimonial and Family Proceedings Act 1984).
157 See n 153, *supra*.
158 See n 153, *supra*; Law Com No 103, paras 73-79 and Law Com No 112, paras 28-30.
159 For analysis of the application of the clean break principle in practice see Wright [1991] Fam Law 76.
160 See Matrimonial Causes Act 1973, s 25(2)(f) (as substituted by the Matrimonial and Family Proceedings Act 1984). Whilst reflecting contributions is not specified as a separate model in the Law Commission's 1980 Discussion Paper (Law Com No 103), it is clear that this was one of the main motivations behind the 1970 Matrimonial and Property Proceedings Act, which was consolidated in the Matrimonial Causes Act 1973 (see Law Com No 25, para 69 and, eg, 305 HL Debs at col 862, 18 November 1969 (per Baroness Summerskill) and 794 HC Debs 28.1.70 (2nd reading) at col 1559 (per the Solicitor General)). In particular, the need for the equitable distribution scheme became more acute after the House of Lords rejected judicial attempts (largely by Lord Denning) to introduce a "contribution" approach to determine beneficial ownership in *Pettit v Pettit* [1970] AC 777 and *Gissing v Gissing* [1971] AC 886.

Where the above objectives conflict,[161] the needs approach takes precedence.[162] Thus, where needs cannot be guaranteed by property adjustment,[163] there will not be a clean break.[164]

2. Realisation

In English law, a party can take proceedings at any time during the marriage to claim ownership of their property.[165] The sale of jointly owned property will be ordered[166] once the underlying purpose of the trust for sale[167] no longer exists.[168] However, an order under the discretionary distribution scheme can only be made once a decree of divorce, nullity or judicial separation has been granted. Under the new divorce regime,[169] a court will be able to make a property adjustment order at any time after the proceedings have been started, although such an order will not actually take effect until the decree is granted, unless there are special circumstances making this appropriate.[170] The idea is that once the marriage has broken down, the parties should be encouraged to concentrate on resolving all the practical matters such as property adjustment so that the whole process can be completed by the time the decree is granted at the end of the "period of reflection and consideration".

In the light of the above, it may be argued that the policy of English law is not to allow realisation until a decree has been granted. It is suggested, however, that the English rule does not reflect any particular policy about realisation but rather pragmatic considerations.[171] Therefore, the search for the policy of English law in relation to the issue of realisation should be undertaken in the

161 The 1984 reform has been widely criticised because of its introduction of contradictory objectives (see eg, Symes (1985) 48 MLR 44 and Dewar (1986) Conv 96.

162 Bromley and Lowe (ch 5, n 100, *supra*) at p 766 say: "It is obvious however that the court's primary concern must be for the needs of all the members of the family with priority having to be given to the needs of any child of the family." The Child Support Act 1991 will prevent the courts from "throwing the wife and children onto the state" as they seemed prepared to do in *Ashley v Blackman* [1988] Fam 85 and *Delaney v Delaney* [1990] 2 FLR 457.

163 Conversely, one party may not receive the full value of their contributions if the other party's needs are greater.

164 Maintenance may be ordered immediately or a nominal order made to allow for the possibility of maintenance in the future, should the need arise. See, eg, *Suter v Suter* [1987] 2 FLR; *Whiting v Whiting* [1988] 2 All ER 275; *Hepburn v Hepburn* [1989] 1 FLR 373; and *Waterman v Waterman* [1989] 1 FLR 373.

165 Married Woman's Property Act 1882.

166 Under Law of Property Act 1925, s 30.

167 A trust for sale is imposed by law in the case of all jointly owned property: Law of Property Act 1925, ss 34 and 36.

168 *Jones v Challenger* [1961] 1 QB 176. The purpose may be to provide a home for the children, in which case it will continue after the breakdown of the marriage. See *Re Evers Trust* [1980] 3 All ER 399 and Schuz (1982) 12 Fam Law 108.

169 See s 23A Matrimonial Causes Act 1973 (inserted by Family Law Act 1996).

170 See *ibid* s 23B.

171 Eg, if property adjustment took effect on separation, what would happen in the event that the parties became reconciled? Under the new regime, s 31A Matrimonial Causes Act 1973 (inserted by Family Law Act 1996) gives the court power to order property transferred under a property adjustment order to be transferred back where the order is discharged on joint application by the parties.

wider context of the policy behind divorce law generally. We have already seen that one of the most fundamental objectives of modern divorce law is to enable dead marriages to be buried.[172] The sooner the property issues between the parties can be sorted out, the sooner the marriage can be buried.

Thus, it is suggested that it is the policy of English law to allow realisation of matrimonial property rights as soon as practicable after a marriage has broken down. In English domestic law, it is not practicable to allow realisation before the decree, but if it is practicable under other systems then this should be encouraged.

IV. APPLICATION OF POLICY

A. Sharing of Post-Decree Acquisitions

What are the implications of the objectives identified above[173] for the sharing of post decree acquisitions? The contribution principle would tend towards non-sharing because the non-owning spouse cannot normally be said to have made a contribution to any post-separation acquisitions. The clean break doctrine would also seem to favour non-sharing. The needs principle would involve sharing of post-decree acquisitions where there are insufficient pre-decree acquisitions to satisfy reasonable needs. We saw that in English domestic law, where the objectives conflicts, the needs approach takes precedence. By analogy, in the "conflict of rules" situation, where needs cannot be guaranteed without recourse to post decree acquisitions,[174] the latter should be included.

How can such a result be obtained by use of a preference rule? Under a discretionary scheme, it is possible to provide for distribution of the appropriate proportion of the post-decree acquisitions. In contrast, a rule-based system can only produce an "all or nothing" situation. If we adopt the rule which does not recognise the decree, *all* the post-decree acquisitions must be shared. If we adopt the rule which recognises the decree, *none* of the post-decree acquisitions can be shared.

It is suggested that the desired policy can be implemented by adoption of the "differential rule", which always results in non-sharing of post-decree acquisitions, subject to an exception where reasonable needs cannot be met without recourse to such acquisitions.

Such an exception can be achieved by use of the doctrine of preclusion, as defined for our purposes above.[175] In other words, the owner spouse is precluded from relying on the decree in order to claim the pecuniary advantage of not providing for the reasonable needs[176] of the other out of his post-decree

172 At ch 4, III, *supra*.
173 At III B 1 (B), *supra*.
174 Where the foreign scheme provides for a discretion to vary the shares, reasonable needs can be met by increasing the share in the pre-decree acquisitions.
175 At ch 5, II A 4, *supra*.
176 It does not matter if the applicable matrimonial property regime does not have a reasonable needs principle, because the doctrine of preclusion is a rule of English law being used to help solve the "conflict of rules" problem. It determines to what extent post-decree acquisitions, which are not normally included within the relevant matrimonial property regime, should be included in a situation where there is a dispute about the recognition of the decree.

acquisitions. There are two possible methods of dealing with the "all or nothing" problem. The first is to define pecuniary advantage as being the advantage of not providing for the reasonable needs of the non-owner spouse, rather than as the advantage of not sharing the post-decree property.[177] Only in relation to that part of the post-decree acquisitions required to satisfy reasonable needs is the owner precluded from relying on the decree. Alternatively, if the preclusion doctrine is treated as discretionary, as suggested above, the court can simply apply it to such part of the post-decree acquisitions as it sees fit.

B. Realisation

The domestic policy in relation to realisation deduced above would require the application of whichever rule would allow realisation. We saw above[178] that this result can be achieved by application of the differential rule, which ensures recognition of the decree.

177 In other words, the pecuniary benefit is only the *illegitimate* pecuniary advantage.
178 At II C, *supra*.

Chapter 7

Torts

I. THE SCOPE OF THE PROBLEM

A. Introduction

There are two issues in torts[1] in which marital status may be relevant: inter-spousal immunity and wrongful death claims.

In England, a statutory choice of law rule for tort has recently been enacted[2] providing for application of the *lex loci delicti*, as defined in the legislation, subject to a flexible exception.[3]

However, since the common law rule may still be applicable in other Commonwealth countries, it is appropriate to consider the "conflict of rules" problem both in relation to the new and old choice of law rules.

B. The Position at Common Law

1. The Choice of Law Rule

The House of Lords in *Boys v Chaplin*[4] upheld the choice of law rule in tort enunciated by Wills J in *Phillips v Eyre*:[5]

> "As a general rule, in order to found a suit in England for a wrong alleged to have been committed abroad, two conditions must be fulfilled. First, the wrong must be of such a character that it would have been actionable if committed in England; . . . Secondly, the act must not have been justifiable by the law of the place where it was done."

However, case law has shown that a number of different interpretations may be placed on these words. In *Boys v Chaplin* itself, their Lordships arrived at the unanimous decision in favour of the plaintiffs by a number of different routes

1 A spouse's claim for loss of consortium was abolished by the Administration of Justice Act 1982. Under the rule in *Philips v Eyre* (see at B, *infra*) even if such a cause of action was recognised under the *lex loci delicti*, it could not be given effect to because there would not be actionability in England.

2 In the Private International Law (Miscellaneous Provisions) Act 1995, Part III.

3 Section 12(1) provides: "If is appears, in all the circumstancs, from a comparison of—
(a) the significance of the factors which connected a tort or delict with the coutnry whose law would be the applicable law under the general rule; and
(b) the significance of any factors connecting the tort or delict with another country,
that it is substantially more appropriate for the applicable law to be the law of the other country, the general rule is displaced and the applicable law is the law of that other country."

4 [1971] AC 356.

5 (1870) LR 6 QB 1 at 28-29.

and the *ratio decidendi* of the case is far from clear.[6] Subsequent English case law[7] supports the view that the *Philips v Eyre* test requires civil actionability between the parties under both the *lex fori* and the *lex loci delicti,* but that this general rule may be departed from in appropriate circumstances.

Case law provides us with little guidance on the scope of the exception. In *Boys v Chaplin* itself and in the more recent case of *Johnson v Coventry Churchill*[8] the *lex loci delicti* was displaced in favour of the *lex fori* on the basis that England had the closest and most real connection to the particular issue in question and that the policy behind the particular foreign rule did not apply to a case where both parties were English.[9]

Two important questions were left unanswered by their Lordships. Firstly, can the *lex loci delicti* be displaced in favour of a third law? Most commentators answer this question affirmatively. Secondly, can the first limb of the rule in *Philips v Eyre* be displaced where it is found that a foreign law, which would usually be the *lex loci delicti* or the law displacing it, is much more closely connected to the issue in question? This question was eventually answered in affirmative by the Privy Council in the case of *Red Sea Insurance v Bouysunes SA*.[10]

Thus, because of the flexibility injected into the common law rule by the judges, the new statutory rule will make little difference in most cases. The main purposes of the reform seem to be simplification and clarification of the law. Since the first limb of the *Philips v Eyre* test has been abolished, it will not be necessary, in a case like *Red Sea Insurance*, to prove that the *lex fori* should be displaced. In relation to the second limb, the main improvement is the resolution of the problem of determining the *lex loci delicti* in multi-forum torts. Also, the test for displacement of the *lex loci delicti* is defined more precisely than was possible in case law. However, it is thought that the exception will continue to operate in very much the same way as under the common law. Therefore, it will be appropriate to use the phrase the "flexible exception" to refer both to the statutory exception and the *Boys v Chaplin* displacement of the *lex loci delicti.*

2. The "Conflict of Rules" Scenario

At first sight it might be thought that the "conflict of rules" cannot arise in relation to the common law choice rule because the *lex fori* is part of the rule. However, under the double-barrelled choice of law rule, the *effective* branch of the rule is that which denies liability. Thus, where under the second branch liability is denied, the *lex loci delicti* is the *effective* choice of law rule. This

6 See, eg, Briggs (1984) 12 Anglo-Am LR 237; Collins (1977) 26 ICLQ 480; Karsten (1970) 19 ICLQ 35; McGregor (1970) 33 MLR 1.

7 Eg, *Coupland v Arabian Gulf Co* [1983] 1 WLR 1136 at 1146-1148 and *Johnson v Coventry Churchill* [1992] 3 All ER 14. See also Law Com WP 87 at para 2.17.

8 [1992] 3 All ER 14.

9 In *Warren v Warren* [1971] Qd R 386 and *Corcoran v Corcoran* [1974] VR 164, the displacement of the *lex loci delicti* was also in favour of the *lex fori.*

10 [1994] 3 All ER 749.

means that where there is a dispute as to the recognition of a decree as between the *lex fori* and the *lex loci delicti*, the "conflict of rules" may arise.

Moreover, the fact that the *lex fori* can also be displaced under the flexible exception[11] increases the scope for a conflict between the choice and recognition rules.

C. Inter-Spousal Immunity

Inter-spousal immunity in tort was virtually abolished in England by the Law Reform (Husband and Wife) Act 1962. A court may still stay an action in tort between a married couple where no substantial benefit would accrue to either party or it could be more conveniently disposed of under s 17 of the Married Women's Property Act 1882. However, inter-spousal immunity still exists in other jurisdictions.[12]

There are no English conflicts cases involving inter-spousal immunity. Authority can be found in US and Australian[13] case law for classifying the question of whether one spouse can sue the other in tort as a question of procedure;[14] of tort[15] or of domestic relations because it requires determination of the incidents of the marital relationship.[16]

If the issue is procedural, immunity could never be claimed in an English court. If the issue is one of domestic relations, it will be governed by the *lex domicilii*.[17] If the issue is treated as one of tort, then if the *lex loci delicti* provides immunity there will not be sufficient actionability[18] by that law and the action will fail. However, the flexible exception may be invoked in order to displace the *lex loci delicti* in favour of the *lex domicilii*.[19] None of the cases considers the situation where the spouses have different domiciles. It is suggested that the best solution is to apply the *lex loci delicti* unless the spouses have the same domicile or the laws in their respective domiciles are the same (and different from the *lex loci delicti*).

11 See *Red Sea Insurance* case, *ibid.*

12 Eg, in the USA, inter-spousal immunity has only been fully abolished in 35 jurisdictions. In a further five, the immunity has only been removed for intentional torts (See Clark (ch 4, n 75, *supra*) at 11.1).

13 Since the Australia cases, federal legislation (Family Law Act 1975, s 119) has been enacted stating that spouses can sue each other in tort. However, the constitutional validity of this provision has not yet been determined.

14 As, eg, in *Mertz v Mertz* 3 NE 597 (1936), where it was held that since there was no remedy for a wife against a husband under the law of the New York forum, she could not succeed even though there was actionability under the *loci delicti*.

15 See *Gray v Gray* 174 A. 508 (1934) and *Dawson v Dawson* 138 So 414 (1931) and other cases cited in Clark (ch 4, n 75, *supra*) at 11.1, n 40).

16 *Warren v Warren* [1972] Qd R 386; *Haumschild v Continental Casualty Co* 95 W 2d 814 (Wisconsin 1959) and other cases cited in Clark (ch 4, n 75, *supra*) at 11.1, n 41.

17 *Ibid.*

18 Cf *Corcoran v Corcoran* [1974] VR 386. In some Australian cases it was held that it was sufficient if the conduct was civilly actionable but this approach is irreconcilable with the judgments in *Boys v Chaplin* in which it was made explicit that there must be actionablity between the *same parties* under the *lex loci delicti*.

19 *Corcoran v Corcoran* [1974] VR 164; *Warren v Warren* [1972] Qd R 386.

To avoid confusion, in the ensuing discussion we will simply refer to the *lex causae*.

The "conflict of rules" situation can be seen from example T1.[20] Here, there is actionability under English law. Whether or not there is actionability under the law of Florida, the *lex causae*, depends on whether the parties are considered to be still married or not. If this issue is governed by the choice rule, then the law of Florida will hold that the parties are still married and thus there will be no actionability under the second limb of the rule. On the other hand, if the recognition rule is applied, the *lex fori* will decide that they are not married and that there can be no immunity.

It is less clear whether the conflict can arise in the reverse situation, ie if the decree is recognised by the *lex loci delicti* and not by the *lex fori*.[21] It may be argued that if the law of Florida recognises the decree, then there is no immunity under Florida law and thus there is actionability. On the other hand, it may be argued that the issue of actionability under Florida law has to be decided without determining the status of the parties. Thus, on the basis of the immunity there would be no liability if these parties are still married. We then have to decide which rule should answer the question of whether the parties are to be considered as still married.

The first approach may seem to be more consistent with the double actionability rule as defined in *Boys v Chaplin*. Thus, what is required is real actionability between these parties. Whether this exists can only be determined after ascertaining whether the parties are in fact still married.[22] But this approach produces a *fait accompli* in favour of the choice of law rule. It is suggested that this choice should not be made without proper consideration as to whether it is the appropriate preference rule.

Under the second approach, the issue of status is first decided according to the rule indicated by the preference rule. *Then* it is possible to determine whether there is in fact actionability under both limbs. It is suggested that this approach is to be preferred.

The Law Commission recommended keeping silent about the issue of inter-spousal immunity in reforming legislation because neither the law of the domicile nor the applicable law in tort have strong credentials to apply. The removal of the *lex fori* from the choice of law test does not in fact have any impact here since we have seen that the issue can only arise where there is immunity according to the *lex loci delicti* or displacing law.

D. Wrongful Death Claims

Under many systems of law, a tortfeasor who wrongfully causes death is liable in damages[23] to certain dependants or relatives of the deceased, including a

20 At ch 1, IV B, *supra*.
21 If, eg, the decree in Haiti was *inter partes*, but neither party was a national of that country.
22 However, the statutory provisions (n 3, *supra*) do not refer to actionability.
23 Usually, there is a requirement that the deceased himself could have sued if he had been injured rather than killed by the tort.

surviving spouse.[24] In England, such liability is governed by the Fatal Accidents Act 1976, as amended. Originally, divorced spouses[25] were not included in the list of eligible dependents. However, following the recommendations of the Law Commission, a "former wife or husband[26] of the deceased" was added to the list of dependants[27] by the Administration of Justice Act 1982.

Thus, where there has been a disputed decree, the "spouse" will be able to claim under English law without determining whether the decree is recognised or not. However, most other jurisdictions still limit wrongful death claims to the present spouse of the deceased.

In England, entitlement to damages by bereaved relatives is based on the actual injury caused to them as a result of the death.[28] Thus, only those statutory "dependants" who can show that the deceased would have provided them with financial support will be able to recover. As we shall see, assessment based on likely future dependency can solve problems of unmeritorious claims in cases where there is a doubt about the validity of the relationship between the claimant and the deceased. However, in some jurisdictions, designated beneficiaries have a right to a claim for wrongful death whether or not they can prove dependency.[29]

The questions of whether a beneficiary has to prove dependency and whether damages are based on the level of dependency would seem to be questions of substance and not procedure and so governed by the *lex causae*.[30]

There are no English conflicts cases dealing with wrongful death claims. The better view would seem to be that under the rule in *Philips v Eyre*, the dependant can only claim where (s)he has a right to do so *both* under English law and under the *lex loci delicti*. Assuming that all the other criteria are fulfilled, the "spouse" will be able to claim under English law either as a current spouse or as an ex-spouse and thus again the *effective* choice rule is the *lex loci delicti* or the law displacing it. This will be referred to as the *lex causae*.

As we saw above in relation to inter-spousal immunity, the preferable analysis is that whilst the *lex causae* determines whether a spouse can claim it does not necessarily determine whether a claimant is a spouse. This is an issue to be determined by the law chosen by the preference rule. Thus, the "conflict

24 The better view is that all the surviving wives of a valid polygamous marriage would be able to claim, although there is no English authority on the point. See, eg, Morris (ch 1, n 6, *supra*) at p 178.

25 *Payne-Collins v Taylor Woodrow Construction Ltd* [1975] 1 QB 300.

26 Defined to included persons whose marriage had been annulled or declared void: s 1(4).

27 Cohabitees who had lived with the deceased as husband and wife for at least two years were also added to the list.

28 Fatal Accidents Act 1976, s 3(1).

29 Eg, in the United States, there are a number of different approaches to wrongful death. See Speiser, *Recovery for Wrongful Death* (2nd edn, 1975) at 10.1-10.2.

30 The majority in *Boys v Chaplin* [1971] AC 356 held that the question of whether a particular head of damage is available as opposed to the actual quantification of the damages is a question of substance. Thus, whether damages are based on dependency or status is a question of substance; whereas the actual calculation of the level of dependency is a question of procedure.

31 At ch 1, IV B, *supra*.

of rules" can arise whenever the decree is recognised by the *lex causae* and not the *lex fori*, as in example T2 above,[31] or *vice versa*.[32]

We might add that the new legislation does not affect the present issue. Since there is actionability under English law whether or not the decree is recognised, removing the requirement of actionability under the *lex fori* does not make any difference.

II. POSSIBLE SOLUTIONS[33]

A. Prefer the Choice Rule

1. Theoretical Basis

The rationale will depend on what the choice of law rule is. To the extent that the rule is the *lex loci delicti*, we might rely on the words of Hancock quoted by Cheshire and North,[34] to the effect that the commission of a tort abroad is "of more acute concern to the foreign community than to the community of the forum". Thus, it may be argued that the foreign community should decide the extent of the tortfeasor's liability including whether a particular person is to be treated as a "spouse" either for the purposes of claiming for wrongful death or for claiming immunity in tort.

To the extent that any other law is applicable under the "flexible exception", the close connection which justifies its applicability in place of the *lex loci delicti* would provide support for applying it to determine whether the party in question is to be treated as a "spouse" in connection with this tort. Where the displacing law is the law of the domicile, the status theory[35] may also be used to justify preferring the choice rule here.

Whatever law is applicable, it may be argued that if the *lex causae* gives a particular immunity or right to a spouse, it only envisages their application to persons who are considered to be spouses according to its law.

2. Authority

There are no reported tort cases where the conflict between recognition rules and choice of law rules has arisen. Indirect support for application of the choice rule may be provided by the US case of *Meisenholder v Chicago NW Ry*.[36] This involved a claim under the Workman's Compensation Acts by a "widow". It was held that the claim failed because the marriage was not recognised by the law of Illinois where the accident happened, although the marriage was valid under the conflicts rules of the Minnesota forum[37] because it was valid according to the law of Kentucky, where it was contracted.

32 Prior to 1982 the conflict could not arise where the decree was recognised by the *lex fori* because the claimant could not be a "spouse" under either the recognition rule or the choice rule (because the *lex fori* was part of the choice rule) unless the *lex fori* was displaced under the exception in *Boys v Chaplin*.

33 For tabular illustration of results of applying the different preference rules, see Tables 6A and 6B in the Appendix, *infra*.

34 *Op cit* (ch 1, n 6, *supra*) at p 546.

35 See ch 4, II A 1, *supra*.

36 213 NW 32 (1927).

37 See Harper (1959) 59 Col LR 440.

Harper[38] hypothesises about the result in this case if the doubt about the status of the widow arose because of a Mexican divorce which was not recognised in some fora. He concludes that the validity of the divorce should be determined by the place of the wrong because the reference to "widow" in the wrongful death statute of the *loci delicti* is assumed to mean a "widow" as understood by that law and not as understood by the domestic or conflicts rules of the forum.

3. Results in Relation to Inter-Spousal Immunity

(A) WHERE THE *LEX CAUSAE* DOES RECOGNISE THE DECREE

The effect of preferring the choice rule is to deny immunity.

(B) WHERE THE *LEX CAUSAE* DOES NOT RECOGNISE THE DECREE[39]

The effect of preferring the choice rule will be to uphold the immunity. In cases where the tortfeasor "spouse" is unmeritorious, the doctrine of preclusion could be applied to prevent him/her obtaining a pecuniary benefit from denying the validity of the decree.

4. Results in Relation to Wrongful Death

(A) WHERE THE *LEX CAUSAE* RECOGNISES THE DECREE[40]

Application of the choice rule here would lead to denial of the "wrongful death" claim because the claimant is not considered to be a spouse by the *lex causae.*

(B) WHERE THE *LEX CAUSAE* DOES NOT RECOGNISE THE DECREE

Since the claimant is still considered to be a spouse by the *lex causae,* (s)he can claim.

B. Prefer the Recognition Rule

1. Theoretical Basis

The only rationale here would seem to be the familiar "full effect" argument. It might be noted that this argument would seem to have less validity in the wrongful death situation where we are concerned with a third party. It hardly lies in the tortfeasor's mouth to insist upon the strict logic of giving full effect to a matrimonial decree.

2. Authority

The American case of *In Re Degramo's Estate*[41] may be seen as providing authority for the use of the recognition rule in a wrongful death claim. The facts were as follows:

38 *Ibid* at 456.
39 As in example T1.
40 As in example T2.
41 33 New York Supplement (1895) 502.

The deceased, who was resident in Michigan at the date of her death, was killed negligently in a railroad accident in Ohio. The issue arose in a New York case as to how the damages received from the railroad company should be distributed. The deceased had obtained a divorce from her husband in Michigan, but this was not recognised in New York because the husband was not served and did not appear in the action.

The New York court held that the distribution of the damages was governed by the law of Ohio where the accident took place. Since the divorce was not valid, apart from in Michigan, the husband was entitled to the damages.

Thus, it appears that the court applied the recognition rules of the forum. However, the court found that the husband remained the husband of the deceased "except as to his status in the state of Michigan". Two possible interpretations might be given to this finding. Firstly, it might seem to be a finding that the divorce was not valid under the law of Ohio. But, it is difficult to see how the court could make such a finding when no evidence was brought as to whether the divorce would have been recognised in Ohio.[42] The second is that it is simply a statement of New York law. Thus, a New York court will not give effect to any incidents of the divorce decree other than those which are governed by the law of Michigan.

If the latter interpretation is correct, then the case would seem to support the application of the *lex fori* where the decree is not recognised. However, since there is no evidence that the result would have been any different if the *lex causae* had been applied, it is relatively weak authority.

3. Results in Relation to Inter-Spousal Immunity

(A) THE DECREE IS RECOGNISED[43]

The application of the recognition rule would result in denial of immunity.

(B) THE DECREE IS NOT RECOGNISED

Here, application of the recognition rule would result in upholding the immunity. This result would seem absurd because neither of the two relevant laws would in fact allow immunity. The *lex causae* would not allow immunity because it considers the parties are no longer married. The *lex fori* would not allow immunity because no such immunity exists under its domestic law.

4. Results in Relation to Wrongful Death

(A) WHERE THE DECREE IS RECOGNISED

The application of the recognition rule would result in denial of the claim because the *lex causae* does not allow claims by divorced spouses. Again, this result is absurd because neither system would have denied the claim. The *lex fori* would have allowed it because it allows claims by ex-spouses. The *lex causae* would have allowed it because it considers the parties are still married.

42 The husband did not apppear and was not served with process.
43 As in example T1.

(B) WHERE THE DECREE IS NOT RECOGNISED[44]

The application of the recognition rule would result in upholding of the claim because the parties are treated as still married for the purpose of applying both limbs. This result is in accordance with the *lex fori* but not the *lex causae*.

C. The "Differential Rule"[45]

1. Inter-Spousal Immunity

The differential rule will lead to denial of immunity in all situations.

2. Wrongful Death

The differential rule will lead to denial of the claim in all situations.

D. Upholding Tort Claims

It may be argued that the fundamental policy of the law of tort is to provide compensation for the plaintiff. Only where some other policy objective overrides this basic principle should there be a valid defence or exception to liability.

This argument would militate in favour of a result which upheld the claims. In relation to inter-spousal immunity, this would achieve the same result as the "differential rule". In relation to wrongful death, the "differential rule" does not produce the correct result and thus we would have to rely on the express result-selecting rule, which can conveniently be referred to as the presumption in favour of upholding tort claims.

III. POLICY

A. Inter-Spousal Immunity

There was considerable debate about the nature of the inter-spousal immunity at common law. In particular, it was unclear whether it negatived liability or enforcability. Whilst it seems to have originated from the theory of unity between spouses,[46] in more recent years[47] it was justified on the basis that it was unseemly for one spouse to litigate against the other and that to tempt one spouse to claim compensation from the other might endanger the stability of the marriage.[48]

These rationales were undermined by the advent of widespread, frequently compulsory, use of liability insurance. Where the tortfeasor was insured, then

44 As in example T2.
45 See ch 4, II C 3, *supra*.
46 This has now been said to be fully dead and buried: *Midland Bank v Green (No 3)* [1982] Ch 529.
47 See per McCardie J in *Gotliffe v Edelston* [1930] 2 KB 378 at 392.
48 Law Reform Committee, 9th Report Cmnd 1268 (1961), paras 7-10. See also, Clark (ch 4, n 75, *supra*) at para 11.1.

a tort claim by his/her spouse was effectively a claim against the insurance company.[49] Thus, there would generally be a common interest rather than a conflict of interest between the parties.

Furthermore, it seemed unjust that the insurance company should benefit from the fact that the victim was married to the tortfeasor. In addition, if one spouse was jointly liable with a third party, the third party would have to bear the full liability and could not claim a contribution from the tortfeasor spouse. These concerns about justice as between the spouses and third parties outweighed any residual reluctance to sanction litigation between spouses and the immunity was abolished[50] by the Law Reform (Husband and Wife) Act 1962. The only trace of the former immunity lies in the court's power[51] to stay a case where it considers that there would be no benefit to either party.

B. Wrongful Death

The common law rule forbidding claims arising out of wrongful death has been changed by statute throughout the common law world. The English Fatal Accidents Acts are typical of the legislation, which generally allows particular classes of dependents to claim sums which are quantified on the basis of the level of their dependency on the deceased.[52]

The policy behind the legislation is clear. The tortfeasor should not benefit from the fact that (s)he has killed the deceased rather than severely maimed him/her. Whilst the deceased him/herself can no longer suffer any loss as a result of the tort, those who were dependent on him/her may suffer substantial loss as a result thereof. The limitation on the class of claimants seems to reflect the requirement of foreseeability in relation to tort damages. Thus, the tortfeasor can only be expected to compensate the sorts of people whom (s)he might reasonably have foreseen would have been dependent on the deceased. Furthermore, requiring a particular relationship may prevent bogus claims, although it may also exclude meritorious beneficiaries.[53]

49 In some Australian jurisdictions, the exception was at first expressly limited to cases where the cause of action arose from the driving of a motor vehicle registered in that state. As in such cases insurance was mandatory, no non-insurance cases could arise. Difficulties arose where accidents took place involving vehicles registered in other states. See *Schmidt* [1973] 1 NSWLR 59; *Warren v Warren* [1972] Qd Rev 386; and *Corcoran v Corcoran* [1974] VR 164.

50 Following the report by the Law Reform Committee (n 48, *supra*). See comments by Stone (1961) 24 MLR 481; Khan Freund (1963) 25 MLR 695.

51 See Law Reform Committee Report (n 48, *supra*) at para 11. There is no reported case in which this has been exercised.

52 Some US jurisdictions base quantum on loss to the estate. See Speiser, *Recovery for Wrongful Death* (2nd edn, 1975) vol I.

53 Prior to the Administration of Justice Act 1982 cohabitees, even of many years standing, could not sue. The only remedy to this injustice was through legislation.

IV. APPLICATION OF POLICY

A. Inter-Spousal Immunity

It seems clear that the policy of English law would militate against upholding the immunity in the "conflict of rules" situation. Where there is liability insurance, then there is no basis for the immunity. Where there is no such insurance, the very fact that a matrimonial decree has already been pronounced between the parties would seem to remove any argument based on "seemliness" or stability of marriage. However, the Law Reform Committee[54] specifically stated that the power to stay should apply even after the spouses had ceased to cohabit so long as they were still married because–

> "there may even in these circumstances be some possibility of reconciliation between them or, where there is not, litigation may serve only as an excuse for the airing of matrimonial grievances and bitterness."

In any event, as the power to stay is a procedural provision,[55] the court could stay the proceedings provided that the decree was not recognised by the *lex fori*, irrespective of the position under the *lex causae*. This does not affect the conclusion that domestic policy requires a result which denies effect to the foreign immunity.

However, this policy may conflict with the principle of "conflicts justice" in the sense of upholding the reasonable expectations of the parties. Thus, in example T1, Florida is clearly the law most closely related to the relationship between the parties and to the tort and thus the parties would reasonably expect that since their divorce is not recognised by the law of Florida the tort immunity continues. It may seem unfair that Jane can successfully claim because of the fortuitious fact that Kevin is now living in England. On the other hand, it hardly lies in Kevin's mouth to complain that he has no immunity when he has chosen to obtain a divorce in Haiti. However, in the reverse situation where Jane was Haitiain and had been the one to obtain the unilateral divorce, Kevin might justifiably protest that he had assumed, relying on the law of Florida, which was the law which had the closest connection both to the parties' relationship and to the tort, that the marriage was still valid and therefore the immunity still stood.

It is generally accepted that reasonable expectations are less relevant in relation to non-intentional events where the parties have not modified their behaviour in reliance on a particular law. Furthermore, the policy of Florida law creating inter-spousal immunity must be very weak in a situation where a divorce has actually taken place, even if such divorce is not recognised in Florida. Therefore, it is suggested that it is not inappropriate to determine the outcome in accordance with the domestic policy of the forum.

54 *Op cit* (n 48, *supra*) para 13.
55 *Ibid*, para 16.

The desired result can be achieved by the differential rule. As we have already seen, this rule has the advantage of consistency with the 'full effect' principle where recognition is granted and otherwise giving precedence to the law governing the issue. This rule avoids the need to rely on the doctrine of preclusion and avoids the absurdity of allowing immunity which would not be allowed by either system alone.

B. Wrongful Death

Until 1982, ex-spouses could not claim. If we had been considering this issue before 1982, we might have had difficulty in determining how to apply English policy to the "conflict of rules" situation. On the one hand, it might have been argued that if the "spouse" could prove dependency, (s)he should have been able to claim. There is no reason why the tortfeasor should benefit from the fact that a decree has been obtained, if there is a dispute as to whether it should be recognised. In other words, the policy of compensation requires that the claimant should be given the benefit of the doubt about the decree. On the other hand, it might have been argued that to allow a claim where there has been an attempt to obtain a divorce decree, even though this the decree is not universally recognised, would be against the intention of the legislation which did not cover former spouses and could give rise to abuse. It is suggested that the former argument is more convincing.[56] It was reasonably foreseeable that the "spouse" in the disputed decree situation might suffer loss of dependency. (S)he should not be in a worse position than a separated spouse[57] simply because there had been an attempt at divorce, the outcome of which was disputed. Abuse would have been unlikely where there was a requirement of dependency and in other cases could have been prevented by the doctrine of preclusion.

56 It might be argued that both positions are too simplistic and that everything depends on the circumstances surrounding the decree. If the "spouse" had not obtained financial provision because of the doubt surrounding the decree, (s)he should be entitled to claim. His/her dependency would reflect what financial provision (s)he would be able to claim in the future. If the "spouse" had obtained financial provision in connection with the divorce/nullity decree, then arguably (s)he is in the same position as any other ex-spouse and should not have been able to benefit because there is a dispute as to whether the decree should be recognised.

57 There do not seem to be any English decisions on the position of the separated spouse under the Fatal Accidents Act, but there is a significant amount of American case law. The majority view seems to be that separation does not affect eligibility (see, eg, *Schilling v Gall* 33 Wis 2d 14, 146 NW 2d 390 (1966) and cases quoted therein and at 18 ALR 1409 supplemented by 90 ALR 920), although there is some authority that a deserting spouse cannot claim (see Speiser, n 52, *supra* at para 6.2). Claims have been allowed where a divorce suit was pending (*Wright v Dilbeck* (1970) 122a Ga App 214, 176 SE 2d 175) and where an interlocutory divorce order entitling the claimant to a final decree in six months had been made (*Piland v Yakima Motor Coach Co* (1931) 162 Wash 456, 298 P 419). However, the state of the marriage at the time of the death will usually be relevant in quantifying the amount of dependency (see Speiser *op cit* at para 6.6). The Royal Commission on Liability and Compensation for Personal Injury (the Pearson Commission) (1978, Cmnd 7054-I at para 417) recommended that the possibility of divorce should not be taken into account in assessing damages for lost dependency where it would be detrimental to the plaintiff to do so.

Since the extension of the class of dependents to cover former spouses, the position seems clearer. The reason for the reform was[58] that former spouses might have lost valuable rights of maintenance[59] as a result of the death of the deceased.[60]

Where an award is based on dependency, an ex-spouse who has already received financial provision in a lump sum in lieu of maintenance will not be able to get a "second bite of the cherry". Thus, the policy of English law requires that the "spouse" should be able to claim in all situations. This result can be achieved by applying the presumption in favour of upholding tort claims.

However, where under the *lex causae* the award is not based on dependency, there is a possibility of abuse by a spouse who has received financial provision in one jurisdiction, but whose divorce is not recognised in another jurisdiction. Here, the doctrine of preclusion could apply to prevent him/her denying the validity of the decree as (s)he has derived financial benefit therefrom.

58 Law Com 56, para 259.

59 Maintenance payments cease on the death of the payer unless they are secured.

60 This extension is consistent with the theory suggested above because it is reasonably foreseeable that an ex-spouse will suffer loss.

Chapter 8

Adoption

I. THE SCOPE OF THE PROBLEM

A. Introduction

The "conflict of rules" can potentially arise following a foreign adoption wherever it is necessary to determine the status of the child in a case governed by a foreign law. The conflict will in fact arise where the foreign adoption order is recognised by the law of the forum and not by the *lex causae* or *vice versa*. An analogous problem may arise where an English adoption is not recognised by the *lex causae*. As we saw in relation to divorce, here the conflict is between a rule of domestic law and the choice of law rule, but some of the applicable policy considerations will be the same.

A child's status is most commonly questioned in relation to succession and custody/guardianship. However, there are other possible situations, such as in relation to wrongful death claims, immigration, taxation, social security and rights under pension or life insurance schemes. It may also be relevant to determine a child's status in relation to the prohibited degrees of marriage and the requirement of parental consent to marriage. In English law, custody/guardianship, immigration, social security and taxation are governed by the law of the forum and thus the "conflict of rules" cannot arise. In this chapter, we will be concentrating on the issues of succession and wrongful death claims.

It is important to appreciate that such cases may arise out of the death of either the child, the adoptive parents or the natural parents. The likelihood of the child claiming following the death of the natural parents has been increased by the right of adopted children to see their original birth certificate[1] as well as by the increase in "older children" adoptions.[2]

The choice of law rules in relation to succession and wrongful death claims have been set out above. In order to understand when the conflict is likely to arise, we will need to explain the rules for recognising foreign adoptions, which are materially different from and more complicated than those for recognising foreign matrimonial decrees.

In the past there has been much debate about which law governs the incidents of a foreign adoption. Some cases[3] suggested that the law of the place where the adoption was granted determined what was meant by the phrase "adopted child"

1 Adoption Act 1976, s 51.
2 Eg, the proportion of non-parental adoptions where the child was aged over 10 increased from 8% in 1975 to 27% in 1986; Bromley and Lowe (ch 5, n 100, *supra*) at p 411 n 3.
3 Eg *Re Marshall* [1957] Ch 507. For discussion of Commonwealth cases, see Kennedy (1956) 34 Can BRev 507 at 547 *et seq*.

and thus what incidents were attached to the adoption. Academic writers[4] were critical of this approach and claimed that it was inconsistent with the approach taken in other areas, such as legitimation.[5] It now seems to be established[6] that the law governing the succession or other "main" issue must determine what incidents attach to adoption. What has not been decided is which law should determine whether the child in question has been successfully adopted.[7] It is to this question that this chapter is directed.

B. Recognition of Foreign Adoptions under English Law

There are now four different sets of recognition rules, three of which are statutory. A new Hague Convention on Inter-Country Adoptions was concluded in 1993, but is not yet in force. We will consider each of the sets of rules in turn.

1. Adoptions in the British Isles

All adoption orders made in Northern Ireland, the Channel Islands and the Isle of Man are automatically recognised.[8]

2. "Overseas Adoptions"

Adoption orders made in any country listed in a Statutory Instrument[9] made by the Secretary of State under powers granted to him under the Adoption Act 1976 are entitled to automatic recognition[10] subject to the following limitations:

(i) The adoption was made under the statutory law and not common or customary law of the foreign country.[11]
(ii) The adopted person is under 18 and has not been married.[12]
(iii) The authority which purported to authorise the adoption was competent to do so.[13]
(iv) Recognition is not contrary to public policy.

The most salient features of these provisions are that no reciprocity of treatment of English adoptions is required and that no connecting factor is required between the adopters or the adopted person and the foreign country. The latter may not be so surprising since countries will only be included in the order where the Secretary of State is satisfied with the arrangements for adoption there. His primary considerations will presumably be the methods of safeguarding the

4 See Kennedy *ibid* and Taintor (1954) 15 U of Pitts L Rev 222 at 243 *et seq.*
5 Although no cases are cited which raise this issue squarely.
6 *Re Valentine's Settlement* [1965] Ch 831 at 843-845. See Cheshire and North (ch 1, n 6, *supra*) p 770.
7 Dicey and Morris (ch 1, n 6, *supra*) at p 901 suggest that an English court *might* refer the whole question to the *lex successionis*.
8 Adoption Act 1976, ss 38(1)(c).
9 The relevant order is SI 1973/19.
10 Either on a request for a declaration or where the issue arises in other proceedings: Adoption Act 1976, s 53(2)(3).
11 SI 1973/19, para 3(3).
12 *Ibid.*
13 Adoption Act 1976, s 53(2)(a).

interests of the child and preventing abuse. The latter should include the requirement of some connection with the foreign court.

It should be remembered that whilst a large number of countries[14] are included in the order, there are still many which are not.

3. Convention Adoptions

The Adoption Act 1976 provides that adoptions made under the Hague Convention on Adoptions 1965 and known as "regulated adoptions" are to be recognised as "overseas adoptions". The rules providing when adoptions may be made under the Convention are complex, but in practice they are of little significance since the Convention is only in force with Austria and Switzerland[15] and both of these countries are designated under the 1973 order.

4. Other Adoptions

Any adoptions which are not recognised under the above headings may be recognised at common law. There has been much academic debate over the common law rules. The leading case is the Court of Appeal decision in *Re Valentine's Settlement*.[16] The majority stated that foreign adoptions will only be recognised where the adopters are domiciled in the country where the order is made *and* the child is ordinarily resident there. Danckwerts LJ was "not sure" whether the latter requirement was in fact necessary.[17]

There are some indications in the judgment that the South African order would have been recognised if it had been recognised by the law of the domicile, which was Southern Rhodesia. Thus, it has been suggested,[18] by analogy with the rule in *Armitage v A-G*,[19] that an adoption order should be recognised if it would be recognised by the law of the domicile of the adopters.

Other writers[20] have gone further and suggested that the rules in *Travers v Holley*[21] and *Indyka v Indyka*[22] might apply to adoptions. Under the former, a foreign adoption would be recognised where there was a connection with the foreign court which would *mutatis mutandis* have given the English court jurisdiction. Under the Adoption Act 1976,[23] the English Court may grant an adoption order where one of the applicants is domiciled in the United Kingdom, the Channel Islands or the Isle of Man and the child is in England when the

14 See SI 1973/19. The list includes most of the Commonwealth and UK Dependant Territories, all Western European countries, Yugoslavia, Greece, Turkey, South Africa and the USA.
15 SI 1978/1431.
16 [1965] Ch 831.
17 *Ibid* at 846.
18 Morris (ch 1, n 6, *supra*) at p 249.
19 [1906] P 135.
20 Cheshire and North (ch 1, n 6) at p 769; Khan Freund, *The Growth of Internationalism in English Private International Law* (1960) pp 82-88. Kennedy (1956) 34 Can BRev 507, although writing before *Indyka*, would clearly have advocated the applicability of that decision to adoptions.
21 [1953] P 246.
22 [1969] 1 AC 33.
23 Section 62.

application is made.[24] Thus, the recognition rule is substantially similar[25] to the jurisdictional rule and application of the *Travers v Holley* rule would not lead to any significant widening of the former. By contrast, application of the rule in *Indyka v Indyka* would allow all adoptions to be recognised provided that there was a "real and substantial connection" with the granting court. Thus, for example, the habitual residence or nationality of the adopters and maybe even of the child[26] would probably be sufficient.

It has also been suggested[27] that since the requirement for the child to be resident has been removed from the English jurisdiction rule, it should also be dropped from the recognition rule if it is part of the latter.

Finally, it should be mentioned that, as with "overseas adoptions", recognition may be refused at common law where it would be contrary to public policy. No doubt this power would only be invoked in extreme circumstances.

5. The Hague Convention on Protection of Children and Cooperation in Respect of Intercountry Adoptions

This Convention primarily seeks to regulate the procedures for inter-country adoptions to ensure that such adoptions are made in the best interests of the child and in particular to prevent international trafficking in children.[28] Article 23 provides that an adoption certified by the competent authority of the state of the adoption as having been made in accordance with the Convention shall be recognised by operation of law in the other contracting states.

C. Recognition of Foreign Adoptions in Other Countries

It is not practicable here to undertake a survey of recognition provisions worldwide,[29] which seem to vary more than conflicts rules in other areas of family law.[30] All that is required is sufficient information to show that there is a real likelihood of a situation arising in which an adoption order will be recognised in England and not by the *lex causae* of the succession or tort claim or *vice versa*.

24 In practice, the applicants and the child have to be resident in England because otherwise it is not possible for the relevant authorities to carry out the assessment during the trial period. See *Re Y Minors* [1985] Fam 136.

25 The recognition rule refers to the domicile of *both* parties. This is no doubt because at that time the domicile of a married woman was dependent on that of her husband. The jurisdiction rule does not formally require ordinary residence of the child, but see n 24, *supra*.

26 The US Restatement (Conflict of Laws) para 78 provides for jurisdiction where *either* the child or the adopters is domiciled or resident in the forum.

27 Cheshire and North (ch 1, n 6, *supra*) p 769.

28 See art 1 and the Preamble.

29 Lipstein (1963) 12 ICLQ 835 seems to be the most comprehensive work, but there have been significant changes in the last 30 years.

30 This may explain the limited success of the Hague Convention on Adoption. See Lipstein *ibid*. Scoles and Hay (ch 4, n 18, *supra*) at pp 546-549 conclude that the Convention "is of limited usefulness in addressing the problems raised by international adoption cases".

In the common law world, many jurisdictions[31] still require a jurisdictional link between the adopters and the jurisdiction in which the order is granted. At the other extreme, some jurisdictions recognise all adoptions[32] effected according to the law of another jurisdiction. There are a variety of positions in between. Some states adopt the approach of the English Adoption Act 1976 and prescribe which countries' adoptions should be recognised.[33] Others specify that foreign adoptions will only be recognised where certain incidents attach to them under the *lex adoptionis*.[34]

The position in the civil law world is more complicated because generally adoption is governed by the personal law[35] of the parties. Foreign adoptions will only be recognised where they are in accordance with the personal law.

The Hague Convention on Adoption 1965 was only ratified by three countries. If the recent Convention on inter-country adoption enjoys more success, the potential for the "conflict of rules" arising in relation to inter-country adoptions will be substantially reduced.

In summary, a number of situations in which the "conflict of rules" may arise can be identified:

1. "Overseas adoptions" recognised in England may not be recognised by common law countries requiring a jurisdictional link.
2. "Overseas adoptions" recognised in England may not be recognised in civil law countries if the adoption was not in accordance with the personal law of the parties.
3. Adoptions recognised under English common law may not be recognised in civil law countries if the adoption is not in accordance with the national law of the parties, even though it is in accordance with their domiciliary law.
4. Adoptions recognised in "liberal" common law countries may not be recognised in England if they are not "overseas adoptions" and the adoption is not granted or recognised in the country of the adopters' domicile.
5. Adoptions recognised by civil law countries, which are not "overseas adoptions", may not be recognised in England if they are not granted or recognised in the country of the adopters' domicile.

31 Eg, the Australian uniform legislation requires *inter alia* that the applicant(s) be resident or domiciled in the foreign country where the order is made (although there is a presumption that this requirement is met), but some of the states have abolished this requirement (see Sykes and Pryles (ch 2, n 246, *supra*) at p 524). Newfoundland and Nova Scotia have similar jurisdictional requirements (see Castel (ch 4, n 17, *supra*) at p 387). Most American states will recognise an adoption granted in the court of the adopter's or the child's nationality or residence (see Scoles and Hay (ch 4, n 18, *supra*) at p 548).

32 Eg, Alberta, British Columbia, Saskatchewan and Ontario (see Castel ch 4, n 17, *supra*) p 389).

33 Eg New Brunswick. In some Australian states, there is provision for a proclamation to be made declaring that adoptions made in a particular country are *conclusively* presumed to comply with the recognition requirements. See Sykes and Pryles (ch 2, n 246, *supra*) at p 525.

34 Eg, Manitoba, New Zealand. Under the Australian uniform legislation, the adoptive parents must have a right of custody superior to that of the natural parents and must be placed generally in relation to the adopted person in the position of parent(s). However, there is a presumption that such requirements are satisfied. See Sykes and Pryles (ch 2, n 246, *supra*) pp 524-525.

35 The prerequisites for adoption will usually be governed by the personal law of the adopters, but some aspects, such as the need for the consent of the natural parents and the child, will be governed by the personal law of the child. See Lipstein (1963) 12 ICLQ 835.

The application of the *Indyka* rule would reduce the likelihood of conflicts arising under categories 4 and 5 above. However, to the extent that it increased recognition of adoptions made in the place of residence, as opposed to nationality, it might increase the likelihood of conflicts under category 3.

II. POSSIBLE SOLUTIONS

Most of the analysis of the possible rules in Chapters 5 and 7 in relation to succession and wrongful death claims by spouses will be relevant here. For example, the rationale for applying the choice of law rule would not seem to be any different, since we are concerned with exactly the same choice rules. However, there may be some material differences in respect of the rationale behind application of the recognition rule because we are concerned with a different type of foreign judgment.

A. Rationale for Applying the Recognition Rule

1. Where the Foreign Order is Recognised

The "full effect" doctrine would in the present context seem to require that, in order to give full effect to a foreign adoption, it is necessary to treat the adopted child as the natural born child of the adoptive parents for the purposes of succession[36] and wrongful death claims. In other words, it is logically inconsistent to recognise such adoptions without according them the incidents which we accord to English adoptions.

It is submitted that there are two problems in applying the "full effect" doctrine to adoptions. Firstly, it is far from clear what is meant by giving full effect to an adoption. It will be remembered that the "full effect" theory was propounded in relation to capacity to remarry.[37] It was seen as logically inconsistent to recognise a divorce and not allow remarriage because the right to remarry is universally seen as the main purpose and essential effect of divorce.[38] By contrast, there would not seem to be international agreement about the essential effect of adoption and, if this could be determined,[39] it would most probably not include full rights of succession.[40]

Secondly, it is arguable that the institution of "adoption" is not universal in the same way as marriage and divorce. Thus, whilst the relationship created by the foreign court may be called an adoption it should not necessarily be

36 Apart from the hereditary titles, see the Adoption Act 1976, s 44(1).

37 We saw above (in sections II B 1 of chs 5, 6 and 7 respectively) that the theory is less persuasive in relation to other issues.

38 A form of dissolution which relieves the parties of matrimonial obligations but does not in principle allow the right to remarriage (although sometimes the right may be delayed), is a "divorce *a menso et thoro*" and not a "divorce *a vinculo matrimonii*". In modern usage only the latter is referred to as a divorce.

39 The lowest common denominator would seem to be that the adoptive parents acquire parental authority and a duty of support in respect of the child during his minority. See Krause, "Creation of Relationships of Kinship", *International Encyclopedia of Comparative Law* (1976) vol IV, ch 6 at para 6-185.

40 Krause *ibid* para 6-186 shows that the effect of adoption on inheritance rights varies greatly from system to system.

assimilated to the English status of the same name.[41] Thus, recognition of the foreign adoption simply requires giving effect to the status which has been created. This argument would favour determining the effect of the adoption by the *lex adoptionis*[42] rather than the *lex fori*. Thus, it is suggested that the "full effect" doctrine is a weak rationale for preferring the recognition rule in respect of succession and wrongful death claims following foreign adoptions.

2. Where the Foreign Order is not Recognised

Does the policy of the "non-recognition" rules require that they be given precedence to ensure that all effects of adoption be withheld from the parties to a non-recognised adoption?[43] In order to answer this question we need to examine the various "non-recognition" rules.

(A) LACK OF JURISDICTIONAL LINK

We saw above that there has been a general trend[44] liberalising the jurisdictional[45] bases for adoption. In England, no jurisdictional link is required in respect of "overseas adoptions". However, the common law recognition rules still depend on domicile, although it has been suggested that these rules be widened.[46] Thus, it is feasible that a situation like *Re Valentine*[47] could arise where the adoption was not an "overseas adoption".[48]

The purpose of jurisdictional rules is to prevent forum shopping and consequent prejudice to the defendant. In the case of adoption, whilst it is clearly preferable *ab initio* that the adoption takes place in an appropriate forum, it is difficult to see why *ex post facto*, after the child has been treated as an adopted child, incidents of adoption should be withheld because of lack of jurisdictional link[49] even where English law is the *lex causae*. *A fortiori*, where the adoption is recognised by the *lex successionis*, the lack of jurisdictional link should not prejudice the parties' rights.

(B) PUBLIC POLICY

Pubic policy restrictions on recognition of foreign adoptions will usually be designed to protect the child. For example, it would seem to be against public policy to recognise an adoption where the child had effectively been bought by

41 Krause (n 39, *supra*) at para 6-1767 *et seq* shows that in some systems adoption is much more limited and that in some countries there are two types of adoption available: full adoption and limited adoption.
42 Cf discussion at text accompanying nn 3-5, *supra*.
43 We saw above (ch 2, IV C) that the policy of non-recognition of a divorce did not necessarily require invalidation of the second marriage.
44 Cf the 1965 Hague Convention on Adoption. The complicated jurisdictional rules probably explain why the Convention has not been successful.
45 See McClean and Patchett in (1970) 19 ICLQ 1.
46 See nn 18 and 20, *supra*.
47 [1965] Ch 831.
48 Today *Re Valentine* would be decided differently because South Africa is one of the countries listed in SI 1973/19.
49 If the lack of a jurisdictional link is evidence of lack of *bona fides*, the adoption should also be refused recognition on public policy grounds.

the parents for the purposes of providing services for them and no doubt in this situation a court would refuse to give custody of the child to the parents. However, if the issue of recognition arose in relation to succession to the estate of one of the parents, there would seem to be no reason to prevent the child from succeeding. On the contrary, the child would be better protected by recognition of the order.

Where the adopted person was an adult, it may be more likely that public policy would require that the parties should not benefit from an adoption, where the parties' intention was not *bona fide*.[50] Morris[51] suggests that the "facts would have to be extreme before public policy demanded the *total* non-recognition of a foreign adoption *for all purposes*" (my emphasis).

Thus, whether the non-recognition is based on lack of jurisdiction or on public policy, there is no justification for giving it automatic precedence. In any event, whichever preference rule is chosen, the residual public policy defence will always be available.

B. Authority

There are no English decisions in which the "conflict of rules" has arisen in relation to adoption. However, there are two types of case which may provide us with some guidance.

1. Legitimacy/Legitimation Cases

The literature on the incidental question generally tends[52] to refer to problems arising out of legitimacy/legitimation rather than adoption. However, there is clearly a strong similarity between the two types of situation[53] and "conflicts of rules" cases concerning legitimacy/legitimation would be of persuasive authority in relation to adoption.

The legitimacy/legitimation cases properly belong to Part III of this book, because they do not involve any issue of recognition of a foreign judgment, and will therefore be discussed below.[54] It is sufficient to say at this stage that these cases are all consistent with the view that the law governing the succession should apply its rules to determine whether the claimant is legitimate(d), but the cases are of weak precedent value because no actual conflict arose.

2. Effect of "Foreign Adoption" Cases

After much debate, it now seems to be established[55] that in adoption cases it is the *lex successionis* which determines the extent of succession rights to and

50 Eg, where the motive was to evade immigration rules or to exclude another person from their legitimate share of an inheritance, recognition would be against public policy.

51 *Op cit* (ch 1, n 6, *supra*) pp 249-250.

52 While in his discussion Gottlieb (1977) 26 ICLQ 734 at 762 assimilates adoption with succession, one of his model problems (no 8 at p 788) does specifically refer to adoption.

53 For discussion of the similarities and differences, see Ch 10, III A, *infra*.

54 Ch 10, III B, *infra*.

55 *Re Valentine's Settlement* [1965] Ch 831, in which earlier case law to the contrary was stated to be wrong. See also the US case of *Anderson v French* (1915) 77 NH 509, 93 Atl 1042.

from adopted persons and not the *lex adoptionis* or for that matter the *lex fori.*[56] It can perhaps be logically inferred from this that the *lex sucessionis* should also determine whether the "adopted person" in question should in fact be treated as an adopted person for the purposes of succession.

C. Results[57]

The results will have to be analysed according to four possible types of cases which might arise:

1. Child claims after death of "adopted" parent or other "adopted" relative.
2. "Adopted" parent or other "adopted" relative claims after death of child.
3. Child claims after death of natural parents or other natural relative.
4. Natural parent or other natural relative claims after death of child.

1. Child Claims After Death of "Adoptive" Parent/Relative

Here, it will be helpful to refer to examples A1 and A2[58] which are based on the facts of *Re Valentine's Settlement.* The results of the application of the various rules may be summarised as follows.

(A) PREFERENCE FOR THE CHOICE RULE

Where the order is recognised by the *lex causae* but not the *lex fori,* as in example A2, where South Africa is the *lex successionis,* the claimant will succeed. On the other hand, where the order is recognised by the *lex fori* but not the *lex causae*, as in example A1, where Rhodesia is the *lex successionis*, the claimant will not succeed.

(B) PREFERENCE FOR THE RECOGNITION RULE

The opposite results will be achieved. Thus the claim will be successful where the order is recognised by the *lex fori* and not the *lex causae* (as in example A1), but not in the opposite situation (as in example A2).

(C) THE "DIFFERENTIAL RULE"

Under the "differential rule"[59] the recognition rule will apply where it leads to recognition of the foreign adoption and otherwise the choice rule will prevail. This will result in successful claims in every case.

(D) PRESUMPTION OF UPHOLDING SUCCESSION RIGHTS OR TORT CLAIMS

This would produce the same result as the "differential rule".

56 Although the *lex successionis* seems to have been the *lex fori* in all the decided cases.
57 For tabular illustration of the results of applying the different preference rules, see Tables 7A and 7B in the Appendix, *infra*.
58 At ch 1, IV B, *supra*.
59 See ch 4, II C 3, *supra*.

2. "Adoptive" Parent/Relative Claims After Death of the Child

The results will be the same as under 1. above.

3. Child Claims after Death of Natural Parent/Relative

This type of case can only arise where, under the relevant law, the adoption extinguishes rights of succession between child and natural parent. Assume, in examples A1 and A2, that the child wishes to claim against his natural parents whose domicile at death is the same as Dorothy's in each case.

(A) PREFER CHOICE RULE

The child can only claim if the adoption is *not* recognised by the *lex successionis*. This is the situation in example A1, but not A2.

(B) PREFER THE RECOGNITION RULE

Here the child can claim where the adoption is not recognised by the *lex fori,* as in example A2, but not A1.

(C) THE "DIFFERENTIAL RULE"

The child would not be able to claim in any situation.

(D) PRESUMPTION OF UPHOLDING SUCCESSION RIGHTS/TORT CLAIMS

This would ensure that the child could succeed against the natural parents where the adoption was not recognised by one of the relevant laws.

4. Natural Parents/Relative Claims After Death of Child

The conflict can only arise in this situation where under the relevant law the adoption order extinguishes the natural parent's succession rights and/or rights to claim for wrongful death in respect of the child. It may be noted that in some domestic laws there may not be reciprocity of treatment. Thus, a child may retain succession rights in respect of the natural parent, whilst the natural parent loses his/her rights in relation to the child on adoption.[60] Where the conflict arises, the results will be the same as in 3, above.

III. POLICY

A. The Law

Adopted children are treated as the children of their adopted parents and no longer as the children of their birth parents from the date of the adoption,[61] for nearly all purposes.[62] Thus, the child may succeed under a will or on intestacy

60 Eg, in Israel under the Adoption Law 1981, s 16(3).

61 Adoption Act 1976, s 39.

62 The main exception relates to descent of peerages and there are particular rules relating to the adoption of an illegitimate child by one of his parents as the sole adoptive parent.

as a child of the adoptive parent, but not as a child of the birth parents.[63] The adoptive parents will have reciprocal rights on the death of the child, whereas the natural parents will not have any rights arising from the death of the child after the making of the adoption order. Similarly, for the purposes of discretionary family provision[64] and wrongful death claims it is the adoptive relationship and not the natural relationship which is relevant.

The recent Adoption Law Review[65] has affirmed that despite certain trends towards "open adoption",[66] adoption orders should continue to effect a complete legal transplant of the child from the natural family to the adoptive family.[67] However, we may still need to bear in mind that changes in adoption practice may increase the chance that there is a continuing relationship between the child and the natural parent and this may be relevant in application of policy.

In order to consider how we should deal with the "conflict of rules" situation where there is a dispute as to whether an adoption order should be recognised, we need to consider the policy of inheritance and tort law respectively in relation to succession and wrongful death claims arising out of the parent-child relationship as well as the policy of the adoption law rule explained above.

B. Wills

We saw above[68] that the prime policy objective in relation to wills is to give effect to the wishes of the testator.[69] This policy is equally pertinent in relation to bequests to and by doubtfully adopted children.

C. Provision for Dependants

The Inheritance (Provision for Family and Dependants) Act 1975, provides that "any other person whom the deceased has treated as a child of the family in relation to any marriage to which he had any time been a party"[70] is entitled to claim.[71] Thus, where an adoption order is not recognised, but the child has been treated as if he were adopted, the child will be eligible to claim without having

63 Although he will not lose "any interest already vested in possession or interest expectant (whether immediately or not) upon an interest so vested at the date of the adoption." (Adoption Act 1976, s 42(4)).

64 It has been held that a child who has been adopted after the deceased's death cannot apply for an order in relation to his/her natural parents: *Re Collins* [1990] Fam 56.

65 Department of Health, Consultative Document on Adoption Law (1992).

66 *Ibid*, para 4.1.

67 *Ibid*, para 2 (R1).

68 At ch 5, III A, *supra*.

69 The principle of treating references to relatives in wills as including adoptive relatives is consistent with this objective. In particular, it should be remembered that this principle will not apply if contrary intention can be shown from the will.

70 Hereinafter such a child shall be referred to as a *de facto* child and the parents as *de facto* parents.

71 Section 1(1)(d). This may be seen as an extension of the provision of support rights in favour of minor children who are treated as a child of the family during a marriage (Domestic Proceedings and Magistrates Court Act 1978, s 2 and on divorce, see Matrimonial Causes Act, ss 23, 24 and 52 (as amended by Children Act 1989, Sch 12, para 33). However, the category here is wider, as can be seen from the decisions in *Re Leach* [1986] Ch 226 and *Re Callaghan* [1985] Fam 1.

to meet the additional requirement of proving that (s)he has been maintained by the deceased immediately before his death.[72]

We may conclude that the policy of ensuring that proper provision is made for dependants of the deceased includes both *de jure* and *de facto* children.[73] Of course, in relation to both categories, whether the child succeeds will depend on all the circumstances of the relationship between the parties.[74]

D. Intestacy

1. On Death of Parents

Where there is no surviving spouse, the children of the intestate take the whole of the estate. Where there is a surviving spouse, the issue take half of the residue of the estate (after the statutory legacy) absolutely and the remainder (following the surviving spouses's life interest) in the other half.

It is suggested that the two[75] most persuasive rationales for the intestacy rights of children are as follows.

(A) THE PRESUMED WISHES OF THE INTESTATE[76]

The intestate is presumed to wish his/her property to be divided in the same way as the average testator bequeaths his/her property. The present intestacy laws are based on an analysis of wills in the 1950s.[77] It is not surprising to find that after providing for a remaining spouse, the average testator makes provision for his/her children.

(B) THE MORAL OBLIGATION OF THE INTESTATE

Whilst the legal obligation of parents to support their children ends when the children reach the age of 18, there is a continuing moral obligation of support, arising from the parent's responsibility for bringing the child into the world. Clearly, the extent if any of this obligation depends on the respective financial position of the parents and children. On death, the parent no longer has any further personal need of his/her assets and therefore, subject to making provision for any other more needy dependants,[78] the children can be considered to have first[79] claim on those assets.

72 See s 1(1)(e) and s 1(3).

73 It may be noted that parents are not listed as a separate category of claimants in s 1 of the Act. Thus, natural and adoptive parents can only claim if they can show that they were being maintained by the deceased immediately before his/her death under s 1(1)(e).

74 Thus, eg, where an adoption order is invalid the child could claim against the natural parents. However, where all the parties had acted on the reasonable assumption that the adoption order was valid it seems unlikely that an award would be made, except perhaps where there has been a continuing relationship between them.

75 The rationales of need and desert, mentioned in the Law Commission's Working Paper No 108, are less useful because they depend more on the behaviour and financial circumstances of the particular child. In any event, the moral obligation rationale clearly reflects need and desert.

76 See Law Commission WP No 108, paras 4.2-4.3.

77 Report of Committee on the Law of Intestate Succession (Morton Committee) Cmnd 8310, para 3.

78 The moral obligation could be enforced under the Inheritance (Provision for Family and Dependants) Act 1975.

79 This hypothesis does not take into account the moral obligation to give to charity because the law of intestacy cannot make charitable donations where the deceased himself failed to do so by testamentary bequest.

The Law Commission mooted the possibility of extending intestacy rights to *de facto* children.[80] Their main reason for not recommending such a reform was that one of the main requirements of intestacy law is that it should be simple and to include *de facto* children would mean that "administrators would have to make complex decisions of fact".[81] They were also concerned that it would be unfair to allow such children to share both in the estate of their *de facto* parents and their *de jure* parents and that it would be complicated to prevent the latter. However, it may be noted that they did not suggest that *de facto* children did not come within the policy of intestacy provision.

2. On Death of Children

If there is a surviving spouse and no issue, the parents of the deceased take half of the residue of the estate after the statutory legacy. If there is no surviving spouse and no issue, the parents of the deceased take the whole estate. In both cases, where the deceased has been validly adopted, the adoptive parents take to the exclusion of the natural parents.

It is suggested that the rights of parents to take on the intestacy of their children can also be explained on the basis of presumed wishes[82] and moral obligation.

3. On Death of More Distant Relatives

It is more difficult to explain the basis for the order in which more distant relatives may claim on intestacy.[83] The list seems to be based on the closeness of the blood tie. Although rather speculative, the intestate might be presumed to wish closer relatives to take in preference to more distant ones. It is more difficult to base succession by more distant relatives on moral obligation, although it has been suggested that the notion of family property would provide more distant relatives with a moral claim.[84]

E. Wrongful Death

In 1982 the category of eligible dependants under the Fatal Accidents Act was expanded[85] to include, *inter alia*:

(i) a person who has been treated as a child of the family by the deceased victim; and
(ii) a person who was treated by the deceased as his parent.

80 For definition, see text accompanying n 73, *supra*.
81 Law Com No 187, para 49.
82 Although it may be argued that the deceased may have preferred to benefit his/her siblings as in the long-term this would be tax advantagous. The Law Commission did not think that tax considerations should be relevant, see Law Com No 187 at para 50-51.
83 See Law Com WP 108, para 4.11.
84 *Ibid.*
85 See Fatal Accidents Act 1976, s 1(3), substituted by Administration of Justice Act 1982, s 3.

Thus, it can be seen that the policy behind wrongful death provision is to compensate *de facto*[86] as well as *de jure* children and parents for the loss of dependency arising from the defendant's tortious actions.

F. Adoption Law

Finally, we should consider the policy of the domestic rule, which will be referred to as a rule of adoption law, that adopted children are treated[87] for nearly all purposes as the natural born legitimate children of the adopters. Perusal of the legislative history of the provision shows that the main rationale behind this principle[88] is to facilitate the full integration[89] of the child into the adoptive family because this is believed[90] to be in the best interests of the child.[91]

Since the very question is whether the child should be treated as an adopted child, it is not clear how much weight should be attached to the policy of adoption law. However, it is suggested that in the situation where there is some doubt as to the policy of succession or tort law, this may be resolved by application of the "full integration" principle.

IV. APPLICATION OF POLICY

We now need to examine how the policy we have identified applies in relation to cases which have a foreign element and where there is a dispute about the validity of the adoption order between the forum and the *lex causae.*

A. Wills

1. "Adoptive" Parent as Testator

It is suggested that the "adoptive" parent would normally intend the word "child" in his will to include a child whom he had adopted, even though there was a dispute about the validity of the adoption order. If (s)he was not aware that the decree would not be recognised in some countries, then (s)he would clearly intend the child to be treated as a legally adopted child. If (s)he was aware of the doubt and did not want the child to succeed, this would surely be stated specifically in the will.

86 For definition, see text accompanying n 70, *supra.*

87 Full assimilation of treatment was only achieved by the Children Act 1975.

88 See Hougton Committee Report (1972) at, eg, para 326.

89 Full integration is seen by the judiciary as the main advantage of adoption over other methods of disposal, principally because of the security and stability it provides for the child and the adoptive family. See, eg, *Re S* [1987] Fam 98 at 107; *Re B (MF)(an infant), Re (SL) (an infant)* [1972] 1 All ER 898 at 899-900; *Re L (A Minor)* [1987] 1 FLR 400 at 403; and *Re A (A Minor)* [1987] 2 FLR 184 at 189.

90 On the basis of empirical research showing that children who are adopted fare better than children who remain in long-term foster care. See Tizard, *Adoption: A Second Chance* (1977) and Seaglow *et al, Growing Up Adopted* (1972).

91 It is clear that the promotion of the welfare of the child is the main, although not the sole, policy objective in modern adoption legislation. See Adoption Law Review (n 65, *supra*) para 7.1 *et seq.*

2. Relative/Friend of Adoptive Parents as Testator

The position is perhaps less clear in relation to third parties who are not themselves involved in the adoption process. By analogy with the reasoning adopted above in relation to "former" spouses,[92] it could be assumed that the testator intended to benefit a child whose adoption is recognised by the law governing the interpretation of his/her will.

However, it might be argued that the analogy is false since the fact that the adoption is not recognised will not usually affect the *de facto* relationship[93] between the adoptive parent and the child or between the testator and the child. Thus, the testator would intend to benefit the child irrespective of the validity of the adoption or at least provided that the adoption is valid by some relevant law.

It is suggested that the latter approach should be preferred because it is more consistent with the adoption law policy of "full integration".

3. Natural Parent or Relative/Friend as Testator[94]

Similarly, the natural parent or his/her relatives/friends will not usually intend a reference to a child to include a child who has been adopted. Even if the testator believes the adoption order to be invalid, if (s)he wishes to include the child, surely the child would be mentioned expressly by name in order to avoid any doubt.

4. Adoptive Child as Testator

By analogy with the reasoning in 1. above, where the "adopted" child has made testamentary provision for his/her parent, it should be assumed that (s)he intended to refer to the adoptive parents, unless contrary intention can be seen from the will.

Again, the situation is less clear where the "adopted" child makes testamentary provision for other relatives. However, unless (s)he actually has a continuing relationship with his/her natural relatives it would seem clear that the intention must be to refer to the "adoptive" relatives.

The desired results[95] in each of the four situations can be achieved by use of the "differential rule" under which the rule which recognises the adoption will be applied.

92 At ch 5, IV A 2, *supra*.
93 We saw above (*ibid*) that the position is more speculative where third parties have made provision for "spouses".
94 Assuming that, under the relevant law, a valid adoption extinguishes all succession rights between the child and the natural parent. There are a number of legal systems where this is not the case. See Krause (n 39, *supra*) para 6-184.
95 It may be noted that these are all consistent with the "full integration" principle.

B. Provision for Dependants

1. Discretionary Provision

It will be remembered that in fact the "conflict of rules" situation will only arise if an English court is prepared to apply a foreign discretionary provision statute.[96] It is assumed that the foreign statute only allows claims by adopted children if there is a recognised order and does not allow validly adopted children to claim against the estate of the natural parents.

We saw above that the policy of the English discretionary provision statute is to ensure that proper provision is made on death for the *de facto* children[97] of the deceased. Thus, it is clear that the preference rule should ensure that the "adopted" child can claim against the "adoptive" parents.

Should the "adopted" child be able to claim against his/her natural parents? Under English domestic law, where the adoption order is invalid the child would be eligible to claim but would be unlikely to succeed unless there had in fact been a continuing relationship between the parties. It would seem inappropriate to allow the child to claim against his/her natural parents where the *lex causae* itself recognises the adoption. However, where the *lex causae* does not recognise the adoption, there would not seem to be any good reason[98] not to apply the choice rule and allow the child to claim, even though his chances of success are slim. Since such a right would not affect that child's position in the adoptive family, allowing a claim is not inconsistent with the "full integration" principle.

The above results could be achieved by applying the "differential rule" in the case of a claim against the estate of an adoptive parent and the choice rule in a claim against the estate of a natural parent.

2. Fixed Shares

An English court may be faced with the situation where the *lex successionis* provides a fixed share for a child,[99] including an adopted child, but there is a dispute as to the validity of the adoption. It was argued above[100] that the policy of English law in relation to discretionary provision should in principle be equally applicable in relation to fixed shares since the two "systems" are simply different methods of achieving the same purpose.

Thus, in the present context, the policy of allowing a claim against the adopted parents should apply equally in fixed share cases. This result is supported by the "full integration" principle.

However, it is more problematic to apply the policy of allowing claims against the natural parents where the *lex causae* does not recognise the

96 See ch 5, I C, *supra*.
97 For definition, see text accompanying n 70, *supra*.
98 There can be no concern about an unfair result, since an award will only be made in a deserving case and the court will take into account *inter alia* the possibility of the child having a claim against both parents' estates (which was of concern to the Law Commission, n 81, *supra*). Allowing the child to claim in this very specific situation will not lead to a proliferation of bogus claims.
99 This is analogous to the position in relation to spouses. See ch 5, III B 4, *supra*.
100 *Ibid*.

adoption,[101] to "fixed share" cases. One of the reasons that we gave in favour of allowing a claim against natural parents was that under the discretionary system unmeritorious cases would be rejected. However, in "fixed share" systems there is no such filter mechanism.[102] The result of allowing a claim against the natural parents would be to entitle the child to a full "fixed share" in the estate of both sets of parents, irrespective of his/her relationship with them.

It is suggested that such "double succession" is against the policy of English law.[103] Thus, the corollary of allowing a claim against the "adoptive" parents is to disallow a claim against the natural parents.

The suggested desired results of allowing claims against "adoptive" but not natural parents can be achieved by use of the "differential rule", under which the recognition rule is applied where it recognises the adoption and otherwise the choice rule.

C. Intestacy

It is assumed throughout the following discussion that, under the *lex successionis*, where there is a valid adoption this extinguishes the succession rights between natural parents and children. Where this is not the case, there will be succession between the natural relatives whether or not the adoption is recognised. The only issue will be whether the "adopted child" and the adoptive relatives can claim *inter se*.

1. On Death of the "Adoptive" Parents

On the assumption that intestate provision for children is based on the presumed wishes and moral obligations of the intestate, should the "adopted" child be able to claim against the estate of either his "adoptive" or natural parents?

It is suggested that the average testator would wish his/her "adopted" children to take whether or not the adoption is legally recognised by either the *lex successionis* or the *lex fori*. Failure to make a will may reflect the intestate's belief that the adoption is legally effective in the relevant jurisdiction(s).

To the extent that intestacy rights are based on a moral obligation does that obligation extend to "adopted" children? It was suggested earlier that the moral obligation to provide for children on death is a continuation of the legal obligation of support in respect of minor children.[104] Since *de facto* parents

101 There will not be any problem where the *lex causae* allows adopted children to take fixed shares in both their adoptive parents and natural parents' estates, see Krause (n 39, *supra*) at para 6-183.

102 It will be remembered that in relation to spouses, the difficulty caused by the lack of flexibility of the fixed share system was to a large extent solved by the use of the doctrine of preclusion (see ch 5, IV B 2, *supra*). This doctrine is inappropriate in the case of a claim by an adopted child because the child was not a party to the adoption order.

103 See Law Com No 187 at para 49. The Adoption Law Review's (n 65, *supra*) recommendation that a child whose natural parents have died intestate should not lose his contingent interest under the statutory trusts by virtue of adoption might seem to contradict this. However, this situation is different because the succession rights against the two sets of parents are successive rather than concurrent.

104 See III C 1 (B), *supra*.

have support duties in respect of children who have been treated as children of the family,[105] such children should be included within the scope of the moral obligation on death.

We saw above that the Law Commission rejected the idea of giving intestacy rights to *de facto* children because of the complexity this would cause. It is suggested that their reasoning is inapplicable in the present context. Firstly, the situation where the decree is recognised in one jurisdiction and not in another is unusual and complexity is unavoidable. Secondly, it will usually be beyond doubt that the "adopted" child has been treated as the child of the family. Thirdly, if the preference rule prevents succession to the estate of the natural parent,[106] there is no danger of a double portion.

Thus, it is submitted that on intestacy of the adoptive parent the doubtfully adopted child should succeed, without having to rely on discretionary family provision legislation.[107]

2. On Death of "Adopted" Children

The presumed wishes and moral obligation principles would seem to require that the "adoptive" parents should be able to take on the intestacy of their "adopted" child. If the child did indeed wish to benefit his natural parents, surely he would make specific testamentary provision for them.

If the "adoptive" parents are no longer living, the child may also be assumed to prefer that his/her adoptive relatives should succeed in preference to the natural family which has rejected him/her.

3. On Death of Other Adoptive Relatives

It is not so clear that other relatives can be presumed to wish the doubtfully adopted child to succeed on the same basis as if the adoption order is valid. In particular, there may be a situation where the question is whether the doubtfully adopted child or a more distantly related blood relative succeeds to the whole estate. Indeed if moral obligation here is seen as reflecting the notion of family property, it may be argued that a person with a doubtful legal relationship has a weaker claim than a more distant relative, whose relationship is not in doubt.

Thus, it might be more appropriate to presume that the deceased wishes to benefit only children whose adoption is recognised in his own country, the law of his domicile.

In relation to movables, the *lex domicilii* will also be the *lex successionis.* Thus, application of the choice rule would produce the desired result. However, intestate succession to immovables is governed entirely by the *lex situs.*[108]

105 See n 71, *supra*.

106 See at 4, *infra*.

107 The Law Commission (Rept No 187 at para 50) suggested that the *de facto* child was adequately protected by the Inheritance (Provision for Family and Dependants) Act 1975. However, as this only provides for maintenance, it is difficult to see how it can be equated to intestacy rights.

108 It is unlikely that the intestate would expect the *situs* to determine the validity of the adoption. Moreover, since the use of the *lex situs* to govern intestate succession to immovables is widely criticised (see ch 5, n 8, *supra*) it would seem inappropriate to extend its function.

None of the existing preference rules would enable the domicile to determine whether the adopted child could take. Whilst it is possible to create a new rule to the effect that in relation to intestacy by distant relatives, the domicile of the deceased at the time of his death determines whether the adoption order is valid, this is difficult to fit within the existing conflict of laws framework. A speculative assumption about the wishes of the deceased would not seem to justify such an innovation.

Since none of the approaches based on intestacy policy is satisfactory, we should consider the application of the "full integration" policy of adoption law. It is suggested that in this context this policy would seem to require that an "adopted" child be able to claim from distant adopted relatives.

4. On Death of Natural Parents/Relatives

What is the position in relation to birth relatives? By analogy with the will situation, the intestate will be presumed not to wish to benefit a natural child/relative who has been adopted. Arguably, any moral obligation is extinguished by the adoption order[109] whether it be legally recognised or not.[110]

From the above discussion we may conclude that the policy of intestacy law would be to allow claims between "adopted" children and "adoptive" parents/relatives. However, claims by and against the estates of natural relatives should not be allowed.

Thus, again the desired results can be achieved by the "differential rule", which will apply whichever rule results in recognition of the adoption order.

D. Wrongful Death

Since the policy of English law is to allow claims by *de facto* children and parents, it seems clear that the "adopted child" and "adoptive parent" should be able to claim in respect of the wrongful death of the adoptive parent in the "conflict of rules" situation. This result can be achieved by application of the "differential rule".

The more difficult question is whether the "adopted" child be allowed to claim in relation to the death of the natural parent and *vice versa*. The problem only arises where under the *lex causae*, a valid adoption would prevent a claim.[111]

Under English domestic law, a valid adoption will prevent a claim, but an invalid adoption will not prevent a claim if it can be shown that the claimant

109 Although in a number of countries the natural parents' support obligation is retained, although it is subsidiary to that of the adoptive parents': Krause (n 39, *supra*) para 6-184.

110 If the natural parent has in fact been maintaining the child before his/her death, there will be a claim under discretionary family provision.

111 Speiser (ch 7, n 52, *supra*) at pp 141-143 brings cases where it was held that the right to recover was not cut off by the adoption, although the fact of the adoption might well reduce the size of the award.

would have received financial support from the deceased. Thus, in the case where there is a doubt about the validity of the adoption, there is no difficulty in allowing a claim based on dependency.[112] However, it will be rare that dependency can be proved. An "adopted" child will not be doubly compensated in the unlikely event that both sets of parents are wrongfully killed, since (s)he will only receive what (s)he would have received if they had all remained alive. The desired result can be achieved by application of the presumption in favour of tort claims.

However, where under the *lex causae* the award is not based on dependency, the position is more difficult. If the presumption in favour of tort claims is adopted, unmeritorious claimants may recover for losses they have not suffered simply because the adoption is technically invalid by the law of one country. On the other hand, if the "differential rule" is applied, then even in the case where the claimant is dependent on the deceased, (s)he will not be able to claim because the law of one country has a liberal policy in relation to recognising foreign adoptions.

Since no solution can ensure a result which will always be consistent with forum policy, it is suggested that the most logical option should be sought. The *lex causae* allows a wrongful death claim based purely on status and therefore the *lex causae* should determine that status.[113] In other words, the choice of law rule governing the tort should be applied to determine whether the "adopted" child can claim on the wrongful death of his/her natural parent and *vice versa* where the award is not based on dependency.

112 It may be noted that in some countries adopted children can inherit from both adoptive and natural parents. See Krause (n 39, *supra*) at para 6-183.

113 Furthermore, this solution avoids the possibility of a result which is inconsistent with the law of both countries where the *lex causae* does recognise the adoption and the *lex fori* does not recognise the adoption, but only allows claims based on dependency.

PART III

SPECIFIC SOLUTIONS IN CASES WHERE THERE IS A CONFLICT BETWEEN TWO CHOICE OF LAW RULES

Chapter 9

Invalidity of Marriage *ab initio*

I. SCOPE OF THE PROBLEM

A. Introduction

We are concerned with the situation where the incidental question is the initial validity of the marriage and the forum would determine this differently from the *lex causae* governing the main question.[1] The "critical question" is whether the party is "single" or "married" for the purpose in question. Under the "conflict of rules" analysis, there is a conflict between the forum's choice of law rules governing marriage and its choice of law rules governing the main question because the latter lead to application of the rules[2] of the *lex causae* to determine whether one of the parties is considered married for the purpose in question.

In order to determine how likely this conflict is to arise, it is necessary to consider the differences between English choice of law rules governing validity of foreign marriages and foreign choice rules. Thus, it will be convenient to look at some foreign rules and then to make a comparison.

B. Comparison between English and Foreign Choice of Law Rules

Three main models for choice of law rules governing validity of marriage can be found. Under the first and simplest, the *lex loci celebrationis* governs all questions concerning the validity of a marriage. The other two models involve distinguishing between issues of formal validity and issues of essential validity (also referred to as capacity) with the former being governed by the *lex loci celebrationis* and the latter by the personal law of the parties, the *lex patriae* and the *lex domicili* respectively. English law belongs to the third category and thus the "conflict of rules" is most likely to arise where the *lex causae* adopts one of the other models. However, even within each model there is room for differences of detail and therefore potential for conflicts. It is only necessary here to provide a very general survey[3] so as to give some indication of the types of conflicts that might arise.

It should be mentioned that, in some systems, distinctions may be drawn between the law to be applied to determine whether the parties may be permitted to marry and those that are applied to determine whether a marriage which has

1 See example M11 at ch I, IV B, *supra*.
2 Usually its conflicts rules.
3 A comprehensive survey of choice of law rules relating to marriage can be found in Palsson (ch 1, nn 42 and 119, *supra*) and Rabel, *The Conflict of Laws, A Comparative Study* (2nd edn, 1958) vol 1, ch 8.

been entered into is to be recognised as valid. In the incidental question situation, whilst the main question may relate to the *a priori* position, the subsidiary question will always *ex hypothesi* be concerned with the *ex post facto* situation.

1. The Lex Loci Celebrationis Model

This is the model traditionally favoured in the United States.[4] However, over the years it has been necessary to make inroads into the *lex loci* approach[5] in order to avoid evasion of local marriage restrictions by out of state marriage celebration[6] and to recognise the interests of other states in the validity of the marriage.[7]

However, despite the problems encountered in the United States, the *lex loci* model was adopted by the Hague Convention on the Celebration and Recognition of the Validity of Marriages in 1978. The main reason seems to be that this model may be seen as a compromise between those common law countries which use domicile and civil law countries where nationality is the prevalent connecting factor. However, like many compromises it seems to have pleased very few and only three countries[8] have ratified and a further three[9] joined the Convention.

The Australian implementation of the Convention[10] is not simply adoption of the *lex loci celebrationis* choice rule in place of the existing rules. The common law rules are saved. Thus, whilst most marriages celebrated abroad[11] are recognised if they are formally and essentially valid or validated by the *lex loci celebrationis*, marriages which are valid at common law will also be recognised.

4 And in South Africa (see Forsyth, *Private International Law* (1981) pp 230 *et seq*).

5 See discussions in Reese (1977) 26 ICLQ 952; Baade (1972) 72 Columbia Law Rev 329; and Scoles and Hay (ch 4, n 18, *supra*) at pp 342 *et seq*.

6 Eg, Marriage Evasion Statutes, reproducing or resembling the Uniform Marriage Evasion Act 1912 (which was withdrawn as an approved Act in 1943) were enacted in a number of jurisdictions (see Scoles and Hay *ibid* at p 437). A similar result was also sometimes achieved by case law as in *Lanham v Lanham* 136 Wis 360, 117 NW 787 (1908).

7 Thus, a marriage which is valid by the *lex loci* "will be held invalid if it would be regarded as such by the court of the State having the requisite degree of interest in the matter" (Reese (1977) 26 ICLQ 952 at 955). Reese goes on to point out that this exception has only been applied to invalidate a marriage if the *lex domicili* of one of the parties hold the marriage invalid. The Uniform Marriage and Divorce Act, s 210 provides that a marriage will be valid if valid either by the *lex loci* or by the *lex domicili*. The Restatement (2nd) para 283, whilst providing in sub-para 1 that validity is determined by the law which "with respect to the particular issue has the most significant relationship to the spouses and the marriage", goes on to state a presumption that a marriage which is valid by the *lex loci celebrationis* should be recognised everywhere unless "it violates the strong public policy of another State which has the most significant relationship to the spouses and the marriage at the time of the marriage".

8 Australia, Luxemburg and the Netherlands.

9 Egypt, Finland and Portugal.

10 In the Marriage Amendment Act 1985.

11 The few exceptions are listed in s 88D of the Marriage Act 1981 (as introduced by the Marriage Amendment Act 1985).

2. The Lex Loci/Lex Patriae Model

This is still the prevalent model on the Continent,[12] although in some countries reforms have widened recognition of marriages involving foreign elements.[13] Whilst the common *lex patriae* of the parties will invariably be applicable, the situation where they have different and conflicting *leges patriae* is more difficult.[14] Some countries apply the two laws cumulatively,[15] which will increase the chance of invalidity of the marriage. Others have rules for giving preference to one of the rules[16] or use a third law to resolve the conflict.[17]

The distinction between the laws governing issues of formal and essential validity, whilst creating classification problems which are well known, is widely justified.[18] However, it should be pointed out that domestic laws of "nationality" countries do not always abide by this distinction in relation to requirements which for policy reasons are considered by them to be fundamental. Thus, occasionally, domestic legislation applies requirements, which appear to be formal, to all nationals.[19]

3. The Lex Loci/Lex Domicili Model

This is still the prevalent model[20] in England and Wales and most of the Commonwealth. Whilst formalities are governed by the *lex loci celebrationis*, as in the preceding two models, capacity is governed by the domicile of each party.

(A) FORMAL VALIDITY

In relation to formalities, there are two main deviations from the *lex loci* rule. Firstly, under the Foreign Marriages Act 1892 as amended by the Foreign Marriage Act 1947 and the Foreign Marriage (Amendment) Act 1988, consular marriages and marriages of member of British forces serving abroad will be recognised where they are performed abroad in accordance with the requirements

12 See, eg, arts 17 and 9 of the Austrian Private International Law statute which came into force on 1 January 1979 (a translation appears at (1980) 28 Am J Comp Law 222). For the position in Germany, see Dickson (1985) 34 ICLQ 231.

13 Eg, art 43 of the new Swiss code provides that a foreign marriage will be recognised in Switzerland if it is valid under the law of the state of celebration or of the domicile, habitual residence of nationality of the spouse (see McCaffrey (1980) 28 Am J Comp Law 235 at 265).

14 This situation is more common than marriages between persons of same nationality and different domicile (See Dyer Report, *Actes et documents de la troizieme session* Tome III, p 28).

15 This usually means applying each party's national law to govern his/her capacity except in the case of bilateral impediments. See Dyer Report (n 14, *supra*) at pp 31-32 and Palsson (ch 1, n 42 *supra*) at pp 83-84.

16 Eg, where one party is a national of the forum, preference for the *lex fori*. For other options, see Palsson *ibid* at p 84 *et seq*.

17 Eg, the *lex fori* or the common matrimonial domicile (see Dyer Report (*supra*, n 14) at pp 32-33).

18 See, eg Dyer Report (*supra*, n 14) at p 24.

19 Perhaps the most well known is the former Greek requirement that all nationals who are members of the Greek Orthodox church must marry in accordance with religious rites of that church and that otherwise their marriage is void. This provision was repealed in 1982 and marriages performed in contravention of this requirement prior to that date are retrospectively valid provided that no second marriage has been entered into by either party.

20 For discussion of alternatives see ch 4, I C, *supra*.

of the statute, notwithstanding that they do not comply with the formalities of the *lex loci celebrationis*.[21] Similar provisions are found in many other systems including those belonging to the previous two models.

Secondly, under the so-called "common law marriage" exception, parties who comply with the simple common law formalities of agreeing in each other's presence to marry each other (*per verba de praesenti*) will be recognised as married where compliance with the local law is impossible[22] or where one party is serving as a member of an occupying or associated military force in a country which is under belligerent occupation.[23] This exception, whilst followed in other common law jurisdictions,[24] is not known in civil law countries.[25] Indeed in such cases, *ex hypothesi* the marriage is invalid by the *lex loci celebrationis* and thus if this is the *lex causae* of the main question, there will be a conflict.

(B) ESSENTIAL VALIDITY

Whilst continuing with the assumption that essential validity is still governed by the dual domicile test,[26] we should bear in mind that where this test would lead to invalidity and the marriage is valid according to some law which is more closely connected, the court may well apply the latter.[27] This will reduce the scope for conflict. Also, the exception to the domicile rule created in *Sotomeyer v De Barros (No 2)*,[28] under which a foreign impediment will not invalidate a marriage celebrated in the forum where one party is domiciled in the forum, will reduce the scope for conflict where the *lex causae* of the main question is the domicile of the foreign spouse. Whilst this rule has been widely criticised as parochial,[29] it is still applicable in England and Wales and Canada.[30]

Thus, the scope for the "conflict of rules" to arise in England in relation to the initial validity of marriage may be summarised as follows:

1. Where the *lex causae* applies the *lex loci celebrationis* to matters of capacity and the party whose capacity is in issue is not domiciled in the *lex loci*.
2. Where the *lex causae* applies the law of a third country (other than that of the domicile of the party whose capacity is in issue) to matters of capacity by way of exception to the *lex loci* principle.

21 Although in relation to a consular marriage the marriage officer must be satisfied *inter alia* that the authorities of the *lex loci* will not object to the marriage (see Foreign Marriage Order, SI 1970/1539).
22 See discussion in Law Com WP 89 at paras 2.23-2.25 and Australian cases of *Savenis v Savenis* [1950] SASR 309 and *Kuklycz v Kuklycz* [1972] VR 50.
23 See, eg, *Taczanowska v Taczanowski* [1957] P 301.
24 For Australia, see Sykes and Pryles (ch 2, n 246, *supra*) at pp 420-425. For Canada, see Castel (ch 4, n 17, *supra*) at pp 286-288.
25 It is not even clear to what extent it applies in Scotland. See Law Com WP 89 at para 2.29.
26 See ch 4, I C, *supra*.
27 *Ibid*.
28 (1879) 5 PD 94.
29 See, eg, Cheshire and North (ch 1, n 6, *supra*) at p 597; per Cumming-Bruce J in *Radwan v Radwan (No 2)* [1975] Fam 35 at 50; and by the Law Commission (WP No 89 at para 3.17 and Report No 165, paras 2.7-2.8 and 2.15).
30 However, the rule was not adopted in Scotland (*Lendrum v Chakravati* 1929 SLT 96 at 102-103 and it is doubtful whether it is part of Australian law (see *Miller v Teale* (1954) 92 CLR 406 at 414).

3. Where the *lex causae* applies the law of the nationality to determine essential validity and the party whose capacity is in issue is not a national of the country where he is domiciled.
4. Where the *lex causae* applies the law of the domicile, but disagrees with the forum as to where the party whose capacity is in issue is domiciled.
5. Where the marriage is not formally valid by the *lex loci celebrationis* but it is recognised in England under an exception which is unknown to the *lex causae*.
6. Where the *lex causae* characterises the alleged defect as one of forum and the *lex fori* treats it as one of capacity or vice versa.

II. PREFERENCE FOR THE CHOICE OF LAW RULE GOVERNING THE VALIDITY OF THE "FIRST" MARRIAGE

A. Theoretical Basis

1. Generally

In Part II of this book, we examined the theoretical basis for giving preference to each of the two rules which were in conflict, ie the choice rule (governing the main question) and the recognition rule respectively in relation to each chosen subject. In the situation currently under consideration, instead of the recognition rule, there is a choice of law rule governing the validity of the "first" marriage. Thus, we need to examine the theoretical basis for preferring this rule where it conflicts with the result of applying the *lex causae* of the main question.

By analogy with the arguments adopted in relation to recognition rules, it can be contended that where the forum's choice of law rules require recognition of the validity of the "first" marriage then "full effect" must be given to the status resulting from application of those choice of law rules. Where necessary this will require overriding the application of choice of law rules governing the main question which lead to a conflicting result. It may also be claimed that the choice rule governing the validity of the "first" marriage needs to be applied in order to ensure internal consistency. Questions of the validity of this marriage can arise in many contexts and it seems absurd that this marriage may be considered valid for some purposes and not for others.

However, these arguments rest on the premise that marriage is universal, a proposition on which doubt has already been cast.[31] Furthermore, it has already been pointed out that often the apparently problematic inconsistency is purely theoretical.[32] Thus, the theoretical basis for giving preference to the choice rule governing the "first" marriage must depend on its superiority over the particular competing choice of law rule governing the main question. Accordingly, it is necessary to examine each type of main question which might arise separately. We will restrict our discussion to the topics which have been chosen for analysis in this book. Matrimonial property regimes usually only apply where there has

31 When discussing remarriage after a foreign divorce (ch 4, II A 1, *supra*).
32 Chapter 4, II A 3 (a), *supra*.

been a matrimonial decree and thus the relevant subjects for present purposes are: capacity to remarry; succession and tort.

2. Capacity to Remarry

Here the conflict is between the choice of law rules governing the remarriage and those governing the "first" marriage. Since the same conflicts rules are involved in relation to both questions, priority cannot be claimed by reference to the nature of the rules themselves.

The real issue is one of timing. Are the choice of law rules governing capacity to marry to be applied at the time of the "first" marriage or the time of the remarriage. There is a certain logic in insisting that the matter should be considered from a historical chronological perspective and that therefore the validity of the first marriage has to be tested by reference to the rules applicable at the date when it was celebrated. It may further be argued that justice requires the validity of the first marriage to be ascertained according to a law appropriately connected at the date of its alleged inception because that is what the parties would have legitimately expected.

On the other hand, the situation looks rather different if we focus on the "critical question" of whether the party remarrying is "single" at the time of the second marriage. Arguably, everyone would expect a law closely connected with him/her at this later date to apply for this particular purpose.

3. Succession

Here it may be argued that the choice of law rule governing the "first" marriage is more important than the choice of law rule governing succession, because the former concerns status. Presumably, the basis for such a contention is that determination of status has wide implications whereas succession simply determines how much money or property a person receives on the specific occasion of the death of a particular individual. However, again it is clear that such reasoning is based on the doubtful premise that marriage is universal.[33]

The argument in favour of the choice rule governing the "first" marriage seems strongest in the case of succession between the "spouses" themselves. In theory, this choice rule should lead to application of the substantive law which they would reasonably expect to apply to issues dependent on the validity of their marriage. Conversely, the argument is weakest in the case of a third party testator or intestate, who has never had any connection with the law indicated by the forum's choice of law rule for validity of marriages.

4. Tort

If the tort choice of law rule is a mechanical application of the *lex loci delicti*, then it might be argued that the marriage choice rule should be preferred because it provides for application of a law which has a more significant connection with the parties. However, where the tort choice of law rule allows

33 Chapter 4, II A 3, *supra*.

for the displacement of the *lex loci delicti* by a more closely connected law,[34] this point is inapplicable. Again, the argument in favour of the choice rule governing the "first" marriage seems stronger where the tortfeasor is the "spouse" than where (s)he is a third party.

B. Authority

1. Case Law

There is very little reported case law concerning where the incidental question is the validity *ab initio* of the "first" or only marriage.[35]

Perhaps the clearest authority is the US tort case of *Meisenholder v Chicago NW Ry*,[36] which supports application of the *lex causae* of the main issue.

In this case, a "widow" claimed in Minnesota under the Workman's Compensation Acts following the death of her "husband" in an accident which took place in Illinois. The parties, who were first cousins resident in Illinois, had got married in Kentucky. First cousin marriages were allowed by the law of Kentucky, but not by the law of Illinois. Under the Uniform Marriage Evasion Act in force in Illinois the marriage was not recognised. However, by the law of the Minnesota forum, the marriage was valid under the *lex loci celebrationis* rule. It was held that the claim failed because by the *lex loci delicti*, the claimant was not the widow of the deceased.

The Australian case of *Haque v Haque*,[37] discussed earlier, also provides authority in favour of application of the *lex causae* governing the main question. Whilst Azra could not succeed as the deceased's wife because of the divorce, her children could take if her marriage to their father was valid. The marriage, which was actually polygamous, was not valid in the Western Australian forum, where it had been celebrated. However, the court held that, irrespective of this fact, Muslim law, which was applied by the Indian *lex successionis*, did recognise the marriage and that the children could therefore take.[38] Similarly, the attempted remarriage between Azra and the deceased in Western Australia was not recognised because it was invalid under Muslim law rather than because it would not be recognised in Western Australia.

2. Statutes and Conventions

Whilst, as we saw above, the problem of capacity to remarry after a foreign matrimonial decree has been addressed by statute in a number of countries, the legislation in none of them extends to cover the case where the first marriage is alleged to be void *ab initio*, but no decree has been obtained confirming this.

34 As under the exception in *Boys v Chaplin* [1971] AC 536 and as provided for by in the Private International Law (Miscellaneous Provisions) Act, s 12.

35 Dicta of Lord Greene MR in *Baindail v Baindail* [1946] P 122 at 127 suggest that whether or not a Hindu marriage was recognised in England, where the succession was governed by Indian law as the law of the deceased's domicile, effect would have to be given to the rights of the Hindu widow.

36 213 NW 32 (1927).

37 (1962) 108 CLR 230.

38 *Ibid* at 248.

It will be remembered that the statutes in question only concerned capacity to remarry and did not deal with any of the other main questions which may arise.

However, the Hague Conference, whilst avoiding the problem of the incidental question for many years, was finally forced to confront it in the Convention on Celebration and Recognition of Marriages.[39] It was appreciated that the question of validity of marriage very frequently arises as an incidental question. The prevailing view at the Third Commission was that if nothing was included in the Convention on the point, the implication would be that the Convention rules applied in all cases. In other words, the Convention would provide for application of the conflicts rules of the *lex fori*. Thus, it was decided to make express provision, which was finally contained in Article 12 and reads as follows:

> "The rules of this Chapter[40] shall apply even where the recognition of the validity of a marriage is to be dealt with as an incidental question in the context of another question. However, these rules need not be applied where that other question, under the choice of law rules of the forum, is governed by the law of a non-Contracting State."

This provision is a compromise in the sense that it simply allows national courts to follow their own practice in cases where the *lex causae* of the main question is the law of a non-contracting state. In fact, where the law of a contracting state governs the main question, there should not be any conflict because both laws will apply the Convention to determine the validity of the marriage. Thus, the first part of the Article seems to be redundant and the provision cannot be seen as decisive authority on which of the two choice rules should govern where the incidental question is the validity of the "first" or only marriage.

C. Results

The results discussed in the relevant chapters in Part II of this book can be applied *mutatis mutandis* to the current situation by substituting the results of applying the choice of law governing the "first" or only marriage for the recognition rule, except that all references to the differential rule should be ignored.[41] Example M11[42] provides an illustration.

III. CONSTRUCTING PREFERENCE RULES

A. General Comparison with the Matrimonial Decree Situation

In both situations the "conflict of rules" arises because the subsistence of the "first" marriage at the relevant date is in dispute. In the matrimonial decree

39 For summary of the debate and final provision in relation to the incidental question, see Malmstrom Report (ch 1, n 11, *supra*) at para 25.

40 Ie ch II, dealing with recognition of the validity of marriages (as opposed to ch 1, which deals with the celebration of marriages).

41 See Tables 8a, 8b, 8c and 8d in the Appendix. For construction of an appropriate differential rule in the present context, see III B, *infra*.

42 Chapter 1, IV B, *supra*.

situation the dispute arises because one relevant jurisdiction recognises a decree dissolving, annulling or declaring the marriage void and the other does not. In the situation currently under discussion, the doubt arises because one relevant jurisdiction considers the marriage valid whereas the other considers it void *ab initio*.

The difference between the two scenarios may appear to be purely formal. Thus, a case where a nullity decree has been granted may come within both categories. If the applicable recognition rules do not allow a nullity decree to be recognised, the question of the validity of the marriage *ab initio* will arise. This may lead to the result that, although the decree is not recognised, the marriage is held to be void *ab initio*. In the same way, a foreign nullity decree may be recognised even though the marriage would not have been considered void under either of the potentially applicable choice of law rules.[43]

However, it is suggested that there is at least one significant difference of substance between the two types of case. In the decree situation, invariably one or both of the parties do(es) not wish the marriage to continue;[44] whereas if there has been no decree both parties *may* wish to assert that the marriage has always and continues to subsist.

We will consider below[45] to what extent the parties attitude to the "first" marriage affects policy and the application thereof in relation to each of the three "main question" situations with which we are concerned.

B. A "Differential Rule"

In Part II of this book, we examined a number of possible differential rules[46] which might be applicable where the incidental question concerned recognition of a matrimonial decree. It was concluded that the only differential rule which could be supported was to apply the recognition rule where this led to recognition of the decree and otherwise to apply the choice of law rule. The theoretical justification for this differential rule was that it was consistent with the need to give "full effect" to a recognised decree, but where there was no recognised decree allowed the whole of the *lex causae* to apply. The fact that such a rule seemed to represent the current English law in relation to capacity to marry after a matrimonial decree was seen as providing some authority for such a rule.

The question which needs to be addressed here is whether there is some other differential rule which might be appropriate where there is no matrimonial decree. It would be possible to provide that the choice of law rule governing the validity of the "first" marriage should apply where it leads to the recognition

43 This situation would have arise in *Vervaeke v Smith* [1983] 2 All ER 144 if there had been no earlier English decision and the Belgian decree was not contrary to public policy. Ie the Belgian decree would have been recognised even though the marriage would not have been valid by the choice of law rules of either the forum or the *lex causae* governing the validity of the second marriage (both of which were English).

44 The only exception might be where a declaration is sought to clarify whether a doubtful marriage is valid or not.

45 In sections C, D and E.

46 See ch 4, III C, *supra*.

of the marriage in question and that otherwise the choice of law rule governing the main question should apply. A rationale for such a rule, analogous to that for the recognition situation, would be that "full effect" should be given to the forum's choice of law rule where it recognises the creation of a status but that otherwise the whole of the law governing the main issue should apply. The proposed rule is also consistent with a presumption in favour of the validity of marriages.

It is suggested that this rule may be an appropriate preference rule in relation to succession or tort, where the concern is in relation to only one marriage.[47] Even where there has been a subsequent marriage, the particular tort or succession question usually[48] depends only on whether the "first" marriage created the status of "spouse".[49] In order to avoid confusion, this differential rule will be referred to as the "first marriage validation rule".

C. Capacity to Remarry

Where the question of capacity to remarry arises, the first marriage has already broken down and thus the policy of "burying dead marriages" and "looking to the future" require that the validity of the second marriage is recognised. As emphasised in Chapter 4, this does not mean that the first marriage may not still be subsisting for other purposes. This point is likely to be more important in relation to invalidity *ab initio* than where there has been a matrimonial decree because the first "spouse" may not have recourse to financial relief.[50]

In Chapter 4 the desired result was achieved by the differential rule which preferred the recognition rule where it led to recognition of the decree and otherwise preferred the choice rule. In the present context the desired result may only be achieved by an express result selecting rule in favour of the validity of the most recent marriage.[51]

D. Succession

In the succession situation it is more than likely that the marriage whose validity is in dispute has never broken down. Where succession between the parties is concerned, the "marriage" will have been terminated by death. Where succession from third parties is in issue, the parties may still be living together and their marriage *de facto* very much alive despite the legal doubts as to its validity. However, we shall see that for most purposes succession law is not concerned with whether the marriage has broken down and therefore this apparently significant difference may have less influence than expected on the construction

47 Cf in relation to capacity to remarry the main issue is itself a question of creation of status.
48 Cf where the surviving "spouse" has remarried before the fatal accident.
49 The approach taken in this book is that the rights of the "second" spouse depend on the question of the validity of the remarriage. See ch 5, I D, *supra*.
50 In England and Wales, it will always be possible to petition for a decree declaring the marriage void and therefore to obtain ancillary relief. However, there are countries where no financial provision is available for parties to void marriages.
51 See ch 4, II D and Swisher and Jones (ch 4, n 155a, *supra*).

of preference rules. We will now examine the different methods of succession in turn.

1. Wills

(A) WHERE THE TESTATOR IS THE OTHER "SPOUSE"

Where a testator who has not contracted a subsequent marriage refers to his/her spouse in the will, (s)he must assume that the marriage is valid and intend to benefit the "spouse", whether or not the parties are still living together in domestic harmony.[52] This result can be obtained by preferring whichever choice rule upholds succession rights.

Where a testator has contracted a subsequent marriage without obtaining a decree, the position is more complicated. In English law, a valid or voidable marriage has the effect of revoking a former will, unless the will is expressed to be made in contemplation of the marriage.[53] However, not all laws have such a provision[54] and thus an incidental question of the second degree[55] appears to arise. In order to determine whether the "first" spouse can take under the will, we need to determine whether the subsequent marriage has the effect of revoking the will. Is this question to be determined by the conflicts rules of the forum or the conflicts rules of the *lex successionis* governing the main question. In England, it has been held that the question of whether a marriage revokes a will of movables is one of matrimonial law to be governed by the domicile of the testator at the time of the marriage and not the *lex successionis*.[56] This either means that the *lex fori* approach has been preferred or that because the issue is considered to be a matrimonial one and not a testamentary one it is seen as independent of, rather than as incidental to, the main issue.[57] Thus, the incidental question does not arise. However, there is English authority that in relation to immovables the *lex successionis* governs the issue of revocation,[58] in which case there is potential for the incidental question to arise.

If the relevant substantive law holds that a valid marriage does revoke a will, it then becomes necessary to determine whether the post-will marriage is valid, which will depend on the validity of the "first" marriage. Which law determines

52 Thus, s 18A of the Wills Act 1837 (as amended by FLA 1986) does not apply unless there has been a dissolution or annulment of the marriage.

53 Wills Act 1837, s 18 (as substituted by the Administration of Justice Act 1982, s 18).

54 According to Cheshire and North (ch 1, n 6, *supra*) at p 850, few other legal systems have adopted the revocation rule.

55 This term is used by Schmidt (ch 1, n 1, *supra*) at p 321.

56 In *Re Martin, Loustalan v Loustalan* [1900] P 211.

57 In Schmidt's terminology (ch 1, n 1, *supra*) at p 410, the "incidental question falls clearly outside the scope of the choice-of-law rule regarding the main question".

58 See *Re Caithness* (1890) 7 TLR 354, where it was implicit in the decision that the will in relation to immovable property in England was revoked by the marriage of a domiciled Scotsman despite the fact that the will was not revoked by Scots law. Cf Australian decision of *Re Micallef's Estate* [1977] 2 NSWLR 929 and Canadian decision of *Davies v Davies* (1915) 24 DLR 737, which are preferred by Cheshire and North (ch 1, n 6, *supra*) at p 859.

these questions?[59] It is submitted that in the present context it is not necessary to consider all the possible permutations of laws which might be applied to determine the critical question of whether the first "spouse" should be considered as "married" so as to take under the will. We have seen that the applicable policy is to give effect to the intention of the testator. It can surely be presumed that the testator does not intend[60] to benefit the first "spouse".[61] After all, (s)he has entered into a subsequent marriage in reliance on the invalidity of the "first" marriage.

(B) WHERE THE TESTATOR IS A THIRD PARTY

In this situation, it is less clear whether the doubt about the validity of the marriage affects the testator's wish to benefit the "spouse". It is suggested that, as in the case of a matrimonial decree, the question of validity should be seen through the eyes of the testator.[62] After some discussion, it was concluded[63] that the law of the testator's domicile at the time of the making of the will, which is the choice of law rule governing interpretation of the will both in relation to movables and immovables, best reflects the testator's idea of what is a "spouse". This conclusion is equally applicable in this context.

2. Provision for Dependants

(A) DISCRETIONARY SCHEMES

Under the Inheritance (Provision for Family and Dependants) Act 1975, a spouse includes a person who has entered into a void marriage with the deceased in good faith, provided that (s)he did not enter into a subsequent marriage during the deceased's lifetime.[64] Thus, where the question of succession is governed by English law and this Act is applicable[65] the surviving "spouse" will be able to claim without it being necessary to determine whether the marriage was valid, provided that (s)he entered into the marriage in good faith. We have seen that the policy of English domestic law is to make provision for a survivor of a void marriage subject to narrow exceptions.

However, there are foreign schemes where a party to a void marriage cannot claim. Thus, assuming that an English court would be prepared to apply a foreign discretionary scheme,[66] it may be necessary to determine which law

59 If the question whether a valid marriage revokes a will were seen as an incidental question of the second degree, the validity of the post-will marriage and the "first" marriage might be viewed as incidental questions of the third and fourth degree respectively.

60 Just as (s)he is presumed not to intend to benefit a divorced spouse (see Wills Act 1837, s 18A (as amended by FLA 1986) and ch 5, III A 1, *supra*).

61 The position of the second spouse depends on whether the remarriage is valid. Under the preference rule suggested at B above, the marriage would be valid and therefore the "second" spouse would take.

62 See ch 5, IV A 2, *supra*.

63 *Ibid.*

64 Inheritance (Provision for Family and Dependants) Act 1975, s 25(4). Where the marriage has been dissolved or annulled the claimant may qualify as a "former spouse" (see ch 5, III B 2, *supra*).

65 It will be remembered that even in relation to succession to immovables, the Act only applies where the deceased died domiciled in England and Wales, s 1(1) of the 1975 Act (see ch 5, III B 1, *supra*).

66 See ch 5, I D, *supra*.

should determine whether the claimant is a "spouse" for the purposes of the scheme.

Application of the forum policy, outlined above, would require preferring the choice of law rule which upholds the succession right. Since the provision is discretionary, an award will only be made where the claimant is meritorious. Thus, presumably the claim of a "spouse" who had remarried during the lifetime of the decease would fail. Similarly, the claim of a "spouse" who had not entered into the marriage in good faith could be denied if it was considered to be unmeritorious.[67]

(B) FIXED SHARE SCHEMES

On the basis of the earlier conclusion that the policy behind fixed share schemes was the same as that behind discretionary provision schemes,[68] the choice of law rule which upholds the succession right should also be preferred in this situation.

However, as was seen above,[69] the difficulty with fixed share schemes is the lack of the discretionary element which provides a safeguard against providing a "windfall" for the unmeritorious. The problem in this context is less severe since there are less likely to be claimants who are trying to take unfair advantage of the doubt as to their status. There are not likely to be many circumstances other than those specified as exceptions in the English legislation[70] where the fact that there was a doubt about the validity of the marriage might cause the claim to be unmeritorious.[71] Perhaps a claimant who has obtained pecuniary benefits from third parties[72] by claiming that his/her marriage is invalid might also be considered umeritorious.

Nonetheless, it is still necessary to consider whether it is possible to frame the preference rule in such a way as to prevent the few umeritorious claims to fixed shares which would otherwise succeed. In relation to matrimonial decrees, it was suggested that a limited use of the doctrine of preclusion could to a large extent make up for the inflexibility of the fixed share scheme.[73] Since this doctrine prevents one "spouse" from attacking the validity of a matrimonial decree, it is inapplicable in the present context.

However, an analogous equitable doctrine might be devised to prevent a spouse from claiming that a marriage is valid where (s)he has acted in a way which is inconsistent with such a claim. The clearest example would be where (s)he has contracted a subsequent marriage during the lifetime of the deceased in reliance on the invalidity of the first marriage. The situation mentioned above

67 Such a claim should not be considered automatically unmeritorious just because the claimant originally "knew" that the marriage was invalid provided that there was at some stage a genuine *de facto* relationship between the parties. After all, the marriage is considered valid according to a relevant legal system.
68 See ch 5, III B 4, *supra*.
69 Chapter 5, IV B 2, *supra*.
70 See at 2(A), *supra*.
71 Of course, the claims might not seem meritorious for other reasons, such as the claimant's behaviour during the marriage, but this is irrelevant under fixed share schemes.
72 Eg, tax and social security benefits for single parents.
73 See ch 5, IV B 2, *supra*.

where (s)he obtained pecuniary benefits in reliance on the invalidity of the marriage might also be included. It is more difficult to include the situation where the claimant did not enter into the marriage in good faith because the mere fact that (s)he did not believe that the marriage was valid is not in fact behaviour inconsistent with the validity of the marriage.[74]

No doubt the same, if not more serious,[75] objections as those levelled at the doctrine of preclusion, could be raised against this extension of the doctrine. However, again it must be emphasised that the doctrine has a very limited operation, is discretionary and only prevents reliance on the validity of the marriage for the limited purpose of succession to the estate of the "first" spouse. Thus, it does not prevent the surviving "spouse" from asserting the validity of the "first" marriage for other purposes.

3. Intestacy

The intestacy rights of a surviving spouse are confined to a spouse who was validly married to the deceased. As we have seen, where the marriage is void the surviving "spouse" may claim under the Inheritance (Provision for Family and Dependants) Act 1975 for the court to vary the intestacy. Even if analogous provisions are found in similar foreign schemes, the court has to take into consideration all the circumstances of the case including the interests of the other potential beneficiaries in exercising their discretion. Also, under many schemes it is only possible to award maintenance. Thus, an award under a discretionary scheme may be substantially less than would be received if the claimant could take as surviving spouse under the relevant foreign intestacy legislation. Thus, where the marriage is valid according to one choice of law rule and not according to the other, it will be critical to determine which rule prevails.

It was concluded above that the main policy behind intestacy provision in English domestic law seems to be to make adequate provision for the surviving spouse. Thus, as in relation to matrimonial decrees, this policy would be best reflected by giving preference to the choice of law rule which results in upholding the succession rights. This will, of course, be the rule which holds that the marriage is valid.

Again, as in relation to fixed schemes, the difficulty with this solution is that it allows unmeritorious claimants, including the "surviving spouse" who remarried during the lifetime of the deceased in reliance on the invalidity of that marriage, to succeed in full. Again, the extension of the doctrine of preclusion seems to be the best solution to ensure an equitable result in these exceptional cases.

74 In any event, such a claimant is not necessarily unmeritorious (see n 67, *supra*).

75 *Inter alia*, because here to prevent a claimant from relying on the validity of a marriage goes against the policy in favour of upholding marriages.

E. Torts

As with succession, it should be pointed out that in the tort situation it is very likely that the doubtfully valid marriage is *de facto* alive immediately before the tort in question.

1. Inter-Spousal Immunity

The arguments for the immunity are clearly stronger where the parties are living together as man and wife, even though there is some doubt as to the validity of the marriage. However, it was seen above that English law has abolished the immunity in all cases and therefore forum policy requires denial of the foreign immunity.

In the matrimonial decree situation, it was suggested that this policy could be given effect to by means of the differential rule, which always resulted in recognition of the decree. However, such a rule is inapplicable where there is no decree. Thus, it is necessary to resort to the express result selecting preference rule in favour of upholding the tort claim.

2. Wrongful Death

Under the Fatal Accidents Act 1976,[76] the definition of spouse does not include a party to a void marriage. However, as seen above, such a party will be treated as a former spouse where the marriage has been annulled or declared void. Furthermore, provided that the claimant has been living together with the deceased for two years immediately prior to the fatal accident, (s)he will be able to claim as a cohabitee. Nonetheless, there seems to be a lacuna in respect of the party to a void marriage who has not acquired a decree and who was not living with the deceased prior to his/her death. It is suggested that this reflects the fact that such a claimant would not have had any claim for financial support against the deceased during his/her lifetime until such a declaration had been obtained. However, it seems unfair that the claimant should lose out because (s)he had not got round to obtaining such a decree, especially if the deceased has been providing maintenance under an agreement or voluntarily. Perhaps (s)he had no idea that the marriage was invalid. Whilst such a claimant is eligible for an award under the Inheritance (Provision for Family and Dependants) Act 1975, this will not help if the deceased left little property.

Thus the question arises whether it would be sufficient for the declaration of nullity to be obtained after the fatal accident. Whilst in principle it seems that the eligibility of the claimant should be assessed at the date of the accident, justice requires that a subsequent declaration suffice. However, if neither of the parties had been domiciled or habitually resident in England and Wales for one year at the relevant date, it may not be possible to obtain a declaration of nullity in England. Preferably, the legislation should be amended to include expressly a party to a void marriage with the deceased.

76 As amended by the Administration of Justice Act 1982.

Despite the lacuna discussed above, it is suggested that the policy of English law may still be said to favour compensating the "spouse" in the doubtful marriage situation where dependency can be shown.

The "first marriage validation rule"[77] would give effect to this policy. In other words, whichever rule upheld the validity of the marriage would be applied. It is suggested that even where the deceased had contracted a subsequent marriage, this rule would be appropriate. As seen above,[78] it is not unfair to require the tortfeasor to pay to two "spouses" where damages are based on the level of dependency of the claimant on the deceased. Thus, since the deceased only had a finite income, the more claimants there are, the smaller is each one's dependency, but the total is not increased. Indeed, the English legislation envisages the tortfeasor being liable to a former wife and a current wife.

However, where the award is not based on dependency, the position is more complicated. Neither the "first marriage validation rule" nor the presumption in favour of tort claims can ensure a result which is consistent with forum policy. Thus, the most logical option would be to apply the *lex causae* governing the tort.

What is the position where the surviving "spouse" has contracted a second marriage? Prima facie, it appears that (s)he will not be able to show dependency since (s)he would no longer have been entitled to maintenance from the deceased.

However, the Fatal Accidents Act 1976 (as amended), s 3(3) provides that no account shall be taken of the remarriage of a widow in assessing the damages payable to her in respect of her husband's death.[79] The Pearson Commission[80] recommended that this rule should be abolished because of the "manifest absurdity of awarding damages for a loss which is known to have ceased".

In effect, in this situation the award is not based on dependency and thus the rule suggested above for such cases (ie apply the choice of law rule) would seem to be appropriate.

77 See B, *supra*.
78 In ch 7, IV B.
79 As this provision appears to be procedural, it will apply even where the tort is governed by a foreign law.
80 Chapter 7, n 57, *supra* at para 412.

Chapter 10

Legitimacy and Legitimation

I. THE SCOPE OF THE PROBLEM

A. Introduction

It may be thought that questions of legitimacy and legitimation are no longer of practical relevance in the light of the modern trend to remove discrimination against children born out of wedlock.[1] Whilst the importance of the subject has admittedly decreased substantially in recent years, situations involving foreign elements may still arise in which it is necessary to determine whether a particular child is to be considered legitimate or illegitimate for a particular purpose.[2] In some of these situations, such as determination of nationality, the main issue will always be governed by the *lex fori*[3] and thus no incidental question can arise. However, where succession or a tort claim for wrongful death is governed by a foreign law according to which only a legitimate or legitimated child may take, a true incidental question may be presented which can be analysed as a potential conflict between the choice of law rule governing the main question and the choice of law rule governing legitimacy or legitimation.[4] However, this potential will only be realised where one of these rules leads to the child being illegitimate and the other results in him/her being legitimate/legitimated.

Thus, in order to ascertain the actual scope of the problem, it is necessary to compare English choice of law rules governing legitimacy and legitimation with foreign rules.

1 Twenty years ago, Krause's survey in *Encyclopedia of Comparative Law* vol IV, ch 6 showed that most countries had some form of discrimination against children born out of wedlock. However, perusal of the pages of the Journal of Family Law's Annual Survey of Family Law and a recent article by Meueusson ((1995) 43 Am J Comp Law at 119) reveal that the situation has now been virtually reversed. Indeed, in recent years the shift of emphasis has moved from concern about the lack of rights of such children to concern about how they can prove paternity in order to enjoy the rights they now possess. Many of the countries whose laws still discriminate against illegitimate children may well have to remove them in order to comply with their international obligations under the widely adopted UN Convention on the Rights of the Child 1990.

2 See Sykes and Pryles (ch 2, n 246, *supra*) at p 499. The present author adopts their decision (at p. 500) to continue to use the traditional terminology rather than more neutral but clumsy expressions.

3 Eg, in English law a child whose parents are not married does not take the nationality of his/her father (British Nationality Act 1981, s 1(1) and s 59(2)-(5),(9) and see *Motala v A-G* [1990] 2 FLR 261) and cannot succeed to a title of honour (Family Law Reform Act 1987, s 19(4)).

4 Where the choice of law rule for legitimacy is the validity of the parents' marriage an incidental question of the second degree is raised.

B. The English Choice of Law Rules

1. Legitimacy

The question of which law governs a child's legitimacy has never been satisfactorily resolved. As a matter of principle, it seems that the child's domicile of origin should govern. Such a rule is perfectly practicable where the child's parents are both domiciled in the same place at the time of the child's birth[5] or if they are domiciled in different places, but there is no conflict between the two laws about the status of the child at birth.

The difficulty arises where the parents are domiciled in different countries and according to one the child is legitimate and according to the other (s)he is illegitimate. Under the current English rules governing domicile, it is not possible to determine the child's domicile of origin without knowing whether (s)he or is legitimate.[6] Some commentators attempt to break this vicious circle by preferring the domicile of the father[7] and there are some judicial dicta to support such an approach.[8] This apparently arbitrary discrimination[9] might be justified on the basis that it is the child's relationship with the father which is in issue.[10] However, this is incorrect. If the child is held to be illegitimate, (s)he is also the illegitimate child of the mother and, for example, claims to succeed through the mother may be affected.[11]

The older authorities appear to support the view that a child is only legitimate if his/her parents are validly married.[12] Some commentators have alleged that this is not a choice of law rule at all, but simply the common law domestic rule. Such a rule is clearly inconsistent with *Re Bischoffsheim*[13] and *Motala v A-G*,[14] in which the parents' relevant marriage was invalid according to English choice of law rules. Dicey and Morris have accommodated these cases by adding a rider to their traditional "born in wedlock" rule. Such a pragmatic approach might, when it was first put forward over 40 years ago, have been justified on the basis that the *lex fori* rule should be used where there was a conflict between the laws of the parents two domiciles. However, English law now recognises that the offspring of certain void marriages as legitimate.[15] Thus, the Dicey and Morris formula is difficult to justify.

5 As in *Re Bischoffsheim* [1948] Ch 79 and *Motala v A-G* [1990] 2 FLR 261.
6 This would change under the Law Commission's proposals (Rept No 168) under which a child's domicile would be in the country with which he is for the time being most closely connected (with rebuttable presumptions where his parents are domiciled in the same country or where he only has a home with one parent).
7 Most notably, Cheshire and North (ch 1, n 6, *supra*) at pp 752-754.
8 Eg, *Re Grove* (1888) 40 Ch D 216 and, more recently, *Hashmi v Hashmi* [1972] Fam 36.
9 However, as we shall see below, it is clear that whether a child is legitimated depends on the domicile of the father and that the English putative marriage doctrine only applies where the father is domiciled in England (Legitimacy Act 1976, s 1(2)).
10 Thus, Wolff (ch 2, n 13, *supra*) at section 381 argues that if the child is legitimate under the *lex domicili* of the father, it is irrelevant that he may be illegitimate under the *lex domicili* of the mother. See also Gutman (1959) ICLQ 678 at 687-688.
11 Eg, in the famous case of *Shaw v Gould* (1868) LR 3 HL 55, the question was whether the child was the legitimate child of Elizabeth.
12 See Morris (ch 1, n 6, *supra*) at pp 233-234.
13 [1948] Ch 79
14 Note 3, *supra*.

It is suggested that a better solution which is more in keeping with modern domestic policy is that a child should be recognised as legitimate if (s)he is so recognised by the law of either of his parents domiciles.[16] However, there is no authority in support of such a view and it is still not clear how a case similar[17] to *Shaw v Gould* would be decided today.[18]

2. Legitimation

The position regarding legitimation is much simpler. At common law, foreign legitimations were recognised provided that the father was domiciled in the country providing for legitimation *both* at the time of the birth and the legitimating event.[19] Under the Legitimacy Act 1976,[20] a foreign legitimation by subsequent marriage will be recognised where marriage has the effect of legitimating the child by the law of the father's domicile at the time of the marriage. Legitimations, including those other than by subsequent marriage, may still be recognised at common law.[21]

C. Foreign Choice of Law Rules

1. Legitimacy

(A) COMMON LAW SYSTEMS

The application of the domicile principle is facilitated by legislation in some states under which a child's domicile at birth can be ascertained without reference to whether or not he was born legitimate.[22]

Otherwise, it seems that most common law systems would, like English law, apply the child's domicile of origin where both parents have a common domicile or there is no conflict between the law of their two domiciles as to the status of the child.[23] Where there is such a conflict, application of the domicile of the father seems to be favoured.[24]

15 Legitimacy Act 1976, s 1 (the so-called "putative marriage" doctrine).
16 This is analogous to the provision in art 19 of the German Civil Code under which it is sufficient if the child is legitimate by the *lex patriae* of either parent, where the parents have different nationalities.
17 Where a foreign divorce decree was not recognised either by the forum or the domicile of the remarrying party. Of course, today a Scottish decree would be automatically recognised under the Family Law Act 1986, s 44(2).
18 Note, the putative marriage doctrine in Legitimacy Act 1976 s 1 would not apply because the father was domiciled in Scotland.
19 See *Re Goodman's Trusts* (1881) 17 Ch D 266; *Re Wright's Trusts* (1856) 2 K & J 595; and *Re Luck's Settlement* [1940] Ch 864.
20 Re-enacting former legislation, originally the Legitimacy Act 1926.
21 See Legitimacy Act 1976, s 10(1) and *Re Hurll* [1952] Ch 722.
22 Thus, eg, under the Family Law Reform Act in Ontario, s 2, where the parents have different domiciles the child takes the domicile of the father unless he is habitually resident with the mother only. Similarly, see the New Zealand Domicile Act 1976, s 6.
23 The decision in *Re Bischoffsheim* [1948] Ch 79 was approved by the Privy Council in *Bambgose v Daniel* [1955] AC 107 at 120. See also Castel (ch 4, n 17, *supra*) at p 382. Sykes and Pryles (ch 2, n 246, *supra*) at p 509, whilst approving the result achieved in *Re Bischoffsheim* cast doubt on the logic of applying the law of the domicile of the parties if under that law legitimacy depends on the validity of the marriage.
24 See Sykes and Pryles (ch 2, n 246, *supra*) at p 501. See also the Canadian cases of *Yuen Tse v Minister of Employment and Immigration* (1983) 32 RFL (2d) 274 and *R and McDonnel v Lenny Ba Chai* [1954] 1 DLR 401 at 403 and the Australian case of *Perpetual Executors and Trustees Association of Autralia Ltd v Roberts* [1970] VR 732 at 756-757.

The US Restatement[25] offers a novel approach to break the vicious circle by providing that a child's legitimacy is to be determined by the domicile of the parent whose relationship with the child is in question. This view assumes that the status of legitimacy is not universal but should be determined in respect of each issue as it arises.

Thus, it can be seen that in a case where there is a conflict between the laws of the parents' domicile as to the status of the child, there is scope for the "conflict of rules" to arise as between the English forum and the a common law *lex causae*. In particular, the English court may still apply the "lawful wedlock" rule, whereas the foreign *lex causae* may apply the domicile of the father or the domicile of the child where this can be ascertained without reference to legitimacy. It should also be reiterated that "domicile" does not have the same meaning in all common law countries.[26] Thus, there is always the possibility that the *lex causae* may consider that the relevant party/parties are domiciled in a different country from that which English law regards as the domicile.

(B) CIVIL LAW SYSTEMS

Traditionally, in most civil law countries, matters of personal status are governed by nationality. The application of the nationality at birth to determine legitimacy causes the same problems as that of the domicile of origin because nationality is dependent on the legitimacy or otherwise of the child.[27] In a number of European states, the circle was broken by application of the nationality of the husband. It seems that husband should be interpreted to mean "pseudo husband" where the mother's marriage is void.[28]

In some countries, recent reforms in private international law have provided more rational solutions. In Germany, the child's legitimacy is governed by the law governing the matrimonial relationship between his/her parents at the time of birth.[29] However, if the parents are of different nationalities, it will be sufficient if the child is legitimate by one of the *leges patriae*.[30] Similarly, under the Austrian IPRG, art 21,[31] where the parents are nationals of different countries, legitimacy is governed by the national law which is most favourable to legitimacy.

25 Para 287 of the Restatement Second, Conflict of Laws (1971).

26 In particular, the revival of the domicile of the origin is not known in the United States and has been repealed in Australia by the Uniform Domicile Acts 1982.

27 Except where nationality is obtained by the fact of birth within the territory. However, it is argued that it is illogical to base status on the fortuitious occurrence of birth within a particular state (see Gutman (1959) ICLQ 678 at 680).

28 See detailed discussion by Gutman (1959) 8 ICLQ 678 at 685-688.

29 Article 19(1). (Art 14(1) provides that the law governing the matrimonial relationship is the law of the spouses' last common nationality if one spouse retains such nationality. Otherwise the law of the last common habitual residence applies provided that one spouse still resides in that place. If neither of these two rules are applicable, the law of the country most closely connected to the spouses together applies.)

30 *Ibid.*

31 See translation attached to Palmer's article, (1980) 28 Am J Comp Law 197 at 222.

In any event, it is clear that there is scope for the "conflict of rules" to arise as between England and a civil law country even in the relatively straightforward situation where the parents are both domiciled in country X and are nationals of country Y if the child is legitimate according to the law of X, but not according to the law of Y or *vice versa*.

2. *Legitimation*

(A) COMMON LAW SYSTEMS

Originally, the English common law rule was followed in Australia[32] and Canada.[33] In Australia, s 90 of the Federal Marriage Act 1961 is modelled closely on the English legislation.[34] In Canada, state legislation[35] makes no reference to the domicile of the father or any other person. Thus, it appears that a child will be considered as having been legitimated by the subsequent marriage of his parents wherever the substantive law of the forum is applicable to the main issue, irrespective of whether the law of his domicile at either the date of birth or marriage would treat the marriage as having this effect.[36]

In the United States, it seems that any form of legitimation will be recognised where it is effective under the law of the domicile of the father or of the child at the time of the legitimating event.[37] In California, it has been held to be sufficient in succession cases that the legitimation is recognised by the *lex successionis*, at least where that is Californian law.[38]

Thus, again there are some differences between the approach of common law jurisdictions in respect of recognition of legitimation and there is therefore some scope for a "conflict of rules" to arise. It should again be borne in mind that such a conflict might be caused by a divergence in the concept of domicile between the *lex causae* and the *lex fori*.

(B) CIVIL LAW SYSTEMS

Traditionally, the nationality of the father would determine whether a particular event had the effect of legitimating a child. This rule still applies in most civil law countries.

However, some recent reforms have attempted to remove the paternal bias. For example, the reformed German Civil Code distinguishes between different types of legitimation. Thus, legitimation by subsequent marriage will be recognised where the marriage has a legitimating effect either by the law

32 Eg, marriages before the English Legitimacy Act 1926 were only recognised as legitimating the children of the parties if the father was alive and domiciled in England at the date of the birth, the date of the marriage and the date of the coming into force of the Act (eg *Re Williams* [1936] VLR).

33 *R and McDonnell v Leong Ba Chai* [1954] 1 DLR 401 at 403.

34 In *Heron v National Trustee Executors and Agency Co of Australia Ltd* [1976] VR 733 it was held that a legitimation by earlier marriage under the English 1926 Act could be recognised under this section.

35 Based on a Uniform Act prepared by the Uniform Law Conference in 1919-20 (see Castel (ch 4, n 17, *supra*) p 273, n 26).

36 See Castel (ch 4, n 17, *supra*) at pp 273-274.

37 Restatement, Second, Conflict of Laws, para 287, comments (f) and (g).

38 See *In re Lund's Estate* 26 Cal 2d 472, 159 P 2d 643 (1945) and *In the Estate of Bassi* 234 Cal App 2d 529, 44 Cal Reprt 541 (1965).

governing the matrimonial relationship,[39] or where the spouses have different nationalities, by the *lex patriae* of either. In cases of legitimation by recognition, the *lex patriae* of the recognising parent governs. Similar provisions are found in the Austrian and Swiss conflicts codes.[40]

II. PREFERENCE FOR THE CHOICE OF LAW RULE GOVERNING THE LEGITIMACY/LEGITIMATION

A. Theoretical Basis

In Part II we examined the theoretical basis for giving preference to the choice of law rule governing the main question both in relation to succession and tort.[41] In Chapter 8, we considered the rationale for preferring the recognition rule in relation to foreign adoptions. In the situation under discussion in this chapter, instead of a recognition rule there is a choice of law rule governing the status of the child. Thus, it is now necessary to examine the theoretical basis for giving preference to the choice of law rule governing the legitimacy/legitimation of the child, where it conflicts with the result of applying the choice of law rule governing the main question.

Again, it may be argued that where a status is recognised, "full effect" should be given to this status by ensuring that the child obtains all the benefits thereof. Further, it may be contended that the status of legitimacy is more fundamental than that of marriage because it is permanent and cannot be terminated. Therefore, it should be treated as universal.[42] The difficulty with this argument is that the incidents of the status are not universal. In particular, a legitimated child may not always be entitled to the same rights as a child born legitimate. Therefore, it might seem to be more logical for the law determining the incidents also to govern the status. Indeed, since the status of legitimacy or legitimation is nowadays less likely to have daily practical significance[43] than the status of marriage, it is arguably less problematic for a child to be considered as legitimate(d) for some purposes and not others.

In relation to succession, the argument in favour of applying the choice rule governing the child's status seems to be strongest where the testator or intestate is the parent or child. The deceased would be deemed to have expected the law indicated by the forum's choice of law rule relating to status to determine the relationship between them. Conversely, the argument is at its weakest where the deceased is a third party who may have had no real connection with either the forum or the law chosen by the forum to govern the status of the child.

39 See n 29, *supra*.
40 Article 22-23 and art 71-73a respectively.
41 See ch 5, II A 1, *supra* and ch 7, II A 1, *supra* respectively.
42 This seems to be the basis of the German Bundesgerichtshof's decision to apply the *lex fori* to determine the child's legitimacy in their decision of 9 July 1986 (see Schmidt (ch 1, n 1, *supra*) at pp 411-412).
43 Cf where a child's surname depends on whether he is legitimate or not (see Schmidt *op cit*) or where his/her right to maintenance from the father is so dependent.

B. Authority

Two English succession cases support application of the *lex causae* governing the main question rather than the forum's choice of law rules governing legitimacy/legitimation.

In the case of *Re Johnson*,[44] the *lex successionis* was Maltese law,[45] under which the deceased was legitimated and therefore her next of kin could succeed. Under English law, she was not treated as legitimated[46] and therefore the next of kin could not succeed. It was held that Maltese law should apply to determine how the estate should be distributed.

Re Stirling[47] is a weaker authority because the claimant was illegitimate by all relevant laws. However, the court referred to the Scottish law as the *lex successionis*,[48] which would not have been necessary if the question of legitimacy was to be determined by the conflicts rules of the *lex fori*.[49]

Similarly, in the Australian case of *Haque v Haque (No 1)*[50] the question of the children's legitimacy for the purposes of succession under Indian law (which applied Muslim law in this case) was referred to that law and not determined by the conflicts rules of the forum.

Old American cases classifying legitimation provisions as inheritance rather than status statutes[51] might also be cited as indirect support in favour of the application of the *lex causae* governing the main question.

44 [1903] 1 Ch 821. The case of *Dogliani v Crispin*(1866) LR 1 HL 301 is also sometimes cited as favouring the *lex successionis*. However, in fact, there was no conflict in this case. Both English law and Portugese law agreed that the son was illegitimate. The difference was that Portugese law, which was the *lex successionis*, allowed the natural son of the deceased to succeed provided that the deceased was not "noble'. In any event, the real basis for the decision in this case was that the English court was bound to recognise the decision of the Portugese court regarding the administration of the estate as it was the court of the domicile.

45 The deceased died domiciled in Baden, under which law succession was governed by nationality. The deceased was a British subject. It was held that Maltese law should govern as the law of her domicile of origin was Maltese. There seem to be two alternative grounds for this decision. Either, the change of domicile was ineffective because Baden disregarded domicile. Alternatively, reference to the law of the nationality was a reference to how English law would apply to this particular propositus. The first ground has been held to be wrong (see *Re Annesley* [1926] Ch 692; *Re Askew* [1930] 2 Ch 259; and *Casdagli v Casdagli* [1918] P 89). But the refusal to follow *Re Johnson* on this point does not weaken the case as an authority in favour of the choice of law rule.

46 Her father was domiciled in England.

47 [1908] 2 Ch 344

48 Under the Scottish law, there was an issue as to whether the claimant should be treated as legitimate under the putative marriage doctrine. It should be noted that in *Shaw v Gould* (1868) LR 3 HL 55, English law was the *les successionis* and thus determined the question of legitimacy. Thus, the Scottish doctrine was not relevant unless the English choice of law rules on legitimacy referred to Scottish law as the law of the domicile.

49 See Gottlieb (1955) 33 Can Bar Rev 523 at 539 and n 59. Gottlieb also refers to the old Kentucky case of *Sneed v Ewing* (1831) 5 JJ Marsh 460. Again, the claimant was illegitimate both by the *lex fori* and the *lex successionis* but the court expressly applied the latter.

50 (1962) 108 CLR 320.

51 See Taintor (1940) XVIII Can Bar Rev 691 at 703 *et seq*.

C. Results

The results discussed in Chapter 8[52] in relation to claims against and by adoptive parents can be applied *mutatis mutandis* to the current situation by substituting the results of applying the choice of law rule governing the legitimacy/legitimation for the rule governing the recognition of the adoption.[53] Examples L1 and L2 provide an illustration of a typical legitimation "conflict of rules" situation.[54]

III. CONSTRUCTING PREFERENCE RULES

A. General Comparison with the Adoption Decree Situation

In many ways, the legitimacy/legitimation situation is analogous to the adoption situation. In both cases, the claimant's success depends on whether or not the relationship of parent and lawful child exists between two persons. The similarity with the legitimation situation is stronger because the creation of the status depends upon acts done by the parents after the birth of the child. Thus, arguments based on the parties' expectations which were used in relation to adoption are likely to be equally valid in relation to legitimation. Legitimacy is largely determined by facts in existence at the time of the birth. Where different legal systems attribute different legal consequences to those facts, the question arises as to which legal system is expected by the parties to apply.

Similarities may also be found in the development of the legal treatment of adopted and legitimated children. At common law neither adoption nor legitimation were recognised, although foreign created status would be respected. In the 1920s both categories of status were introduced into English law. At first there were considerable restrictions on the rights of adopted and legitimated children. These have gradually been eroded and today the policy of the law is to assimilate the legal position of such children to those of children born legitimate. Similarly, the common law position of the illegitimate child as *filius nullius* has been reversed in recent years[55] and, whilst some differences in the position of the child born out of wedlock remain, the overall policy is one of equalisation of treatment.

The main material difference between the adoption and legitimacy/legitimation situation for our purposes is that in the former two sets of parents were involved. The validity or otherwise of the adoption order affected the rights and duties of both sets and therefore it was necessary to formulate separate preference rules to govern the relationship between the child and the "adoptive" parents on the one hand and between the child and the natural parents on the other hand; whereas in the legitimacy/legitimation situation only one set of parents is involved. The question arises as to whether the position of

52 At II C.
53 The differential rule should also apply *mutatis mutandis*. See discussion at III B, *infra*.
54 See ch 1, IV B, *supra* and Table 9 in the Appendix, *infra*.
55 See n 1, *supra*.

these parents is more analogous to the "adoptive" or the natural parents in the adoption situation.

There is a technical similarity with the natural parents, since in both cases we are concerned with what incidents, if any,[56] the law attributes to the biological relationship between the parent and child. However, the analogy is only superficial because in the adoption situation the question is essentially negative, ie has the attempt to sever the relationship between the child and the natural parent been successful; whereas in the case of legitimacy/legitimation the question is positive, ie whether the circumstances surrounding the birth or events occurring thereafter are such that the child is considered legitimate/ legitimated. This is clearly more analogous to the position of the adoptive parents and thus the preference rules for legitimation/legitimacy should be based on those governing the relationship between the child and the "adoptive" parents.

B. A "Differential Rule"

Analogical deduction from the "first marriage validation differential rule" developed in the previous chapter,[57] would produce a "differential rule" under which the choice of law rule governing legitimacy/ legitimation was preferred where this rule recognised the creation of the status and otherwise the choice of law rule governing the main question was applied. The "full effects" rationale expounded there is equally applicable here. It should also be mentioned that such a "differential rule" is consistent with the traditional presumption[58] in favour of legitimacy/legitimation.[59] The rule can simply be called "the legitimacy differential rule".

C. Succession

1. Wills

(A) PARENT AS TESTATOR

Where it is clear that the parent only wishes to benefit his/her legitimate(d) offspring, the question arises as to which law (s)he would expect to determine whether such offspring are legitimate(d).

The position in relation to legitimation seems to be analogous to that in relation to adoption.[60] Thus, where the father has carried out some act with the intention of legitimating the child, he and the mother will assume that it is

56 A valid adoption has the effect of removing all legal recognition of that biological relationship.

57 Chapter 9, III B, *supra*.

58 Thus, even at common law all children born during the subsistence of a valid marriage where presumed to be the legitimate children of the parties to that marriage. This presumption still applies (see Bromley and Lowe (ch 5, n 100, *supra*) at pp 240-244).

59 Schmidt (ch 1, n 1, *supra*) pp 327-328) refers to a number of German authors who advocated alternative application of the *lex fori* and the *lex causae* principle in the context of legitimacy depending on the validity of the marriage. Whichever approach resulted in the child being legitimate should be applied in accordance with the "commonly acknowledged maxim *in favorem legitimitatis*".

60 See ch 8, IV A 1, *supra*.

effective. If there was some doubt in their minds about this, then the will could have been drafted in such a way so as to include the "legitimate(d)" child, whilst still excluding other illegitimate children.

The position regarding legitimacy is slightly different, in that the status arises automatically at birth. The parent will have a close connection with both the law governing legitimacy and that governing the succession. If according to either of these laws the child is illegitimate and the testator does not wish an illegitimate child to take, then (s)he might be expected to frame the will in such a way as to exclude the child in question. In the absence of such express provision it should be assumed that (s)he would wish to benefit a child who is considered legitimate by either of the two relevant systems.

The desired results can be obtained by applying the choice of law rule which applies the law recognising the child as legitimate(d). The "legitimacy differential rule" ensures this outcome.

(B) THIRD PARTY RELATIVE AS TESTATOR

It was argued[61] that a third party on the side of the adoptive parents should be assumed to wish to intend to benefit the adopted child even if the order was not recognised by the law governing the interpretation of the will.

It might be argued that a similar principle should apply *a fortiori* in relation to legitimacy/legitimation because whether or not the child is legitimate(d) does not affect any biological relationship with the third party. On the other hand, in some circles there is a greater social stigma attaching to illegitimacy[62] than to adoption.

The situation is less clear than on the death of the parent, because the third party testator may not have any connection with the law governing the legitimacy. Nonetheless, it is suggested that where there is doubt about the testator's intention, forum policy requires solving the doubt in favour of the legitimacy of the child.

Thus, it should be assumed that the testator would have been satisfied provided that the child is legitimate by one of the relevant legal systems.[63]

Thus, the desired results could again be achieved by applying the "legitimacy differential rule".

2. *Provision for Dependants*

(A) DISCRETIONARY PROVISION

No foreign discretionary provision scheme has been found which requires that those claiming as children of the deceased must be legitimate(d).[64]

61 See ch 8, IV A 2, *supra*.

62 However, a dispute about the legitimacy of the child will generally arise where the parents marriage is invalid rather than where the parents never made any attempt to marry. It is the latter situation which is usually more stigmatic.

63 See section (a), *supra*.

64 Some schemes specifically provide for inclusion of children born out of wedlock provided that the relationship was admitted by the deceased or established in his lifetime. See, eg, Western Australian Inheritance (Family and Dependants Provision) Act 1972, s 7(1)(e).

(B) FIXED SHARE SCHEMES

Where fixed shares can only be claimed by legitimate(d) children or where the illegitimate child receives a smaller share,[65] forum policy would require that the child be treated as legitimate(d) wherever possible. As with adoption, this result could be achieved by the "legitimacy differential rule", under which the choice of law rule which leads to recognition of legitimacy/legitimation would apply.

3. Intestacy

(A) ON DEATH OF THE PARENT OR CHILD

Most countries now allow illegitimate children to succeed on a par with illegitimate children,[66] but some do not allow the same rights to the parents of such children.[67] Where the *lex successionis* does not allow illegitimate children and/or their parents the right to succeed on intestacy, the position is analogous to that on adoption where succession rights on intestacy depend on the validity of the adoption.[68]

Thus, it is submitted that where there is doubt as to the legitimacy or legitimation of the child, the intestate should be presumed to intend the surviving parent or child to succeed. To the extent that intestacy rights are based on moral obligations, since parents are usually obliged to maintain their minor illegitimate children, there would be a continuing obligation to make provision for such adult children after death.

The desired result in relation to intestacy of parent or child can be achieved by application of the "legitimacy differential rule".

(B) ON DEATH OF OTHER RELATIVES

In relation to adoption,[69] there was some concern that relatives may prefer their property to be inherited by a more distant blood relative than by a closer "adopted" relative where there was doubt as to the validity of the order. This concern hardly seems relevant in relation to legitimacy/legitimation because there is a biological relationship between the deceased and the claimant,

65 Many such provisions have now been abolished. See, eg, the Turkish Civil Code 1990 and decision of Tokyo High Court declaring provision restricting succession to illegitimate children to half as unconstitutional. However, such restrictions still exist in countries applying the classical Muslim law of succession (see Coulson, *Succession in the Muslim Family* (1971) pp 172-174). Thus, in *Haque v Haque* (1962) 108 CLR 230, where the deceased had provided in his will for distribution according to Muslim law, the children of Azra could only share in the inheritance if their parents marriage was valid.

66 See n 1, *supra*.

67 One of the rationales seems to be that the parents took the risk when procreating outside marriage, whereas the children are not responsible for being born out of wedlock and so should not be subject to discrimination. The South American Convention of San Jose de Costa Rica, which outlaws discrimination against illegitimate children, specifically allows the retention of restrictions on the succession rights of ascendants. In reliance on this, the Uruguay Law of 25 March 1987 (No 15.855) only allows ascendants to inherit on intestacy where they have recognised child and never as obligatory heirs (see Ferreiral (1994-5) 33 Journal of Family Law, Annual Survey of Family Law at 555).

68 See ch 8, IV C 1 and 2, *supra*.

69 See ch 8, IV C 3, *supra*.

whether or not the claimant is legitimate(d). It may be assumed therefore that even where the applicable intestacy rules only allow claims by legitimate(d) persons, the intestate would wish the claimant to succeed where (s)he is recognised as legitimate(d) by a relevant system of law.

Thus, again, the "legitimacy differential rule" is the appropriate preference rule.

D. Tort

Most countries allow[70] illegitimate children to claim for wrongful death of their parents and for parents to claim for the wrongful death of their natural children.[71] However, where claims are only allowed where the claimant is the legitimate child of the deceased or vice versa, the "conflict of rules" situation may arise. As found in relation to adoption, the policy of the forum is to provide compensation for dependants irrespective of whether the claimant or deceased was born in wedlock. Thus, whichever law recognises the child as legitimate(d) should be applied.

This result can be achieved either by application of the "legitimacy differential rule" or the presumption in favour of tort claims. As stated earlier,[72] the former should be preferred, since the rule as well as the result can be justified.

70 Such provision often predates recent equalisation of status legislation (eg, English Law Reform (Miscellaneous Provisions) Act 1934; Manitoba Fatal Accidents Act RSM 1970 and Australian states' fatal accidents legislation). In the USA, the Supreme Court held in *Levy v Lousiana* (1968) 391 US 68, 20 L Ed 436 that illegitimate children who had been cared for by their mother could claim for her wrongful death. The same right was given in respect of the wrongful death of the father in *Re Estate of Niles* (1975) 81 Misc 2d 1075, 386 NYS 2d 995.

71 In some states the wrongful death action is for the benefit of those persons entitled to take the intestate personal property of the deceased. Thus, whether an illegitimate child or his/her parent can recover for wrongful death depends on whether such a person has succession rights.

72 See ch 4, IV, *supra*.

Chapter 11

Parenthood in Relation to Children Born as a Result of Artificial Insemination or Egg/Embryo Transfer

I. THE SCOPE OF THE PROBLEM

A. Introduction

Until relatively recently the question of parenthood, as opposed to the "legitimacy", "legitimation" or official recognition of the child-parent relationship, was essentially a question of proof and therefore did not raise issues of substantive law. The common law rebuttable presumption that the husband of a married woman is presumed to be the father of her child is a presumption of fact and therefore procedural. Since questions of procedure are governed by the law of the forum, no conflicts of law issues appear to arise and the Anglo-American textbooks do not deal with the subject.[1]

However, a combination of recent law reforms and the advances of modern medical technology creates the possibility of conflicts between the law of different countries as regards the legal parenthood of children born as a result of artificial insemination, egg and embryo transfer.[2]

1. Artificial Insemination by Donor

Artificial insemination by donor[3] is a method of enabling a couple to have a child despite the husband's infertility.[4] Whilst the phenomenon is not new, until recently the practice remained unregulated by law. Generally, all the parties concerned shared the common interest of pretending that the child was the natural born child of the mother and her husband and the child was registered as such. However, if the presumption of legitimacy could be rebutted by blood tests showing that the husband could not be the biological father, at common law the husband could not be considered as the child's father,[5] although he

1 Cf continental systems seem to have treated paternity as a separate substantive issue and therefore do provide choice of law rules. See *infra*.

2 The word "transfer" is preferred because "donation" suggests that the reason is to provide an egg for a woman who cannot produce eggs; whereas in fact the procedure may equally well be used to provide a womb for a woman who cannot carry a fetus at all or sufficiently long that (s)he can be borne alive.

3 Artificial insemination by husband does not raise any questions of parenthood.

4 It might also be used as part of a surrogacy arrangement, which is designed to overcome the woman's infertility.

5 See Law Commission WP No 74, paras 10.1 and 10.3. Although in the US some cases seem to suggest that the husband may be estopped from denying paternity where he has agreed to the insemination, at least where there is "ratification" following the birth. See, eg, *R v S* 9 Kan App 2d 39, 670 P 2d 923 (Ct App 1983); *In re Marriage of Adams* 174 Ill App 3d 595, 528 NE 2d 1075 (Ct App 1988) reversed on other grounds (see *infra* at n 45 and accompanying text) and *KB v NB* 811 SW 2d 634 (Tex App San Antonio 1991). See also *In Re Adoption Anonymous* 345 NYS 2d 430, where it was held that the AID child should be treated as the legitimate child of the marriage and that therefore his adoption required the husband's consent.

might owe certain obligations if he had treated him/her as a child of the family.[6] In theory, the donor was the father,[7] although anonymity would usually prevent claims arising between him and the child.

The Human Fertilisation and Embryology Act 1990[8] now provides that in the case of artificial insemination by donor, the husband of the mother[9] would be treated for all purposes as the father of the child unless he could show that he did not consent to the insemination and that the donor is not treated as the father.

Similar provisions are found in a number of other countries, although there may be significant variations. In particular, in some countries the legislation only relates to married women; whereas in other countries it relates to all women.[10] In the latter situation, the effect is that the child does not have a legal father at all. Furthermore, applicability of the statutory regime may depend upon whether the insemination is performed through a physician or not[11] and whether or not the donor is known to the mother or not.[12] In addition, in some jurisdictions, written consent of the parties to the insemination may be required.[13]

On the other hand, many countries still adhere to the traditional strictly biological test of paternity.

2. Egg and Embryo Transfer

Recent developments in the field of artificial reproduction allow a woman to give birth to a child in respect of which she is not the genetic mother after an unfertilised or fertilised egg of another woman has been implanted into her. This procedure may be used either where the "genetic mother" wants a child, but cannot carry the child in her own womb[14] or where the carrying mother wants a child but cannot produced eggs.[15]

6 The cases at n 5, *supra*, may be interpreted as simply estopping the father from denying a support obligation (see *KB v NB ibid* at 637, n 6). See also earlier cases of *People v Sorensen* 68 Cal 2d 280, 437 P 2d 495 (1968); *Gursky v Gursky* 242 NYS 2d 406 (Sup Ct 1963); *In re Baby Doe* 291 SC 389, 353 877 (1987) and Annotation, Legal Consequences of Human Artificial Insemination, 25 ALR 3d 1103 (1969). See also the Israeli case of *Selma v Selma* (Civil Appeal 449/79) 34 (2) PD 779, where it was held that the husband had entered into an implied contract to support the child.

7 Cf Californian case of *People v Sorenson* 68 Cal 2d 280; 68 Cal Rptr 7 (1968),where it was held that the donor was not the father because he was not responsible for the use of his sperm by the doctor.

8 Section 28, replacing s 27 of the Family Law Reform Act 1987.

9 The details of the provisions in relation to unmarried women are discussed in section III, *infra*.

10 Eg s 5 of the US Uniform Parentage Act provides that the AID child born to a married women who was inseminated with the consent of her husband is treated as the child of the husband only and not the child of the donor. However, a number of states, in enacting this provision, omitted the word "married".

11 Compare the Californian case of *Jhordan C v Mary K* 224 Cal Reptr 530 (Ct App 1986) with the Oregon case of *McIntyre v Crouch* 780 P 2d 239 (Or Ct App 1989).

12 Compare the New Jersey case of *CM v CC* 377 A 2d 821 (NJ Sup Ct Juv & Dom Rel Div 1977) with the Colarado case of *In re RC* 775 P 2d 27 (1989).

13 In *In Re Marriage of Adams* 551 NE 2d 635 (Ill 1990) (discussed in detail at text accompanying n 45, *infra*), Justice Miller held that whilst both the Illinois and Florida statutes required written consent, because of a variation in the wording, the effect of lack of written consent might be different in each state.

14 The so-called "rent a womb" scenario, known technically as "gestational surrogacy". This is distinguished from full surrogacy where the surrogate mother's own egg is fertilised by the commissioning husband's sperm. In the latter there is no doubt as to who is the mother of the child.

15 Known as egg or embryo donation.

The effect of this major technological advance is that determination of motherhood is no longer merely a biological fact. Each legal system must decide whether the genetic connection or the birth connection is determinative of motherhood and whether such rule is absolute or may vary depending on the factual circumstances. Whilst in most legal systems giving birth to a child is still considered to be conclusive proof of maternity, there has been at least one American case, a decision of the Supreme Court of California,[16] which held that in the case of a gestational surrogacy arrangement the genetic mother whose eggs were used to form the embryo may be the legal mother where this accords with the intention of the parties.

The English legislation enables the same result to be achieved by a different method. Whilst the gestational mother is treated as the legal mother,[17] the court may make a parental order in favour of the commissioning parents where at least one of them is the genetic parent of the child borne by the surrogate mother.[18] Such an order must be made within six months of the child's birth and the consent of the carrying mother and the father of the child must be obtained.[19] The fundamental difference between the English statutory approach and that in the Californian case mentioned above is that in the former the court order *creates the status*; whereas in the latter the order was merely *declarative*. The implications of the Californian decision is that if the surrogate mother is happy to hand over the child to the commissioning parents, the latter can be treated as the legal parents for all purposes without the need for any court order or formal legal step. Whilst the decision was controversial, it is likely that the approach will bė adopted in some other jurisdictions because of its flexibility.

Many countries are still considering legislation on the question of parenthood in surrogacy situations[20] and it is likely that the solutions reached in different systems will not be identical.

Since conflicting results are only likely to be obtained in relation to gestational surrogacy as opposed to egg/embryo *donation*, the discussion will be restricted to the former.

3. How Can the Incidental Question Arise?

In cases where the parties have connections with more than one country, it will be necessary to create choice of law rules to determine which country's parenthood rule should apply or recognition rules to determine whether a foreign parental order should be recognised. Where the parenthood issue arises as an incidental question, for example in a succession case, there may be a conflict between the choice of law or recognition rules of the forum regarding the determination of parenthood and those of the *lex causae* and it will be necessary to determine which should prevail.

16 See *Johnson v Calvert* 19 Cal Reptr 2d 494; 851 P 2d 776 (1993).

17 Human Fertilisation and Embryology Act 1990, s 27.

18 *Ibid*, s 30. This section came into force on 1 November 1994.

19 This procedure is also available where the surrogate's own egg was fertilised.

20 In Israel legislation was enacted in 1996 which provided for the regulation of surrogacy agreements and the making of a parental order in favour of the commissioning parents.

Clearly, the incidental question in a parenthood case has much in common with the matters of legitimacy, legitimation and adoption, which have already been discussed. However, because of the novelty of the subject, it is useful to consider the scope of the problem. Also, since the subject, of parenthood raises strong issues of public policy, it is appropriate to consider whether different solutions may be required.

B. The English Choice of Law and Recognition Rules

To the author's knowledge there are no reported English parenthood cases[21] which have raised conflicts issues and therefore it will be necessary to assume choice of law rules and recognition rules based on rational deduction from existing rules.

1. Recognition of Foreign Orders

(A) PARENTAL ORDERS

It might seem logical to extend the current regime applicable to recognition of foreign adoptions orders[22] to parental orders, since the two orders have the same effect. The parental order creates a legal child-parent relationship between the commissioning parent(s) who is/are not the legal parent(s) of the child and destroys the relationship between the child and the gestational mother in the same way that an adoption order creates a legal relationship with the adoptive parent(s) and terminates the relationship with the natural parent(s).

The difficulty of this solution is that recognition of foreign adoptions is to a large extent based on statutory provisions, which do not apply to parental orders. Whilst such provisions might be legislatively extended to parental orders, such a development seems unlikely unless and until the existence of such parental orders in foreign countries becomes considerably more widespread. Thus, it would seem necessary to fall back on the common law rules as stated in *Re Valentine's Settlement*,[23] which require that the order be made by the court in which the adoptive parents were domiciled and the child was ordinarily resident at the date of the adoption.

These requirements might give rise to a number of problems in the context of parental orders. For a variety of reasons, the child might not be born in the state of the parents' domicile.[24] However, it might well be appropriate for the order to be obtained in the state where the child was born,[25] even though this state is neither the child's residence nor the parents' domicile.

As noted above,[26] some ambivalence about the requirement that the child should be ordinarily resident in the granting state can be found in *Re Valentine's*

21 No cases concerning the relevant provisions of the Human Fertilisation and Embryology Act have been found.
22 See ch 8, I B, *supra*.
23 [1965] Ch 831.
24 Eg: (i) the parents do not currently reside in the place of their domicile; (ii) a suitable surrogate was found in another state; (iii) facilities for egg/embryo transplant do not exist in their state.
25 Eg, otherwise the commissioning parents may be unable to remove the child from the state.
26 Chapter 8, n 17, *supra* and accompanying text.

Settlement.[27] *A fortiori*, the requirement should not be necessary in the case of a parental order. In particular, the whole idea of a parental order is to obviate the procedure of obtaining an adoption order and thus, for example, there will not be a required trial period as with an adoption order.[28] Therefore, there is no need for the granting state to be able to supervise the process. This argument is supported by the fact that the jurisdiction provision in the 1990 Act does not make any requirement about the residence of the child.[29]

The problem of the restrictiveness of the domicile requirement might be resolved by following suggestions[30] that the adoption recognition rule should be extended in the same way that the divorce and nullity recognition rules were extended at common law.[31]

It is an open question as to what extent public policy would prevent recognition of foreign parental orders in cases where the safeguards of the English system were not satisfied.[32]

(B) FOREIGN DECLARATORY ORDERS

There is a dearth of authority on the rules which govern recognition of foreign judgments declaring status. Since none of the statutory regimes applies, it is assumed that the common law domicile principle would be used. Since the focus is on the child it is assumed that the requirement is that the order is made in the state where the child is domiciled. However, the vicious circle appears again because it is not possible to determine what is the child's domicile until the issue of parenthood is decided. A similar problem arose in recognising nullity decrees at the time when a married woman's domicile was dependent on her husband. One solution was to decide the validity of the marriage by English law in order to determine her domicile.[33] If she was domiciled in the country which gave the judgment then the judgment annulling the marriage would be recognised. Similarly in the present context it would be possible to determine the child's parenthood and therefore its domicile by English law and then to determine whether the foreign court had international jurisdiction to grant the order.

Even if this solution is accepted, using domicile as the only accepted basis for recognition seems unduly restrictive and it would seem appropriate to extend it in the same way as done in relation to divorce and nullity. In addition, the use of the more liberal rules obviates the problem of determining domicile.

27 Note 23, *supra*.

28 Although the Act does state that regulations may provide for any provision of the enactments about adoption to have effect in relation to parental orders with such modifications as are specified.

29 The jurisdiction requirements are that at least one of the applicants must be domiciled in the UK or the Channel Islands or the Isle of Man at the time of the application and making of the order: s 30(3)(b). Whilst it is provided in s 30(3)(a) that the child must have a home with the husband and the wife, there is no requirement that any of them must be resident in the UK.

30 See references in ch 8, n 20, *supra*.

31 Ie by application of the rules in *Armitage v A-G* [1906] P 135; *Travers v Holley* [1953] P 246; and *Indyka v Indyka* [1969] 1 AC 33.

32 Eg, if the surrogate mother does not agree or where the surrogate mother is paid for agreeing (as opposed to payment for her service in carrying the baby).

33 See, eg, *Lepre v Lepre* [1965] P 52, per Simon P at 59-60.

2. Paternity of AID Children and Maternity of Children Born as a Result of Gestational Surrogacy Arrangements

Where there is a conflict between the "parenthood rule" of two or more relevant countries, a choice of law rule will be required to determine which system's parenthood rule applies. To what extent can such a rule be deduced from the common law legitimacy choice of law rule?

(A) *LEX FORI*

As explained above, the view which seems to have been adopted in the cases is that legitimacy of a child depends on the validity of his/her parent's marriage. As this is the domestic law rule, it may be asserted that the choice of law rule was effectively the law of the forum. Adoption of a similar approach in relation to parenthood would seem to result in application of the English common law rules as amended by the Human Fertilisation and Embryology Act 1990 in all cases.

Some support for this may be found in the fact that the 1990 Act does not state any limitations on the applicability of its status provisions. On the contrary, these provisions are expressly stated to apply whether or not the insemination or implantation was carried out in the United Kingdom.[34] However, no reference is made to the place of birth or residence or domicile of the parties. This is particularly significant, since s 27 of the Family Law Reform Act 1987, which governed the paternity of AID children until the enactment of the HFEA, specifically stated that it applied only to children born in the United Kingdom. It may be assumed that the omission of this limitation means that the Act applies wherever the children are born.

However, it is submitted that the lack of any limitation in the Act does not means that it is of universal application. All provisions of English internal law only apply to cases involving a foreign element where the relevant choice of law rule indicates that English law is applicable.[35] It is suggested that the *lex fori* approach is a less appropriate choice of law rule in relation to parenthood than in relation to legitimacy. Firstly, the *lex fori* approach is likely to lead to inconsistency between the child's status in English law and in systems which are more closely connected to him and his parents. The consequence of being considered to be the child of Fl in one country and the child of F2 in another country[36] is arguably far more problematic than being considered legitimate in one country and illegitimate in another. Secondly, whilst parties will generally not consider in advance the status of a child born naturally, they will almost

34 See ss 27(3) and 28(3).

35 See Bromley and Lowe (ch 5, n 100, *supra*) at p 262. See also HC Deb 517 (20/3/90) at col 208, per the Lord Chancellor.

36 A situation which might be referred to as a "limping" parental relationship. The *lex fori* approach is criticised for this reason by Justice Miller in *In Re Marriage of Adams* (n 45, *supra*) at 639 as follows: "Whether a parent-child relationship exists between a husband and a child born to the wife as a result of heterologous artificial insemination should not depend on the laws of every state in which the family members may find themselves in the future." Furthermore, English law may govern the main question (eg succession to the estate of a third party) even though neither the child nor the parents have any connection with England.

certainly consider the legal consequences of using artificial reproduction techniques. Thus, it is appropriate to apply the law or a at least one of a number of laws which they will legitimately expect to apply[37] to determine the parenthood of the resulting child.

(B) DOMICILE

It will be remembered that the alternative choice of law in relation to legitimacy was the domicile of the child and that the major difficulty was that this led to circular reasoning. In other words, the domicile of the child could not be determined until his legitimacy had been determined. A similar problem arises in the parenthood context in that it is impossible to determine the child's domicile until it is known who are his parents.

Many writers solved the problem in relation to legitimacy by preferring the father's domicile to the mother's. In the present context such a discriminatory approach is not needed since the question of parenthood is not an absolute status like legitimacy but must be decided separately in relation to each parent. Therefore, it seems eminently logical to refer to the domicile of the parent in respect of whom parenthood is in question.[38] Thus, the question of whether a person is a parent of a child should be determined by the domicile of that person at the date of the child's birth. Since in English law questions of personal status are still generally decided by the law of the domicile,[39] a person will most likely[40] expect the question of whether he is a parent to be so determined in an English Court.[41]

Such a split approach might, however, cause problems in the case where the commissioning parents are domiciled in different states. Assume that according to the law of the commissioning husband's domicile the husband of the surrogate mother is the father as this is treated like a case of AID; whereas assume that under the law of the commissioning wife's domicile she, the donor of the egg, is treated as the mother in accordance with the intention of the parties. The absurd result is that the commissioning wife and the husband of the surrogate are the legal parents of the child.

37 See per Justice Miller *ibid.*

38 This "dual" approach is taken by the Restatement, art 287(1) in relation to legitimacy, but the connecting factor is significant connection rather than domicile.

39 The Lord Chancellor (at HL Debs vol 517 (20/3/90) col 208) seems to have assumed that the domicile of the parents at the time of the birth is the relevant connecting factor.

40 As is well known, because of the technical rules of domicile a person may not have any real connection with the place of his/her domicile. However, this problem should be solved by reforming the law of domicile and not by avoiding or qualifying the use of domicile as a connecting factor.

41 The Law Commission in Rept 118, para 12.26 discussed the possibility of limiting the application of their recommendation that the husband should be treated as the father of the AID child to the situation where the husband was domiciled in the UK. They dismissed this because they thought that it was undesirable for a child's paternity to depend on the ascertainment of the domicile of his father at a particular time. Thus they recommended that the rule apply to all children born in England and Wales. However, this did not solve the problem of children born abroad. Since many questions of personal status depend upon ascertainment of domicile at a particular time, it is not clear why determination of paternity should be any different. In any event, without legislation it is difficult to see how a court could do otherwise than fall back on the common law domicile principle.

However, it is suggested that the potential for such absurdity[42] in certain situations should not invalidate the separate domicile approach completely. Rather, there should be an exception to the domicile rule where it would lead to absurdity as a result of the combined application of the laws of each party's domicile. In such a case, perhaps the law which has the most real and significant connection to the conception and birth of the child might apply.[43]

C. Other Countries' Choice and Recognition Rules

1. Recognition Rules

In common law countries, in the absence of legislation analogous to that governing recognition of foreign adoption orders, it will be necessary to resort to the common law rules.

In civil law countries, it seems likely that, as with adoption, a foreign parental order will only be recognised if it is in accordance with the personal law of the parties, which will usually be the *lex patriae*.

The Swiss law is unusual in providing an express and liberal rule for recognition of foreign judgments concerning judicial establishment of a parent-child relationship. Such judgments will be recognised when they are rendered or would be recognised in the state of the domicile, habitual residence or nationality of the child or either parent.[44]

Again, it must be remembered that public policy may prevent recognition of foreign parental orders. For example, a country which outlaws surrogacy may refuse to recognise foreign parental orders following surrogacy arrangements on the basis that such recognition might encourage what they consider to be an immoral or unethical practice.

2. Choice of Law Rules

(A) UNITED STATES

The Illinois Supreme Court was faced with the question of determining which law should govern the paternity of a child born as a result of AID in *Re Marriage of Adams.*[45] The court applying para 287 of the Restatement (Second), which deals with legitimacy, held that the law which has the most significant relationship to the paternity dispute should determine the child's paternity. In the instant case, this was Florida, the country where the parties were resident at the time of the conception and birth and where the child was conceived and born. Therefore, the parties' stipulation that Illinois law should apply was unreasonable and was not upheld.

One of the reasons that the court may have referred to the legitimacy provision is that the relevant Florida statute provided that the child born by AID

42 The opposite result, ie that the surrogate mother and the commissioning husband are the natural parents, would not be absurd.
43 In much the same way as the exception to the common law tort rule in *Boys v Chaplin* [1971] AC 356.
44 Article 70 of the Swiss Conflicts Law (McCaffrey (1980) 28 Am J Comp Law 235 at 271).
45 133 Ill 2d 437,141 Ill Dec 448, 452; 551 NE 2d 635,639.

was irrebuttably presumed to be the legitimate child of the husband and wife provided that they had consented in writing.

However, application of the significant relationship test to the question of parenthood can be justified independently. In particular, it will lead to application of the law which the parties would legitimately expect to apply.[46] Thus, whilst not all artificial reproduction situations raise the question of legitimacy,[47] it is likely that the significant relationship test will also be used to determine issues of parenthood in such cases, at least in states where the Restatement approach is applied in relation to choice of law matters.

(B) THE CONTINENT

As parenthood is a matter of status, most Continental countries are likely to rely on the law of the nationality as the personal law of the parties.[48] Thus, for example, in Germany paternity is governed by the nationality of the mother or the father at the time of the child's birth.[49]

(C) PUBLIC POLICY

States which take a traditional approach to parenthood and insist on a strict biological (as opposed to genetic) link may find that it is against their public policy to apply foreign laws under which determination of motherhood depends partly on intention or under which the husband is treated as the father of an AID child even though it is conclusively proved that he is not the biological father. It is less likely that "liberal" states will find it against public policy to apply the law of the "traditional" jurisdictions because their law was once "traditional" too.[50]

3. Summary of Possible Conflict Situations

There are three main types of situation where the English choice of law rules or recognition rules in relation to parenthood postulated above[51] will differ from those of a foreign *lex causae* of the main question:

46 See per Justice Miller in *In Re Marriage of Adams, ibid*, at 639.

47 Eg, artificial insemination of a female cohabitee. The child is clearly illegitimate, but it is necessary to determine whether the father is the partner of the mother who agreed to the insemination or the donor or neither. Similarly with gestational surrogacy, the question may be whether the child is the legitimate child of the commissioning (genetic) parents or the legitimate child of the surrogate mother and her husband.

48 Although the Swiss conflicts law also allows reference to the habitual residence or the domicile and also allows this such a law to give way to the domicile, habitual residence or nationality at the time of the action where case bears a closer relationship to the latter or where the application of one of these laws would be in the interest of the child (Arts 66-69; see McCaffrey, *supra*, n 44).

49 Article 20(1) of the Introductory Law to the Civil Code (see Dickson (1985) 34 ICLQ 231.

50 Lord Goff in *De Dampierre v De Dampierre* [1987] 2 All ER 1 at 12 was not prepared to criticise the French law under which financial provision on divorce depended on fault because it was similar to the position under the previous English law.

51 Even if these choice of law rules are not correct it is inevitable that there will be differences between English choice of law rules and those of some other jurisdictions and therefore the potential for the "conflict of rules" situation would still exist.

(a) Where the *lex causae* applies the law of the nationality in relation to recognition or choice of law and the nationality is different from the domicile.
(b) Where the *lex causae* uses a flexible significant relationship test and on the facts of the case the domicile is not the country with the most significant relationship.[52]
(c) Where application of a particular foreign rule or recognition of a particular foreign parental order is against the public policy of the forum, but not against the public policy of the *lex causae* or vice versa.

II. CONSTRUCTING PREFERENCE RULES

A. General Comparison with the Legitimacy/Adoption Situations

1. Parental Orders

The effect of a parental order in English law is identical to the effect of an adoption order.[53] The only formal difference in the two types of order is that the procedure to obtain a parental order is shorter and that there is no provision for dispensing with the consent of the legal birth parents.

In relation, therefore, to cases involving the relationship between the child and the commissioning parents in whose favour a parental order is made, the preference rules formulated in relation to adoption should apply *mutatis mutandis*. The only question to be considered is whether the fact the relationship between the child and the legal birth parents should be any different in the surrogacy situation as opposed to the normal adoption situation.

2. Determination of Parenthood

We saw in the previous chapters that in relation to adoption and legitimacy the overall policy was one of equalising the treatment of adopted, illegitimate and legitimate children with that of legitimate children. When constructing preference rules there was not found to be any contradiction between this policy and the objectives of the relevant succession and tort rules.

The position in relation to determination of parenthood in relation to children born as a result of artificial reproduction is different because, as shall see below, the policy of "equalisation" is qualified. This creates the possibility of conflict between the policy in relation to parenthood and the objectives of the relevant succession and tort rules.[54] In order to resolve such conflicts it is necessary to consider to what extent the specific policy of the forum in relation to the legal

52 It is of course unclear to what extent the English courts will sacrifice the certainty of the domicile principle in favour of the flexibility of a significant relationship test.

53 Human Fertilisation and Embryology Act 1990, s 30(9)(b).

54 Eg, in the situation of a private insemination of a cohabiting mother, there may be a conflict between the desire to give effect to the wishes of a testator who is a relation of the mother's cohabitee and the policy of the 1990 Act which treats the donor as the only father in this situation. Even though the cohabitee may be registered as the father of the child and the testator may so believe, a third party who was able to prove that the child was born as a result of AID could prevent the child receiving under the will.

consequences of artificial reproduction techniques is relevant to situations involving foreign elements.

On the one hand it may be argued that since succession and tort rules are mainly based on general principles, such as the intentions or expectations of the parties, they are of wider relevance than the specific rules relating to AID and egg/embryo transfer. On the other hand, the question of parenthood raises fundamental moral issues.[55] Therefore, the clearly expressed policy of the forum on these matter may override more general objectives. These conflicting positions will be considered below in relation to the application of policy to particular situations.

B. "Differential Rules" and Result Selecting Rules

1. Parental Orders

The "differential rule" used in relation to adoption and matrimonial decrees can be adopted here. In other words, the conflicts rule which leads to recognition of the order is preferred.

2. Paternity and Maternity

Analogy with the differential rules used in relation to validity of marriage and legitimacy/legitimation does not provide us with a suitable rule in the present context because the question will usually not simply be one of whether the status was created but in relation to whom it is created. In other words, the question is which of two potential "fathers" or "mothers" is the legal one.

It is possible to suggest differential rules, such as preference for the rule which ensures that paternity of the social father is recognised. However, such a rule is in fact based purely on express result selection and cannot be justified independently. Thus, in this chapter, where an automatic preference for one of the choice of law rules is inappropriate, preference rules will recommended on the basis of result selection. The analysis of policy in the next section will form the basis of the formulation of such rules.

III. POLICY

A. In Relation to Parental Orders

As stated above, the only area in need of discussion is the relationship between the child and the surrogate parent(s) who are treated legally as the birth parents. It might be argued that because the surrogate parent(s) never intended to keep the child, their position in the case of a disputed parental order might be different from that of natural parents in the case of a disputed adoption order. However, the policy of English law in relation to parenthood is to ascribe to the surrogate parent(s) the same rights and duties as other natural parents, even to the extent that the husband of the surrogate mother is treated as the father on the basis that the child was born as a result of artificial insemination.

55 See Warnock's "Introduction" in Warnock, *A Question of Life*.

We will have to consider below whether the policy of succession and tort law requires any distinction between the treatment of surrogate parents and other natural parents.

B. In Relation to Paternity of AID Children

1. The Rules

Under the Human Fertilisation and Embryology Act 1990 (hereinafter referred to as "the 1990 Act"), the paternity of an AID child depends on whether the mother is married and if she is not married whether the insemination was carried out as part of treatment licensed under the 1990 Act.

As already stated above, where the mother is married, her husband, and not the donor, is treated as the legal father for all purposes unless he can show that he did not consent to the insemination.[56] The same rule applies in relation to the partner of an unmarried woman where the insemination was carried out in the course of treatment licensed under the Act which was provided for the couple together.[57] Where a single woman is inseminated as part of licensed treatment, the donor will not be the father of the child,[58] which means that the child is fatherless. However, in the case of private insemination (sometimes referred to as DIY insemination), the donor will be treated as the father in all cases where the mother is not married.

2. Policy behind the Rules

The policy behind these rules can be found in the reports of the Law Commission preceding the Family Law Reform Act 1987, the Warnock Committee upon whose recommendations the 1990 Act is based, the Green and White Paper preceding the Act and debates in Parliament. They can be summarised as follows:

(a) Previously, AID children were in practice registered as the legitimate children of the mother and her husband. The difference between the *de jure* system and the *de facto* system was undesirable. In particular, parties were in practice encouraged to make a false declaration on registering the birth, which brings the law into disrepute. In addition, they would be unlikely to reveal to the child his origins, even if they wished to do so, because of the legal implications. Express provision that the husband is to be treated as the father and may be registered as the father on the birth certificate would discourage dishonesty and encourage openness.[59]

56 Two reasons for imposing the burden of proving lack of consent on the husband can be found from a perusal of Hansard. Firstly, the Warnock Committee received evidence of hardship among some women (especially from ethnic minorities) who sought AID without the knowledge of their husbands to avoid being divorced for childlessness (see Baroness Warnock HL Debs vol 515 (13.2.90) col 1344). Secondly, the provision was intended to protect the child who would suffer if the issue of legal paternity depended upon proof that the father had consented. In particular, where the issue arose many years later it might be difficult to obtain such proof (per the Lord Chancellor *ibid* at col 346, citing comments of the Law Commission in Rept No 118 at p 175).

57 Section 28(3). There is no requirement that the mother and the partner are cohabiting, although in practice treatment might only be provided where they can show that they have a stable relationship.

58 Section 28(6).

59 See Warnock Committee, paras 4.25 and 4.28.

(b) Social fatherhood[60] is more important than biological fatherhood. It is in the child's interests that the person who is acting as his father should also be treated in law as his father. Furthermore, the effect of not treating the husband as the father would leave the child effectively fatherless, since he would not normally be able to trace the donor.
(c) A man whose wife[61] or cohabitee[62] has AID treatment should have the responsibility of maintaining the child. In the words of the Lord Chancellor, "the responsibility travels with the benefit".[63]
(d) Donors neither wish nor expect to have any connection with the child who is born as a result of their donation. Many donors would be discouraged from donating their sperm if they thought that this might later involve them in liability to the resulting child. This consideration requires that donors should not be treated as the father[64] even if no other person is treated as the father.[65]
(e) Private DIY insemination should be discouraged[66], *inter alia*, to ensure that the recipient receives proper counselling and to reduce the chance of infected semen. Whilst the Warnock Committee did not distinguish between the legal position of the donor in the case of private treatment as opposed to licensed treatment, the legislative restriction of the rule that donors are not treated as the father of the child to cases of licensed treatment in respect of unmarried woman[67] is clearly based on this policy of "discouraging private inseminations".[68]

It is clear that in some situations the reformers had to choose between two conflicting policies. Thus, for example, in the case of private insemination the policies of discouraging dishonesty and recognition of social fatherhood conflict with that of discouraging private inseminations. In the case of married couples the former was preferred;[69] whereas in the case of unmarried couples the latter was preferred.

C. Maternity Following Egg/Embryo Transfer

1. The Rule

The Human Fertilisation and Embryology Act 1990, s 27 provides that in all situations the carrying mother is treated as the mother of the child.

60 Law Commission WP No 74 at para 10.8 refer to giving effect to the "social truth".
61 Provided that he cannot show that he did not consent to the treatment.
62 Provided that he sought the treatment with her.
63 517 HL Deb (20.3.90) col 210.
64 See Warnock Committee para 4.22 and HL Deb vol 513 (7.12.89) col 1009.
65 Ie where the mother is single.
66 The Warnock Committee, at para 4.16, recommended that provision of unlicensed services be an offence.
67 An unmarried woman may be more tempted to resort to private arrangements as she may find it harder to obtain licensed treatment. See Lowe and Douglas, " Becoming a Parent In English Law" in Eekelaar and Sarcevic (eds) *Parenthood in Modern Society* at p 150, n 18.
68 See Dewar, *Law and the Family* (2nd edn, 1992) at p 90.
69 Unless the husband could show that he did not consent to the treatment.

2. Policy behind the Rule

Three main reasons for the rule can be found:

(a) As mentioned above,[70] egg/embryo transfer may be used to cure either the infertility of the carrying mother (referred to as egg/embryo donation) or to remedy the genetic mother's inability to carry the child (referred to as gestational surrogacy). The egg/embryo donation situation is far more common[71] and was approved by the Warnock Committee,[72] whereas they had severe reservations about the use of surrogacy.[73] The statutory provision ensures protection of donors and recognition of social motherhood in the donation situation.

(b) The "carrying mother" rule can be justified on grounds of pragmatism, certainty and simplicity.[74] Whilst it is possible to prove that the commissioning mother is the genetic mother, it is more immediately obvious who is the gestational mother. Accordingly, it is much simpler to treat her like all other mothers who give birth and to allow the normal registration of birth procedure to apply as in the past.

(c) It might be argued that this rule reflects the policy of disapproval of surrogacy. Indeed, the majority of the Warnock Committee recommended banning all organisations involved in surrogacy arrangements and declaring all surrogacy agreements illegal contracts unenforcable in the courts. A dissenting opinion held that only commercial arrangements should be banned, that each agreement should be considered on its merits by the courts and that licensed agencies should be able to provide surrogacies service in appropriate situations.

The subsequent legislation has taken a *via media*. The Surrogacy Arrangements Act 1985 only banned commercial agencies and advertising of and for surrogacy services. The approach of the Human Fertilisation and Embryology Act 1990 is ambivalent. On the one hand there is a provision[75] stating that surrogacy agreements are unenforcable. On the other hand, a special procedure is created to enable commissioning parents to obtain parental orders.[76] The former might be thought to discourage surrogacy arrangements, whilst the latter might be thought to encourage them because both parties know that there is a quick and easy method of regulating the consequences very soon after the birth.

Therefore it is suggested that there is no policy of discouraging surrogacy *per se*[77] in English law. The rule that the surrogate mother is treated as the mother can

70 At I A 2, *supra*.
71 See HL Deb vol 517 (20.3.90) at col 207, per the Lord Chancellor.
72 They argued that there was no significant difference between egg/embryo donation and semen donation: paras 6.6 and 7.4.
73 See (c) *infra*.
74 See HL Deb vol 517 (20.3.90) at col 206, per the Lord Chancellor.
75 Section 36.
76 This was a late addition to the Bill as a result of a well-publicised case (*Re W (Minors) (Surrogacy)* [1991] Fam Law 180), in which the granting of a parental order was seen as the just solution (see Douglas and Lowe (n 67, *supra*) at pp 151-152.
77 As opposed to commercial exploitation of surrogacy.

be explained on grounds (a) and (b) above. This means that there is no automatic[78] public policy reason for not giving preference to a foreign rule which treats the genetic mother as the mother.

IV. APPLICATION OF POLICY

A. Introduction

It should be stated at the outset of this section that the recommendations in this chapter are rather more tentative than those in the earlier chapters. The main reason for this is that the whole area of the legal effects of artificial reproduction is still relatively new and controversial. Therefore it is not always easy to determine how to apply the apparent policy of the law. Furthermore, in a number of situations the policy behind the parenthood rules appears to conflict with the policies of succession and tort law already discussed. Finally, the need to rely on express result selecting rules is not entirely satisfactory.

B. Parental Orders

As stated above, the preference rules in relation to the relationship between "adopted" children and their "adoptive" parents should apply *mutatis mutandis* in the parental order situation. However, some thought needs to be given to the relationship between the child and the surrogate parents.

In Chapter 8, on adoption, it was recommended that in two situations there should be the opportunity for claims between the child and the natural parents where there was a dispute about the validity of the adoption order. Do these conclusions hold good in relation to surrogate parents where there is a dispute[79] about the validity of the parental order?

1. Discretionary Provision Schemes

Whilst the chances of success were slim, it was thought that if the *lex causae* did not recognise the adoption, then there should be a possibility[80] of a claim against the estate of the natural parents. It is suggested that the surrogacy situation should be distinguished.

There is no genetic link between the child and the surrogate parents and the latter's involvement in the birth process was on the basis that they would not raise the child themselves.

2. Wrongful Death

Again, a distinction should be made with the adoption situation. The chance of dependency between the child and surrogate parent is so remote that no provision needs to be made for it.

78 Although on the facts of the particular case there may be some public policy reason not to do so; eg, where this would be thought to be against the welfare of the child.
79 Ie it is recognised by the forum and not the *lex causae* or *vice versa*.
80 Eg, in the case of "open" adoption.

Thus, in both cases the "differential rule" should be applied, which will result in application of the rule which recognises the parental order.

C. Determination of Paternity

It will be necessary to distinguish between the different fact situations in accordance with the 1990 Act.

1. Where the Mother is Married or is Unmarried but has Received Treatment from an Official Agency Together with her Partner

The policies of discouraging dishonesty and recognising social fatherhood would require that in all situations preference should be given to the choice of law rule which results in the husband or partner of the mother being treated as the father of the child. We will consider to what extent this policy is consistent with the objectives of the various relevant succession and tort rules and then recommend appropriate preference rules.

(A) WILLS

(i) Husband/Cohabitee as Testator

The husband/cohabitee will have a connection with both the law governing the succession and the law governing paternity, if either of these laws treats him as the father.[81] Thus, it should be assumed that a reference in his will to his children is intended to include the AID child.[82] This assumption is in accordance with the forum's policy in relation to AID children. The desired result can be achieved by applying the express result selection rule in favour of social fatherhood (to be called "the social fatherhood preference rule").

(ii) Third Party Relative as Testator

In the legitimacy situation, it was concluded that even where the testator has restricted the bequest to legitimate children, (s)he should be assumed to intend to benefit the child provided that the latter was legitimate by a relevant system. This conclusion was based partly on the fact that the doubt about the child's legitimacy did not affect the testator's biological link with the child; whereas in the AID situation there is no blood relationship between the child and a testator who is related to the husband/cohabitee.

There was considerable debate in the House of Lords as to whether the rule that an AID child should be treated as the child of the husband should apply retrospectively to wills and deeds executed before the provision comes into force. The Lord Chancellor took the view that most testators would not wish to exclude a beneficiary simply because (s)he was born as a result of semen donation.[83] Other Lords, seeking an amendment to the Bill, expressed the opinion that the effect of the Bill was that children would benefit who were

81 There is a close analogy with the legitimacy situation (see ch 10, III C 1 (a), *supra*).
82 Even if he did not know that the child was an AID child.
83 At HL Deb vol 516 (6.3.90) col 1152 and at HL Deb vol 517 (20.3.90) at col 218.

never intended to benefit[84] and that donor children would be "retrospectively foisted" onto testators contrary to their wishes.[85] On a vote, the amendment was not passed[86] and thus the Lord Chancellor's view would seem to have been accepted.

It is suggested that this approach can in fact also be supported by the practical argument that since AID children are generally registered as the children of the husband/cohabitee and that other family members may well not know that they are donor children, the testator takes and has always taken the risk that any child born to the wife/cohabitee of the apparent father may really be an AID child.

Thus, in reality, it is submitted that, whatever the law about AID children in his/her own jurisdiction, the testator must be assumed to expect, even if (s)he does not so desire, that the bequest may include AID children. This result is in accordance with English policy in relation to AID children and can be achieved by applying the "social fatherhood preference rule".

(iii) Donor as Testator

In practice, this issue can only arise if the child can identify the donor. There has been much academic discussion about what information a child should be able to receive concerning his/her donor parents.[87] In England records of treatment and donors must be kept[88] and the Human Fertilisation and Embryology Authority must, on request, disclose to any person over 18 whether (s)he was born as a result of treatment services and provide certain non-identifying information.[89] In particular, the applicant must be informed whether any stated person whom (s)he proposes to marry would but for the status provisions of the Act be related to him/her.[90] If the answer to the latter question was in the positive, it may be practicable for the child to identify the donor. Moreover, there are some legal systems[91] which do provide access to identifying information. Thus, the possibility of a donor child claiming against the estate of the donor, although small, is not completely unrealistic, even where the treatment was obtained through an official agency.

Thus, the question arises whether a donor will intend a reference to his children to include a reference to the children born as a result of his donation. It is suggested that this is extremely unlikely. In those systems where donors are still treated as legal fathers, identifying information will not be available, and in those systems where such information is available, donors are not treated as

84 See, eg, at HL Deb vol 517 (20.3.90) at cols 213-220, per Lords Keith and Roskill and Lady Saltoun. See also at HL Deb vol 516 (6.3.90) at cols 1149-1152, per Lord Jauncey and Lady Saltoun.
85 HL Deb vol 516 (6.3.90) at col 1152, per Lady Saltoun and at col 1151, per Lord Jauncey.
86 See HL Debs vol 517 (20.3.90) at cols 220-222.
87 See, eg, O'Donovan (1988) 2 Int J of Law and the Family; and Haimes (1988) 2 Int J of Law and Family 46.
88 Section 31(1) and (2) of the 1990 Act.
89 *Ibid*, s 31(3)-(5).
90 *Ibid*, s 31(4)(b). Such information must also be given to minors proposing to marry: s 31(6)-(7).
91 Eg Sweden, Germany and Switzerland: see Guillod (1993-4) 32 Journal of Family Law Annual Survey 465 at 466.

legal fathers. Thus, the donor will either have assumed that he is not liable or that he cannot be traced by the children born as a result of his donation.

Thus, the policy of succession law is in accordance with the policy of protecting the donor in the situation under discussion. Therefore the choice rule which leads to application of the law which does not treat the donor as father should be applied. The result can be achieved by applying an express result selection preference rule ensuring donor protection (to be referred to as "the donor protection preference rule").

(B) PROVISION FOR DEPENDANTS

We saw above[92] that the policy in relation to discretionary provision and fixed share schemes is to ensure that proper provision is made for *de facto* children of the deceased. On the death of the husband/cohabitee, this policy is consistent with the policy in relation to AID children and can be achieved by the "social fatherhood preference rule".

On the death of the donor, the policy of providing for *de facto* children does not apply. Thus, "the donor protection preference rule" should be applied to prevent such a claim.[93]

(C) INTESTACY

(i) On Death of the Husband

By analogy with the testate situation, it should be assumed that the husband/cohabitee would wish an AID child born to his wife/partner to inherit, where the child is treated as his by either of the relevant legal systems. If he does not so intend it would be reasonable to expect him to make a will to exclude succession by such a child. The moral obligation theory supports this view since the husband will be obliged to maintain the children of the family.

This situation can be seen from example AID1.[93a] The desired result is application of the Illinois (the *lex causae*) choice rule, which can be achieved by the "social fatherhood preference rule".

(ii) Death of the Child

The presumed wishes, moral obligation, social fatherhood and protection of donor policies all lead to inheritance by the husband and not the donor. There do not seem to be any conflicting policies. The desired results can be achieved by application of the "social fatherhood" and "donor protection" preference rule respectively.

(iii) Death of the Donor

The position seems to be the same as in relation to testate succession.

92 At ch 8, III C.

93 This is the opposite conclusion to that reached in relation to adoption (ch 8, IV B 1, *supra*). The difference is that there is no policy of protecting natural parents whose children are "adopted" and thus the door should be left open to allow a claim in exceptional circumstances.

93a Ch 1, IV B, *supra*.

(D) WRONGFUL DEATH

We saw above[94] that the policy of English law is to provide for *de facto* children and *de facto* parents of the deceased. In the case of the death of husband/cohabitee, this is consistent with the policy in relation to AID children and the desired result can be achieved by application of the "social fatherhood preference rule".

Since there will be no financial dependency between the donor and the child, there is no basis for allowing a claim on the wrongful death of either[95] and the "donor protection preference rule" should be applied.

2. Where the Mother is Single, but has Received Treatment from a Recognised Agency

Assume the situation where the application of one choice of law rule results in the child being fatherless and the other results in the donor being the father, if he can be identified. The policy of protecting donors would require preference for the former rule. Whilst it may be argued that English law has no interest in protecting foreign donors, it similarly has no reason to impose liability on such donors.

We saw in situation 1, above, that the objectives of the relevant succession and tort rules were consistent with the English policy of protecting donors. Therefore, the "donor protection preference rule" should apply in all circumstances.

3. Where the Mother is not Married and the Insemination was Done Privately

This scenario is illustrated by example AID2,[96] where the dispute is between a choice of law rule (here the forum's domicile rule leading to the application of Zebraland law) which results in the donor being treated as the father and the conflicting choice of law rule (here the *lex causae's* significant connection rule leading to application of Quickland law) under which either the cohabitee is treated as the father or no person is treated as the father.

This is the most problematic situation because, as we shall see, there is a potential conflict between the objectives of succession and tort rules and the policy of the forum in relation to AID children.

(A) WHERE THE DONOR HAS NOT DISPLAYED ANY DESIRE TO BE TREATED AS THE FATHER OF THE CHILD

In 1, above, we saw that the policy of succession and tort law would not allow the child to inherit from or claim on the wrongful death of the donor or *vice versa*.[97] However, in the domestic situation, the policy of discouraging private

94 Chapter 8, IV E, *supra*.
95 Cf the position in relation to adoption at ch 8, IV D, *supra*.
96 Chapter 1, IV B, *supra*.
97 It could be argued that the position is different where there is a private insemination because the donor is not anonymous and ought to know that he will be treated as the father. However, even if this argument has some validity in the entirely domestic situation, it can be of little weight in a "conflict of rules" situation where, *ex hypothesi*, the donor is not treated as the father by a relevant system.

inseminations is overriding[98] and the donor is treated as the father for all purposes.

In the "conflict of rules" situation, the position is less clear-cut. According to one of the relevant laws, the donor is not treated as the father of the child and therefore he may legitimately expect not to incur any liability. Unless the forum has any real interest in discouraging private inseminations which take place outside the United Kingdom, it would seem appropriate to prefer the more general policies of succession and tort law and of protecting the donor.

It may be argued that to the extent that private inseminations may result in the transmission of inherited diseases, and in particular the HIV virus, discouraging them is a matter of international and not just national interest. On the other hand, the attitude of the English court is unlikely to have any significant effect on the practice of private insemination abroad by parties not connected with England at the time of the insemination.

Thus, it is suggested that in the "conflict of rules" situation in relation to private inseminations where one of the parties has a real connection with England or the insemination was carried out in England, policy requires application of the rule which treats the donor as the father of the child. On the other hand, in cases of insemination where there is no real connection with England, the rule which treats the child either as fatherless or as the child of the mother's partner should be preferred.

In the first case, the desired result can be achieved by an express result selection preference rule in favour of donor fatherhood (to be referred to as the "donor fatherhood preference rule"). In the second case, the "donor protection preference rule" is appropriate.

(B) WHERE THE DONOR HAS BEEN TREATED AS THE FATHER OF THE CHILD

If the donor wishes to be treated as the father of the child,[99] he will have to apply to court for a declaration of parental rights unless the mother agrees that he may be treated as the father. If there is a court order, then the question becomes one of recognition of the court order.

Where the donor is treated as the *de facto* father, then the policy of succession and tort law would seem to require that on his death the child should have rights of inheritance and to claim on wrongful death where appropriate and *vice versa*. The result is consistent with the English domestic position, although it fails to promote the policy of discouraging private inseminations. In this case the "donor fatherhood preference rule" and the "social fatherhood preference rule" both produce the desired result.

98 This policy also overrides the policy of protecting donors and in the case of cohabitees the policies of social fatherhood and discouraging dishonesty.

99 See, eg, US cases of *Thomas S v Robin Y* 599 NYS 2d 377 (Fam Ct 1993); *In re C* 775 P 2d 27; and *CM v CC* 377 A 2d 821.

D. Determination of Maternity in the Surrogacy Situation[100]

It will be remembered that we are here only concerned with the situation where the surrogacy arrangement has been successful and the baby handed over to the genetic mother without any court order or other formal legal step. According to one relevant system, the child is still treated as that of the surrogate mother whereas in the other system the child is treated as that of the genetic and social mother.

We have seen that forum policy is to treat the gestational mother as the mother for all purposes. This policy may conflict with the policies of succession law and tort law.[101] Whilst in the domestic situation the former will automatically prevail, it is suggested that this need not be the case in the "conflict of rules" situation. In particular, we saw that it is not contrary to public policy to apply a foreign rule under which the genetic mother is treated as the mother. English law is prepared to treat the genetic mother as the mother after the simple expedient of obtaining a parenthood order. It would seem absurd to end up with a different result because in a foreign systems the genetic mother is treated as the legal mother without the need for a parental order.

Therefore, in the "conflict of rules" scenario, in relation to questions of succession or tort, where the policy is to reflect the intention or presumed intention of the mother or a third party relative[102] or to make provision for *de facto* children,[103] the genetic mother should be treated as the mother and the surrogate mother should not be treated as the mother. The desired results can be achieved by application of an express result selection rule in favour of the genetic mother (to be referred to as the "genetic motherhood preference" rule).

100 We will not deal with the egg donation situation because to the best of the author's knowledge all systems treat the carrying mother as the mother.

101 Which, as we have seen, are generally designed to reflect the intentions of the parties or to make provision for *de facto* children or parents.

102 Ie wills and intestate succession.

103 Ie family provision and wrongful death.

Chapter 12

Conclusion

I. SUMMARY

The purpose of this book has been to find a solution to the vexed problem of the incidental question by analysing the problem as a conflict between two conflict of law rules of the forum. In Chapter 2 we concluded that global solutions were no more appropriate under this analysis than under traditional analyses.

Thus, it was necessary to develop a methodology for determining which of the conflicting rules should prevail in a given situation. The chosen methodology was explained in Chapter 3. The majority of the book has been devoted to the application of this methodology to the most common situations in which the incidental question arises.

In order to give legitimacy to the search for preference rules in relation to each given topic, evidence was presented in each chapter of the situations in which the "conflict of rules" might arise in an English court. This research confirms the view that the incidental question arises far more often than is recognised. It is hoped that this work will increase the awareness of the problem among lawyers. Whilst, no doubt, frequently just results are achieved when the problem is not recognised,[1] it is surely preferable that those giving advice and making decisions in relation to legal problems should do so on the basis of an understanding of all the legal issues involved.

As explained in Chapter 3, the methodology used in the book is based on a result-orientated approach. Thus, in each type of situation it was necessary to determine which result was in accordance with the forum's policy and then to formulate the preference rule which would give rise to this result. The role of the preference rule is to determine which of the conflicting conflicts rules should apply. In a few situations, the desired result would be achieved by applying one of the conflicting rules in every case. However, in most situations the desired result could only be guaranteed by use of a "differential rule", which mandated the application of the conflict rule which recognised the decree or the particular status in question.

It is suggested that the recommended preference rules, which are set out below, could be enacted in a national code dealing with private international law or in multinational conventions designed to harmonise the conflicts rules of different countries. Even without enactment, it is hoped that judges might adopt these rules, since in most cases there is no binding authority in cases where the incidental question arises.

1 Eg in *Perrini v Perrini* [1979] Fam 84.

II. LIST OF RECOMMENDED PREFERENCE RULES

A. Following a Matrimonial Decree Whose Validity is in Dispute

1. In relation to capacity to re-marry, the recognition rule should prevail where the decree is recognised and otherwise the choice rule should prevail (the "differential rule").
2. (a) In relation to testate succession between spouses, the "differential rule" should apply.
   (b) In relation to testate succession of a third party, the choice of law rule for interpretation of the will should be applied.
3. In relation to discretionary and fixed share family provision schemes, there should be a presumption in favour of whichever rule upholds succession rights. In the case of fixed shares, this should be subject to the doctrine of preclusion.
4. On intestacy, there should be a presumption in favour of whichever rule upholds succession rights, subject to the doctrine of preclusion.
5. In relation to matrimonial property, the "differential rule" should apply subject to the doctrine of preclusion, in the situation where sharing of post-decree assets is required in order to meet reasonable needs.
6. In relation to inter-spousal immunity in tort, the "differential rule" should apply.
7. In relation to claims by a "spouse" for wrongful death, the presumption of upholding tort claims should apply to determine which rule prevails. However, this should be subject to the doctrine of preclusion in cases where under the *lex causae* the award is not based on dependency.[2]

B. Following an Adoption Decree Whose Validity is in Dispute

8. In relation to testate succession, the "differential rule" should apply.
9. In relation to discretionary family provision:
   (a) Where the deceased is the "adoptive" parent, the "differential rule" should be applied.
   (b) Where the deceased is the natural parent, the choice of law rule should prevail.
10. In relation to fixed shares, the "differential rule" should be applied.
11. On intestacy, the "differential rule" is also the most appropriate rule.
12. On a claim for wrongful death, the presumption in favour of tort claims is the appropriate preference rule. However, where the claim is not based on dependency, the choice of law rule should apply to determine the validity of the adoption for the purpose of claims by the child on the death of the natural parents and *vice versa*.

2 In order to prevent claims by "spouses" who have already received lump sum financial provision in lieu of maintenance.

C. Where the Validity of a Marriage *Ab Initio* is in Dispute

13. (a) In relation to testate succession between the "spouses" the presumption in favour of succession rights should be applied.
    (b) In relation to testate succession of a third party, the choice of law rule for interpretation of the will should be applied.
14. In relation to discretionary and fixed share family provision schemes, there should be a presumption in favour of whichever rule upholds succession rights. In the case of fixed shares, this should be subject to an equitable exception where the claimant has acted in a way which is inconsistent with the claim that the marriage is valid.
15. On intestacy, there should be a presumption in favour of whichever rule upholds succession rights, subject to the equitable exception in 14 above.
16. In relation to inter-spousal immunity in tort, the presumption in favour of upholding tort claims should apply.
17. In relation to claims by a dependent "spouse" for wrongful death, the rule which results in the marriage being recognised (the "first marriage validation rule") should apply.

D. Where the Legitimacy of a Child or the Validity of a Legitimation of a Child is in Dispute

18. In relation to all issues of succession and tort claims, the rule should be applied which results in the child being treated as legitimate (the "legitimacy rule") should be applied. This results in application of the rule which recognises the child as legitimate(d).

E. Where the Legal Parenthood of a Child Born as a Result of Artificial Reproduction Techniques is in Dispute

19. Where a parental order has been made
    (a) As between the child and the parents in whose favour the order is made the preference rules applicable between "adopted" children and their "adoptive" parents should apply *mutatis mutandis.*
    (b) As between the child and the natural/surrogate parent(s), the "differential rule" should be applied, which will result in application of the rule which recognises the parental order.
20. Where the child has been born as a result of artificial insemination
    (a) Where the mother is married or is unmarried but has received treatment from a recognised agency together with her partner,
        (i) the rule which results in the husband or cohabitee being treated as the father (the "social fatherhood preference rule") should apply to claims arising from the relationship between the husband/cohabitee and the child.
        (ii) the rule which results in the donor not being treated as the father (the "donor protection preference rule") should apply to claims arising from the relationship between the donor and the child.

(b) Where the mother is single, but has received treatment from a recognised agency, the "donor protection preference rule" should apply to all claims

(c) Where the mother is not married and the insemination was done privately,

  (i) if there is a relevant connection between the insemination and England or the donor displays a desire to be treated as the father, the rule which results in the donor being treated as the father should be applied;

  (ii) otherwise, the "donor protection preference rule" should apply to all claims

21. Where the child has been born as a result of a gestational surrogacy arrangement, the rule which treats the genetic and not the surrogate mother as the mother should be applied (the "genetic motherhood preference rule") to all claims.

III. CONCLUDING REMARK

Perhaps more important than the actual preference rules themselves is the methodology developed in this book, which has implications beyond the narrow issue of the incidental question. Whilst there have been some efforts to use result-orientation to form choice of law rules, there does not seem to have been any serious attempt to formulate a comprehensive set of result-orientated rules based on a systematic analysis of policy. Whilst it may not always be possible to obtain uniformity between all countries because they have differing policy needs, this is equally true of present conflicts rules. It may be argued that result orientated rules are ephemeral because the policies behind them will change. However, this is equally true of all legal rules, which need to be updated from time to time to take account of changing attitudes and values. Thus, the use of result oriented rules answers the criticisms levelled against traditional mechanical jurisdiction selecting rules and yet avoids the uncertainty which characterises *ad hoc* result selecting methods. It is therefore suggested that future research in private international law should concentrate on the development of appropriate result oriented rules based on a proper examination of policy.

Appendix

Table 1: Conflicts Rules in Statutory Form in England

A. RECOGNITION RULES (excluding bi-lateral treaties)

1. Administration of Justice Act 1920 (recognition of certain Commonwealth judgments).

2. Foreign Judgments (Reciprocal Enforcement) Act 1933 (recognition of judgments of specified countries).

3. Arbitration Act 1950, Part II (recognition of arbitration awards coming within the Geneva Convention).

4. Arbitration Act 1975 (recognition of arbitration awards coming within the New York Convention).

5. Adoption Act 1976 (recognition of certain adoption orders).

6. Child Abduction and Custody Act 1985 (recognition of foreign custody decisions – gives effect to Council of Europe Convention).

7. Family Law Act 1986, Part I (recognition of United Kingdom custody orders).

8. Family Law Act 1986, Part II (recognition of British Isles and overseas matrimonial decrees).

9. Civil Jurisdiction of Judgments Act 1982 (recognition of judgments of EC member countries – gives effect to Brussels Convention).

10. Civil Jurisdiction and Judgments Act 1991 (recognition of judgments of EFTA States – gives effect to Lugano Convention).

B. CHOICE RULES

1. Foreign Marriages Act 1892 (as amended) (formal validity of consular marriages abroad and marriages of British forces serving abroad).

2. Wills Act 1964 (formal validity of wills).

3. Legitimacy Act 1976, s 3 (legitimation by subsequent marriage).

4. Recognition of Trusts Act 1987 (choice of law rules for trusts – gives effect to Hague Convention on Law Applicable to Trusts and on their Recognition).

5. Contract (Applicable Law) Act 1991 (choice of law rules for all contracts to which the Act applies – gives effect to Rome Convention).

Table 2: Conflicts Rules in Statutory Form in Israel

A. RECOGNITION RULES

1. Enforcement of Foreign Judgments Law 1958.
2. Regulations to Give Effect to New York Convention (Recognition of Foreign Arbitrations) 1978.

B. CHOICE RULES

1. Palestine Order in Council 1922, art 64(2) (validity of marriage)
2. Family Law Amendment (Maintenance) Law 1959, s 17 (maintenance).
3. Legal Capacity and Custody Law 1962, s 77 (capacity of persons).
4. Succession Law 1965, ss 137-144.
5. Dissolution of Marriages (Special Cases) Law 1969 (divorce in civil court).
6. Spouses' Property Relations Law 1973, s 15 (matrimonial property).

Table 3: Results of Applying the Possible Preference Rules to Validity of Remarriage after a Disputed Matrimonial Decree

	A *English lex fori does not recognise, lex causae does recognise decree*	*B* *English lex fori does recognise, lex causae does not recognise decree*
1. Apply choice rule	v	x
2. Apply recognition rule	x	v
3. Apply "differential rule"	v	v
4. Presumption in favour of upholding validity of marriage	v	v

v = remarriage is valid
x = remarriage is invalid

Table 4: Results of Applying the Possible Preference Rules to the First Spouse's Right to Inherit after a Disputed Matrimonial Decree

	A *English lex fori does not recognise, lex causae does recognise decree*	*B* *English lex fori does recognise, lex causae does not recognise decree*
1. Apply choice rule	x	v
2. Apply recognition rule	v	x
3. Apply "differential rule"	x	x
4. Presumption in favour of upholding succession rights	v	v

v = "spouse" can inherit
x = "spouse" cannot inherit

Table 5a: Results of Applying the Possible Preference Rules to the First Spouse's Right to Share in Post-Decree Acquisitions under Immediate/Deferred Community Scheme[1]

	A *English lex fori does not recognise, lex causae does recognise decree*	*B* *English lex fori does recognise, lex causae does not recognise decree*
1. Apply choice rule	x	v
2. Apply recognition rule	v	x
3. Apply "differential rule"	x	x

v = "spouse" can share
x = "spouse" cannot share

1 On the assumption that there is entitlement to share in post-separation assets.

Table 5b: Results from Applying the Possible Preference Rules to the First Spouse's Right to Immediate Realisation of Share under Immediate/Deferred Community Scheme[2]

	A *English lex fori does not recognise, lex causae does recognise decree*	*B* *English lex fori does recognise, lex causae does not recognise decree*
1. Apply choice rule	v	x
2. Apply recognition rule	x	v
3. Apply "differential rule"	v	v

v = "spouse" entitled to immediate realisation
x = "spouse" not entitled to immediate realisation

2 On the assumption that realisation is only available on termination of the marriage.

Table 6a: Results of Applying the Possible Preference Rules to the Defence of Inter-Spousal Immunity

	A *English lex fori does not recognise, lex causae does recognise decree*	*B* *English lex fori does recognise, lex causae does not recognise decree*
1. Apply choice rule	v	x
2. Apply recognition rule	x	v
3. Apply "differential rule"	v	v
4. Presumption in favour of upholding tort claims	v	v

v = P can claim (ie no immunity)
x = P cannot claim (ie is immunity)

Table 6b: Results of Applying the Possible Preference Rules to Wrongful Death Claims by First Spouses

	A *English lex fori does not recognise, lex causae does recognise decree*	*B* *English lex fori does recognise, lex causae does not recognise decree*
1. Apply choice rule	x	v
2. Apply recognition rule	v	x
3. Apply "differential rule"	x	x
4. Presumption in favour of upholding tort claims	v	v

v = P can claim
x = P cannot claim

Table 7a: Results of Applying the Possible Preference Rules to Succession and Wrongful Death Claims between Child and Adoptive Parents.

	A *English lex fori does not recognise, lex causae does recognise decree*	*B* *English lex fori does recognise, lex causae does not recognise decree*
1. Apply choice rule	v	x
2. Apply recognition rule	x	v
3. Apply "differential rule"	v	v
4. Presumption in favour of upholding succession and tort claims	v	v

v = child/adoptive parent can claim
x = child/adoptive parent cannot claim

Table 7b: Results of Applying the Possible Preference Rules to Succession and Wrongful Death Claims between Child and Natural Parents

	A *English lex fori does not recognise, lex causae does recognise decree*	*B* *English lex fori does recognise, lex causae does not recognise decree*
1. Apply choice rule	x	v
2. Apply recognition rule	v	x
3. Apply "differential rule"	x	x
4. Presumption in favour of upholding succession rights	v	v

v = child/natural parent can claim
x = child/natural parent cannot claim

Table 8a: Results of Applying the Possible Preference Rules to Validity of Remarriage Where the Validity *ab initio* of the First Marriage is in Dispute

	A *Law governing the validity of the first marriage* ***does*** *recognise that marriage but the law governing the validity of the second marriage* ***does not*** *recognise the validity of the first marriage*	*B* *Law governing the validity of the first marriage* ***does not*** *recognise that marriage but the law governing the validity of the second marriage* ***does*** *recognise the validity of the first marriage*
1. Apply choice rule governing validity of first marriage	x	v
2. Apply choice rule governing validity of second marriage	v	x
3. Apply "first marriage validation rule"	x	x
4. Apply presumption in favour of upholding validity of marriage which is last in time	v	v

v = remarriage is valid
x = remarriage is invalid

Table 8b: Results of Applying the Possible Preference Rules to Inheritance Where the Validity of the Marriage *ab initio* is in Dispute

	A *Law governing the validity of the marriage* ***does*** *recognise the marriage but the law governing inheritance* ***does not*** *recognise the validity of the marriage*	*B* *Law governing the validity of the marriage* ***does not*** *recognise the marriage but the law governing inheritance* ***does*** *recognise the validity of the marriage*
1. Apply choice rule governing validity of the marriage	v	x
2. Apply choice rule governing inheritance	x	v
3. Apply "first marriage validation rule"	v	v
4. Apply presumption in favour of succession claims	v	v

v = "spouse" can inherit
x = "spouse" cannot inherit

Table 8c: Results of Applying the Possible Preference Rules to Inter-Spousal Immunity[3] Where the Validity *ab initio* of the Marriage is in Dispute

	A *Law governing the validity of the marriage* ***does*** *recognise the marriage but the law governing the tort* ***does not*** *recognise the validity of the marriage*	*B* *Law governing the validity of the marriage* ***does not*** *recognise the marriage but the law governing the tort* ***does*** *recognise the validity of the marriage*
1. Apply choice rule governing validity of the marriage	x	v
2. Apply choice rule governing tort	v	x
3. Apply "first marriage validation rule"	x	x
4. Apply presumption in favour of upholding tort claims	v	v

v = "spouse" can claim (ie no immunity)
x = "spouse" cannot claim (ie is immunity)

3 It is assumed that the law governing the tort does provide for inter-spousal immunity

Table 8d: Results of Applying the Possible Preference Rules to Wrongful Death Claims Where the Validity *ab initio* of the Marriage is in Dispute

	A *Law governing the validity of the marriage* ***does*** *recognise the marriage but the law governing the tort* ***does not*** *recognise the validity of the marriage*	*B* *Law governing the validity of the marriage* ***does not*** *recognise the marriage but the law governing the tort* ***does*** *recognise the validity of the marriage*
1. Apply choice rule governing validity of the marriage	v	x
2. Apply choice rule governing tort	x	v
3. Apply "first marriage validation rule"	v	v
4. Apply presumption in favour of upholding tort claims	v	v

v = "spouse" can claim
x = "spouse" cannot claim

Table 9: Results of Applying the Possible Preference Rules to Succession and Wrongful Death Claims[4] between Child and Parents Where the Child's Legitimacy or the Validity of His/Her Legitimation is in Dispute

	A *Law governing the child's status* ***does*** *recognise the legitimacy/legitimation but the law governing the succession/tort* ***does not*** *recognise legitimacy/legitimation*	*B* *Law governing the child's status* ***does not*** *recognise the legitimacy/legitimation but the law governing the succession/tort* ***does*** *recognise the legitimacy/legitimation*
1. Apply choice rule governing status	v	x
2. Apply choice rule governing succession/tort	x	v
3. Apply "legitimacy" differential rule	v	v
4. Apply presumption in favour of upholding succession/tort claims	v	v

v = child/parent can claim
x = child/parent cannot claim

4 It is assumed that the law governing the tort/succession only allows claims between parents and legitimate/(d) children.

Bibliography

Bromley PM and Lowe NV, *Bromley's Family Law*, 8th edn (1992) London, Butterworths.

Castel J-G, *Canadian Conflict of Laws* 5th edn (1978) Toronto, Butterworths.

Castel J-G, *Canadian Conflict of Laws*, 2nd edn (1986) London, Butterworths.

Cavers D F, *The Choice of Law Process*, (1965) Ann Arbor, University of Michigan Press.

Cheshire G, *Private International Law*, 7th edn (1965) London, Butterworths.

Clark H H, *The Law of Domestic Relations*, 2nd edn (1987) St Paul, Minn, West.

Clark J B and Ross Martyn J G, *Theobald on Wills*, 15th edn (1993) London, Sweet & Maxwell.

Collier J G, *Conflict of Laws*, 2nd edn (1994) Cambridge, Cambridge University Press.

Collins L *et al*, *Dicey and Morris' Conflict of Laws*, 12th edn (1993) London, Stevens.

Committee on the Law of Intestate Succession (Morton Committee) (1951) Cmnd 8310.

Cook WW, *The Logical and Legal Bases of the Conflict of Laws*, (1942) Cambridge Mass, Harvard University Press.

Coulson N, *Succession in the Muslim Family* (1971) Cambridge, The University Press.

Cretney S and Masson J, *The Principles of Family Law*, 5th edn (1990) London, Sweet and Maxwell.

Currie B, *Selected Essays on the Conflict of Laws* (1963) Durham NC, Duke University Press.

Department of Health, *Consultative Document on Adoption Law* (1992).

Dewar J, *Law and the Family* 2nd edn (1992) London, Butterworths.

Dicey A V, *The Conflict of Laws*, 4th edn (1927) London, Stevens.

Edgar S G G, *Craies on Statute Law*, 7th edn (1971) London Sweet & Maxwell.

Eekelaar J, *Regulating Divorce* (1991) Oxford, Clarendon Press.

Ehrenzweig A A and Jayme E, *Private International Law*, Vol 1 (1967) Leyden, Sijthoff.

Freedman J *et al*, *Property and Marriage: An Integrated Approach*, Institute of Fiscal Studies Reports Series No 29 (1988).

Gordon D M, *Foreign Divorces: English Law and Practice* (1988) Aldershot, Avebury.

Glendon M-A, *New Family and New Property* (1981) Toronto, Butterworths.

Graveson, *The Conflict of Laws*, 7th edn (1973) London, Sweet & Maxwell.

Gray K, *Reallocation of Property on Divorce* (1977) Abingdon, Professional Books Ltd.

Green D, *Maintenance and Capital Provision on Divorce: A need for precision* (1987) London, The Law Society.

Hoggett B M and Pearl D S, *The Family Law and Society Cases and Materials*, 3rd edn (1991)London, Butterworths.

Jaffey AJ E, *Introduction to the Conflict of Laws* (1988) London, Butterworths.

Kahn Freund O, *The Growth of Internationalism in Private International Law* (1960) Jerusalem, Magnes Press, Hebrew University.

Kahn Freund O, *Problems in Private International Law* (1977) Leyden, Sijthoff.

Law Commission, *The Field of Choice*, Rept No 6 (1966).

Law Commission, *Report on Financial Provision in Matrimonial Proceedings*, Rept No 25 (1969).

Law Commission, *Hague Convention on Recognition of Divorces and Legal Separations*, Rept No 34 (1970).

Law Commission, *Report on Personal Injury Litigation – Assessment and Damages*, Rept No 56 (1973).

Law Commission, *First Report on Family Property: a New Approach*, Rept No 52 (1973).

Law Commission, *Second Report on Family Property: Family Provision on Death*, Rept No 61 (1974).

Law Commission, *Third Report on Family Property: The Matrimonial Home (Co-ownership and Occupation Rights) and Household Goods*, Rept No 86 (1978).

Law Commission, *Illegitimacy* , WP No 74 (1979) London, HMSO.

Law Commission Discussion Paper, *The Financial Consequences of Divorce: The Basic Policy*, No 103 (1980).

Law Commission, *Financial Relief After Foreign Divorce*, WP No 77 (1980) London, HMSO.

Law Commission, *The Financial Consequences of Divorce*, Rept No 112 (1981) London, HMSO.

Law Commission, *Financial Relief after Foreign Divorce*, Rept No 117 (1982) London, HMSO.

Law Commission, *Illegitimacy* , Rept No 118 (1982) London, HMSO.

Law Commission Consultation Paper, *Recognition of Foreign Nullity Decrees and Related Matters,* (1983) (unpublished).

Law Commission, *Recognition of Foreign Nullity Decrees and Related Matters*, Rept No 137 (1984) London, HMSO.

Law Commission, *Choice of Law Rules in Marriage*, WP No 89 (1985) London, HMSO.

Law Commission, *Choice of Law Rules in Marriage*, Rept No 165 (1987) London, HMSO.

Law Commission, *The Law of Domicile*, Rept No 168 (1987) London, HMSO.

Law Commission Discussion Paper, *Ground for Divorce*, No 170 (1988) London, HMSO.

Law Commission, *Matrimonial Property*, Rept No 175 (1988) London, HMSO.

Law Commission, *Distribution on Intestacy*, WP No 108 (1988) London, HMSO.

Law Commission, *Distribution on Intestacy*, Rept No 187 (1989) London, HMSO.

Law Commission, *Ground for Divorce*, Rept No 192 (1990) London, HMSO.

Law Commission Consultation Paper, *The Effect of Divorce on Wills* (1992) London, HMSO.

Law Reform Committee, 9th Report, *Liability in Tort Between Husband and Wife*, Cmnd 1268 (1961) London, HMSO.

Law Reform Committee's 22nd Report, *Making and Revocation of Wills,* Cmnd 7902 (1980) London, HMSO.

Law Society, *Maintenance and Capital Provision on Divorce* (1991).

Levontin A V, *Choice of Law and Conflict of Laws* (1976) Leyden, Sijthoff.

Lord Chancellor's Department, *Looking to the Future (Mediation and the Ground for Divorce: A Consultation Paper)* Cmnd 2424 (1993).

Lorenzen E, *Selected Articles on the Conflict of Laws* (1947) New Haven, Yale University Press.

Marsh H, *Marital Property in the Conflict of Laws* (1952) Seattle, University of Washington Press.

McClanahan W S, *Community Property Law in the United States* (1982) Rochester, Lawyers Co-Operative Publ Co.

McClean J D, *Recognition of Family Judgments in the Commonwealth* (1983) London, Butterworths.

McClean J D, *Morris: The Conflict of Laws*, 4th edn (1993) London, Sweet & Maxwell.

McLeod J, *The Conflict of Laws* (1983) Calgary, Carswell.

Morris J H C, *Dicey and Morris' Conflict of Laws* 9th edn (1973) London, Stevens.

North P M, *The Private International Law of Matrimonial Causes in the British Isles and the Republic of Ireland* (1977) Amsterdam, North-Holland Publishing Co.

North P M, *Essays in Private International Law* (1993) Oxford, Claredon Press.

North P M and Fawcett J J, *Cheshire and North's Private International Law*, 12th edn (1992) London, Butterworths.

Palsson L, *Marriage in Comparative Conflict of Laws: Substantive Conditions* (1971) Leyden, Sijthoff pp 229 – 232 and 244 – 250.

Patchett K W, *Recognition of Commercial Judgments and Awards in the Commonwealth* (1984).

Piggott Sir F, *Foreign Judgments* (1908) Hong Kong, Kelly and Walsh.

Rabel E, *The Conflict of Laws: A Comparative Study*, vol 1, 2nd edn (1958) Ann Arbor, University of Michigan.

Read H E, *Recognition and Enforcement of Foreign Judgments* (1938) Cambridge, Harvard University Press.

Royal Commission on Civil Liability and Compensation for Personal Injury (The Pearson Commission), Cmnd 7054-I (1978).

Scoles E F and Hay P, *Conflict of Laws* (1982) St Paul, Minn, West.

Scottish Law Commision, *Report on Succession*, No 124 (1989).

Seglow J *et al*, *Growing Up Adopted* (1972).

Shapira A, *The Interest Approach to Choice of Law* (1970) The Hague, Nijhoff.

Silberg M, *Personal Status in Israel* (1958) (Hebrew).

Speiser S M, *Recovery for Wrongful Death*, 2nd ed, Vol 1 (1975).

Rochester, NY, Lawyers Co-Operative Pub Co.

Royal Commission on Liability and Compensation for Personal Injury (the Pearson Commission) (1978, Cmnd. 7054-I).

Spencer Bower G and Turner Sir A K, *The Doctrine of Res Judicata*, 2nd ed (1969)London, Butterworths .

Sykes E I and Pryles M C, *Australian Private International Law*, 3rd edn (1991)Sydney, Law Book Co.

Tizard B, *Adoption: A Second Chance* (1977) London, Open Books.

Von Mehren A T and Trautman D T, *The Law of Multistate Problems* (1965) Boston, Little, Brown.

Warnock M, *A Question of Life* (The Warnock Report on Human Fertilisation and Embryology) (1985) Oxford, Blackwell.

Wolff M, *Private International Law*, 2nd edn (1950) London, Oxford University Press.

Articles and Essays

Allen C K, *Status and Capacity* (1930) 46 LQR 277.

Anton A E, *The Recognition of Divorces and Legal Separations* (1969) 18 ICLQ 620.

Baade H W, *Marriage and Divorce in American Conflicts Law: Governmental-Interests Analysis and the Restatement (Second)* (1972) 72 Col LR 329.

Battersby G *The Doctrine of Preclusion in Canada* (1977) 16 UWOnt LR 163.

Baxter I F G, *Family Law Reform in Canada* (1987) 35 Am J Comp Law 801.

Bellet P and Goldman B, *Explanatory Report of Hague Convention on Recognition of Divorces and Legal Separations*, transalated into English at (1971) 5 Fam LQ at p 321.

Berkovits B (1988) *Transnational Divorces: The Fatima Decision*, (1988) 104 LQR 60.

Bishop W, *Choice of Law for Impotence and Wilful Refusal* (1978) 41 MLR 512.

Carswell, *The Doctrine of Vested Rights in Private International Law*, (1959) 8 ICLQ 268.

Carter P B *Recogntion of divorces: denial of natural justice and the doctrine of estoppel* (1971) 45 BYBIL 410.

Carter P B, *Capacity To Remarry After a Foreign Divorce*, (1985) 101 LQR 496.

Carter P B, *Choice of Law in Tort and Delict* (1991) 107 LQR 405.

Carter P B, *The Role of Public Policy in Private International Law*, (1993) 42 ICLQ 1.

Castel J-G, *Choice of Law – Matrimonial Regimes – Recognition in Ontario of Foreign Express or Implied Marriage Contract or Settlement* (1982) 60 Can Bar Rev 180.

Cavers D, *The Choice-of-Law Problem* (1933) 47 Harvard LR 173.

Cohn E J, *The Form of Wills of Immovables* (1956) 5 ICLQ 395.

Collins L, *Vicarious Liability and the Conflict of Laws* (1977) 26 ICLQ 480.

Comment, *United States Recognition of Foreign Nonjudicial Divorces* (1969) 35 Minn LRev 612.

Clarkson C M V, *Marriage in England: favouring the lex fori* (1990) 10 Legal Studies 80.

Davie M, *Matrimonial Property in English and American Conflict of Laws* (1993) 42 ICLQ 855.

Deech R, *Financial Relief – Retreat from Precedent* (1982) 98 LQR 621, 630-632.

Dickson B, *The Reform of Private International Law in the Federal Republic of Germany* (1985) 34 ICLQ 231.

Downes T A, *Recognition of Divorces and Capacity to Remarry* (1986) 35 ICLQ 170.

Engdahl D E, *Proposal for a Benign Revolution in Marriage Law and Marriage Conflicts Law* (1969) 55 Iowa L Rev 56.

Fasberg C, *The Intertemporal Problem in Choice of Law Reconsidered: Israeli Matrimonial Property* (1990) 39 ICLQ 856.

Fawcett J J *Is American Governmental Interest Analysis the Solution to English Choice of Law Problems?* (1982) 31 ICLQ 150.

Fentiman R, *The Validity of Marriage and the Proper Law* [1985] CLJ 256.

Ferreiral E V, *Uruguay: Ending Discrimination between Birth in and out of Wedlock*, Annual Survey of Family Law (1994-5) 33 J of Fam Law 555.

Forder C, *Might and Right in Matrimonial Property Law: A Comparative Study of England and the German Democratic Republic* (1987) 1 Int J of Law and the Family 47.

Forsyth C F, *Section 7 of the Matrimonial Property Act 1976: A Choice of Law Rule?* (1977) 7 NULR 397.

Frank R, *Family Law After Unification* (1991) 30 J Fam Law 335.

Goldberg G D, *The Assignment of Property on Marriage* (1970) 19 ICLQ 557.

Goldwater C I, *Some Problems Relating to Choice of Law in Matrimonial Property* (1981) 16 Isr LR 368.

Goodhart A L, *The Doctrine of Divisible Divorce* (1957) 73 LQR 29.

Gottlieb A E, *The Incidental Question in Anglo-American Conflict of Laws* (1955) 33 CanBar Rev 523.

Gottlieb A E, *The Incidental Question Revisited* (1977) 26 ICLQ 734.

Guillod, *Switzerland: Everyone has the right to know his origins* (1993-4) 32 Journal of Family Law Annual Survey 465.

Gutman E, *The Status of Legitimacy in Compartive Conflict of Laws*, (1959) ICLQ 678.

Haimes E, *Secrecy: What Can Artificial Reproduction Learn from Adoption?* (1988) 2 Int J of Law and Family 46.

Hancock M, *Three Approaches to the Choice of Law Problem*, in Nadelman K *et al* (ed), *Legal Essays in honour of H E Yntema* (1961).

Harper F V, *Torts, Contract, Property, Statute Characterization and the Conflict of Laws* (1959) 59 ColLR 440.

Hartley T C, *Bigamy in the Conflict of Laws* (1967) 16 ICLQ 680.

Hartley T C, *The Policy Basis of the English Conflict of Laws of Marriage* (1972) 35 MLR 571.

Jaffey A J E, *Recognition of Extra-Judicial Divorces* (1975) LQR 320.

Jaffey A J E, *The Essential Validity of Marriage in the English Conflict of Laws* (1978) 41 MLR 38.

Jaffey A J E, *The Foundations of Rules for the Choice of Law* (1982) 2 OJLS 368.

Jaffey A J E, *Recognition of Foreign Nullity Decrees* (1983) 32 ICLQ 500.

Jaffey A J E, *The Incidental Question and Capacity to Remarry* (1985) 48 MLR 465.

Khan Freund, *Law Reform (Husband and Wife) Act 1962* (1962) 25 MLR 695.

Karsten I G F, *Chaplin v Boys: Another Analysis* (1970) 19 ICLQ 35.

Karsten I G F, *Capacity to Contract a Polygamous Marriage* (1973) 36 MLR 291.

Kegel, *Fundamental Approaches*, International Encyclopedia of Comparative Law, Vol III, Chapter 3.

Kennedy G D, *Adoption in the Conflict of Laws*, (1956) 34 Can BRev 507.

Krause H D, *Creation of Relationships of Kinship* International Encyclopedia of Comparative Law (1976) Vol IV Chapter 6.

Levontin A V, *Foreign Judgments and Foreign Status in Israel* (1954) 3 Am J Comp Law 199.

Levontin A V, *Two Paradoxes in the Recognition of Foreign Judgments* (1967) 2 Isr LRev 197.

Lipstein K, *Adoption in Private International Law* (1963) 12 ICLQ 835.

Lipstein K, *Conflict of Laws 1927-71 – the Way Ahead* [1972B] CLJ 67.

Lipstein K, *Recognition of Divorces, Capacity to Marry, Preliminary Questions and Depecage* (1986) 35 ICLQ 179.

Llwellyn Davies D J, *The Influence of Huber's De Conflictu Legum on English Private International Law* (1957) 18 BYBIL 49.

Lowe N and Douglas G, "Becoming a Parent in English Law" in Eekelaar and Sarcevic (eds) *Parenthood in Modern Society: Legal and Social Issues for the 21st Century* (1993) Dordrecht, Kluwer.

McCaffrey S, *The Swiss Draft Conflicts Law* (1980) 28 Am J Comp Law 235.

McClean D and Patchett K W *English Jurisdiction in Adoptions* (1970) ICLQ 1.

McGregor H, *The International Accident Problem* (1970) 33 MLR 1.

Meeussen J, *Judicial Dissapproval of Discrimination Against Illegitimate Children: A Comparative Study of Developments in Europe and the United States* (1995) 43 Am J Comp Law 119.

Miller J G, *Provision for a Surviving Spouse* (1986) 102 LQR 445.

Miller J G, *Family Provision on Death – the International Dimension* (1990) 39 ICLQ 261.

Morris J H C *Intestate Succession to Land in the Conflict of Laws* (1969) 85 LQR 339.

Nott S M, *Capacity to Marry Following Foreign Divorce or Nullity Decrees* (1985) 15 Fam Law 199.

O'Donovan K, *A Right to Know One's Parentage* (1988) 2 Int J of Law and the Family 27.

Palmer E, *The Austrian Codification of Conflicts Law*, (1980) 28 Am J Comp Law 197.

Palsson L, *Marriage and Divorce in Comparative Conflict of Laws* International Encyclopedia of Comparative Law, Vol III Chpt 16.

Pearl D S, *Capacity for Polygamy* [1973] CLJ 143.

Pearl D S, *Family Law Act 1986 Part II* [1987] CLJ 35.

Pederson I M, *Matrimonial Property Law in Denmark* (1965) 28 MLR 137.

Pilkington M, *Transnational Divorces under the Family Law Act 1986* (1988) 37 ICLQ 131.

Rafferty N, *Matrimonial Property and the Conflict of Laws* (1982) 20 UWOL Rev 177.

Reese W, *Marriage in American Conflict of Laws* (1977) 26 ICLQ 952.

Rheinstein M and Glendon M-A, *Interspousal Relations* (1980) International Encyclopedia of Comparatative Law Vol IV, Chapter 4.

Robertson A H, *The 'Preliminary Question' in the Conflict of Laws* (1939) 55 LQR 565.

Russell M J, *Fluctuations in Reciprocity* (1952) 1 ICLQ 181.

Schreter H H, *Quasi-Connunity Property in the Conflict of Laws* (1962) 50 Calif LR 206.

Schuz R G, *Section 30 Law of Property Act 1925 and Unmarried Cohabitees* (1982) 12 Fam Law 108.

Shaki A, *The Criterion 'Domicile' and its Preference over the Crtierion of Nationality in Israel Private International Law* (1966) 16 *Scripta Hierosolymitana*, Studies in Israel Legislative Problems (eds Tedeschi and Yudin) at p163.

Shava M, *Connecting Factors in Matters of Personal Status in Israel* (1983) 5 Tel Aviv University Studies in Law 144.

Shava M, *The Dissolution of Marriage (Special Cases) Law* (1970) 26 Hapraklit 302 at p 304)(Hebrew).

Shava M, *Israeli Conflict of Laws Relating to Matrimonial Property – A Comparative Commentary* (1982) 31 ICLQ 307.

Stone O, *Ninth Report of the Law Reform Committee (Liability in Tort Between Husband and Wife)* (1961) 24 MLR 481.

Swisher P N and Jones M D, *The Lost-in-Time Marriage Presumption* (1995) 29 Fam Law Q 409.

Symes P *Indissolubility and the Clean Break* (1985) 48 MLR 44.

Taintor C W, *Adoption in the Conflict of Laws* (1954) 15 U Pitts LR 222.

Taintor C W, *Legitimation, Legitimacy, and Recognition in the Conflict of Laws* (19) 18 Can Bar Rev 691.

Vitta, *Codification of Private International Law in Israel* (1977) 12 Isr LRev 129.

Voegeli W and Wilenbacher B, *Property Division and Pension-Splitting in FRG* in Weitzmann L and Maclean M (eds) *Economic Consequences of Divorce The International Perspective* (1992).

Von Mehren A T and Trautman D T, *Recognition of Foreign Adjudications: A Survey and A Suggested Approach* (1968) 81 Harv L Rev 1601.

Von Mehren A T, *Choice of Law and the Problem of Justice* (1977) 41 Law and Contemporary Problems 27.

Waters D, *Matrimonial Property Entitlements and the Quebec Conflicts of Law* (1970) 22 McGill LJ 315.

Wengler W, *The Law Applicable to Preliminary (Incidental Questions* International Encyclopedia of Comparative Law, Vol III Chapter 7.

Wright A, *Financial Provision, the Clean Break and the Search for Consistency* (1991) Fam Law 76.

Young J, *The recognition of extra-judicial divorces in the United Kingdom* (1987) Legal Studies 78.

Young J, *Foreign Nullity Decrees: Perrini v Perrini* (1980) 29 ICLQ 515.

Index